Hospital Costs and Health Insurance

Hospital Costs
and Health Insurance

Martin Feldstein

Harvard University Press
Cambridge, Massachusetts
and London, England
1981

Library of Congress Cataloging in Publication Data

Feldstein, Martin S
    Hospital costs and health insurance.

    Bibliography: p.
    Includes index.
        1. Insurance, Health — United States — Addresses,
essays, lectures. 2. Hospitals — United States — Rates —
Addresses, essays, lectures. I. Title.
[DNLM: 1. Economics, Hospital — United States.
2. Insurance, Health — United States. WX157 F312h]
HD7102.U4F44   368.3′82′00973   80-18226
ISBN 0-674-40675-3

To Kate, Margaret, and Janet

Preface

The explosion of hospital costs and the restructuring of health insurance have become the central issues of national health-care policy. In 1978 and again in 1979, Congress has considered and almost enacted plans to implement direct controls on the costs of many of the seven thousand individual hospitals. Now that Medicare and Medicaid provide benefits for the aged and the poor, it is the rapid increase of hospital costs that provides the primary impetus for national health insurance. Unfortunately, the current policy initiatives generally reflect a misunderstanding of the reasons for the rapid rise in hospital costs and of the difference between hospital-cost inflation and the general inflation that troubles the economy.

I hope that this volume will contribute to a better understanding of the nature of hospital-cost inflation and of the desirable direction for restructuring health insurance in the United States. The book brings together twelve papers published between 1971 and 1977 in journals, conference volumes, and government reports. The introduction summarizes the conclusions and implications of the analysis and provides a guide to the chapters in which particular issues are discussed. Part One (chapters 1–5) deals with the behavior of hospitals and hospital costs. Chapters 6–8 examine the role of private health insurance, and the last three chapters deal with more specific aspects of national health insurance.

I have of course learned more about the health-care system and hospital costs since I wrote these papers. I have also thought of technical improvements that could be made in the studies themselves. But if I were to start making revisions in the original articles, it would be difficult to know where to stop. Since I believe in the basic analysis and conclusions of this research, I have resisted the temptation to modify any of the articles that follow the introductory chapter.

I hope that this volume will be of interest to noneconomists who are concerned about the health-care sector and public policy in this area as well as to fellow economists. Each chapter can be read independently of the others. Someone with no knowledge of economics and a strong aversion to mathematics can read the introduction and chapters 1, 7, and 9 with no difficulty and will find chapters 2, 5, 10, and 11 quite accessible. Although chapters 3 and 4 present a formal model with statistically estimated parameters that cannot be fully understood without some background in economics and statistics, the general analytic framework and empirical findings will be of interest to a broader group of readers. Chapters 6 and 8 are best reserved for readers with a knowledge of economics. The introductions to the three parts present brief summaries of the chapters in each part.

Four of the chapters were originally written with coauthors: chapter 1 with Amy Taylor, chapter 7 with Elisabeth Allison, chapter 10 with Bernard Friedman and Harold Luft, and chapters 8 and 11 with Bernard Friedman. I am grateful to them for collaborating in the original research and for permitting me to include our joint papers in this volume.

Grants from the Carnegie Foundation and the Robert Wood Johnson Foundation supported a seminar on the economics of health care at Harvard University during several of the years when I was engaged in this research. The students in the seminar and the economists from other institutions who visited the seminar were a source of stimulation and suggestions. Discussions with several colleagues at Harvard and with economists at other universities contributed significantly to the final product. I also benefited from the opportunity to discuss hospital costs and health insurance with noneconomists who were actively engaged with these problems: physicians, hospital administrators, insurance officials, and individuals in the state and federal governments who are responsible for health-care policy.

The research reported in these chapters would not have been possible without the help of several able research assistants: Virginia Ambrosini, Eva Ewing, Bernard Friedman, Harold Luft, Anthony Pellechio, and Amy Taylor. Judy Frink prepared the final manuscript and bibliography. I am grateful to all of them for their help.

I began this research with a plan to estimate an econometric model of the health-care sector that would be useful for guiding public policy. I specified and estimated a simple prototype model and published the results in 1968. A grant from the Department of Health, Education, and Welfare permitted me to develop that prototype into the research presented here. Although the full model was never completed, it provided the organizing framework for estimating what I believe are the key relationships between the demand for hospital care, the price of that care, and the extent of insurance for hospital expenses. It is perhaps noteworthy that a research project that began with the idea of developing an econometric model in order to increase the government's ability to control the health-care sector ended with the conclusion that the government should interfere less in order to allow the natural forces of the competitive market to function more effectively.

Contents

Hospital Costs and Health Insurance

Introduction

The increase in hospital costs has been overwhelmingly greater than the general rise in consumer prices. From 1950 to 1978 the overall consumer price index, which measures the cost of all goods and services bought by consumers, rose about 171 percent. During the same period medical care services as a whole rose more than twice as much, 378 percent. But the upsurge in the cost of hospital care was much more dramatic. Average cost per patient-day was only $16 in 1950. By 1978 it was about $214, an increase of more than 1,200 percent.

Although everyone is aware that hospital costs have risen rapidly, there is little understanding of why they have risen at such an unprecedented rate. Much has been written about the rise in hospital wage rates and the supposedly low rate of increase in productivity among hospital staff. But such "explanations" miss the real nature of the problem, for there are two—and really only two key ingredients to understanding the rise in hospital costs: the changing nature of the hospital product and the impact of insurance. Of these, the second is the more crucial—and largely explains the first.

The Changing Hospital Product

The most obvious characteristic of hospital care today is that it is very different from what it was twenty-five years ago. Today's care is more complex, more sophisticated, and, it is to be hoped, more effective.

The rapid rise in hospital costs unquestionably reflects this rapidly changing product. The rate of hospital-cost inflation, therefore, cannot be compared without qualification to the rate of inflation of most

This chapter draws heavily on my article "The High Cost of Hospital Care—And What to Do about It," reprinted with permission from *The Public Interest,* no. 48 (Summer 1977), pp. 40–54. © by National Affairs, Inc.

other goods in the consumer price index. The consumer price index tries to measure the cost of buying an unchanged bundle of goods and services. But cost inflation in hospital care does not mean that consumers are paying much more for the same old product; it means that they are buying a different and much more expensive product. Hospital-cost inflation is therefore quite different from other types of inflation. To understand the nature of this problem, we must ask why hospital care has become much more sophisticated and therefore much more expensive.

Higher incomes and greater education have undoubtedly played some role in increasing the demand for sophisticated hospital care, and scientific discoveries have obviously changed the technological possibilities in hospitals. But the major reason, I believe, for hospital-cost inflation has been the very rapid growth in insurance.

In addition to providing protection against unforeseen medical expenses, health insurance substantially lowers the net price of care that the patient pays out of pocket at the time he consumes services. There is now substantial evidence that patients, guided by their doctors, demand more services and more expensive services when a large part of the cost is offset by insurance.[1]

Some simple but striking numbers illustrate this point. In 1950, when average cost per patient-day was a little less than $16, private insurance and government programs paid 49 percent of hospital bills; on the average the net cost to a patient of a day of care was just under $8. By 1975 average cost per patient-day had jumped to about $152 — but private and public insurance were paying 88 percent of the hospital bill, leaving a net cost to the patient of only $18. Thus, although the cost of providing a day of hospital care had increased more than ninefold (from $16 to $152), the net cost to patients had just about doubled (from $8 to $18). Moreover, the general increase in the prices of all goods and services meant that $18 in 1975 could buy only as much as $8 in 1950. So in real terms, the net cost to the patient at the time of illness has not changed at all during those twenty-five years.

Even without Medicare, Medicaid, and other government programs the picture is not very different. In 1950 private insurance paid 37 percent of private hospital bills; on average the net cost to a private patient for a day of hospital care was therefore just under $10. By 1975 private insurance was paying for 79 percent of privately financed

---

1. Chapter 2 reviews the statistical evidence on the effect of insurance on the demand for hospital care and discusses the doctor's role in determining demand. My own statistical estimates of the demand for hospital care are presented in chapters 3 and 4.

hospital care. The average net cost to the patient at the time of illness, therefore, was only $32 per day—not the $152 incurred by the hospital. In 1950 prices this $32 is equivalent to $14. In real terms the net cost per day to the patient had increased by only $4.[2]

Looked at somewhat differently, with 79 percent of private hospital bills now paid by insurance, an extra $10 of expensive care costs the patient only $2 out of pocket. It is not surprising, therefore, that patients and their doctors continue to encourage the growing sophistication and expense of hospital care.

I think that this is the essence of the hospital-cost inflation problem. Increased insurance has induced hospitals to improve their product and provide much more expensive and sophisticated care.

Before considering the implications of this explanation, let me contrast it with the usual reasons offered for the rise in hospital costs. These traditionally boil down to four ideas: (1) Hospitals are inefficient. (2) Labor costs have risen particularly rapidly. (3) Hospitals have had a low rise in technical progress. (4) Hospital supply has not kept up with increasing demand. Each of these notions is basically incorrect.

Perhaps the most frequently heard explanation of rising hospital costs is that hospitals are technologically and managerially inefficient. But even if there are good reasons for criticizing the efficiency of hospitals, there is no reason to believe that their inefficiency has been rapidly increasing over the past two decades. Inefficiency cannot account for a 1,200 percent increase in hospital costs. It cannot begin to account for a significant fraction of that overwhelming increase.

Rising labor costs are also frequently cited as the primary cause of hospital-cost inflation. It is true that wages and salaries constitute a large share of hospital costs and that hospital wages have risen more rapidly than wages in the general economy. Nevertheless, this rise does not begin to account for the rise in hospital costs. From 1955 to 1975 labor cost per patient-day rose at a rate of 9 percent a year. But as a fraction of the total hospital bill, labor costs actually decreased from 62 percent in 1955 to 53 percent in 1975. In other words, nonlabor costs rose faster than labor costs. Moreover, about one-third of the increase in labor costs was due to a rise in the number of personnel per patient-day rather than to an increase in hospital wage rates. The earnings of hospital employees rose at 6.3 percent a year from 1955 to 1975, while the average earnings of all private nonfarm workers rose at 4.5 percent. If the rate of increase of hospital wages had been held to this 4.5 percent national average, the overall rise in the

2. These figures are discussed more fully in chapter 1.

average cost of a day of hospital care would have been reduced from 9.9 percent a year to 8.8 percent. In other words, the rise of hospital wages in excess of the national average rate of wage increase can account for only about one-tenth of the high rate of hospital-cost inflation.[3]

The third common explanation is that hospital-cost inflation is the result of a low rate of technical progress. I think that this is clearly and obviously false. Hospitals have been the scene of extremely rapid technical changes, but these changes differ from those in other industries: they have not reduced costs. Technological progress in hospitals does not involve making the old product more cheaply but making a new range of products that are more expensive.[4]

Why have hospitals moved toward increasingly expensive ways of providing more services for patients rather than toward providing old services more cheaply? Although some of this change merely reflects the path of scientific progress, I believe that it is the method of financing health services that primarily determines the pattern of technological change. Hospitals would not be buying the latest, expensive medical technology if they could not afford it. What permits them to afford it is the mode of insuring against hospital costs.

The final traditional explanation is that hospital costs have risen because supply has not kept up with demand. Economic analysis of ordinary markets usually emphasizes that prices rise because supply does not increase as rapidly as demand. But in the case of hospitals, I think the opposite is true. It is precisely because supply has kept pace with demand that hospital costs have gone up. Hospitals have responded to the increased demand and increased willingness to pay for sophisticated services by providing them, and costs have gone up accordingly. The increase in demand has induced a rapid rise in the supply of a more expensive type of hospital care.[5]

This brings me back to my original contention that the rise in hospital costs reflects a change in the product, induced largely by the growth of insurance. But this explanation of the rise in hospital costs raises an awkward question. Implicit in every discussion of hospital-cost inflation is the assumption that the rise in cost has been excessive and should not be allowed to continue at the same rate. But if this rise

3. Hospital wages and the contribution of labor costs to the general increase in hospital costs are discussed in chapter 1.

4. On the relation between hospital costs and the real volume of resources used per patient day, see chapters 1 and 5.

5. A formal model of the links between insurance, demand, and hospital costs is presented in chapter 3 and developed more fully in chapter 4.

reflects a change in product rather than an increase in inefficiency or a low rate of technological progress, why is it a problem?

The answer in brief is that the current type of costly medical care does not correspond to what consumers or their physicians would regard as appropriate if their choices were not distorted by insurance. Prepaying health care through insurance, both private and public, encourages hospitals to provide a more expensive product than consumers wish to pay for. In the end, consumers do pay for it — in ever higher insurance premiums.

Although the consumer eventually pays the full cost of the expensive care through higher insurance premiums, at the time of illness the choice of the patient and his physician reflects the net out-of-pocket cost of the care. Because this cost appears so modest, the patient and the physician choose to buy more expensive care than they would if the patient were not so well insured. In this way, the current method of financing hospital care denies patients and their physicians the opportunity to choose effectively between higher-cost and lower-cost hospital care.[6]

Why Patients Overinsure

If insurance is responsible for such an inappropriate expansion in the demand for expensive care, why has insurance grown so rapidly? In part, this growth reflects a family's rational demand for protection against unexpected illness. It is unfortunate but inevitable that this process tends to be self-perpetuating. The high cost of care induces families to buy more complete insurance, and the growth of insurance induces the hospital to produce more expensive care.

This demand for protection cannot explain the comprehensive "first-dollar insurance" — insurance for all costs up to a specified limit — that now exists. Current insurance is often inadequate in protecting the family against the substantial bills that can cause real hardship. Why have Americans bought such complete coverage for relatively small bills? Why have they been willing to pay for insurance that provides little real protection against catastrophic illness but induces them to buy more expensive and sophisticated care for less serious illnesses?

Most insurance is now group insurance and, more specifically, insurance bought for employee groups. Decisions on the scope of cover-

6. A formal analysis of the waste or "economic inefficiency" involved in this distortion of patient demand is presented in chapter 6.

age and on coinsurance rates and deductibles are generally made in collective bargaining by expert representatives of labor and management. Why would such experts forego higher wages in order to obtain excessive, shallow insurance? The answer, I believe, lies in the tax treatment of premiums.[7]

Government policies encourage insurance by a tax deduction and exclusion that now cost the Treasury more than $10 billion a year. Individuals can deduct a portion of the premiums they pay for health insurance. More important, employer payments for insurance are excluded from the taxable income of the employee as well as the employer. These premiums are also not subject to Social Security taxes or state income taxes.

Thus, even for a family with relatively low income, the inducement to buy insurance can be substantial. Because of the income and payroll taxes, a married man who has two children and earns $8,000 a year will take home an additional $70 for each $100 the employer adds to his income. If the employer buys health insurance instead, the full $100 can be applied against the premium and there is no tax to be paid. In this case the dollar buys nearly 50 percent more in healthcare services if paid through an insurance premium than if paid in wages to individuals who then buy the care directly. For workers in high tax brackets, the incentive is stronger.

I believe the subsidy is strong enough to induce employees and unions to choose higher insurance instead of higher wages. The primary effect of this insurance is to distort the pattern of medical care and to exacerbate the rising cost of hospital care. Moreover, this subsidy, which costs taxpayers several billion dollars a year, is regressive. The subsidy is greatest for middle- and upper-income employees in high-wage industries.[8] In short, the current tax treatment of insurance premiums, particularly the exclusion of employer payments from the employees' taxable incomes, is a costly, regressive, and inefficient aspect of the tax system.

An important step in dealing with high hospital costs must be to change this aspect of the tax system, which now contributes significantly to the underlying problem of excess insurance. More generally, the system of health insurance must be restructured to correct the incentives faced by patients and their doctors. Other proposed "solutions" will only lead us astray.

7. The importance of the tax subsidy is discussed in chapter 7, and a formal model of its effect is presented in chapter 8.

8. Chapter 7 considers the distribution of the tax reductions due to the current tax treatment of health insurance premiums.

Direct Regulation of Hospital Costs

One proposed solution is the direct regulation of hospital costs. At first glance it seems natural to apply the mechanism of public-utility regulation to hospitals. However, a more detailed examination of this proposal shows that controlling hospital costs is fundamentally different. More important, the direct regulation of hospital costs would in the long run make the nature and quality of hospital services completely unresponsive to the preferences of patients and their physicians.

Consider the experience of hospital-cost regulation under the Economic Stabilization Program of 1971–1974. A special subcommittee of the Cost of Living Council continued to regulate hospital costs during the entire period of price controls. At first, controls were limited to hospital wages and to the prices charged for specific types of hospital service (an X ray, a particular laboratory test). The controls were constantly being confounded by rapid increases in the quality or sophistication of services, which called for new (and higher) costs. During the final phase of the Economic Stabilization Program, the regulation of hospital costs was changed to a comprehensive limit on the overall increase in the cost per patient-day (with minor adjustments for changes in occupancy rates, and the like). The American Hospital Association then filed suit against the Cost of Living Council, charging that such control of the quality of hospital care went beyond the legislative mandate of the stabilization program. The issue became moot when the legislation expired in 1974.

The experience of the Economic Stabilization Program confirmed that the central issue in controlling hospital costs is limiting the quality of hospital care. The problem thus differs fundamentally from the usual issues of public-utility regulation. Such regulation is used to control the exercise of monopoly power, to set a fair rate of profit on invested capital, and to assure that minimum quality standards are maintained. In contrast to the typical public utility, most hospitals—being nonprofit institutions—earn no profits, and minimum standards are already regulated through annual accreditation by a professional association.

Direct regulation of hospital costs is inappropriate because there is no "technically correct" way for the regulators to set an appropriate maximum quality of hospital care. Determining the appropriate quality of care is totally different in this respect from fixing the appropriate rate of profit for a public utility. Controlling the quality of medical care is not a technical economic or legal question that can be solved by bureaucrats, by the political process, or by an administrative tribunal.

Nor can it be assigned to the process of physician peer review. Although peer review can try to ensure the application of accepted standards of care, it cannot properly establish what those standards should be in each particular case. Here again we run up against the difference between setting a minimum standard and imposing a maximum standard on the quality of care. Neither patients nor doctors are likely to accept calmly any such bureacratic imposition.

Determining the correct quality and style of medical care requires the involvement of the individual family and its physician in deciding how much they want to spend for medical care and how much for other things. Although direct involvement of households is not possible in determining the appropriate level of spending on public safety or national defense, it is possible for personal health services. Moreover, it is essential. The only limits on health care that a patient can be expected to tolerate are those he sets for himself. Trying to impose them by administrative fiat will lead to particular scandals and general dissatisfaction.

Although imposing an arbitrary limit on the increase in hospital costs might be beneficial for a few years, in the long run it would make the quality of hospital care completely unresponsive to the preferences of the patients. How would a regulatory agency decide whether real hospital costs should rise at an annual rate of 4 percent, or 6 percent, or 8 percent? After adjusting for the increase in wages and in the prices of things that hospitals buy, should costs and therefore quality be allowed to increase at a rate of 2 percent, or 4 percent, or 6 percent? An arbitrary choice would eventually mean that the quality of hospital care will be very different from the level that patients and their physicians would choose.

And what would regulation do about differences among hospitals in the cost and quality of care? Would current differences be "frozen in" by limiting all hospitals to the same rate of cost increase? On what basis would a hospital be granted permission to add new services that increase its quality? Or would regulation seek to make all hospitals have the same levels of quality and cost except for differences in the diagnostic mix of patients?

These questions show two adverse effects of direct regulation. First, to the extent that current differences are maintained by limiting all hospitals to approximately the same rate of cost increase, direct regulation would be unfair to those who now live in the areas served by lower-quality hospitals and who would prefer a more rapid increase in quality during the years ahead. To the extent that all hospitals are required to have the same level of quality, direct regulation would force many lower- and middle-income families to pay for a more expensive style of care than they want while denying many other middle- and upper-income families the opportunity to purchase the higher-quality care that they would prefer. In short, direct regulation of hospital costs is not compatible with allowing a variety of institutions to develop in response to differences in patients' preferences.

More generally, regulation limits the total resources available for hospital care to less than the total amount that patients and their physicians want to buy at the artificially low net-of-insurance prices. How will this conflict between regulated supply and inflated demand be reconciled? Who will decide which demands are to be satisfied and which frustrated? And on what criteria? Regulation inevitably brings shortages, shortages bring rationing, and rationing means a wasteful allocation of resources. It is disturbing that the government presses for regulation of hospital costs at the very time that the public and the Congress have been sharply critical of the adverse effects of regulation in other industries.

Lessons for National Health Insurance

The nature of hospital-cost inflation and the weaknesses of direct regulation have important implications for national health insurance. Whatever form of insurance is developed must face squarely the problem of determining the evolution of the quality and style of medical care.

The long-run problem is not to reduce or to limit the growth of medical spending but to achieve the correct rate of growth of that spending. This must ultimately come down to balancing additional spending on medical care against the alternative uses to which households might put their resources. And this balancing requires comparing the expected gains from additional medical care—gains that are psychological as well as physical—with the satisfaction that households would enjoy from the alternative spending on food, housing, education, or recreation.

It is important to develop an approach to national health insurance that is appropriate to the advanced technology of today's medical care and the ever-increasing affluence of the American people. Too much of the current debate relies on ideas about the delivery of medical care that have been inherited from a period with quite different technological and economic conditions. The challenge today is to find new methods of financing health care that protect families from financial hardship while also making future health care more responsive to their preferences.

Several years ago, I outlined an approach to national health insurance that I still believe can serve these two objectives.[9] The basic idea in this proposal is simple. Provide every family with an insurance policy so that a family's spending on health care need never be more than a moderate fraction of its income but use a system of copayments to make most families conscious of the cost of their use of health-care services.

Any proposed system of financing health care should be judged by six objectives:

1. *It should prevent deprivation of care.* No one should go without medical care because of inability to pay.

2. *It should prevent financial hardship.* No family should suffer substantial financial hardship because of the expense of illness or accident.

3. *It should keep costs down.* A financing system should encourage efficient use of resources and discourage medical-care price inflation. Whenever possible, patients should use relatively low-cost ambulatory facilities rather than high-cost in-hospital care. Hospitals should be induced to moderate the forces that raise the cost of care: increased personnel, unnecessary pay raises, and a proliferation of technical facilities and services. Physicians should not be encouraged to increase their fees by the knowledge that, because of insurance, the cost to their own patients will rise little, if at all. In short, the financing method should encourage cost consciousness in the decisions of patients, doctors, and hospital administrators.

4. *It should avoid a large tax increase.* A national health insurance program that raises substantial funds from taxpayers and returns it in the form of health insurance has a large hidden cost. By reducing the incentive to work, to invest, and to take economic risks, the increased tax rates would lower real national income. The magnitude of total spending on health care makes this an important consideration. In fiscal year 1978 private health-care expenditures approached $100 billion; transferring this private spending to the public sector would require a very large increase in tax rates.

5. *It should be easily administered.* The administration of a health-care system should not require complex procedures that are costly and inconvenient, or permit arbitrary decisions that will be resented.

6. *It should be generally acceptable.* Any new method of financing should be acceptable to physicians and hospitals, as well as the general public. A system that is disliked by any of these would encounter substantial political opposition and, if instituted, would be hampered by a lack of cooperation.

9. The original proposal is reprinted as chapter 9.

Although almost every American is now covered by some form of private or public insurance, the coverage is still often surprisingly shallow. Families incurring huge medical bills too often find that their insurance pays only a relatively small portion of them. A 1970 National Opinion Research Survey, updated to 1976 prices, found that more than 500,000 families had out-of-pocket expenditures of more than $3,000 for medical care. More than 2 million families spent over $1,500, and more than 10 percent of all families spent over $1,200 out of pocket. These are out-of-pocket expenses — *after* private and public insurance payments and reimbursements.

Although hospital insurance pays a high proportion of hospital bills, current policies generally impose ceilings on the use of benefits. The absence of deep coverage leaves a serious residue of financial hardship and prevents some people from seeking potentially expensive care. The current system of financing medical care has contributed to the rapidly rising cost of care. In short, the current structure of health insurance fails by each of the first three criteria.

The most widely debated proposals for national health insurance call for a program of universal, uniform, and comprehensive health insurance, something like an extension of Medicare to the entire population. The most comprehensive of these proposals would even abolish the small deductible and coinsurance provisions of Medicare, eliminate any limit on the length of covered hospitalization, and extend coverage to drugs, dental care, and even housekeeping services.

There is no doubt that under comprehensive insurance no one would be deprived of needed care because of inability to pay or suffer financial hardship because of illness. In terms of the other criteria, however, such plans must be judged unacceptable.

Although comprehensive insurance would remove the current incentive for patients to use inpatient rather than ambulatory care, it would not introduce positive incentives for the efficient use of resources. Whatever cost consciousness now exists among patients, doctors, and administrators would be removed. There would be no incentive to limit the rising cost of hospital care, to use paramedical personnel more widely, or to produce physicians' services more efficiently. With all bills paid by the government, nothing would limit the rise in hospital wage rates and physicians' income. In such a situation the government would be forced to introduce direct controls in an attempt to contain costs.

Detailed controls, fee schedules, and limits on hospital charges might prevent rising costs for a while, but the experience of Canada,

Britain, and Sweden suggests that health costs rise very rapidly even under government health programs with extensive direct controls. Controls could not achieve, and might actually work against, an efficient use of health resources. They would certainly require a large number of arbitrary policy decisions and engender the hostility of the basic providers. Such arbitrary decisions pose more serious questions than may be generally recognized. What is a "reasonable" level of daily hospital cost? At what rate should hospitals improve facilities, add staff, or raise the level of amenities? How many beds should there be per thousand population? How much should different medical specialists earn? These are not technical questions that could be answered objectively if only enough research were done; they involve tastes and value judgments about the relative desirability of different goods and services.

Finally, even if expenditures were not to rise, the provision of comprehensive insurance would require a substantial tax increase — over $57 billion (at 1978 levels) to replace current (1978) private expenditures on physician and hospital services, and an additional $39 billion if drugs and other personal health care were to be included.

If such a $96 billion increase in government spending were financed by increasing the tax rate of the current Social Security payroll tax, the rate would rise from its current level of 12 percent to more than 21 percent. If, instead, the $96 billion were financed by a general increase in the personal income tax, everyone's tax would have had to rise by more than 50 percent of its 1978 level.

Comprehensive insurance would shift the problem of the health-care sector to a conflict between cost inflation and controls. No matter where the balance between these was struck, there would be no natural incentive to efficiency, and there would be a large government expenditure to be paid for by much higher taxes.

The Major-Risk Approach

I favor a different approach to national health insurance. Every family would receive a comprehensive major-risk insurance (MRI) policy with an annual direct-expense limit — a limit on out-of-pocket payments — that increases with family income. A $500 direct-expense limit means that the family is responsible for up to $500 of out-of-pocket medical expenses per year but pays no more than $500, no matter how large the total annual medical bill. Different relations between family income and the direct-expense limit are possible. For example, the expense limit might start at $500 per year for a family with income below $5,000, be equal to 10 percent of family income between

$5,000 and $18,000 and be $1,800 for incomes above that level. The details of the schedule are unimportant at this point. The key feature is an expense limit that few families would normally exceed but that is low relative to family income.[10]

Major-risk insurance is the most important type of health insurance for the government to provide. It concentrates government effort on those families for whom medical expenses would create financial hardship or preclude adequate care. Because relatively few families have such large expenditures in any year, MRI need not be a very costly program. In terms of the six criteria, these are the advantages of MRI.

1. *It would prevent deprivation of care.* If the maximum annual expenditure on health were limited to 10 percent or less of family income, no family would be deprived of care because of inability to pay. If it is believed that certain types of preventive care and early diagnostic tests would not be undertaken as often as is desirable, the MRI policy could be supplemented by specific coverage for these services at relatively little additional cost.[11]

2. *It would prevent financial hardship.* MRI would also prevent financial hardship by limiting a family's financial risk to 12 percent or less of annual income.

3. *It would reduce cost inflation.* An increase in insurance coverage generally exacerbates the inflation of hospital costs. However, the universal provision of MRI should reduce hospital-cost inflation by eliminating or at least decreasing the current use of shallow-coverage insurance. This would be particularly true if, in introducing national health insurance, the government eliminated the current tax subsidy for private health insurance. In any case, after MRI had removed the risk of major expense, families would then have little to gain from such insurance, for the cost of a policy would be high relative to the upper limit on expenses guaranteed by the MRI.

Of course, once a family had exceeded its direct-expense limit, MRI would be equivalent to comprehensive insurance, and the family would then have no incentive to limit its spending for medical care. To ensure that relatively few families exceed their direct-expense lim-

10. Several specific proposals of this type are described and analyzed in chapters 10 and 11. Chapter 10 focuses on the cost and distributional characteristics of different insurance plans, while chapter 11 analyzes the impact of these plans on the price and quantity of care.

11. The availability, in addition, of government-guaranteed loans for the postpayment of medical bills would allow families to spread expenditures below the expense limit over a period of a year or even more. I shall not discuss this "credit card" feature in more detail in order to concentrate on the principle of major-risk insurance.

it, the MRI policy should use a coinsurance feature instead of a deductible. For example, the annual direct limit of $1,800 for families with incomes over $18,000 could be achieved by using a 50 percent coinsurance on the first $3,600 of medical bills. Fewer than one family in fifteen had medical expenses of more than $3,600 in 1978 (including, of course, the expenses now paid by insurance). Therefore, fewer than one family in fifteen would reach an expense limit based on $3,600 of spending. The coinsurance rates could be cut at lower income levels to keep the direct-expense limit to 10 percent of income, for example, a 33 percent coinsurance rate at an income of $12,000. At some income level it would probably be desirable to cut the $3,600 base so that the coinsurance rate did not have to fall too drastically. It is encouraging in this regard that fewer than one family in five had 1978 expenses exceeding $1,800; a 30 percent coinsurance rate would produce a direct-expense limit of $540.

The general principle is that the combination of a coinsurance rate and an expenditure base can be selected in a way that varies with income to make almost all families significantly sensitive to the costs of additional health spending while limiting each family's maximum out-of-pocket expenditure to 10 percent of income or less.

Even for the small number of families who reach their limits, MRI would indirectly help control expenditures. The basic cost per day in hospitals would be determined not by the willingness of a relatively few families to spend but by the preferences of the far larger number of patients who would not be fully reimbursed. MRI could prevent excesses in physicians' fees and hospital durations of stay by requiring that the same care be given and the same fees be charged to these patients as to those who are paying for their care. Because most medical services would be financed with substantial direct payments, the standards of customary charge and customary care would become meaningful reference standards, as they currently are not. In short, MRI would introduce a cost consciousness and a basis for cost comparison that could improve efficiency and contain medical-care inflation.

4. *It would avoid a large tax burden.* The cost to taxpayers of an MRI program would not be large relative to the benefits conferred. The exact amount would depend on the particular schedule of coinsurance and the overall impact of the program on utilization and unit costs. I estimate that an MRI form of national health insurance that covered all personal health care would raise government spending by no more than $25 billion at 1978 levels. Limiting the scope of coverage or introducing a small deductible per spell of illness could reduce this cost more than proportionately.

5. *It would be administratively simple.* MRI would be relatively simple

and inexpensive to administer. Because MRI would act to contain cost inflation and to increase efficiency, there would be no need for detailed controls or essentially arbitrary policy decisions. Planning efforts could be concentrated on problems that cannot be solved by the natural forces of supply and demand.

6. *It would be generally acceptable.* An MRI scheme should be acceptable to physicians, hospitals, and the general public. It would have the virtue of providing full protection against serious financial hardship without the controls or fee schedules that would accompany other forms of insurance. The current freedom of physicians and hospitals would be preserved. If MRI were administered by the same insurance companies that currently provide health insurance, the net effect would be a small increase in their total premium.

The problem of health-care costs is not to reduce or limit the growth of medical spending, but to achieve the correct rate of growth of that spending. This means that the form of national health insurance that the nation adopts should ensure that individual consumers play the central role in guiding the growth and form of their health services. I believe that MRI is the right way to protect families from the risk of financial hardship while preserving individual freedom of choice and thereby making the future development of the health-care system responsive to the preferences of the people.

Part One

The Behavior of Hospitals and Hospital Costs

Part One begins with a nontechnical review of the basic trends in hospital costs since 1950. The analysis of chapter 1 shows that the unusually rapid increase in the cost per patient-day reflects primarily the changing character of care (as indicated by the growing number of employees and the increasing volume of equipment and supplies) rather than the rise in the prices of these inputs. Special attention is given to the rise in hospital labor costs. Although hospital wages continue to rise more rapidly than other wages in the economy, these relatively greater wage increases are responsible for only a small fraction of the overall increase in the cost of hospital care. Evidence on the growth of public and private insurance suggests that patients and physicians demand (and hospitals supply) increasingly expensive and sophisticated hospital services because insurance pays a growing share of the cost of care.

Chapter 3 examines these issues with the help of a formal model of the behavior of the hospital industry that simultaneously determines the availability, use, price, and cost structure of hospital inpatient care. In particular, the demand for care and the input prices that hospitals pay together define the possible combinations of the quality of care and the number of patient-days of care that the hospital can provide. The physicians and others who are responsible for hospital policy select one of these feasible quality–quantity combinations and thereby determine the cost per patient-day. Econometric estimates of the demand equations with data for all individual states and for each year from 1958 through 1967 imply that demand is quite sensitive to the net price of care and therefore to the extent that insurance pays hospital bills. An analysis of these demand equations and the estimated price-adjustment process indicates that the rise in insurance may have been responsible for as much as two-thirds of the increase in the equilibrium relative price of hospital care between 1958 and 1967.

Chapter 4 extends this model in an important way by recognizing that a more expensive quality or style of hospital care increases the demand for hospital services. An increase in demand leads to a rise in the gross price of hospital care. This two-way relation between demand and quality makes the cost of a day of hospital care very sensitive to changes in insurance and is a potential source of explosive instability. This extended model is estimated with data for all individual states and for all years from 1958 through 1973. The estimates indicate that the process was explosively unstable in the period from 1958 through 1965. As quality increased, however, the sensitivity of demand to quality diminished. The system as a whole appears to have become stable after 1966, but prices continued to rise at a rapid rate. The estimates imply that the primary force propelling this increase in the real cost of hospital care has been the growth of insurance.

The models of chapters 3 and 4 must be regarded as stylized approximations of reality rather than as accurate pictures. Moreover, a number of technical problems with this work remain unresolved. Nevertheless, these models indicate how, because of the nature of price and quality determination in this nonprofit sector, the growth of insurance could cause the dramatic increases of the past twenty years.

Chapter 5 focuses on the technical problem of measuring variation in the overall price of hospital inputs and in an aggregate quality index defined in terms of the input of real resources per patient-day. A price index for hospitals' nonlabor inputs is constructed using weights based on the detailed 1963 input–output table of the U.S. economy. The substantial and persistent variation in the overall price of inputs is analyzed with a cross section of time-series data for individual states. The same sample is then used to examine the intertemporal change and the geographic variation in the quality index of hospital services.

In contrast to the original empirical research of these four chapters, chapter 2 combines a broad survey of existing empirical research on the economics of health care (through 1973) with my speculation about such subjects as the role of the physician in determining the demand for hospital care and the implications of the nonprofit character of the hospitals. The analysis extends to several new topics, including the hospitals' demands for inputs, the process of wage determination in the nonprofit industry, and the market for physicians' services. Part of this chapter dealing with the economics of health insurance provides a useful background for Part Two.

1 The Rapid Rise of Hospital Costs

The sustained increase in the cost of hospital care is without parallel in any other sector of the U.S. economy. The cost of a day of hospital care is currently increasing at an annual rate of more than 15 percent. This cost doubled in the short span between the summer of 1970 and the end of 1975 in spite of the wage and price controls that were in operation for the hospital industry during half of this period. While the general level of consumer prices has risen 125 percent since 1950, the cost of a day of hospital care has climbed more than 1,000 percent. An understanding of the cause of this abnormal rate of cost increase is a necessary first step in the development of appropriate government policies to deal with rising health-care costs and with the financing of health care.

The increases in hospital costs is fundamentally different from the problem of inflation in other sectors of the economy. The unusually rapid increase in the cost of a day of hospital care reflects a change in the character of hospital services rather than a higher price for an unchanged product. To understand hospital-cost inflation therefore requires understanding why hospitals now provide a much more sophisticated and expensive service than they did five, ten, or twenty years ago. The primary reason is that patients are now more willing to pay for expensive care, and doctors are much more willing to order it, because insurance finances a much larger share of those payments. The growth of public and private insurance has been so rapid that the net-of-insurance cost of hospital care has remained essentially unchanged relative to the general price level.

This chapter was written with Amy Taylor and published as a Staff Report of the Council on Wage and Price Stability, Executive Office of the President, January 1977.

Cost per Patient-Day

Hospital cost per patient-day has continually increased at a rate substantially greater than the rate of increase of consumer prices in general. The number of days of hospital care per capita has increased at an annual rate of 1.2 percent over the past twenty-five years, but the increase in the cost per patient-day is responsible for nearly all the rise in the per capita expenditure on hospital care.[1] Attention here is limited to short-term general hospitals and excludes psychiatric, tuberculosis, and other long-term care hospitals. Hospitals owned by the federal government are excluded, but all other ownership categories (nonprofit, state and local, and investor-owned) are included.[2]

Two measures of the daily cost of hospital care are now in general use: the Bureau of Labor Statistics' index of hospital service charges (IHSC) and the American Hospital Association's average cost per patient-day (ACPPD). The index of hospital service charges, which is part of the medical-care component of the consumer price index, is a weighted average of separate price indexes for the basic charge for room and board in the most common type of accommodation (a semiprivate room), for the use of the operating room, and for eight specific common services (a particular laboratory test, a particular diagnostic X ray, a particular physical therapy service, and so forth). This composite index is an improvement over the earlier average daily service charge (ADSC) index that was based only on the charge for room and board.[3] In contrast, the American Hospital Association's average cost per patient-day is not an index of separate prices but is calculated by dividing total hospital expenses (excluding the costs of capital investments) by the number of inpatient-days of care provided.[4]

1. The number of patient-days in short-term hospitals rose from 895 per thousand population in 1950 to 1,209 per thousand population in 1975, an annual rate of increase of 1.2 percent. By comparison, the average cost per day increased at an annual rate of 9.5 percent. The increase in the cost per patient-day is thus responsible for 89 percent of the average annual increase in the cost of hospital care per capita.

2. In the terminology of the American Hospital Association, the study deals with nonfederal short-term general and other special hospitals. The category "other special" includes hospitals specializing in the care of children or women, eye hospitals, and other specialty hospitals not involved in long-term care.

3. The earlier index is continued as the semiprivate room charge component of the new index.

4. Since some of the costs are incurred to provide outpatient services, ACPPD overstates the cost of inpatient care. Since 1963, the American Hospital Association has also estimated the average cost per "adjusted" patient-day by a rather arbitrary division of costs between inpatient and outpatient care. For 1975 the average cost per adjusted day is 12 percent less than ACPPD. Since the adjusted and unadjusted costs have increased at very similar rates and the unadjusted figure is available for a long period, the focus here is on ACPPD.

Table 1.1. Average cost per patient-day in current dollars and 1967 dollars

Year	Average cost per patient-day (ACPPD), current dollars	Consumer price index (CPI), 1967 = 100	Average cost per patient-day (ACPPD/CPI), 1967 dollars
1950	15.62	0.721	21.66
1955	23.12	0.802	28.83
1960	32.23	0.887	36.34
1963	38.91	0.917	42.43
1966	48.15	0.972	49.54
1969	70.03	1.098	63.78
1970	81.01	1.163	69.66
1971	92.31	1.213	76.10
1972	105.21	1.253	83.97
1973	114.69	1.331	86.17
1974	128.05	1.477	86.70
1975	151.53	1.612	94.00
1976	175.08[a]	1.711	102.33

a. The 1976 value of average cost per patient-day is estimated using the annual percentage increase from July 1975 to July 1976 for community hospitals in the American Hospital Association monthly survey.

These two measures differ conceptually in an important way. The index of hospital service charges is an attempt to measure the changing price of a fixed bundle of hospital services, just as the consumer price index in general attempts to measure the changing price of a fixed bundle of consumer products and services. In contrast, the ACPPD reflects the changing mix and volume of services as well as changes in the price of each type of service. Although each measure is interesting in its own right, the ACPPD is the more appropriate measure here since our interest is ultimately in the total increase in hospital cost. Moreover, the index of hospital service charges is only partly successful at measuring the price of a fixed bundle of services, because many of the improvements and increases in the quality of care are not priced separately but are built into the basic room charge. The IHSC is in reality a hybrid between a true price index and an alternative to the ACPPD measure of the changing cost of care. Finally, the IHSC has been available only since January 1972.

The first column of table 1.1 traces the average cost per day during the past twenty-five years. In 1950 the average cost per patient-day was less than $16; by 1976 ACPPD had reached $175.[5] This repre-

5. These figures do not separate outpatient costs; the American Hospital Association's suggested adjustment would lower the 1976 cost to approximately $154.

sents an average compound annual rate of increase of 9.7 percent. During the past decade alone, ACPPD rose more than 250 percent, an annual rate of increase of 13.8 percent.

Of course, it is inappropriate to consider the increase in the cost of hospital care apart from changes in the general level of prices. The second column of table 1.1 shows that the general level of consumer prices rose 137 percent between 1950 and 1976 (that is, the CPI rose from 0.721 to 1.711). The last column of table 1.1 therefore restates the average cost per patient-day in 1967 dollars by dividing ACPPD by the CPI. Measured in this way, average cost per day rose five times from 1950 to 1976, from $21.66 at 1967 prices to $102.33 at 1967 prices. This represents an average annual rate of increase in the relative cost of hospital care of 6.2 percent. The relative cost of hospital care more than doubled in the past decade, an average annual rate of increase of 7.5 percent.

Table 1.2 presents the annual rates of change for selected intervals since 1950. Before the introduction of Medicare and Medicaid in 1966, ACPPD rose at about 7 percent per year. More significant, the rate of increase of ACPPD exceeded the rise in the CPI by more than 5 percent during these sixteen years. The rates of increase after 1966 have been significantly higher. Although part of the increase shown

Table 1.2. Annual percentage changes in cost per patient-day

Interval	Average cost per patient-day (ACPPD)	Average cost per patient-day relative to consumer price index (ACPPD/CPI)
1950–1955	8.2	5.9
1955–1960	6.9	4.7
1960–1963	6.5	5.3
1963–1966	7.4	5.3
1966–1969	13.3	8.8
1969–1970	15.7	9.2
1970–1971	13.9	9.2
1971–1972	14.0	10.3
1972–1973	9.0	2.6
1973–1974	11.6	0.6
1974–1975	18.3	8.4
1975–1976	15.5[a]	8.9[a]

a. The 1976 value of average cost per patient-day is estimated using the annual percentage increase from July 1975 to July 1976 for community hospitals in the American Hospital Association monthly survey.

in the first column reflects the general inflation that has troubled the economy in recent years, the relative cost of hospital care is also rising more rapidly than before, as the second column shows. The relative ACPPD rose at more than 8 percent every year since 1966 except during the years of price and wage controls, 1972–73 and 1973–74.

The rates of increase for 1974–75 and 1975–76 indicate that there has been no lasting decline in the rate of cost increase. To assess whether the change is due to a "making up" of ground lost during the control period, it is useful to examine more detailed monthly data for the very recent period. The monthly figures presented in table 1.3 are calculated on the basis of an American Hospital Association survey of community hospitals; thus the coverage is not as broad as the data used to compute ACPPD. There is a strong seasonal pattern in the average cost per day, reflecting in particular the relatively small number of patient-days provided in December and the correspondingly high cost per day. To avoid misleading inferences, it is best to compare the cost in any month with the cost for the same month in previous years.

As table 1.3 shows, the rate of increase in cost per day has averaged

Table 1.3. Rates of increase of cost per patient-day in community hospitals in 1975–76

Year, month	Average cost per patient-day	Average cost per patient-day, one year earlier	Percentage change over previous year	Percentage change in relative price over previous year
1975:7	162.92	135.66	20.1	9.5
1975:8	164.35	138.81	18.4	9.0
1975:9	161.16	141.37	14.0	5.7
1975:10	159.07	139.61	13.9	5.9
1975:11	163.40	141.93	15.1	7.2
1975:12	179.60	154.01	16.6	9.0
1976:1	159.50	137.98	15.6	8.2
1976:2	161.87	142.13	13.9	7.2
1976:3	164.55	144.90	13.6	7.0
1976:4	172.83	149.62	15.5	8.9
1976:5	174.75	160.00	9.2	2.8
1976:6	183.72	158.37	16.0	9.5
1976:7	185.65	162.92	14.0	8.1
1976:8	186.49	164.35	13.5	7.5
1976:9	190.94	161.16	18.4	12.2

more than 18 percent for the twelve months ending in September 1976, an increase of more than 12 percent relative to the general level of consumer prices. Although the higher rate of price increase in the period just after price and wage controls were lifted in April 1974 might be attributed to some form of catching up, there is no evidence that the rate of relative price increase has slowed in more recent months.

These cost increases are national averages of the experiences of individual hospitals.[6] There is substantial variation among the individual hospitals around this overall average. During the period 1965–1974, approximately one-fourth of hospitals increased their average cost per patient-day by more than 14.0 percent, while an equal number had cost increases of less than 10.6 percent. Larger hospitals and teaching hospitals tended to have higher than average rates of increase.[7]

Hospital Wage Rates

Hospital wage rates have risen more rapidly than wages in other parts of the economy. The average earnings per hospital employee rose 237 percent between 1955 and 1975, while average earnings of all private nonfarm production workers rose only 142 percent. But these relatively greater wage increases are responsible for only a small part of the overall increases in the cost of hospital care. If the earnings of hospital employees had increased at the same rate as that of all private nonfarm production workers, the annual rate of increase of average cost per patient-day would have been 8.8 percent instead of 9.9 percent. During the past decade the rate of increase of hospital earnings in excess of the general rise in earnings has been responsible for only about one-fourth of the increase of hospital costs in excess of the general rise in consumer prices.

The first two columns of table 1.4 compare the increase in the average annual earnings per full-time equivalent hospital employee with the average for all private nonfarm production workers. The earnings of hospital employees rose from \$2,563 in 1955 to \$8,649 in 1975. During the same period the full-time annual earnings of all private nonfarm production workers rose from \$3,521 to \$8,522.[8] Hos-

---

6. Since ACPPD is calculated by dividing total cost by total patient-days, this is equivalent to a weighted average of the ACPPD for individual hospitals, with the weights proportional to the numbers of patient-days.

7. Other significant patterns can also be discovered. An analysis of the cost increases of 3,065 individual hospitals was presented in Feldstein and Taylor (1976).

8. These earnings figures exclude the cost of fringe benefits. Since fringe benefits

Table 1.4. Earnings and labor costs

Year	Average annual earnings per full-time equivalent hospital employee (1)	Average annual earnings, all private nonfarm employment[a] (2)	Full-time equivalent employment per patient-day (3)	Labor cost as percentage of ACPPD (4)
1955	$2,563	$3,521	2.03	61.7
1960	3,240	4,195	2.26	62.3
1963	3,639	4,600	2.41	61.7
1966	4,097	5,139	2.61	61.1
1969	5,380	5,960	2.80	59.8
1970	5,921	6,212	2.92	58.8
1971	6,530	6,619	3.01	58.6
1972	7,062	7,080	3.10	56.8
1973	7,388	7,562	3.15	55.9
1974	7,803	8,031	3.26	54.3
1975	8,649	8,522[b]	3.39	53.1

a. *Economic Report to the President,* 1976; published weekly figures have been convert-ed to full-time equivalent annual rates. Data relate to production or nonsupervisory workers.

b. Preliminary.

pital workers thus went from earning less than three-fourths of the national average to earning slightly more than the national average. Since the mix of education levels and occupations of hospital workers differs from that of the rest of the economy, there is no particular significance to the current equality of earnings. Moreover, the rising level of earnings for hospital workers and for workers in general reflects changes in the mix of education, experience, and occupations and not just increases in the wage rate for an unchanged group of employees.

The greater increase in the average earnings of hospital employees has frequently been cited as the primary cause of the unusually rapid rise in hospital costs. Such an interpretation is not supported by a more detailed examination of the evidence. The third column of table 1.4 shows that a substantial part of the increase in labor cost per patient-day is due to the rising number of employees rather than to their

---

have grown relative to cash earnings, the calculations presented in this section under-state the rates of increase of both hospital earnings and other earnings.

higher wage rates. The number of full-time equivalent employees per patient-day rose form 2.03 in 1955 to 3.39 in 1975. The number of employees per patient-day thus rose at an average annual rate of 2.6 percent while the average earnings per employee increased at a rate of 6.3 percent. The increase in the number of employees therefore accounts for some 30 percent of the overall increase in labor cost per patient-day. Moreover, hospital spending for nonlabor inputs has increased even more rapidly than the expenditure for labor. As the final column of table 1.4 shows, labor costs have been a declining fraction of total cost per patient-day; payroll accounted for 62 percent of hospital costs in 1955 but only 53 percent in 1975.

These indications of the limited importance of the rise in hospital wage rates suggest the following question: what would the rise in the average cost per patient-day have been if the earnings of hospital employees had only increased at the same rate as the earnings of all private employees? The figures in table 1.5 show that earnings of hospital employees rose 10.8 percent between 1974 and 1975. Since payroll expenses accounted for 54.3 percent of total cost at the beginning of this period, this 10.8 percent increase in earnings by itself would raise the average cost per patient-day by 5.9 percent.[9] The remainder of the 18.3 percent rise in the average cost per patient-day reflects the increased number of employees and the greater expenditure on nonlabor inputs. If the increase in earnings of hospital employees had been limited to the 6.1 percent experienced by all private sector employees, the increase in earnings would have raised the average cost per patient-day by 3.3 percent instead of 5.9 percent. The average cost per patient-day would therefore have risen by 2.6 percentage points less than it actually did, that is, by 15.7 percent instead of 18.3 percent.[10] The difference is clearly not very large, only about one-seventh of the actual rate of cost increase.

A comparison of columns 3 and 4 shows that this result for 1974–75 is quite typical of the entire twenty-year period. For the period 1955–1975 the ACPPD rose at the rate of 9.9 percent. If the rate

9. That is, 5.9 percent is 54.3 percent of 10.8 percent. This calculation assumes that the increase in earnings per employee has no effect on the number of employees or on the use of nonlabor inputs. If higher earnings induce a reduction in the number of employees, the calculation overstates the effect of the earnings increase. Similarly, if higher earnings induce an increase of nonlabor inputs to substitute for employees, the calculation understates the effect of the earnings increase. On balance, ignoring induced changes can be expected to lead to an overstatement of the effect of the wage increases on the average cost per patient-day.

10. This method of calculation probably overstates the difference in the total cost increase that would result from limiting the increase in the earnings per hospital employee.

Table 1.5. Annual rates of change in earnings and labor costs

| Interval | Annual percentage rates of change of | | | | | |
	Earnings of hospital employees (1)	Earnings of all private nonfarm employees (2)	ACPPD (3)	ACPPD if hospital employee earnings increased as all private nonfarm earnings (4)	ACPPD in 1967 dollars (5)	ACPPD in 1967 dollars if hospital employee earnings increased as all private nonfarm earnings (6)
1955–1960	4.8	3.6	6.9	6.2	4.7	4.0
1960–1963	3.9	3.1	6.5	6.0	5.3	4.8
1963–1966	4.0	3.8	7.4	7.3	5.3	5.2
1966–1969	9.5	5.1	13.3	10.6	8.8	6.1
1969–1970	10.1	4.2	15.7	12.2	9.2	5.7
1970–1971	10.3	6.5	13.9	11.7	9.2	7.0
1971–1972	8.1	7.0	14.0	13.5	10.3	9.8
1972–1973	4.6	6.8	9.0	10.2	2.6	3.8
1973–1974	5.6	6.2	11.6	12.0	0.6	0.2
1974–1975	10.8	6.1	18.3	15.7	8.4	5.8
1955–1966	4.4	3.5	6.9	6.3	7.8	7.2
1966–1975	8.7	5.8	13.6	11.8	7.4	5.6
1955–1975	6.3	4.5	9.9	8.8	7.6	6.5

of increase of hospital employees' earnings had been limited to 4.5 percent instead of 6.3 percent, the ACPPD would have risen at 8.8 percent instead of 9.9 percent. The evidence in columns 1 and 2 shows that the gap between the increase in hospital earnings and other earnings has been greater in the last ten years of the period than in the preceding decade. But even if the 8.7 percent rate of increase in hospital earnings from 1966 to 1975 had been held to the 5.8 percent rise in general earnings, the annual increase in ACPPD would only have been cut from 13.6 percent to 11.8 percent.

The last two columns of table 1.5 repeat these calculations for the increase in hospital costs relative to the general price level. The last line of the table shows that the increase in the relative ACPPD (ACPPD divided by the consumer price) was 7.6 percent for the twenty-year period 1955–1975 and would have been reduced to 6.5 percent if the increase in hospital earnings had been limited to the economy-wide rate of increase. For the most recent decade the corresponding figures are 7.4 percent and 5.6 percent. The rate of increase of hospital earnings in excess of the general rise in earnings is therefore responsible for about one-fourth of the increase of hospital costs in excess of the general rise in consumer prices.

The Changing Character of Hospital Care

The unusually rapid increase in the cost per patient-day reflects the changing character of hospital care and therefore the growing number of employees and the increasing volume of equipment and supplies rather than the rise in the price of these inputs.

The four basic components of hospital-cost inflation are an increased number of personnel per patient-day, higher wage rates, an increased use of nonlabor inputs per patient-day, and higher prices for those nonlabor inputs. Decomposing the overall rise in cost into these four components is a useful first step toward understanding why costs have risen so rapidly. The analysis developed in this section shows that about 75 percent of the increase in average cost per patient-day relative to the general price level has been due to the increase in inputs per patient-day; only about 25 percent has been due to the increase of input prices in excess of the general increase in consumer prices.

It is useful to consider first the relative importance of increases in labor and nonlabor costs. Line 1 of table 1.6 shows that labor cost per patient-day rose from $14.26 in 1955 to $80.39 in 1975, an average annual increase of 9.0 percent. In contrast, the nonlabor cost per patient-day (line 4) rose from $8.86 to $71.14, an average annual increase of 11.0 percent. The overall increase of ACPPD of 9.9 percent is a weighted average of the rates of increase of the two components, with each component weighted by the corresponding share in total cost. Thus the 9.0 percent increase in labor cost contributes 5.13 percent to the total cost increase (9.0 times 0.57, the average labor share in total cost), and the 11.0 percent increase in nonlabor cost contributes 4.73 percent to the total cost increase. The increases in labor and in nonlabor costs therefore each account for about half of the rise in ACPPD.

The 9.0 percent annual increase in labor cost per patient-day can be divided into a 6.3 percent increase in earnings per employee (line 2 of table 1.6) and a 2.6 percent increase in the number of employees per patient-day (line 3). These figures imply that the 5.13 percent contribution of labor cost to the overall cost increase can be divided into 3.63 percent due to higher earnings per employee and 1.50 percent due to the increase in the number of employees.

It is more difficult to divide the 11.0 percent annual increase in nonlabor cost per patient-day into increases in the price of inputs and increases in the volume of inputs. Changes in the use of nonlabor inputs cannot be measured in physical terms in the same way that changes in labor inputs can be measured by the number of employees. If an index of the prices paid by hospitals for nonlabor inputs were available, it would be possible to construct an index of the quantity of nonlabor inputs by dividing nonlabor costs by the index of prices that hospitals paid for those inputs. Such an index of the price of nonlabor inputs was developed by using the information on hospitals' purchases of different inputs that is contained in the most detailed input–output table for the American economy.[11] This composite price index incorporated thirty-five types of inputs and used the corresponding disaggregated components of the wholesale and consumer price indexes. The price index defined in this way was then evaluated for the years 1958–1967. An analysis of the resulting index showed that it was very highly correlated with the consumer price index;[12] changes in the prices paid by hospitals for nonlabor inputs closely followed the general movement of consumer prices. This analysis therefore uses the consumer price index to measure changes in these input prices and thereby to determine the relative volume of nonlabor inputs.

11. This index is discussed in chapter 5.
12. The simple correlation between the CPI and this input price index was 0.999 for the period 1958–1967. Its correlation with the wholesale price index was noticeably lower, 0.88.

Table 1.6. Input prices and real inputs per patient-day

Real inputs	1955	1960	1963	1966	1969	1970	1971	1972	1973	1974	1975
1. Labor cost per patient-day ($)	14.26	20.08	24.01	29.41	41.85	47.61	54.13	59.71	64.08	69.57	80.39
2. Earnings per employee ($)	2,563	3,240	3,639	4,097	5,380	5,921	6,530	7,062	7,388	7,803	8,649
3. Full-time equivalent employees per patient-day	2.03	2.26	2.41	2.61	2.80	2.92	3.01	3.10	3.15	3.26	3.39
4. Nonlabor cost per patient-day ($)	8.86	12.15	14.90	18.74	28.18	33.40	38.18	45.50	50.61	58.54	71.14
5. CPI, 1967 = 1.00	0.802	0.887	0.917	0.972	1.098	1.163	1.213	1.253	1.331	1.477	1.612
6. Nonlabor inputs per patient-day, 1967 dollars	11.04	13.70	16.25	19.28	25.66	28.72	31.48	36.31	38.02	39.63	44.13
7. Input price index, 1967 = 100	0.633	0.750	0.811	0.889	1.096	1.188	1.282	1.363	1.434	1.543	1.700
8. Inputs per patient-day, 1967 dollars	36.52	42.97	47.98	54.16	63.90	68.19	72.00	77.19	79.98	82.99	89.14
9. ACPPD	23.12	32.23	38.91	48.15	70.03	81.01	92.31	105.21	114.69	128.05	151.53
10. Relative ACPPD	28.83	36.34	42.43	49.54	63.78	69.66	76.10	83.97	86.17	96.70	94.00
11. AHA input price index, 1967 = 100	—	—	—	—	100.0	108.5	115.3	119.2	125.1	136.8	152.6
12. Inputs per patient-day in 1969 dollars (based on AHA index)	—	—	—	—	70.03	74.66	80.06	88.26	91.68	93.60	99.30

Line 6 of table 1.6 presents the measure of the volume of nonlabor inputs obtained by deflating the nonlabor cost per patient-day (line 4) by the consumer price index. This decomposition implies that the 11.0 percent annual increase in the cost of nonlabor inputs consists of a 7.2 percent rise in volume of those inputs and a 3.6 percent rise in their price. Since the rising cost of nonlabor inputs contributes 4.73 percent to the overall increase in ACPPD, the corresponding contributions for the volume of nonlabor inputs and their prices are 3.15 percent and 1.58 percent.

Thus the overall 9.9 percent increase of ACPPD from 1955 to 1975 can be decomposed into its four components: number of employees, 1.50 percent; volume of nonlabor inputs, 3.15 percent; earnings per employee, 3.63 percent; price of nonlabor inputs, 1.58 percent. A corresponding decomposition can be calculated for individual years or subperiods on the basis of the data presented in tables 1.6 and 1.7.

An overall input price index for hospital inputs can be calculated by combining the consumer price index with an index of earnings per employee obtained by dividing the earnings presented in row 2 of table 1.6 by the 1967 earnings of $4,918. The resulting input price index, presented in row 7, indicates that the prices that hospitals paid for their inputs rose at an annual rate of 5.1 percent between 1955 and 1975.[13] Dividing the ACPPD by this index of input prices yields the volume of hospital inputs per patient-day as measured by their value at 1967 prices (line 8). The volume of hospital inputs rose at 4.6 percent per year, from $36.52 (at 1967 prices) in 1955 to $89.14 in 1975.[14]

Stated in this way, the increase in the volume of hospital inputs is responsible for slightly less than half of the rise in ACPPD. More interesting, however, is to analyze the rise in ACPPD relative to the general level of consumer prices. Line 10 of table 1.6 shows that the relative ACPPD rose at an annual rate of 6.1 percent during the twenty-year period 1955–1975. The 4.6 percent annual increase in real inputs therefore accounts for about 75 percent of the relative rise in hospital costs. The remaining 25 percent comes about because the hospitals' input prices increased at a more rapid rate than the general increase in consumer prices.

A similar decomposition for individual years and subperiods is shown in table 1.7. Line 6 shows the annual rate of increase in the

13. The index uses 1967 quantity weights: 0.60 for the labor price index and 0.40 for the nonlabor price index.
14. These two component rates of increase do not add to the 9.9 percent rate of increase of ACPPD because of the interaction effect: $(1.051)(1.046) = 1.099$.

Table 1.7. Annual percentage changes in input prices and quantities

	1955–1960	1960–1963	1963–1966	1966–1969	1969–1970	1970–1971	1971–1972	1972–1973	1973–1974	1974–1975
1. Earnings per employee	4.8	3.9	4.0	9.5	10.1	10.3	8.1	4.6	5.6	10.8
2. Full-time equivalent employees per patient-day	2.2	2.2	2.7	2.4	4.3	3.1	3.0	1.6	3.5	4.0
3. CPI	2.0	1.1	2.0	4.1	5.9	4.3	3.3	6.2	11.0	9.1
4. Nonlabor inputs per patient-day	4.4	5.9	5.9	10.0	11.9	9.6	15.3	4.7	4.2	11.4
5. Input price index	3.5	2.6	3.1	7.2	8.4	7.9	6.3	5.2	7.6	10.2
6. Inputs per patient-day	3.3	3.7	4.1	5.7	6.7	5.6	7.2	3.6	3.8	7.4
7. ACPPD	6.9	6.5	7.4	13.3	15.7	13.9	14.0	9.0	11.6	18.3
8. Relative ACPPD	4.7	5.3	5.3	8.8	9.2	9.2	10.3	2.6	0.6	8.4
9. Percentage of increase in relative ACPPD due to increased inputs	70	70	77	62	74	58	69	100+	100+	88
10. AHA input price index	–	–	–	–	8.5	6.3	3.4	5.0	9.4	11.5
11. Inputs per patient-day based on AHA index	–	–	–	–	6.6	7.2	10.2	3.9	2.1	6.1

volume of inputs per patient-day, while line 8 shows the corresponding increase in the relative ACPPD. For example, from 1974 to 1975
the relative ACPPD rose 8.4 percent while real inputs per day rose 7.4
percent; this increase in real inputs thus accounts for 88 percent of
the rise in the relative ACPPD, a figure reported in line 9.

The impact of the price and wage controls on the hospital industry
is very clear from the figures of table 1.7. Controls began in August
1971 and were removed in April 1974. The rise in earnings per employee was substantially reduced in 1972 – 73 and 1973 – 74 (line 1).
In both years hospital wages rose substantially less than consumer
prices. While general wages were rising at 6.8 percent in 1972 – 73
(see table 1.5), earnings per hospital employee rose only 4.6 percent;
in 1973 – 74 the corresponding figures were 6.2 percent and 5.6 percent. There was a brief slowdown in the rate of growth of the number
of employees in 1972 – 73 (line 2), the only pair of years for which
controls were continually enforced. Nonlabor inputs per patient-day
also fell sharply, as shown in line 4. The composite index of real inputs per patient-day (line 6) therefore rose at only 3.6 percent in
1972 – 73 and 3.8 percent in 1973 – 74, by far the lowest rates during
the past decade.

The American Hospital Association has developed its own index of
the price of inputs (both labor and nonlabor) purchased by hospitals.
This input price index and the implied measure of real inputs per
patient-day (in 1969 prices) are presented in lines 10 and 11 of table
1.6. The corresponding rates of change are shown in lines 11 and 12
of table 1.7. Because the AHA index has been available only for a relatively short period, we have not analyzed the implications of these
figures. But it is clear from a comparison of lines 5 and 11 (or 6 and
12) of table 1.7 that the AHA index has behaved in a roughly similar
way to the alternative index developed here.

The Growth of Insurance

The previous section showed that approximately three-fourths of the
rise in hospital costs relative to the general price level has been due to
the increased volume of personnel and other inputs. Hospitals use
more inputs to produce an increasingly sophisticated style of hospital
care. This change in the character of the hospitals' service accounts
for the unusually rapid rise in hospital costs.

Why have hospitals changed the character of their product in this
way? The evidence indicates that hospitals have changed their product in response to market pressures from patients and their doctors.
Patients want and are willing to pay for more expensive services.

Physicians also recommend more expensive patterns of care to their patients and try to induce the hospitals with which they are affiliated to provide more staff and facilities. This increased demand for expensive care is primarily the result of the growing share of hospital costs paid by public and private insurance. With insurance now paying approximately 90 percent of all hospital costs, there is a strong incentive for patients and their physicians to seek the "best possible care" almost without concern for its cost.[15]

Table 1.8 traces the dramatic growth of private and public insurance during the past twenty-five years. In 1950 private insurance paid 29 percent of the cost of short-term hospital care and government paid an additional 21 percent; patients financed the remaining 50 percent by direct out-of-pocket expenditure.[16] By 1963 the fraction of costs paid by private insurance had nearly doubled, rising from 29 percent to 56 percent. The fraction financed by direct consumer spending was cut nearly in half, falling from 50 percent to 26 percent. If government payments are excluded from consideration, the fraction of private costs paid by private insurance rose from 37 percent in 1950 to 68 percent in 1963 (line 4). Direct consumer spending fell from nearly two-thirds of the cost of private care in 1950 to less than one-third in 1963.

The growth of private and public insurance during the past decade has reduced direct consumer spending to less than 12 percent of the cost of short-term hospital care. The percentage of costs paid by the government has more than doubled since the introduction of Medicare and Medicaid, rising from 18 percent in the early 1960s to 44 percent in 1974 (line 2). Private health insurance has also grown; private insurance paid 68 percent of private health care costs in 1963 and 79 percent by 1975 (line 4).

15. Hospital technology has also changed because of independent scientific discoveries, but the nature of the scientific developments and technological innovation (quality improving instead of cost saving) reflects the market demand condition. See chapter 4 of M. Feldstein (1971b) for further discussion of these issues.

16. These percentages and the corresponding figures for later years are calculated on the basis of data published by the Social Security Administration and the American Hospital Association. The Social Security Administration estimates total expenditure on hospital care and the proportions financed by government, private insurance, and direct consumer spending. All these amounts refer to care in all types of hospitals, including long-term and psychiatric institutions, and not just the short-term hospitals that are the subject of this chapter. To develop estimates for short-term hospitals, we subtracted the American Hospital Association's measures of the cost of care in federal, long-term, tuberculosis, and psychiatric hospitals from the Social Security values for total and government spending. An alternative estimating procedure that started with the American Hospital Association data to estimate private expenditure directly produced estimates very similar to those presented here.

Table 1.8. Insurance and the net cost of hospital care

	1950	1955	1960	1963	1966	1969	1970	1971	1972	1973	1974	1975
Percentage of hospital costs paid by												
1. Private insurance	29.3	44.7	52.5	56.0	51.4	44.6	45.6	45.7	45.4	45.9	45.4	43.6
2. Government	21.1	19.9	18.8	17.8	25.5	37.6	37.8	40.6	41.1	40.9	42.8	44.5
3. Direct consumer spending	49.6	35.2	28.7	26.2	23.1	17.8	16.6	13.7	13.5	13.2	11.8	11.9
Percentage of private cost of hospital care paid by												
4. Private insurance	37.1	55.9	64.7	68.1	69.0	71.5	73.2	76.9	77.1	77.7	79.4	78.6
5. Direct consumer spending	62.9	44.1	35.3	31.9	31.0	28.5	26.8	23.1	22.9	26.3	20.6	21.4
6. Average cost per patient-day	15.62	23.12	32.23	38.91	48.15	70.03	81.01	92.31	105.21	114.69	128.05	151.53
7. Net cost 1[a]	7.75	8.14	9.25	10.19	11.12	12.47	13.53	12.65	14.20	15.14	15.11	18.03
8. Net cost 2[b]	9.82	10.19	11.38	12.41	14.93	19.96	21.71	21.32	24.09	25.58	26.38	32.43

Note: All figures exclude hospital costs in federal, long-term, tuberculosis, and psychiatric hospitals.
a. Net cost 1 = ACPPD × Direct consumer expenditure ÷ Total expenditure.
b. Net cost 2 = ACPPD × Direct consumer expenditure ÷ Private expenditure.

Although consumers pay the full cost of the more expensive hospital care through higher insurance premiums and higher taxes, at the time of illness the choice of the patient and his physician reflects the net cost of the care. Because of the dramatic growth of third-party payments, the net cost of hospital care to patients at the time that they enter the hospital has grown much more slowly than the gross average cost per patient-day. The cost net of payments by both insurance and government (net cost 1) is an overall measure of the average net cost that affects patients' demand for hospital care at the time of illness. However, since most families do not receive government assistance in paying hospital bills, it is relevant to study cost net of insurance but not net of any government payments. Net cost 2 measures directly the average net cost that private patients pay for hospital care at the time of illness. The values of net cost 1 and net cost 2 are shown in lines 7 and 8 of table 1.8.

The figures for net cost 1 show that when deductions are made for payments by insurance companies and government, the average net cost of a day of hospital care rose from $7.75 in 1950 (49.6 percent of the ACPPD of $15.62) to $18.03 in 1975 (11.9 percent of $151.53). Even if we ignore hospital care paid by government (net cost 2), the rise is still only from $9.82 in 1950 to $32.43 in 1975.

Since net costs 1 and 2 are measures of the net prices that influence demand for care, it is more appropriate to measure these net costs relative to the prices of other goods and services. Table 1.9 shows that the overall net cost of hospital care (net cost 1) actually declined between 1950 and 1974 relative to the cost of all other consumer goods and services. Measured in the prices of 1967, the net cost of a day of hospital care was $10.75 in 1950 and only $10.23 in 1974. The figures imply that purchasing a day of hospital care required a smaller sacrifice of others goods and services in 1974 than it did in 1950. More generally, the figures in the second column of table 1.9 show that the net relative price showed no discernible trend between 1950 and 1975. The average annual rate of increase has been only 0.1 percent.

Even if we ignore the growth of government payments and focus on the cost of privately paid care net of private insurance (net cost 2), the rate of increase has been very small. The third column of table 1.9 shows that net cost 2 in 1967 dollars rose from $13.62 in 1950 to $20.11 in 1975, an average annual rate of increase of 1.6 percent. This is only one-fourth of the 6.0 percent rate of growth of ACPPD in 1967 dollars.

In thinking about the demand for hospital care, it is also useful to compare the cost of hospital care with the earnings of the typical worker. In 1950 the average spendable (aftertax) weekly earnings of

Table 1.9. The net cost of care in 1967 dollars

Year	Average cost per patient-day (1)	Net cost 1 (2)	Net cost 2 (3)	Net cost 2 as percentage of spendable weekly earnings[a] (4)
1950	21.66	10.75	13.62	18.9
1955	28.83	10.15	12.71	16.1
1960	36.34	10.43	12.82	15.6
1963	42.43	11.12	13.54	15.8
1966	49.54	11.44	15.36	16.8
1969	63.78	11.35	18.18	20.0
1970	69.66	11.63	18.67	20.7
1971	76.10	10.43	17.58	19.0
1972	83.97	11.34	19.23	19.9
1973	86.17	11.37	19.22	20.1
1974	86.70	10.23	17.86	19.6
1975	94.00	11.18	20.11	22.2

a. Net cost 2 divided by average spendable weekly earnings for all private nonagricultural employees.

production workers in private nonfarm employment was $52.04. The cost of a day's care net of private insurance (net cost 2) was $9.82, or 18.9 percent of spendable weekly earnings. Although the net cost of care in 1975 had increased to $32.43, spendable weekly earnings had increased to $145.93. As a fraction of earnings, the net cost of care had remained essentially unchanged at 22.2 percent.

The picture that emerges from tables 1.8 and 1.9 can be summarized briefly. Although the cost of producing a day of hospital care has increased rapidly during the past twenty-five years, the real net price to the patient when he goes to the hospital has hardly changed at all. Even if government spending is ignored, the expansion of private insurance has meant that the net cost of privately financed care has not increased relative to average weekly income.

There is now substantial evidence that consumers are responsive to the net price of hospital care, that is, that patients, guided by their doctors, demand more services and more expensive services when a larger part of their costs are offset by insurance.[17] Hospitals respond

17. A variety of evidence is summarized and discussed in chapter 2. For more recent evidence see chapter 4 and Phelps (1975).

to this increased demand for expensive care by raising their cost per patient-day and using the extra revenue to provide a more expensive style of care. This change in the apparent quality of care further increases demand, setting off another round of price and quality increases.[18]

The econometric evidence also indicates that the demand stimulated by increases in insurance occurs only with a lag, as doctors and patients develop new standards and habits. Similarly, hospitals respond to the increasing demand with a lag, as new personnel, equipment, and services are added. As a result of these lags, the increase in the relative cost of hospital care that occurs in any year reflects the increases in insurance during a number of previous years. Even if there were no future increases in the fraction of hospital costs paid by public and private insurance, hospital costs would continue to increase relative to prices in general for a number of years because of past increases in insurance.

Private insurance and government programs now finance approximately equal shares of hospital care; each now accounts for about 45 percent. The growth of government spending has been due primarily to the introduction of Medicare and Medicaid in 1966; as line 2 of table 1.8 shows, before 1966 the fraction of hospital care financed by the government was falling. The growth of private insurance—from paying 37 percent of private hospital spending in 1950 to 79 percent in 1975—reflects in part the rational response of families seeking protection against unexpected and expensive illness. This process tends to be self-reinforcing: the high cost of hospital care induces patients to buy more complete insurance, and the growth of insurance induces the hospital to produce more expensive care.

The purchase of private health insurance is greatly encouraged by tax policies that now reduce tax revenues by more than $6 billion a year. The most important form of this tax subsidy is allowing employers to deduct the cost of health insurance premiums from the company's taxable income while allowing employees to exclude the value of these premiums from their own taxable incomes. These premiums are not subject to Social Security taxes or to state income taxes.

Even for a relatively low income family, the inducement to buy insurance can be quite substantial. Because of the income and payroll taxes, a married man with two children will take home only an additional $70 for each $100 his employer adds to his wage. If the employer buys health insurance instead, the full $100 can be applied against

18. This two-way relation between demand and quality is estimated explicitly in chapter 4.

the premium and there is no tax to be paid. For workers in high tax brackets the incentive is even stronger. In the aggregate, the resulting government subsidy exceeded $6 billion in 1975.[19]

The Continuing Increase in Hospital Wages

Although hospital employees are now paid at least as well as comparable workers in other industries, hospital wages continue to rise more rapidly than other wages in the economy.

The second section of this chapter showed that the wages of hospital employees have increased significantly faster than wages in other sectors of the economy. In the period from 1966 to 1975 hospital wages rose at 8.7 percent a year while the earnings of all private non-agricultural workers increased at 5.8 percent. The higher rate of wage increase for hospital workers added approximately 1.8 percentage points to the rate of increase of the average cost per patient-day. Since the ACPPD relative to the consumer price level rose at 7.4 percent a year, the extra wage increases of hospital employees account for only about one-fourth of the rise in the relative cost of hospital care. Although this higher rate of wage increase is not responsible for most of the increase in hospital cost, as is often alleged, it does contribute significantly to the increasing cost of hospital care. Even a 1.8 percent addition to the annual rate of cost increase raises the average cost by 20 percent in a decade. If this differential had not existed since 1966, the average cost per day in 1976 would have been $149 instead of $175.

Table 1.10 shows that hospital earnings continue to increase more rapidly than earnings elsewhere in the economy. Column 1 presents the annual rate of increase of earnings per full-time employee in community hospitals.[20] The second column converts these figures into an index number with 1967 equal to 100. Because of seasonal variations in earnings, it is best to compare each month with the same month a year earlier. These percentage increases are shown in column 3. The fourth column presents an index of average hourly earn-

19. An estimate of $6.4 billion is developed in Mitchell and Phelps (1975). The estimate of $4.2 billion for fiscal year 1977 made by the staffs of the Treasury and the Joint Committee on Internal Revenue does not include the subsidy that results from excluding premiums from the earnings subject to the Social Security payroll tax. For further discussion of this subsidy and its effect on the demand for health insurance, see chapter 7.

20. The data in this table are based on the American Hospital Association's monthly survey of community hospitals. Total payroll for each month is divided by the number of full-time equivalent employees and rescaled to an annual rate.

Table 1.10. Increases in hospital and nonhospital earnings

Year, month	Annual earnings per hospital employee ($) (1)	Annual earnings per hospital employee (1967 = 100) (2)	Change over previous year (%) (3)	Hourly earnings, private nonfarm production workers (1967 = 100) (4)	Change over previous year (%) (5)
1975:7	9,045	183.9	9.3	173.1	8.7
1975:8	9,074	184.5	8.0	174.6	8.7
1975:9	8,805	179.0	7.6	175.2	8.1
1975:10	9,119	185.4	8.1	176.7	8.2
1975:11	8,953	182.0	8.9	178.2	8.5
1975:12	9,357	190.3	9.9	178.6	8.0
1976:1	9,347	190.1	7.7	179.6	8.0
1976:2	8,845	179.8	10.8	180.8	7.7
1976:3	9,505	193.3	9.5	181.4	7.3
1976:4	9,298	189.1	9.6	182.2	7.6
1976:5	9,533	193.8	10.8	183.7	7.7
1976:6	9,510	193.8	10.8	183.7	7.7
1976:7	9,779	198.8	8.1	185.7	7.3
1976:8	9,792	199.1	7.9	186.9	7.0
1976:9	9,651	196.2	9.6	187.1	6.8

ings for all private nonfarm production workers, and the fifth column gives the annual percentage increase for these earnings.

The average of the fifteen annual changes in hospital wages is 9.1 percent, while the corresponding average for all private nonfarm workers is 7.8 percent. For the available nine months of 1976 these averages are 9.3 percent and 7.4 percent. Since payroll is now 53 percent of total costs, the 1976 wage increase differential of 1.9 percent implies a one percentage point increase in the rate of hospital cost inflation.

The rapid rise in the relative wage of hospital employees suggests five important questions.

1. Does the increase in the average earnings of hospital employees represent a change in the mix of employees toward more skilled persons with higher wages, or have hospital wage rates actually increased faster than average earnings?

2. Are wages rising because lower-paid hospital employees are receiving abnormally high pay increases while the wages of higher-paid hospital employees increase in line with economy-wide averages?

3. Are wage increases a reflection of the hospitals' competition for specialized hospital personnel whose supply cannot be readily increased?

4. How do hospital wages compare with the wages of workers in other industries who have similar occupations or similar demographic and schooling characteristics?

5. Why have hospital wages increased relative to wages in other industries?

The data used to answer these questions are based on surveys of hospital industry wages conducted by the Bureau of Labor Statistics.[21] The surveys have been conducted in an increasing number of metropolitan areas every three years since 1957. In three of the surveys (1963, 1966, 1969) estimates are available for all metropolitan areas of the nation combined. To permit comparability, the wage rate analysis deals only with nongovernmental hospitals in the survey areas. The corresponding national earnings figures are the same as in previous sections and are therefore not exactly comparable.

A detailed analysis of the wage rates for individual hospital occupations suggests that these wage rates rose as fast as or faster than overall earnings per hospital employee. There is no indication that the overall mix of hospital employees changed in the direction of higher skills and higher wages. If anything, the data imply that the number of employees with relatively low pay has grown faster than the number of higher-paid employees.

The reports of the surveys by the Bureau of Labor Statistics[22] provide the numbers of employees and the average wage rates for a detailed list of twenty-eight occupations. These data have been used to calculate the average annual wage change that would have occurred if the relative numbers of employees in different occupations had remained unchanged. More specifically, separate wage rate indexes were calculated for each metropolitan area and for the nation as a whole using the employment mix in 1966 as the basic weights. These wage rate indexes have generally increased more rapidly than the average earnings of all hospital employees, implying that the mix of employees has generally been shifting toward lower-paid occupations.

A simple example illustrates the calculation of the wage rate index. Consider a hospital that has only two types of employees, nurses and maids. The number of nurses in 1963 was $N_{63} = 120$ and the number of maids was $M_{63} = 80$. Their wages in 1963 were $WN_{63} = \$110$ per

21. For an earlier analysis of these issues based on much more restricted data, see chapter 5 of M. Feldstein (1971b).

22. For example, U.S. Bureau of Labor Statistics (1975).

week for nurses and $WM_{63} = \$55$ per week for maids. By 1966 the number of nurses had increased to $N_{66} = 135$ and the number of maids had increased proportionately more to $M_{66} = 105$. Their wages rose to $WN_{66} = \$125$ per week and $WM_{66} = \$65$ per week. These figures imply that the average weekly wage per employee was $88 in 1963 and $98.75 in 1966. This increase of 12.2 percent in the average wage is actually less than the increase of both nurses' wages (14 percent) and maids' wages (18 percent) because the number of lower-paid maids increased relative to the higher-paid nurses. If the number of nurses and maids had been the same in 1963 as in 1966, the average wage in 1963 would have been

$$\frac{(N_{66} \times WN_{63}) + (M_{66} \times WM_{63})}{N_{66} + M_{66}} = \$85.94.$$

Comparing this figure with the $98.75 average for 1966 shows an increase of 15.3 percent, a more appropriate measure of the rate of change than the actual change in average wage per employee. The wage rate index number, with 1966 equal to 100, is defined as the ratio of the calculated average wage for other years based on 1966 employment to the actual average wage for 1966. For 1963 this yields[23]

$$W_{63} = 100 \times \frac{(N_{66} \times WN_{63}) + (M_{66} \times WM_{63})}{(N_{66} \times WN_{66}) + (M_{66} \times WM_{66})} = 87.0.$$

Table 1.11 presents the available wage rate indexes for the individual years between 1956 and 1972.[24] These indexes are based on wages in twenty-eight separate occupations. Data for eight metropolitan areas have been available since 1960. National data were produced only for the years 1963, 1966, and 1969. For comparison, an index is presented for the annual earnings of hospital employees. The annual rates of increase of these wage and earnings indexes are presented in table 1.12.

Consider first the national wage index shown in the next to the last line of table 1.11. This wage index increased from 84.6 in 1963 to 100 in 1966 and 137.0 in 1969. The increase in both periods was greater

23. More generally, the wage rate index for comparing 1966 and some other year t is defined in terms of K different occupations as

$$W = \frac{\Sigma_{i=1}^{K} N_{i,66} W_{i,t}}{\Sigma_{i=1}^{K} N_{i,66} W_{i,66}},$$

where $N_{i,66}$ is the number of employees in occupation i in 1966 and $W_{i,t}$ is the wage rate in this occupation in year t.

24. New data for 1975 were not released in time for this analysis.

Table 1.11. Indexes of hospital wage rates in selected cities

	1956	1957	1960	1963	1966	1969	1972
Atlanta	—	—	66.4	78.0	100.0	140.4	181.8
Baltimore	55.8	—	70.3	81.2	100.0	134.7	190.0
Boston	—	—	75.3	83.5	100.0	142.0	175.0
Chicago	—	—	79.9	86.7	100.0	132.9	175.0
Dallas	—	—	74.4	84.4	100.0	135.5	165.4
Los Angeles	—	—	85.1	87.8	100.0	134.9	168.7
New York	—	53.9	66.8	83.8	100.0	137.1	184.9
St. Louis	—	—	—	—	100.0	139.9	168.9
San Francisco	64.9	—	75.6	86.2	100.0	132.2	174.9
All metropolitan areas	—	—	—	84.6	100.0	137.0	—
National average annual earnings of hospital employees	63.7	65.7	79.1	88.8	100.0	131.3	172.4

than the rise in average earnings per employee; the last line of table 1.11 shows an increase from 88.8 in 1963 to 131.3 in 1969. The corresponding rows of table 1.12 indicate that the wage rates rose at an annual rate of 5.7 percent while earnings increased at 4.0 percent and then rose at 11.1 percent while earnings rose at 9.5 percent. This pattern implies that the number of lower-paid workers has increased relative to the number of higher-paid workers.[25]

The data for the individual cities for a longer interval support the same conclusion that wage rates have increased faster than average earnings. From 1960 to 1966 average national earnings rose at 4.0 percent per year; in six of the eight cities wages rose more rapidly than this. Similarly, from 1966 to 1972 earnings increased at 9.5 percent while wages in six of the nine cities rose more rapidly.

The next three tables look at more detailed wage rate information for particular occupations and occupational groups. Such data are useful for evaluating the assertion that the rise in hospital wage rates reflects rapid increases for the relatively low paid occupations at the base of the skill pyramid while higher-paid professional workers had wage increases in line with changes in the economy-wide averages. The evidence clearly indicates that this assertion is false: the higher-

25. We are comparing wage increases in nongovernmental hospitals in metropolitan areas with earnings increases for all short-term hospitals.

Table 1.12. Annual percentage increases of wage indexes in selected cities

	1957–1960[a]	1960–1963	1963–1966	1966–1969	1969–1972	1960–1966	1966–1972	1960–1972
Atlanta	—	5.5	8.6	12.0	9.0	7.1	10.5	8.8
Baltimore	5.9	4.9	7.2	10.4	12.1	6.0	11.3	8.6
Boston	—	3.5	6.2	12.4	7.2	4.8	9.8	7.3
Chicago	—	2.8	4.9	9.9	9.6	3.8	9.8	6.8
Dallas	—	4.3	5.8	10.7	6.9	5.1	8.7	6.9
Los Angeles	—	1.0	4.4	10.5	7.7	2.7	9.0	5.9
New York	7.4	7.9	6.1	11.1	10.5	7.0	10.8	8.9
St. Louis	—	—	—	11.8	6.5	—	9.1	—
San Francisco	4.4	4.5	5.1	10.0	9.6	4.8	9.8	7.2
All metropolitan areas	—	—	5.7	11.1	—	—	—	—
National average annual earnings of hospital employees	6.4	3.9	4.0	9.5	9.5	4.0	9.5	6.7

Note: A dash indicates that data are not available.
a. 1956–1960 for Baltimore and San Francisco.

paid professional and technical hospital employees have experienced pay increases substantially above the general rise in the earnings of all nonfarm production workers.

The disaggregated data also show that hospital wage rates have increased rapidly even in occupations for which hospitals are not the major industry of employment. Such wage increases therefore cannot be regarded as a reflection of hospitals' competition for specialized personnel whose supply cannot be readily increased.

Consider first the national wage indexes presented in table 1.13. The last two columns show that the relatively highly paid professional nursing staff had the greatest rates of increase in both the 1963–1966 interval and the 1966–1969 interval. These data also show that in 1966–1969 both clerical and housekeeping staff had wage increases substantially greater than the general standard for all private nonfarm production workers, even though in both cases hospitals employ a relatively small fraction of the relevant occupation.

Table 1.14 presents similar information on annual rates of wage increase for these five occupational groups for a longer interval (1960–1972) for the nine cities for which data are available. A general reference standard is the corresponding rate of change of earn-

Table 1.13. National wage increases in occupational groups, 1963–1969

Occupational group	Average weekly wage			Annual percentage change	
	1963	1966	1969	1963–1966	1966–1969
Professional nursing	$92.23	$109.70	$151.92	6.0	11.5
Technical	95.37	110.71	143.81	5.1	9.1
Clerical	65.85	74.07	93.41	4.0	8.0
Nonprofessional nursing	57.08	65.33	88.05	4.6	10.5
Housekeeping	52.80	61.46	80.99	5.2	9.6
All hospital occupations	66.24	78.25	107.22	5.7	11.1
Earnings of all nonfarm production workers	88.46	98.82	114.62	3.8	5.1

ings of private nonfarm production workers. For almost every interval in almost every city, the higher-paid professional nursing and technical staff experienced wage increases substantially greater than the national average. The increases for clerical and housekeeping personnel have exceeded the national average rate of increase.

It is not possible to generalize about the relevant rates of increase of wages for the different occupational groups. For example, professional nurses generally enjoyed the fastest rate of increase in the period immediately after the start of Medicare and Medicaid, but more recently the lower-paid housekeeping, clerical, and nonprofessional nursing staffs have had greater wage gains.

More detailed national data for specific occupations are presented in table 1.15. The figures for 1963, 1966, and 1969 (columns 1, 2, and 3) are based on the national estimates of the Bureau of Labor Statistics. The changes from 1969 to 1972 and 1963 to 1972 shown in the last two columns are weighted averages of the changes in the nine cities listed in table 1.14. These detailed occupational data support the conclusion reached with the information on broader occupational groups.

Some of the highest-paid occupations within each group have experienced wage increases at least as great as those of the lower-paid occupations. Nursing supervisors, chief X-ray technicians, and licensed practical nurses had higher increases for the overall 1963–1972 period than any other occupation within their occupational groups.

Table 1.14. Wage increases in occupational groups, selected cities, 1960–1972

	1960–1963	1963–1966	1966–1969	1969–1972	1960–1966	1966–1972	1960–1972
Earnings of all private nonfarm production workers	3.1	3.8	5.1	5.9	3.4	5.5	4.5
Atlanta							
Professional nursing	3.8	7.9	12.0	7.8	5.9	9.9	7.8
Technical	4.6	7.1	10.4	6.7	5.8	8.5	7.2
Clerical	0.0	4.0	11.3	8.6	2.0	9.9	5.4
Nonprofessional nursing	3.2	9.9	11.7	8.8	6.5	10.2	8.4
Housekeeping	3.4	13.8	13.5	12.7	8.5	13.1	10.8
Baltimore							
Professional nursing	4.3	7.2	11.8	9.6	5.7	10.7	8.2
Technical	4.3	6.7	7.2	10.8	5.5	9.0	7.2
Clerical	3.8	5.9	7.5	10.2	6.5	8.8	7.7
Nonprofessional nursing	5.3	7.2	11.2	13.7	7.3	12.4	9.9
Housekeeping	5.5	8.2	10.4	14.4	6.8	12.4	9.6
Boston							
Professional nursing	3.4	6.6	13.0	7.2	5.0	10.1	7.5
Technical	4.3	5.8	10.8	8.0	5.0	6.1	5.6
Clerical	6.2	4.0	8.3	8.2	5.1	8.2	6.7
Nonprofessional nursing	3.0	6.1	12.7	6.7	4.5	9.7	7.1
Housekeeping	4.0	5.2	10.9	8.2	4.6	9.5	7.0
Chicago							
Professional nursing	3.5	5.5	10.4	8.0	4.5	9.2	6.8
Technical	6.9	6.4	6.6	10.4	6.6	8.5	7.6
Clerical	2.3	5.4	7.1	9.1	3.8	8.1	5.9
Nonprofessional nursing	1.3	4.1	10.6	11.1	2.7	10.8	6.7
Housekeeping	3.1	4.7	10.8	11.2	3.9	11.0	7.4
Dallas							
Professional nursing	3.8	5.0	11.2	7.5	4.4	9.3	6.8
Technical	2.9	3.9	9.9	6.6	3.4	8.2	5.8
Clerical	2.5	5.6	6.3	7.1	3.7	6.7	5.2
Nonprofessional nursing	4.8	6.6	10.8	6.5	5.7	8.6	7.2
Housekeeping	6.6	7.1	10.6	7.9	4.7	9.2	6.9
Los Angeles							
Professional nursing	1.9	5.0	12.6	7.9	3.4	10.2	6.8
Technical	2.9	4.5	8.8	8.4	3.3	8.6	5.9
Clerical	1.7	4.1	6.4	6.3	2.9	7.3	5.1
Nonprofessional nursing	0.0	4.0	8.0	8.2	2.0	8.1	5.0
Housekeeping	−1.3	3.6	7.7	8.1	1.1	7.9	4.5

Table 1.14 (continued)

	1960–1963	1963–1966	1966–1969	1969–1972	1960–1966	1966–1972	1960–1972
New York							
Professional nursing	5.6	7.3	11.8	8.7	6.4	10.2	8.3
Technical	5.3	6.6	10.6	9.0	5.9	10.1	8.0
Clerical	5.6	5.1	8.0	11.3	5.3	9.6	7.5
Nonprofessional nursing	9.6	6.0	10.6	12.5	7.8	11.5	9.6
Housekeeping	9.1	5.8	10.8	12.8	7.4	11.8	9.6
St. Louis							
Professional nursing	–	–	13.6	5.8	–	9.6	–
Technical	–	–	6.4	9.6	–	8.0	–
Clerical	–	–	7.3	8.3	–	7.8	–
Nonprofessional nursing	–	–	11.6	6.6	–	9.1	–
Housekeeping	–	–	9.9	5.9	–	7.9	–
San Francisco							
Professional nursing	4.6	6.9	11.9	8.4	5.7	10.1	7.9
Technical	4.7	5.5	8.6	8.6	5.1	8.6	6.8
Clerical	5.1	3.8	3.9	10.2	4.2	7.0	5.6
Nonprofessional nursing	4.2	4.3	8.5	12.0	4.2	8.0	6.1
Housekeeping	4.6	4.3	7.4	10.8	4.4	9.1	6.8

Note: A dash indicates that data are not available.

Although the wage increases of clerical workers during 1963–1966 were similar to the national average, the wage gains since 1966 have been substantially greater. Switchboard operators, for example, experienced annual wage rate increases of 7.6 percent from 1966 to 1969 and 8.9 percent from 1969 to 1972 despite the wage controls that prevailed during part of this period; the corresponding general earnings increases were 5.1 percent and 5.9 percent. Since hospitals employ very few of the switchboard operators in any city or labor market, it is clear that these wage increases do not reflect hospitals' competition for a fixed number of specialized hospital personnel.

The same general picture emerges for hospital laundry workers (such as machine flatwork finishers), another occupation in which hospitals hire relatively few of the workers in any labor market. In 1966–1969 their wages rose 11 percent, and in 1969–1972 they rose 9.5 percent.

Hospital workers have traditionally been underpaid relative to comparable employees in other industries. It has therefore been natural to regard the more rapid wage increases of hospital workers as an inevitable process of "catching up." An earlier study warned against

Table 1.15. Wage rates and percentage increases by occupation

	Weekly or hourly wage, 1966 (1)	Annual percentage increases			
Occupation		1963–1966 (2)	1966–1969 (3)	1969–1972 (4)	1963–1972 (5)
All private nonfarm production workers	$98.82	3.8	5.1	5.9	4.9
Professional nurses					
Director	$168.00	3.4	9.9	—	8.3
Supervisor	132.50	6.2	11.0	8.3	8.9
Head nurse	116.00	5.6	12.1	8.0	8.8
General duty	103.50	6.2	11.8	7.8	8.7
Instructor	123.00	5.4	11.2	—	8.5
Technical					
Chief X-ray technician	129.50	3.7	9.8	—	8.4
X-ray technician	94.00	4.4	9.5	8.7	8.3
Medical technologist	110.50	5.6	9.9	9.5	8.1
Medical record librarian	122.00	4.6	6.9	—	6.3
Medical social worker	139.50	6.2	7.1	7.3	7.0
Physical therapist	123.50	5.1	8.2	—	7.4
Dietician	120.00	5.0	8.9	7.8	7.5
Clerical					
Payroll clerk	85.00	4.3	7.0	8.9	6.3
Switchboard operator	71.00	4.1	7.6	9.3	7.3
Switchboard-receptionist	63.00	2.8	9.6	—	7.3
Transcriber	78.50	4.1	7.9	7.9	6.4
Nonprofessional nurses					
Aide	61.00	4.5	9.4	10.9	8.6
Practical nurse	74.00	5.0	11.5		
Licensed	75.00	5.4	11.1	9.1	8.7
Unlicensed	65.00	4.1	9.1	—	—
Chief housekeeper	103.50	1.5	11.4	—	8.3
Housekeeping					
Machine dishwasher	1.42	5.8	9.0	—	8.8
Maintenance electrician	2.97	5.3	7.0	—	7.1
Stationary engineer	2.99	3.8	7.3	8.6	7.5
Machine flatwork finisher	1.38	4.5	10.8	9.5	8.7
Kitchen helper	1.47	5.3	9.5	11.2	8.7
Maid and porter	1.51	5.1	9.4	12.0	8.7
Machine washer	1.72	5.4	8.5	—	7.7

Note: Data in columns 1, 2, and 3 based on national wage rate estimates prepared by Department of Labor. Columns 4 and 5 calculated from Department of Labor estimates for nine cities, using 1972 employment weights.

the literal interpretation that rapid relative wage increases would cease when hospital wages had caught up to wages in similar occupations elsewhere.[26] The data through 1969 that were then available already showed some hospital wages exceeding the average wages paid in the same occupation in other industries. The new evidence for 1972 and 1975 indicates that hospital wages continue to climb rapidly even when they have passed the wages paid in other industries.

Of course, most hospital employees do jobs that are not done in any other industry. It is therefore not generally possible to compare the wages of hospital employees with wages in similar occupations in other industries. For a number of clerical and housekeeping activities, however, such direct comparisons are possible. In addition, the wages of general duty nurses can be compared with the wages of nurses who work for industrial companies. The evidence for 1960–1972 in nine cities is presented in table 1.16.[27]

In 1960 hospital workers generally earned 20 percent to 30 percent less than employees in the same occupations in other industries. By 1966 this gap had been reduced somewhat, but differentials of 20 percent were still common. In only five of the sixty-five city-occupation combinations for which data are available did hospital workers earn as much as employees in other industries. But by 1969 hospital wages were greater than the corresponding wages in other industries in twenty-five of the sixty-nine available observations. Moreover, in the vast majority of these twenty-five observations the wages of hospital employees continued to increase more rapidly than wages in other industries. By 1972 forty-six of seventy-six observations showed hospital wages leading wages in other industries.[28]

The data for 1975 were just becoming available at the time of this writing. Information has now been published for three of the original nine cities.[29] In evaluating this evidence, one should bear in mind that hospital wages were subject to controls for a much longer period (until April 1974) than wages in general. In Boston and Baltimore hospital wages continued to rise more rapidly than wages for other

26. M. Feldstein (1971 b).

27. The comparisons use the Bureau of Labor Statistics *Area Wage Surveys* for the individual metropolitan areas in the years indicated.

28. Two of the occupational titles, maintenance electrician and stationary engineer, may describe jobs that are quite different in hospitals. Hospital wages for these occupations are also lower than the wages in all other industries except in New York and San Francisco. If these two occupations are excluded, hospital wages exceed wages in other industries in all but eleven of the city-occupation observations for 1972.

29. The information for hospitals is now published as mean hourly earnings while the earnings in other occupations are weekly. Hospital hourly wages have been converted to weekly wages by multiplying by mean weekly hours.

Table 1.16. Relative wages of hospital and nonhospital employees in selected occupations, 1960–1972

	Hospital wage as percentage of wage in all industries				
	1960	1963	1966	1969	1972
Atlanta					
General duty nurse	73.6	73.2	81.9	94.7	93.8
Payroll clerk	—	—	92.2	103.3	104.4
Switchboard operator	72.5	67.9	80.0	89.7	91.5
Transcribing machine operator	95.3	—	—	108.4	107.0
Maintenance electrician	75.8	—	—	—	78.1
Stationary engineer	89.2	—	—	71.9	77.8
Porter	58.3	60.8	78.3	78.2	103.6
Maid	55.9	59.1	79.4	100.6	123.6
Baltimore					
General duty nurse	75.6	78.5	85.8	97.6	103.6
Payroll clerk	89.7	91.1	90.6	86.3	—
Switchboard operator	78.6	79.9	86.7	92.0	104.7
Switchboard-receptionist	67.7	66.4	—	103.6	100.5
Transcribing machine operator	85.6	91.8	107.4	111.3	119.7
Maintenance electrician	69.3	75.9	—	86.5	86.7
Stationary engineer	75.2	71.8	75.5	87.4	96.6
Porter	61.7	63.9	64.0	92.9	120.6
Maid	68.3	68.5	83.8	101.7	140.7
Boston					
General duty nurse	89.7	90.1	95.0	106.0	103.7
Payroll clerk	92.9	98.7	106.4	106.6	109.6
Switchboard operator	86.6	91.7	91.1	97.7	101.2
Switchboard-receptionist	—	85.9	—	—	102.2
Transcribing machine operator	96.2	98.6	96.8	99.5	109.1
Maintenance electrician	78.6	80.4	—	—	98.0
Stationary engineer	73.3	86.5	78.9	80.2	88.4
Porter	72.5	75.6	86.5	96.5	102.5
Maid	82.5	89.0	89.9	107.2	112.9
Chicago					
General duty nurse	91.4	91.3	95.2	105.0	103.3
Payroll clerk	84.8	89.7	99.5	88.7	103.3
Switchboard operator	79.5	82.5	90.3	96.2	101.3
Switchboard-receptionist	—	75.9	—	—	103.3
Transcribing machine operator	96.2	95.6	102.9	109.5	116.4
Maintenance electrician	86.6	87.0	—	—	100.0
Stationary engineer	88.6	87.8	90.7	90.1	88.8
Porter	64.4	68.6	72.1	85.5	96.5
Maid	67.5	71.4	76.0	89.6	103.0

Table 1.16 (continued)

	Hospital wage as percentage of wage in all industries				
	1960	1963	1966	1969	1972
Dallas					
General duty nurse	84.6	86.5	88.1	97.1	105.1
Payroll clerk	89.4	91.7	88.6	85.6	97.9
Switchboard operator	79.4	77.2	86.3	86.1	87.6
Switchboard-receptionist	—	—	—	—	84.0
Transcribing machine operator	100.8	103.9	102.0	106.1	111.1
Maintenance electrician	70.0	—	—	—	96.2
Stationary engineer	75.6	95.1	96.4	92.6	93.5
Porter	70.5	75.7	83.4	89.4	103.9
Maid	72.1	87.6	89.4	94.1	120.1
Los Angeles					
General duty nurse	83.3	83.7	87.3	101.0	108.0
Payroll clerk	83.7	90.2	88.9	97.1	96.6
Switchboard operator	83.7	85.5	90.4	102.3	98.2
Switchboard-receptionist	84.7	82.7	—	—	97.5
Transcribing machine operator	108.7	109.4	107.2	118.5	113.6
Maintenance electrician	93.1	85.5	—	—	87.9
Stationary engineer	79.2	75.9	84.4	92.3	89.4
Porter	73.7	77.8	79.2	85.4	89.9
Maid	76.5	78.9	76.4	82.4	93.9
New York					
General duty nurse	83.9	88.1	99.2	111.1	116.1
Payroll clerk	85.6	93.3	102.5	102.6	108.7
Switchboard operator	84.1	87.1	93.8	100.5	113.7
Switchboard-receptionist	76.6	—	—	91.3	108.3
Transcribing machine operator	97.2	104.4	106.2	112.9	119.1
Maintenance electrician	79.4	84.4	—	90.6	100.2
Stationary engineer	84.5	95.8	99.7	113.1	109.0
Porter	67.2	78.8	81.0	91.7	105.4
Maid	75.0	88.4	91.4	102.5	110.2
St. Louis					
General duty nurse	—	—	84.1	132.5	97.7
Payroll clerk	—	—	86.2	94.3	92.5
Switchboard operator	—	—	81.2	92.2	100.3
Switchboard-receptionist	—	—	—	—	—
Transcribing machine operator	—	—	86.1	91.0	103.6
Maintenance electrician	—	—	—	—	82.2
Stationary engineer	—	—	70.9	80.2	90.4
Porter	—	—	66.4	77.6	77.1
Maid	—	—	90.7	96.7	97.8

Table 1.16 (continued)

	Hospital wage as percentage of wage in all industries				
	1960	1963	1966	1969	1972
San Francisco					
General duty nurse	86.5	86.0	77.9	104.4	76.6
Payroll clerk	101.1	87.0	100.9	90.0	103.7
Switchboard operator	95.3	101.8	105.1	100.9	117.5
Switchboard-receptionist	95.2	91.0	—	92.3	—
Transcribing machine operator	104.0	112.7	116.9	107.3	126.6
Maintenance electrician	—	—	—	93.5	—
Stationary engineer	88.7	91.3	95.8	91.1	105.6
Porter	75.8	78.0	82.5	85.9	100.0
Maid	78.8	79.4	83.2	86.3	98.8

Note: A dash indicates that data are not available.

industries except for nurses' wages and the wages of electricians and engineers. In Dallas, however, hospital wages rose more slowly than wages in other industries. It will be important to examine the evidence for the remaining cities as it becomes available.

The relation of hospital wages to wages in other industries has been studied in a different way by Fuchs.[30] He used the 1 percent public use samples of the 1960 and 1970 censuses of population to compare the earnings of hospital and nonhospital workers standardized for color, sex, age, and schooling. His analysis showed that even by 1969 the average hourly earnings of all hospital workers were 97 percent of the value expected on the basis of their color, sex, age, and schooling composition; for females, the corresponding figure was over 100 percent. These results support the same conclusion as the occupational comparisons of tables 1.16 and 1.17.

Although it is clear that hospital wage rates have been rising more rapidly than wages in other industries, the reasons for this rise cannot be established unambiguously. The evidence has shown that the faster increase for hospital workers does not represent a shift toward higher-paid occupations or an increase for low-paid workers only. The rapid gains by clerical and housekeeping workers indicate that the wage increases are not just a reflection of hospitals' competition for scarce specialized personnel. Finally, hospital workers are not just catching up to the wages paid in other occupations but are generally

30. Fuchs (1976).

Table 1.17. Relative wages of hospital and nonhospital employees in selected occupations, 1972–1975

	1972	1975
Baltimore		
General duty nurse	103.6	97.1
Payroll clerk	—	101.5
Switchboard operator	104.7	116.4
Switchboard-receptionist	100.5	114.5
Transcribing machine operator	119.7	123.6
Maintenance electrician	86.7	82.5
Stationary engineer	96.6	96.0
Porter	120.6	122.4
Maid	140.7	146.6
Boston		
General duty nurse	103.7	102.0
Payroll clerk	109.6	107.7
Switchboard operator	101.2	103.7
Switchboard-receptionist	102.2	104.7
Transcribing machine operator	109.1	110.6
Maintenance electrician	98.0	96.9
Stationary engineer	88.4	86.0
Porter	102.5	107.4
Maid	112.9	117.1
Dallas		
General duty nurse	105.1	89.1
Payroll clerk	97.9	91.6
Switchboard operator	87.6	91.4
Switchboard-receptionist	84.0	—
Transcribing machine operator	111.1	108.6
Maintenance electrician	96.2	68.8
Stationary engineer	93.5	75.2
Porter	103.9	89.8
Maid	120.1	111.3

better paid than workers in the same occupations in other industries or with the same demographic and schooling characteristics.

Several factors have probably contributed to the rapid wage increases. Hospital employment has increased more rapidly than employment elsewhere in the economy. From 1955 to 1975 hospital employment (on a full-time equivalent basis) rose 4.6 percent a year while total national employment increased 1.5 percent a year. Higher wages were necessary to attract more workers who specialized in hospital occupations and, to a much lesser extent, to attract clerical and housekeeping workers from other industries. Hospitals have frequently established relative wage scales for use in setting wages, and the resulting linking of clerical and housekeeping wages to nursing and technical salaries may have given clerical and housekeeping workers greater wage increases than they would otherwise have obtained. One effect of these rising relative wages may have been to permit hospitals to hire better-quality workers in each occupation. The rising minimum wage may have raised some wages in particular cities but cannot have been important in the aggregate. The role of hospital unions has been growing but still remains relatively small; however, the potential of union activity may be at least as important as unionization itself.

An earlier study explained the unusually rapid wage increases by the idea of "philanthropic wage setting" by hospitals.[31] A hospital, as a philanthropic or public organization, may concern itself with the well-being of its staff as well as of its patients. The tradition of low pay for the hospital staff developed when hospital budgets were very tight. More recently, the rapid rise in demand stimulated by public and private insurance has given hospital administrators much greater budgetary freedom.[32] Hospitals can use this discretionary power to raise the wages of hospital personnel above the levels that would be necessary to obtain the staff they want. Although hospital administrators might dislike the notion that they have willingly contributed to unnecessary increases in hospital costs, they would defend the practice as paying "decent" or "just" wages rather than the lowest wages at which the services could be obtained.[33]

The rise in hospital costs reflects a change in the style or character of the service that hospitals produce, a change induced largely by the growth of insurance. This explanation of the rise in hospital costs raises an awkward question. Implicit in every discussion of hospital-cost inflation is the assumption that the rise in cost has been excessive and should not be allowed to continue at the same rate. But if this rise reflects a change in product rather than an increase in inefficiency, or a low rate of technical progress, or unjustified increases in profit margins or wage rates, why is it a problem?

The answer in brief is that the current type of costly medical care

31. M. Feldstein (1971b), p. 67.

32. This would be particularly true of some types of insurance that simply reimburse hospitals directly for all costs.

33. An econometric study of hospital wages is presented in A. Taylor (1975b). For an econometric analysis of the rise in hospital wages relative to wages in other industries, see A. Taylor (1975a).

does not correspond to what consumers or their physicians would regard as appropriate if their choices were not distorted by insurance. The prepaying of health care through insurance, both private and public, encourages hospitals to provide a more expensive product than consumers wish to purchase.

Although the consumer pays the full cost of the expensive care through higher insurance premiums, at the time of illness the choice of the patient and his physician reflects the net cost of the care. Because this net out-of-pocket cost appears so modest, the patient and physician choose to buy more expensive care than they would if the patient were not so well insured. In this way the current method of financing hospital care denies patients and their physicians the opportunity to choose effectively between higher-cost and lower-cost hospital care.[34]

The nature of hospital-cost inflation has important implications for national health insurance and for government policies to regulate hospital costs. The long-run problem is not to reduce or to limit the growth of medical spending but to achieve the correct rate of growth of that spending. This must ultimately come down to balancing additional spending on medical care against the alternative uses to which households might put those resources. And this balancing requires comparing the expected gains from additional medical care — gains that are psychological as well as physical — with the satisfaction that households would enjoy from the alternative spending on food, housing, or recreation.

Controlling the quality of medical care is not a technical question that can be solved by physician peer review. Although the peer review process can try to ensure the application of accepted standards of care, it cannot be used to establish those standards. Determining the correct quality and style of medical care requires involving the individual family in deciding how much it wants to spend for medical care and how much it wants to spend for other things. Although such direct involvement of families is not possible in determining the nation's spending on defense or on medical research, it is possible for personal health care services. The form of national health insurance should ensure that individual consumers play this crucial role in guiding the growth and form of their health services.

It is important to develop an approach to national health insurance that is appropriate to the advanced technology of medical care and the ever-increasing affluence of the American people. Too much of the current debate relies on ideas about the delivery of medical care

34. For a more technical discussion of this issue, see chapter 6.

that have been inherited from a period with quite different technological and economic conditions. The challenge is to find new methods of financing health care that protect families from the risk of financial hardship while also making the future development of health care more responsive to the preferences of the people.

2 Econometric Studies of Health Economics

The quantity and quality of research on the economics of health care has increased radically in the past decade. Most of these recent studies are applications of econometric methods, either the statistical estimation of economic models or the use of formal techniques of optimization. The purpose of this chapter is to provide a framework for organizing this research and to offer a critical appraisal of the substance of these studies.[1] Since the rapid growth of research on health economics will render any survey of the current state of knowledge obsolete within a very few years, I have tried to emphasize basic questions and general qualitative answers rather than specific findings of individual researchers. I have also suggested questions and areas of investigation that seem worthy of future research.

Two quite different sources of interest have attracted economists to the economics of health. The most obvious has been the emergence of health care as a major object of public expenditure and national policy. The Medicare and Medicaid programs began in 1966. In fiscal year 1971–72 government spent more than $32 billion on health programs. Some form of national health insurance and greater regulation of the health-care industry seem likely developments of the eighties. These changes in the economic status of the health-care sector occurred at the same time that economists were becoming more interested in problems of the public sector and in applied microeconomics.

The second attraction of studying the health-care sector is that it

This chapter was published in *Frontiers of Quantitative Economics*, vol. II, ed. M. D. Intriligator and D. A. Kendrick, North-Holland Publishing Company, 1974, pp. 377–442.

1. Klarman's (1965a) valuable survey summarizes most of the research published before 1965.

provides an opportunity to develop new models for the analysis of what might be called "nonstandard" economic behavior. The suppliers of health-care services are generally nonprofit institutions and professionals. The decisions of households to demand health services are characterized by great uncertainty and by significant reliance on the advice of others, especially of the suppliers themselves. Because of the widespread use of insurance, the net price paid by patients is often substantially less than the gross price charged by suppliers. There is also growing evidence that the usual price mechanism for resource allocation is often supplemented by some form of nonprice rationing. Several other departures from standard market conditions are also present.

Although this combination of nonstandard aspects of economic behavior may be unique to the health-care sector, each of the problems also arises elsewhere. Developing adequate models to deal with such behavior becomes increasingly important as the economy shifts more and more from the production of industrial goods to the provision of human services and as public and quasi-public organizations assume a larger role in economic life. The health-care sector has been one of the principal areas for studying these questions because of the magnitude of the economic problem and the relative abundance of disaggregated data.

In the early sixties economists could debate whether traditional price theory was relevant to health care. That question now seems out of date. It is clear that the basic notions of economic analysis are applicable but that the usual models must be extended to deal with the new problems of nonstandard behavior. Although a consensus has not yet emerged on the correct general specification of a model of the health-care sector, a framework for research has been defined and the range of disagreement in many areas has been substantially reduced.

Most econometric studies in this field have been concerned with understanding the functioning of the health-care sector rather than with assessing the economic impact of health status, the technological relation between care and health, or the effect of economic activity on health.[2] These attempts at modeling the health-care sector have been motivated by the interest in nonstandard behavior and by the desire

2. The focus has thus been very different from the econometric studies of education. There are, of course, exceptions to this general description. Luft (1972) examines the impact of poor health on earnings and family income and the relation between job characteristics and disabling impairments. Barlow (1967) and Newman (1965) consider the general impact of malaria eradication on economic development and population growth. Auster, (1969), Fuchs (1965), and Fuchs and Kramer (1972) estimate aggregate equations relating measures of health (state mortality rates) to the use of health services.

to provide information that might be useful in guiding public policy. A number of studies have been designed to develop models that could predict the effect of possible changes in factors such as the provision of insurance, the stock of beds, or the number of physicians. Other research has attempted to monitor the performance of the current health-care system by asking questions such as, What determines the current geographic distribution of physicians? Or what impact does the federal Medicare program for the aged have on the services received by the rest of the population? Still other studies seek to explain the instances of serious malfunctioning of the health-care system, such as the rapid explosion of health-care costs and the substantial geographic variation in services received under the nominally uniform Medicare program. This concern with issues of public policy has no doubt helped direct attention to useful questions and to sustain researchers who might otherwise have been discouraged by the complexities of the problems and the frustrations of sailing uncharted waters. The real product of this research, however, has been not its contribution to current policy formation but the establishment of a better conceptual and empirical picture of the health-care sector.

Although most studies have dealt with only single aspects of the health-care system, the "invisible hand" that guides researchers to fill existing lacunae is collecting the pieces that will compose an econometric model of the entire sector. This process is still far from complete.[3] Yet it is useful to describe the current econometric research as analyses of three interrelated markets: hospital services, physicians' services, and health insurance.

In addition to the research that examines how the health-care sector functions, a number of studies have applied standard techniques of optimization to problems of health-care planning. There has long been an interest in applying techniques of cost-benefit analysis to the design and evaluation of health activities.[4] A natural extension of this is the use of linear programming to select an optimal mix or time path of activities subject to a variety of constraints. The application of these optimization techniques to health care has led to useful insights and has raised a number of new and interesting problems.[5]

3. Several "complete" sectoral models have been developed to illustrate the use of an econometric model for health-sector analysis and to explore the implications of interdependence of behavior within the sector; see M. Feldstein (1967, 1968); P. Feldstein and Kelman (1970); Yett et al. (1971). Much more work on the specification and estimation of individual equations must be done before such models become more than pedagogical and exploratory material.

4. Recent contributions include Acton (1970), Drèze (1962), Klarman (1967), Rice (1968), Schelling (1968), and Weisbrod (1961, 1971).

5. For applications to a variety of different problems, see M. Feldstein (1967, 1970a),

The Market for Hospital Services

It is not surprising that the demand for and supply of hospital services has been the most common subject of research in health economics.[6] Hospitals account for the largest share of health expenditures and have experienced the most rapid rate of price increase. Insurance, private and public, is much more extensive for hospital services than for other types of health care. The dominant role of the nonprofit institution and the complex nature of the demand for services are the greatest departure from traditional market behavior. Finally, the data on hospital care has generally been much better than on other aspects of the health-care sector.

Econometric analysis of hospital services began with the estimation of short-run and long-run cost functions. A substantial volume of research supports two basic conclusions.[7] First, there are neither significant economies nor diseconomies of scale for hospitals that are larger than some relatively small minimum size. Second, the short-run marginal cost of additional patient care is very much less than the average cost. The currently available data for U.S. hospitals do not contain information on the diagnostic mix of each hospital's patients and therefore do not permit the cross-sectional studies to take into account the multiproduct nature of the hospital's output. Analysis of the costs of British and Canadian hospitals, for which data on output mix are available, indicates that failure to allow for differences in output mix causes an underestimate of the economies of scale.[8] The bias, however, is small, and the conclusion that economies of scale are unimportant is substantiated.[9] Production functions estimated with Brit-

---

M. Feldstein and Luft (1973), M. Feldstein, Piot, and Sundaresan (1973). Hartley, Hartley, and Pondue (1972), ReVelle et al. (1969), and Smith, Miller, and Golladay (1972).

6. Hospital services will denote inpatient services in short-term general hospitals. Outpatient services are discussed with physician care in the next section. Long-term inpatient care, primarily in mental hospitals, has received relatively little attention (Fein 1968; Jones and Sidebotham 1962).

7. Econometric studies of hospital cost functions include Berry (1970), Carr and P. Feldstein (1967), Cohen (1970), M. Feldstein (1967), P. Feldstein (1961), Ingbar and Taylor (1968), and McNerney (1962). There are review articles by Hefty (1969), Mann and Yett (1968) and a summary of methodological issues in M. Feldstein (1967).

8. British data are analyzed in M. Feldstein (1967) and Canadian data in Evans (1970b).

9. None of these studies makes any allowance for differences in the quality of care. If large institutions provide more sophisticated care to each type of patient, the estimated cost functions understate the economics of scale. Berry (1970) has allowed for differences in facilities (for example, intensive care units), but the patient mix is not taken into account at the same time.

ish cross-sectional data also confirm the conclusion of approximately constant returns to scale (M. Feldstein 1967). The absence of data on the quantity of physicians' services used within each hospital has prevented a comparable analysis for U.S. institutions.

More recently, econometric research has turned from the estimation of technological parameters to the analysis of demand and supply behavior. Most of these studies have examined individual relations or particular aspects of those relations (for example, the demand function or the price elasticity of demand) without considering the complete market within which that behavior occurs. The result, I believe, has often been confusion about the way in which the observed quantities and prices are then determined as the outcome of individual and institutional behavior. Because of the nonprofit character of the hospital and the special role of the physician, the issue is much more complex than the usual process of equilibrating supply and demand.

The Demand for Hospital Services

An important but generally neglected question is, What is the role of the personal physician in determining the household's demand for hospital care?[10] The answer is important for the specification of demand behavior and for analyzing the welfare economics of pricing, insurance, and supply behavior. Although the question has rarely been given explicit attention in the literature on the demand for hospital services, a wide range of contrasting answers is implicit.

The most common approach is to ignore the physician and discuss the demand for hospital services in the same way as the demand for other goods and services. Prices, income, and the demographic characteristics of the household are then the basic determinants of demand. At the opposite extreme are those who would argue that patients' preferences are irrelevant and that hospital use is determined by the physician. A patient who comes to a doctor with a symptom lacks the technical information to evaluate alternative options and is acting under substantial stress. The physician determines the demand for hospital care on the basis of his perception of correct medical practice, or on the basis of his own convenience and self-interest, or by seeking to use available resources in a way that optimally balances their potential contribution to the health of his own patient against the use of those resources for other patients. Regardless which is a correct description of the physician's decision rule, the usual household demand variables of price, insurance, and income are irrelevant,

---

10. See P. Feldstein (1966), Joseph (1971), and Klarman (1965a) for surveys of the demand for hospital services.

or, at most, influence the patient's decision to initiate care but do not affect the quantity of care obtained.

An alternative to both models is more useful for understanding demand behavior and more appropriate for analyzing the welfare implications of alternative policies. Instead of considering the physician simply as a supplier of medical services, let us think of the relation between the patient and his physician as one of agency. Because the patient lacks the technical knowledge to make the necessary decisions, he delegates this authority to his physician with the hope that the physician will act for him as he would for himself if he had the appropriate expertise. This agency relationship develops because it is too difficult for the physician to give the patient the information that he needs to make his own decision. It is much easier for the patient to indicate his financial position, insurance coverage, and relevant preferences. Although this communication may be quite imperfect, it is clearly preferable to leaving the patient to make detailed decisions on the basis of grossly inadequate technical knowledge. (It is not surprising that in a market situation in which the costs of exchanging information are extremely high.[11] the optimum will differ from the usual conditions of perfect information. It would be interesting to inquire when the cost of exchanging information leads to an agency relationship).

If the agency relation is complete, that is, if the physician acts solely in the interest of his patient, it would be difficult if not impossible to distinguish the agency relation from the traditional model of independent consumer behavior on the basis of the observed household consumption of hospital services. The only indication in that data could be evidence that demand was less sensitive to the types of variables that are imperfectly perceived by the physician, for example, that demand responds more to variations in the net price of hospital services that are due to differences in the gross price charged by the hospitals than to differences in the extent of insurance coverage. If the agency relation is complete, it can essentially be ignored for the analysis of demand, although it would be important for welfare analysis. Its primary virtue for demand analysis would be to reconcile the use of traditional demand analysis with the obvious fact that patients entrust many of their decisions about medical-care consumption to their physician.

But the agency relation is not complete. The physician's decisions generally reflect, in addition to his patient's preferences, his own self-

11. Consider the cost of the physician's time that would be required to explore fully the patient's preferences, risk aversion, and so forth.

interest, the pressures from professional colleagues, a sense of medical ethics, and a concern to make good use of hospital resources. The balance among these depends on the market relation between patient, physician, and hospital. For example, a physician in a prepaid group practice that owns its hospital facilities cannot act primarily as the patient's agent. Similarly, a surgeon who is also a part owner of a proprietary hospital is likely to offer advice different from that of a general practitioner. Peer group pressure may induce physicians to restrict admissions and durations of stay when and where hospital beds are relatively scarce. General ethical principles may cause each physician to limit the degree to which he treats patients differently on the basis of income or insurance. All these departures from a simple and complete agency relation imply that the observed household demand functions depart from the usual model in several predictable ways. Although all the implications of this idea have not been examined, the available evidence seems to support the notion of a generalized agency model of household demand for hospital services.

The Price Elasticity of Demand. The estimates of the price elasticity of demand confirm that a higher price reduces the consumption of hospital care. Although evidence of a negative own-price elasticity of demand would be unworthy of note for most goods and services, it is of substantial importance for hospital care. It emphasizes the role of household preferences and contradicts the assertion that hospital use is determined by physicians on solely technical grounds.

In evaluating the price elasticity of demand, one must bear in mind that there are two aspects of the relevant price. The net price paid by the patient depends on the gross price charged by the hospital and on the extent of the patient's insurance coverage. If insurance were simply a proportional reduction in price,[12] traditional demand analysis would imply that the elasticity of demand with respect to the gross price charged by the hospital should equal the elasticity with respect to the insurance coverage (to the coinsurance rate). The agency model suggests that the elasticity with respect to insurance coverage may be less. The extent of this differential would depend on the completeness of the agency relation. It may therefore differ between the demand for admissions and the demand for longer durations of stay. The more complete the insurance coverage, the more the physician must depart from his role as the patient's agent and assume the responsibility for the allocation of a public resource. When the insur-

---

12. In the terminology of insurance, this would be true if there were no deductible and a constant coinsurance rate.

ance coverage is nearly complete, the elasticity with respect to insurance would therefore be quite low.

The measurement of gross price and of insurance coverage raises additional conceptual and practical problems.[13] A day of hospital care is not the same product in different hospitals or in the same hospital at different times. A higher gross price may reflect a higher quality of service. This effect will be stronger for a cross section of hospitals within a single market area than through time or across larger geographic areas. But insofar as gross price and quality are positively correlated, the estimated price elasticity of demand can be expected to be biased downward.

Some regression studies have measured the extent of insurance coverage by the percentage of the population with insurance coverage, but this approach obscures variation in the comprehensiveness of coverage and fails to provide an estimate of the price elasticity. The assumption that an individual's insurance coverage can be described by a single effective coinsurance rate is obviously a simplification but is often the most that can be done with available data.[14] The use of an average net price or insurance coverage for an aggregate observation involves a potential source of aggregation bias. Without more detailed microeconomic analyses, it is difficult to assess the magnitude of these problems. While it is necessary to bear these problems in mind, it is important to remember that similar problems prevail in other areas and have not hampered the usefulness of aggregate analysis.

The estimates of the effects of gross price and of insurance have used three types of samples: cross-sectional data on individual households (Rosenthal 1970; Rosett and Huang 1973; Wilensky and Holahan 1972); comparisons of a population before and after a change in insurance (Ginsburg and Manheim 1972; Phelps and Newhouse

13. Several recent studies have emphasized that use of the patient's time is part of the total cost of medical care (Acton 1972; Grossman 1972b; Holtman 1972; Phelps and Newhouse 1972a). Time costs are generally much more important for health care than for most goods and services. One implication of this is that if the elasticity with respect to total price is the same for all persons, the elasticity with respect to money price should be a decreasing function of income. Similarly, if the elasticity of demand with respect to total price is the same at all levels of total price, the observed elasticity with respect to money price would fall as net money price tends to zero. Since there is no reason for the premises of constancy to be correct, the pattern of price elasticities across income classes or net price levels does not constitute a test of the importance of time.

14. The deductible (the amount that the insured pays before receiving any benefits) is relatively small in hospital insurance. The so-called indemnity policies (that pay a fixed dollar amount per day of hospital care) can also be treated as approximately equivalent to policies with fixed coinsurance rates for most studies, although the approximation is not good for studying the patient's choice among hospitals.

1972a; Weisbrod and Feisler 1961); and aggregate data at the state level for which a cross section of time series can be observed (Davis and Russell 1972; chapter 3; Rosenthal 1964). Although individual household observations might in principle give the best estimates, there are a number of problems with the available data. The price paid by an individual household is not really exogenous but reflects the household's choice of a quality level.[15] While the insurance coverage is exogenous for households that automatically receive a particular form of insurance through their employment, it is endogenous for households that buy individual coverage or choose the extent of coverage in an employer plan. At the practical level, the data on insurance benefits have generally been of low quality. The recent release of household data gathered by the U.S. National Center for Health Statistics and the collection of new data by the National Opinion Research Center may permit advances in this area.[16]

The comparison of hospital use by a population before and after an imposed change in insurance coverage generally avoids the problem of self-selection that arises with cross-sectional household data. A recent survey (Phelps and Newhouse 1972a) of such studies concluded that these estimates of the eleasticity of total patient-days with respect to net price clustered around 0.2. There are, however, two reasons to believe that these values underestimate the relevant demand elasticity. First, these studies have generally compared the experience immediately before and after the change in insurance coverage. Since the long-run demand elasticity is likely to be substantially greater than the short-run value, the before-and-after comparisons understate the permanent price effect. Second, in many cases the change in insurance relates to all or a large fraction of the persons in some geograph-

15. The recent study by Wilensky and Holahan (1972) related expenditures per admission to the average coinsurance rate and to family income and demographic characteristics. No gross price variable is included in the equation. Since there is likely to be a positive correlation between the households' insurance coverage and the general level of prices prevailing in the area, this procedure may cause a substantial bias in the estimated price elasticity.

16. Rosett and Huang's (1973) ingenious use of the 1960–61 Survey of Consumer Expenditures provided estimates of the elasticity of total health spending with respect to the average coinsurance rate. Calculating expenditure elasticities made it unnecessary to assume that the price paid by the household is independent of its insurance and income. A serious problem with this study is the ambiguity of the data with respect to employer payments for health insurance. Since these account for a very substantial fraction of all payments, the estimated price elasticity may be subject to a substantial bias. The problem that the local price level may be positively correlated with the insurance coverage would, if the demand elasticity is less than one, cause an upward bias in the expenditure elasticity.

ic area. An increase in insurance coverage can lead to an increase in actual use only to the extent that excess capacity had previously prevailed or only after new capacity is added. A further feature of these before-and-after comparisons is that they generally relate to a situation in which insurance coverage is nearly complete. With the net price near zero and very much less than the gross price, the physician must act not merely as his patients' agent but also as an allocator of hospital resources that would otherwise be in excess demand. The elasticity with respect to insurance is therefore likely to be much less when insurance is virtually complete. Moreover, even an arc elasticity of 0.2 associated with the change from incomplete to complete coverage corresponds to a very substantial 50 percent change in patient-days.[17]

Demand equations estimated with cross sections of aggregate state data have generally implied higher price elasticities than the other two sources. For total patient-days the elasticity with respect to net price has been estimated to be between 0.5 and 0.7.[18] That higher gross price is likely to be associated with higher quality suggests that these estimates may even be biased downward. Some preliminary analysis (chapter 5) indicates that the problem is not serious, at least when the estimates relate to several years of rapidly increasing prices. The pooled cross section of time series permits an examination of adjustment speeds. To date, only a very simple proportional adjustment model, with the same speed of adjustment to all variables, has been estimated. The results imply that the short-run elasticity is on the order of 50 percent of the long-run response. Because individuals use hospital services quite infrequently, the delayed demand response is evidence of the physicians' role in modulating household behavior.

When the net price variable is decomposed into price and insurance, the elasticity with respect to the gross price is substantially greater than the elasticity with respect to the average coinsurance rate, as the generalized agency theory predicts. The physician knows the gross

---

17. Let p be the net price before the increase in insurance coverage and D_0 the associated number of patient-days per capita. Providing complete coverage lowers the net price to zero and increases patient-days to D_1. The elasticity evaluated at 0.5 p and 0.5 $(D_0 + D_1)$ is

$$\eta = \frac{D_1 - D_0}{0.5(D_0 + D_1)} (0.5).$$

If $\eta = 0.2$, the increase in D is 50 percent of D_0.

18. Since price and insurance are endogenous at the aggregate level, these equations have been estimated by an appropriate instrumental variable procedure.

price but may be unclear about the extent of the patient's insurance coverage. Moreover, for ethical reasons physicians may give less weight to insurance than the patient would, especially when there is substantial interpersonal variation in local insurance coverage. Further support for this is that the hospital admission rate appears more responsive to gross price than does the mean stay per case but the opposite is true for the elasticities with respect to the coinsurance rate. Both patient and physician may be more aware of the provisions of the insurance coverage after the patient has been hospitalized. All these inferences must be interpreted cautiously. The data on insurance coverage at the state level are still inadequate. Moreover, working with state data entails all the usual problems of using aggregate data to study microeconomic behavior; unless the microrelations are the same for every household, the aggregate coefficients are not appropriate for predicting the effects of all possible price changes.

Although this survey of price elasticities has concentrated on the limits of the available estimates, there is now much more information and a better sense of the issues than just a few years ago. While the estimated elasticities may seem far apart, there is agreement that price has a significant effect, despite the peculiar nature of this market and the special role of the physician. Moreover, since the lower estimates of the price elasticity are generally associated with nearly complete insurance coverage, the wide range of price elasticities is compatible with the general conclusion that price has a substantial impact on the demand for hospital care. There is some evidence in the pattern of price elasticities to support the generalized agency model in preference to the other theories of household demand.

Effect of Availability. It has become a truism among those concerned with the practical problems of health-sector planning that when additional hospital beds are constructed, they are soon fully occupied (Roemer and Shain 1959). Administrators have learned that the notion of a technologically necessary level of hospital use is chimerical. Although it can hardly surprise any economist to learn that the hospital market tends to eliminate excess demand, there is some evidence that the mechanism is different in this market.

More specifically, the substantial interstate variation in the per capita supply of hospital beds appears to have almost no impact on their utilization rate. The elasticity of patient-days of care consumed with respect to patient-days available is nearly one. Yet the variations in price and in the other factors that influence demand are not sufficient to account for the close relation between use and availability. When the per capita supply of hospital beds is included in the demand equation, it has a substantial and significant effect. The coefficient implies a partial elasticity of use with respect to supply of approximately one-half.

There are three possible reasons for this apparent nonprice rationing. The first is that excess demand prevails in the hospital market, presumably because neither price nor supply responds sufficiently rapidly to increasing demand. Such excess demand implies that the observed quantities are determined by supply. While this would explain why availability is important, it is not consistent with the significant effects of price, insurance, and other demand variables. The important fact about excess demand for hospital services is that changes in the percentage utilization of available beds can act as a buffer, just as inventory changes do for manufactured goods. When demand exceeds desired supply, the percentage utilization of capacity is higher than the hospitals prefer but still permits the level of output to be determined by demand. Although an explanation in terms of general excess demand can therefore be ruled out, it is possible that output has been supply determined in some places and times. If so, the estimated demand equation is adulterated by those observations, and the significant availability effect may reflect only those observations. This problem of estimating demand behavior in the presence of occasional effective constraints on output is clearly worth more attention, not only in this context, but in other areas of applied econometrics.

A second possible explanation is that the demand equation has been incompletely specified. If, in addition, the supply in each area were responsive to local demand, the estimated availability effect would be the spurious result of an incorrect specification. The absence of a usual market-determined supply response and the very slow rate at which local bed availability has actually changed suggest that this is not very likely.

The most plausible explanation of the effect of availability is that it reflects the physician's role and the incompleteness of the agency relationship. Peer group pressures on the physician or a concern for the general welfare of patients in the community can induce physicians to use fewer hospital beds than they would if they were acting solely as the agents of their own current patients. Since these pressures would be stronger where beds are more scarce and occupancy rates higher, hospital admissions and patient-days would respond to bed availability directly as well as through the usual price effect.[19] If this is correct,

---

19. Rafferty (1971, 1972) has examined time-series variation within the same hospital and shown that the mix of case types varies with pressure on capacity. In particular, less serious conditions and postponable treatments are reduced when there is substantial pressure on capacity. He interprets this as evidence of the effect of physicians on the hospital's product mix.

it would be useful to study more explicitly the mechanism by which nonprice rationing operates, the reason that price does not rise to make this unnecessary, and the effect of nonprice rationing on different types of patients.

Other Determinants of Demand. Although most studies of price elasticity have dealt only with the own-price effect, some work is beginning on the important issue of cross-price effects and, more generally, the substitution of in-hospital and out-of-hospital services. Davis and Russell (1972) recently reported that the demand for hospital inpatient care varies directly with the price of care in outpatient departments. A higher price for inpatient care also increases the demand for outpatient services. A physician fee variable was also significantly negative in the hospital admissions equation but insignificant in the outpatient and mean stay equations. Unfortunately, the data on physicians' fees by states or cities are less reliable than prices for hospital services.[20] Moreover, there is evidence that the market for physicians' services may not be clearing and, more important in the current context, that the amount of physicians' services is supply determined (Feldstein 1970c). If so, the actual availability of physicians rather than their price is the relevant variable. Analysis of a cross section of states (chapter 3) indicates that an increase in the number of general practitioners per capita substantially reduces the mean stay per hospital spell and the number of hospital spells per person. Similarly, the relative abundance of medical and surgical specialists, whose services are likely to be complementary with hospital inpatient care, increases the demand for admissions and for longer durations of stay.

The estimated income elasticities have generally been low, almost always less than one.[21] The evidence indicates that the rate of hospital admissions varies much less with income than the mean stay per episode and that total patient-days per capita varies much less than the quality of care or the cost per patient-day.[22] There is, of course, a special problem in assessing income elasticities for health care. In studies using individual household observations, the income elasticity is biased downward, because serious medical conditions often lower family income. Although the use of aggregate data (such as states)

20. Davis and Russell use an estimate of the average gross fee faced by Medicare patients for routine medical care as a proxy for all physicians' fees.

21. See, for example, Anderson and Benham (1970), P. Feldstein and Carr (1964), Davis and Russell (1972), P. Feldstein (1964), Wilensky and Holahan (1972), and chapter 3.

22. The data on total expenditure differences may be distorted by reporting difficulties and variation by income class in the source of payments. See chapter 3.

would reduce the bias due to random differences between measured income and permanent income, it may not correct a bias due to the systematic relation between income and health. A better approach to this problem would be to examine the effect of income on the demand for care for children and for specific acute conditions that are unlikely to affect income.

A number of other factors, including demographic characteristics, educational attainments, and population density have been examined. Inadequate attention has been given to the role of quality differences, to the demand for care for individual disease types, and to the analysis of demand within local market areas. But a general framework of analysis has been established, and new work on these problems can be expected in the future.

Economic Behavior of Hospitals

The supply of hospital services depends on the economic behavior of nonprofit hospitals.[23] Most studies of the economic behavior of hospitals have concentrated on characterizing the motivation of hospitals, of finding an alternative to profit maximization as a determinant of the institution's behavior. The literature on this problem has generally been speculative or analytic but has not faced the problem of testing these theories against the observed behavior of hospitals. It has therefore been easy to forget that an explanation of hospitals' behavior requires more than a theory of the hospitals' maximand. Behavior depends not only on goals but on the constraints imposed by the character of the market. Unfortunately, relatively little attention has been given to analyzing the operation of the market (especially the forms and extent of competition) within which the hospital functions.[24] More analysis of this problem and the accumulation of appropriate data for local market areas should receive high priority in the next few years. The result would be a better understanding of the hospital care market and better models for analyzing the provision of services by other nonprofit institutions.

Probably the most interesting and important question about hospital behavior is what determines the "quality" or "style" of care that the hospital provides. When some hospitals have an average cost per patient-day of $120, while others have an average cost of only $60, the difference is clearly not in technical efficiency or in economies of scale.

---

23. See Davis (1972a) for a valuable critical survey of this subject and some preliminary tests of alternative models.

24. An important feature of the market, to which I shall return, is the extent to which insurers play an active role. See Klarman (1969b).

The cost difference reflects a difference in product. Similarly, the sharp rise in hospital costs—from an average of $16 per patient-day in 1950 to $105 in 1972—reflects a rapidly changing product. Subsidiary questions are of interest in themselves and may shed light on the motivations and constraints that determine hospital behavior: How are hospital prices for each type of service related to the average and marginal costs of those services? What determines the demand for inputs and the wages that hospitals pay for personnel?

The Motives of Hospital Behavior. The motives or maximands of hospital behavior suggested by those who have tried to model the hospital's economic activity include the quantity and quality of care delivered, the net revenue earned by the hospital, and the income of the medical staff. Although the attempt to explain hospital actions as if they were the results of maximizing a utility function with these arguments (subject to technological and market constraints) seems tautological and empty, it may in fact be too restrictive. The hospital is a multi-headed animal whose behavior may fail to satisfy the usual conditions of rationality implied by even an ordinal utility function. Although ultimate authority for a hospital's actions may be vested in a public board of trustees, important independent decision-making power rests with the administrative and medical staffs of the hospital. The same bureaucratic description may also apply to ordinary business firms, but the competitive market and the system of equity ownership may discipline the actions of private firms enough to make profit maximization an adequate approximation to their behavior. Without this discipline of the market, the nonprofit institution may enjoy the luxury of pursuing multiple goals in a decentralized and uncoordinated decision-making structure. The important role of the independent professional reinforces this tendency.[25] Successful analysis of the actions of hospitals and other nonprofit institutions may require replacing the "utility maximizing" model of behavior by a "bureaucratic" theory that explicitly recognizes the existence of several independent sources of decision authority within the institution. Although substantial work on organizational decision making has been done by sociologists and political scientists and some attempts made by economists to apply this work to the business firm, we have no model of bureaucratic behavior with the predictive power of the traditional model of the profit-maximizing firm. The growing significance of nonprofit institutions makes the development of such models particularly important. My task is more modest: to review the "rational" decision models

25. The analogies between the hospital and the private university are obvious.

that have been proposed and examine the empirical analysis of price, output, and input decisions.

A theory that describes the hospital's preferences by a utility func-tion with several arguments is too general to have any predictive val-ue. To be fruitful, a theory must simplify by restricting the number of arguments and, if there are more than two arguments, by specifying properties of the functional form. The suggestion that hospitals act as if they maximize some function of the quantity and quality of their output appears to be one such useful simplification. It has been ap-plied to analyzing the response of British hospitals to changes in the government budget constraint (M. Feldstein 1967) and to predicting the price, input, and output behavior of American hospitals (Evans 1970a; Newhouse 1970a; chapter 3).[26]

A simplification that is useful for some purposes is, of course, not a complete theory. Davis (1972a) has correctly noted that an appropri-ate dynamic theory must recognize that hospitals limit current quanti-ty and quality in order to earn a current surplus that can be used to acquire additional capacity or equipment that can raise future quanti-ty and quality. Evans (1970a) stressed the importance of this intertem-poral trade-off for predicting the response of hospitals to alternative incentive reimbursement proposals. This link between a hospital's earned surplus and its ability to increase its capital stock has not been fully examined, but Ginsburg (1970, 1972a, 1972b) has provided a useful analysis of the sources of capital funds and the way in which an institution's own funds may be leveraged through grants and bor-rowing.

Pauly and Redisch (1973) have proposed a very different model to explain the behavior of hospitals. They suggest that the hospital be viewed as a doctors' cooperative or implicit partnership that seeks to maximize the physicians' money income. While I do not believe that all the hospitals' actions can be explained in terms of this single maxi-mand, the Pauly-Redisch analysis is an important reminder that the professional incomes of the medical staff, although technically not a part of hospital costs, may play an important part in determining the hospital's behavior. If the physicians are assumed to be interested not only in their incomes but also in the style and character of their work and in their sense of professional accomplishment,[27] the Pauly-

26. This specification also appears to be operationally equivalent to Reder's (1965) suggestion of maximizing "weighted" output and to the specification suggested by Klar-man (1965a) and Long (1964) that hospitals maximize output subject to a quality con-straint. See also Lee (1971).

27. The analogy with the university faculties and the professional staff of nonprofit research institutions is again useful.

Redisch hypothesis must be generalized to include the quantity and quality of the hospital's output.

These explanations of hospital behavior imply that the hospital would seek to produce any given output at minimum cost and, in particular, would try to hire all labor inputs at the minimum wage for which they can be obtained. While there is some evidence that hospitals have used their monopsonistic power in the hiring of nurses (Yett 1971), there is also evidence that in recent years hospitals have increased wages by substantially more than was required to obtain the desired numbers of employees (M. Feldstein 1971b). Hospital employees have traditionally earned less than others in the same occupations and cities, but in recent years this differential has disappeared and the reverse has often become true.[28] A nonprofit organization may take a more philanthropic and generous view of employee compensation when its market conditions permit than a profit-making firm would wish or could afford to do.

Finally, the hospital boards of directors generally assume a responsibility to serve the public interest that goes beyond anything that could be expected in the relation between a private firm and its consumers. This implies a reluctance to discontinue individual services that do not cover their own costs and to raise prices sufficiently to eliminate excess demand.

The difficulty of constructing a model rich enough to explain all observed behavior and simple enough to yield new insights into behavior is evident. Perhaps at this time we must make do with a two-level theory. At one level a very general theory reminds us of the full complexity of the institution and behavior with which we are dealing. To deal with particular issues, however, we invoke more specific hypotheses. If we are lucky, the more restricted hypothesis can help us deal with the question at hand without leading to conclusions that would have to be rejected because of considerations suggested by the more general analysis. Only future research on a variety of individual questions will permit us to assess the usefulness of such restricted models.

Technical Change and Price Inflation. The cost of hospital care has been rising rapidly for more than twenty years. The average cost per patient-day in 1970 was five times as high as in 1950. Since 1970, this unit cost has continued to increase at an annual rate of more than 10 percent. Although there have been many popular discussions of this

---

28. This of course relates only to those occupations for which comparable work exists in other industries.

and several attempts to disaggregate the overall increase into individual components, there has been relatively little economic research on this issue.[29]

A traditional analysis in terms of demand and supply has often been suggested but has never been tested empirically. The evidence for a shifting demand curve is clear. The extent of insurance coverage has increased extremely rapidly; by 1970 private and public insurance paid 86 percent of hospital costs. The growth of insurance has been so rapid that the real net cost per patient-day (average cost per patient-day, net of insurance and government payments, and deflated by the consumer price index) was nearly unchanged from 1950 to 1970. While demand increased, the supply of hospital beds remained nearly constant; from 1950 to 1970 the number of short-term beds per capita only rose from 3.4 to 4.2. It is therefore tempting to explain hospital-cost inflation as the result of rapidly shifting demand and inelastic supply. Although such an analysis is plausible, it is undoubtedly wrong. If it were correct, the historical rise in the cost per patient-day would be equivalent to a rise in the price of inputs, and any expansion in the number of hospital beds would be possible only with sharply increasing average costs. Neither of these is true. The wage rate of hospital employees and the average price of hospital nonlabor inputs have increased much less than average cost per patient-day. There is, moreover, no evidence that the total supply of beds could not be increased substantially with little rise in the average cost per patient-day.

The usual supply and demand analysis must be altered substantially to deal with the hospital industry. Price has risen in response to increasing demand not because supply is inelastic but because the supply of higher-quality services is very elastic. The effect of greater demand has been to change the character, quality, or style of hospital care. Increases in the quantity of resource inputs account for the major share of the increased cost per patient-day. Cross-sectional differences in hospital costs are also largely due to differences in the quantity of resource inputs rather than in input prices (chapter 5).

Although the specific way in which quality and price respond to increased demand reflects the competitiveness of the local hospital market, the general character of the response should be the same whenever the hospital has some degree of monopoly power within its

29. The general subject of price and productivity measurement will not be reviewed in this chapter. See Barzel (1969), M. Feldstein (1970b), Reder (1969), and Scitovsky (1967).

market.[30] M. Feldstein (chapter 3) proposed and tested a model in which hospitals respond to greater demand by increasing real resource inputs per patient-day and thus price. More specifically, quality and price adjust with a lag to an equilibrium price that the hospital chooses subject to the constraint on quality and quantity that is implied by the new demand curve. The estimates imply a significant lag in adjustment; only about one-fourth of the gap between actual and equilibrium price is eliminated each year. The model explains interstate variation as well as changes through time. Davis (1972b) found that the basic demand equations of this model also explained five-year observations on a group of 200 individual hospitals and provided a basis for predicting price changes in the post-Medicare period. Other evidence also shows that hospitals respond to higher demand by increasing resource inputs per patient-day.

Some insurers, particularly Blue Cross, not only lower the net cost to the patient but also deal directly with the hospitals. The Blue Cross payment rules and extent of direct control differ among the states. Pauly and Drake (1970) found that these differences had little if any effect on the cost and other performance measures of the hospital. Klarman has emphasized (1969b) the difference between indemnity policies and cost reimbursement, but the studies by Davis (1973) and Salkever (1972) do not find evidence that this difference is important. More generally, the impact of regulatory agencies and government price control has not yet been studied.

This emphasis on demand and on demand-induced technical change should not obscure the fact that increases in hospital wages and input prices have raised the average cost per patient-day and that interstate differences in input prices are reflected in average cost per patient-day. Yett and his associates (1971), in a general econometric model of the health-care sector, related average cost per patient-day to the wage rate, personnel per patient-day, average size of hospital, and other cost determinants. Only the wage rate was significant in this equation, a surprising result considering the symmetrical way in which wages and personnel enter the average cost identity. This may reflect the general disregard of demand in the analysis. Demand was assumed to increase cost only by raising factor prices; changes in quality were ignored. Davis (1972b) attempted to synthesize demand and cost factors by relating the real price of hospital services (average rev-

30. M. Feldstein (1971b) contrasts the extremes of a perfectly competitive market in which only patients' preferences matter and a monopolistic market in which the hospital selects the quality level.

enue per patient-day deflated by the consumer price index) to the demand variables suggested in chapter 3 and to a measure of the real cost per patient-day (average cost per patient-day deflated by the consumer price index). However, by using average cost per patient-day rather than an index of input prices (including wages), Davis treats increases in quality as predetermined rather than as reflections of demand. Not surprisingly, the coefficient of the average cost variable is nearly one (0.93, s.e. 0.015).

The studies of hospital-cost inflation by Lave and Lave (1970) and Salkever (1972) used cross sections of time series for individual hospitals. These analyses were able to identify the characteristics of hospitals in which costs rose most rapidly, for example, teaching hospitals, hospitals in rural areas, hospitals with below-average costs in the beginning of the period, or hospitals with a high proportion of Medicare patients. Because their observations contained information about the individual hospital but not about the patient population in the area or the other hospitals serving that market, the analysis could not be extended to deal with the impact of demand. Davis' (1972b) study showed that microeconomic observations could be combined with data about the population of the surrounding county in a useful way. It would be particularly useful to extend this approach by gathering microeconomic information on each hospital in the market area. This would allow an examination of the effects of market structure on hospital behavior, of the impact of availability on demand, and of the relation of local hospital wages to labor market conditions.

The rapid technical change in hospitals during the past several decades reflects three separate forces: (1) changes in the quality of care induced by shifts in demand and absolute input prices; (2) changes in the technique of production induced by changes in relative input prices; and (3) scientific developments that have altered both the cost-quality opportunity locus and the possibilities for factor substitution. Except for the studies relating demand to quality change, this important set of questions has received relatively little attention and no empirical study. In particular, there has been no attempt to distinguish cost-increasing technical changes that have resulted from demand-induced movements along the cost-quality opportunity locus from cost-increasing technical changes that have resulted from scientific developments that shift the opportunity locus itself.[31] The availability of cross sections of time series should provide a basis for such an analysis.

31. See M. Feldstein (1971b, chap. 4) for a discussion of cost-saving and cost-increasing technical progress.

Input Demand and Wage Determination. Econometric research on the demand for capital and labor inputs has appropriately emphasized the differences between hospitals and the traditional firm. Ginsburg's (1970, 1972a,b) analysis of hospital investment behavior starts with the important observation that voluntary hospitals, unlike industrial firms, do not have access to equity capital. The usual theory of investment, which is derived from maximizing the present value of the shareholders' net equity, is therefore not relevant. In place of equity, the hospital obtains philanthropic contributions and government grants. The availability of these funds constrains the hospital's behavior, while the preferences of donors and grantors influence the form of hospital investment. The absence of equity ownership nevertheless gives the hospital trustees and staff substantial freedom to pursue their own goals and preferences. Ginsburg uses a linear programming model of the hospital to show how capital budget and general revenue constraints influence both the choice of technique and the diagnostic mix of patients treated. Although a model of pricing is not (1972a) suggestion that hospitals earn a surplus in order to finance future investment.

In his empirical work Ginsburg studies a large random sample of individual hospitals for which audited accounts for several years were available. A significant feature of this analysis is the disaggregation of total investment into the expansion of the number of beds and the increase in equipment per bed. The separate analyses showed that the availability of internal and external funds had an important influence on the increase in equipment per bed but substantially less influence on increases in the number of beds. Conversely, past pressure on beds (as measured by the percentage occupancy of available beds) increased the investment in new beds but decreased the expenditure on equipment by a corresponding amount.[32]

The analysis of hospital labor inputs has been concerned primarily with the supply of and demand for registered nurses. Yett (1971) has emphasized that the local monopsony position of many hospitals and the opportunity for (legal) collusion when several hospitals are in the same area, imply that the wage rate will generally be less than the marginal cost of additional nursing services. Yett suggests that the chronic complaint of a "shortage" of nurses may be interpreted as a statement that hospitals would always like to hire more nurses at the prevailing wage (but do not do so because of the higher marginal cost). There has, however, been no specific empirical testing of whether

---

32. For earlier studies of hospital investment, see Brinker and Walker (1962) and Muller and Worthington (1970).

hospitals have substantial potential monopsony power and, if so, whether they have exploited it. It would be useful to examine whether wages are systematically related to local market structure, including the extent of concentration among hospitals and the proportion of nurses who are married women. Because collusion among hospitals is (presumably) legal, market concentration may not be necessary for effective monopsonistic behavior. A theory of the factors that induce collusion may be necessary in order to analyze the use of monopsonistic power.

Benham (1971) developed a model of the market for registered nurses (RNs) with separate equations for their supply and wage rate. The model was estimated with cross-sectional data for individual states. Because many nurses remain outside the labor force, Benham divided the supply determination into separate equations for the stock of RNs in the state and their participation rate. The nurses exhibit the usual labor force participation behavior of married women: their participation rate is depressed by high husbands' income and the presence of children.[33] The number of nurses trained in the state in the recent past apparently has a significant effect on the stock of nurses, but treating even past nursing graduates as a predetermined variable in a cross-sectional analysis may be inappropriate. Positive wage coefficients were found in both supply equations, but the elasticities were very different in the 1950 and 1960 regressions; this instability suggests that the specification of the supply equations is incomplete and that an important omitted variable changed its correlation with relative wages during the decade. The demand function for nurses was not estimated directly but was inverted to yield an equation for the average wage (actually the median annual earnings). This wage variable was inversely related to the supply of nurses and positively related to per capita income and to the median earnings of hospital attendants. The coefficients are quite stable for both years. Benham interprets the personal income variable as a measure of demand and the attendants' wage variable as a measure of the cost of substitutes for RNs. No specific reference is made to monopsonistic behavior, and the evidence is compatible with both monopsonistic and competitive wage setting.

Benham's study provides a coherent analysis and a framework for later work. The wage equation in particular should be extended in several ways. First, per capita income is clearly an insufficient measure of demand. Previous analysis of the demand for hospital services showed that income is generally less important than insurance, the

---

33. Benham's data actually refer to all husbands and children in the state, not just those of nurses.

local stock of beds, population density, and other factors. A more general model of the derived demand for nursing services could be developed along these lines. Second, the possibility that the attendants' wage variable is endogenous should be considered. The supply of those most closely substitutable for RNs (licensed practical nurses, practical nurses, and some technicians) may be subject to many of the same influences as the supply of RNs. Moreover, hospital wage policy may tend to maintain certain wage differentials.[34] Finally, it would be useful to replace the current nurse wage variable (median annual income of female RNs) by some measure of the earnings of hospital nurses per hour or even per week. The Benham variable may reflect in part interstate differences in the extent of part-time or private duty work. Fewer hours per year would lower the current wage variable and increase the number of nurses required to provide any given total quantity of nursing services; this would impart a spurious negative correlation to the quantity variable in the wage equation.

Hospital wage policy may differ from wage determination in private firms in a very important way. A nonprofit organization may take a more philanthropic and generous view of employee compensation when its market conditions permit than a profit-making firm would wish or, in a competitive market, could afford to do. Feldstein (1971b) suggested this philanthropic wage policy as a partial explanation of why hospital wages rose more rapidly than other wages during the 1960s, even in clerical and unskilled labor occupations in which hospitals use a very small fraction of the labor force in the area. For these occupations hospital wages rose more rapidly than the wages paid by other employers in the same area and, by 1969, were often higher than elsewhere. While hospital administrators might not be comfortable with the idea that they paid unnecessarily high wages, they would probably also reject the notion that they hired their staff at the lowest possible wages.[35]

Benham's equation for nurses' wages can be interpreted in this framework. Higher local demand for hospital care not only raises the demand for nurses but also increases hospitals' ability to pay higher wages. A higher level of local per capita income may also raise the level that the hospital administrator thinks is appropriate or just for employees.[36] Since the philanthropic wage policy would extend to all employees, higher wages for attendants would in part be an indicator

34. An alternative interpretation of this variable is considered later.
35. The analogy with universities is again helpful.
36. Stated more formally, the hospital's utility function may have as arguments not only the quantity and quality of care provided to patients but also the wage rate paid to the hospital's staff. An increase in demand permits the hospital to increase all three "desirables."

of the hospital's wage policy; this would explain the positive coefficient even if attendants are generally a very poor substitute for registered nurses. Edelson (1971) has studied this issue by examining differences in the rates of increase in hospital wages in different occupations within each of fourteen metropolitan areas. He assumed that a philanthropic effect would apply only to the four lowest-paid occupations and found evidence for this effect, particularly in the period since the introduction of Medicare. Although this is an interesting result, it does not relate to the general question whether *all* hospital wages rise faster and are higher than they need be to attract the desired flow of labor services. Further research on this question could make a valuable contribution to our understanding of both nonprofit labor markets and of hospital behavior.

The Market for Physicians' Services

It is not clear that the distinction of supply and demand is as appropriate in the current context as in the discussion of the market for hospital care. The generalized agency model showed how the usual income and price variables affect the demand for hospital services even though the actual decisions about the use of the hospital are made by the physician. The same analysis is applicable to the general practitioner's referral of patients to specialists. But the common situation in which the physician (either general practitioner or specialist) prescribes the care that the patient should have and also provides that care may require a different explanation.

The effect of this unusual feature of the demand for physicians' services is reinforced by the special characteristics of the supply of those services. In contrast to the volume of hospital care, the quantity of physicians' services cannot be readily increased. Moreover, individual professional preferences play a large role in determining the care that the physician provides.

The Demand for Physicians' Services
It is useful to distinguish three types of physician care. First, there is the care for which demand is initiated by the patient. This corresponds most closely to the traditional theory of household demand. It differs primarily because the patient may be seeking information and advice rather than care and may therefore recognize the likelihood that additional services will be recommended. The second type of care is prescribed by one physician but rendered by another. Here the first physician may be acting in the role of agent. The third type of care is the service prescribed and provided by the same physician.

The demand for the first two types of care can be studied empirically only if the market for these services is cleared in each observational period (the observed quantity is the quantity demanded at the observed price) or if the price and quantity adjust toward an equilibrium in some regular estimable way. It is meaningful to discuss the demand for the third type only if the physician who prescribes his own services is nevertheless able to act as his patients' agent. The rather perplexing statistical estimates that have been obtained may reflect a failure of these conditions to be met. Even if the market for the first and second types does clear or tend toward a clearing equilibrium, the total output of physicians' services may not reflect demand if the third type dominates in the aggregate. Unfortunately, there has been no attempt to analyze the different types of care separately.

Feldstein (1970c) studied per capita demand for physicians' services using a national time series for 1948–1966. The basic price, insurance, and income variables were either insignificant or had the wrong sign. Also considered was the possibility that the observed quantity of physicians' services (measured as per capita expenditure on physicians' services deflated by an index of physicians' fees) does not measure demand but that the market is tending toward an elimination of excess demand. Dynamic price equations, derived from both Marshallian and Walrasian models of adjustment, were estimated. The Marshallian interpretation of the parameter estimates implied a positive price elasticity of demand, while the Walrasian interpretation implied an equally implausible negative speed of adjustment. Feldstein concluded tentatively that a demand equation could not be estimated, because permanent excess demand had prevailed in the market for physicians' services. To explain this he suggested that medical ethics constrain the doctors' ability to ration demand by price while professional interests encourage doctors to maintain a price at which excess demand enables them to be selective about the patients they treat.

There are two further possible explanations of their inability to identify a demand function. The demand initiated by patients or by referrals from other doctors may be satisfied in the usual way, but the aggregate output may reflect a substantial volume of services prescribed by the providing physicians themselves without regard to the consumer's insurance or other economic characteristics. Fuchs and Kramer (1971) have suggested that the peculiar demand estimates may instead reflect the nature of scientific medical progress during the sample period. From 1948 to 1956 drug therapy advanced rapidly. Fuchs and Kramer view these advances as physician-saving, because in their opinion the improvements in health that resulted from the physicians' increased ability to cure disease led to a net reduction in the demand for physicians' services. Since 1956, there have been no comparable advances and, in the view of Fuchs and Kramer, the technical progress that has occurred has been physician-using. Although such a change in the nature and rate of technical progress may have occurred, Fuchs and Kramer present no estimates of a demand equation to show that a more general specification of technical progress leads to plausible price and income elasticities.[37]

Data for a cross section of states provides greater variation in the explanatory variables and freedom from the problem of changing scientific knowledge. Fuchs and Kramer (1972) used such a cross section for 1966 to estimate a full model of the market for physicians' services. The demand equation that they prefer relates an index of physicians' services per capita to per capita income, average price, and the number of MDs per capita.[38] The estimated income elasticity is low (0.11) and insignificant ($t = 1.3$). The most striking feature of the estimated demand equations is that the alternative insurance variables were always insignificant or the wrong sign. Similarly, when price net of insurance was used instead of gross price, its coefficient was nearly zero and less than its standard error. These results are very similar to Feldstein's inability to obtain "reasonable" coefficients for a demand equation and again raise the question whether the observed quantities actually correspond to amounts demanded.[39]

The significant and substantial elasticity with respect to the number

37. M. Feldstein's (1970c) original equations contained a constant exponential trend to represent technical change and other factors that shift the demand function. To test the suggestion of Fuchs and Kramer, this has been replaced by a variety of alternatives including functions that are discontinuous in 1956, a quadratic time variable, and an index of death rates. None of these alters the original finding of a perverse coefficient on net price and insurance. See M. Feldstein (1973a).

38. The index of physicians' services is gross expenditure on physicians deflated by average price per standard unit of service. Because the consumer price index data are not available by states, Fuchs and Kramer developed a price series based on regional averages estimated in the Health Interview Survey and data on differences in the mix of services among states.

39. These results refer to the original version of the Fuchs and Kramer paper. In a revised version (which I read too late to change the text, the authors find that income elasticity is 0.20 and is significant ($t = 2.5$). The insurance variables in the demand equations are not always insignificant or of the wrong sign. Moreover, the coefficient of net price is, in most specifications, highly significant and it is always negative. The only difference between the revised estimates and the earlier estimates appears to be a smaller set of instrumental variables that, in principle, should reduce the risk of bias. The sensitivity of the results to this small change in method is worrying, but the new Fuchs and Kramer results raise important issues. All further references to Fuchs and Kramer are to the original version.

of physicians per capita (0.41, s.e. 0.07) suggests the type of incomplete agency relationship that explains why the availability of hospital beds affects the demand for hospital care. Alternatively, it may indicate that there is excess demand for physicians' services in some or all states. Fuchs and Kramer reject this and offer as alternatives (1) the possibility that fewer physicians per capita mean greater travel time and longer waiting time in doctors' offices and (2) the idea that the supply of medical resources has generated its own demand. The latter explanation corresponds to the third type of medical services. If this type of care is dominant and if its quantity is supply determined, it is difficult to see why price should be relevant. Indeed, if the quantity is supply determined, the coefficients should be interpreted as a supply equation and the negative coefficient of gross price would indicate that doctors provide more services in states with lower price in order to maintain their income, that is, that the physician's supply curve bends backward in the relevant range.[40]

Scitovsky and Snyder (1972) studied the effect of introducing a 25 percent coinsurance on a particular set of users of a group practice. These patients constituted a relatively small fraction of all users of the group, so it may presumably be inferred that the supply conditions remained unchanged. The 25 percent coinsurance rate reduced physician visits by approximately the same percentage. Phelps and Newhouse (1972b) reanalyzed the data and showed that standardizing for age, occupation, and other demographic factors does not change the conclusion. They also noted the ambiguity of the elasticity implied by this evidence. The arc elasticity is very sensitive to the way in which an increase in price from zero is translated into a proportional change. If the price change is related to the average of the before and after prices, the implied elasticity is −0.13. However, the elasticity may not be a useful summary measure of the demand function. If the price-quantity relation is linear over the relevant range, the implied elasticity rises from −0.13 at the price corresponding to a 12.5 percent coinsurance rate to −0.52 with a 50 percent coinsurance rate. The primary virtue of the Scitovsky-Snyder analysis is that it establishes that coinsurance (and presumably any change in net price) can have a substantial and significant effect in a setting where the quantity is determined by demand.

As Phelps and Newhouse (1972b) also note, the estimated price elasticity may vary substantially with the amount of time used in the

40. I return to this. Note that the argument is not affected by the fact that the dependent variable is services per person and not per doctor, since the number of doctors per person is an explanatory variable and all variables are transformed to logarithms.

consumption of medical care. The total net price that the patient pays for medical care includes the net money price and the value of the time used.[41] In an outpatient setting the value of time may account for a very large portion of the total net price. The elasticity with respect to net money price is then very much less than the elasticity with respect to total net price.

The Economic Behavior of Physicians

Studies of the economic behavior of physicians have dealt with the doctor's personal supply of services and the determination of the price of those services. Unless it is assumed that the physician has no impact on the price of his own services, these two issues cannot be analyzed separately. The need to consider the two issues together is reinforced by the possibility that the market for physicians' services may not clear in the usual way. The implications of the previous studies can be understood best by examining how each of them answers (explicitly or implicitly) the following three questions: (1) To what extent is the doctor a price setter? (2) If the doctor is a price setter, what determines the price that he charges? (3) How does the prevailing price, or the condition of demand if the doctor is a price setter, affect the quantity of services supplied?

Fuchs and Kramer (1972) assume that the physician is a price taker and that the prevailing price is determined by the equilibrium of supply and demand. In this framework they study the relation between the supply of services per physician in each state[42] and a price index of physicians' services, the number of practicing physicians per capita, the number of hospitals beds per capita, the percentage of doctors who are specialists, and the percentage who work in partnerships. Contrary to expectations, in all the equations that they report neither the percentage of specialists not the percentage in partnerships has a significant effect. Both results contradict the usual evidence of substantial differences in earnings between specialists and general practitioners and between solo practitioners and doctors in partnerships. When the supply of beds and the supply of doctors are both included in the equation, the price variable is insignificant. When the supply of beds is omitted, the averate price variable is significantly negative. Fuchs and Kramer are cautious in interpreting this evidence and conclude that while the evidence appears to favor the absence of any ef-

41. For evidence that the time required to consume medical care has a substantial deterrent effect on demand, see Acton (1972), Phelps and Newhouse (1972b), Shannon, Bashur, and Metzner (1969) and Weiss, Greenlick, and Jones (1971).

42. Defined as the ratio of expenditure per practicing physician to the estimated average price of a "GP outpatient visit equivalent."

fect of price on supply, the existence of a positive price effect can be rejected with greater confidence.

The positive effect of local bed supply is interpreted as evidence of a complementary production relation. This is an important new piece of evidence with potential implications about the determinants of hospital bed supply and the measurement of physician scarcity. Unfortunately, no attention is given to the complementary inputs used within the physicians' own practices. Since approximately 50 percent of the gross price of services represents payments for purchased inputs rather than income to the physician, this omission may have a serious effect on the estimated coefficients.[43]

Two related explanations are offered by Fuchs and Kramer for the negative relation between the number of physicians per capita and the volume of services per physician: a local scarcity of physicians may compel doctors to provide more care, while an abundance may imply excess capacity for particular specialties or times. Note that both explanations conflict with the general presumption of the Fuchs-Kramer model that markets are cleared and prices equate supply and demand.

Feldstein's (1970c) analysis is based on combining an extended theory of individual labor supply with a model of the firm in an imperfectly competitive market. The individual physician is assumed to be a price setter, but in contrast to the firm, the doctor does not seek to maximize profits.[44] Instead the physician maximizes utility, which depends not only on his income and leisure but also on the characteristics of his work. The implication of this extension of the theory of labor supply is that the physician does not maximize his income for the number of hours that he works. By charging a lower price, he induces a level of excess demand that enables him to be selective about the patients whom he treats. This model was not analyzed formally but was used as a framework for specifying estimable price and supply equations. According to the preferred price equation, the average price of physicians' services adjusts with a lag to increases in the consumer price index, the prevailing extent of insurance, the average per capita income, and the volume of practice inputs per physician. Although the effects of the first three variables may reflect the pressure of increasing demand, Feldstein (1970c) suggests that the apparent existence of excess demand implies an additional explanation: physicians raise prices when doing so would impose a smaller finan-

43. See, however, footnote 45.
44. For a discussion of profit maximizing by a monopolistic physician firm, see Newhouse (1970b). See also the comments by Frech and Ginsburg (1972a) and Newhouse and Sloan (1972).

cial burden on their own patients. An implication is that excess demand in a local area due to fewer physicians per capita would raise fees less than excess demand due to a higher level of income and insurance, but this implication could not be tested with the aggregate time-series data used by Feldstein. If the existence of excess demand is not accepted, the price equation can of course be interpreted as evidence of the effects of demand. In either case the coefficient of the insurance variable implies that more than one-third of the increased insurance coverage is diluted by induced price increases.

With the physician acting as a price setter, the specification of the supply equation poses a more complex problem. The model implies that the physician selects price and quantity simultaneously from the set of feasible combinations (points at which excess demand would prevail). If so, an equation relating quantity supplied to price is inappropriate. In practice, however, the price and quantity are not likely to be set simultaneously. Supply can be adjusted continuously, while price changes are discrete or "lumpy" and occur with a lag. Moreover, there may be an element of implicit collusion in the setting of common local fees, while the individual physician can adjust his own supply. An equation relating quantity supplied to price and other variables may be a useful approximation to this more complex process of price and quantity setting. Feldstein's estimates with aggregate time series indicate a negative price elasticity of supply and positive coefficients for a time trend (technology), inputs used per physician,[45] and a measure of "reference income." The negative price elasticity suggests that improved insurance coverage increases demand and decreases supply while public policies to restrain increases in physicians' fees may help maintain supply. The reference income variable is an attempt to capture the physicians' rising income aspirations (changes in the marginal rate of substitution of income and leisure); although the income measure used for this (the 95th percentile of the income distribution) is substantially below that of the average physician, the variable does have greater explanatory power than average per capita income. The rather high collinearity among the variables results in large standard errors and implies that the results should be treated as preliminary.

Sloan (1973) has recently developed an ingenious source for analyzing physicians' behavior with microeconomic data. By using the 1960 census 1 percent public use sample, he obtains detailed demographic,

---

45. Brown and Lapan (1972) criticize this use of an endogenous variable, determined by the physician, in the supply equation. The other coefficients are essentially unchanged and their standard errors reduced when it is omitted.

work, and income data for 1 percent of all U.S. physicians. Because each physician's state of residence is also specified, Sloan is able to augment the data for each physician with information relating to the population served by that physician (income, insurance coverage). Sloan presents a theoretical model that extends the standard theory of labor-leisure choice by recognizing that the quantity demanded is a function of price. For his empirical analysis, however, Sloan uses the traditional model in which the physician is a price taker who determines his supply of services. The physician's fee, measured as net income per hour, is related to the physician's own characteristics (age, sex, color, self-employment status) and to attributes of the population in the state (income, insurance). Most individual variables were significant, but variables relating to the state population were generally not; this may reflect the inappropriateness of using state averages to describe each physician's market.[46] A higher physician-population ratio was found to have a negative impact on fees. An unfortunate feature of the data that must be borne in mind in interpreting these results is that there is no information on the extent of individual physician specialization.

Sloan estimates separate physician supply equations for the number of hours worked per week and the number of weeks worked per year. Hours per week is related negatively to the doctor's hourly earnings and to his state's physician-population ratio and positively to a reference income variable (measured as the mean income of physicians in the state). Several other physician and population characteristics also affect supply. Weeks worked per year is related positively to weekly earnings and to the physician-population ratio and negatively to other family income of the physician. The two price elasticities can be combined to obtain an overall negative elasticity of hours worked per year with respect to the hourly wage rate. This measure of supply related only to hours of work, not to the type of work that the physician does, nor to the total volume of services produced by the physician's own efforts and the other inputs in his practice.

Reinhardt (1972) has used a production function for physician services to estimate the effects of employing different amounts and combinations of labor and nonlabor inputs. Alternative measures of output (number of visits and total charges) gave similar results. The estimates indicate substantially decreasing returns to the number of hours worked by the physician. Also noteworthy is the small (5 percent) positive effect of group practice; the use of a multiple regression

---

46. Aggregating the individual observations to state averages did not, however, alter the results.

production function implies substantially less gain from group practice than a simple comparison of unadjusted mean outputs in solo and
group practices.[47] Of particular interest are Reinhardt's estimates of
the effects of physicians' aides (nurses, technicians, office aides); Reinhardt concludes that the sample average of 1.9 aides per physician is
approximately half of the level that would maximize net practice income. To explain the apparent "inefficiency," he notes that physicians may attach a psychic cost to the administrative burdens and to
the departure from the traditional mode of practice. This evidence
seems to fit well with the suggestion that the doctor does not maximize
his income for the hours that he works but has preferences about his
professional life that may influence his pricing and input decisions.

The Supply of Doctors
The total number of doctors in the United States depends primarily
on the number of graduates of American medical schools.[48] This in
turn is determined by the number of places offered by those schools
and not, as in almost every other field, by the demand for professional
education by the prospective students. The total number of applicants
to U.S. medical schools has been about twice the number of available
places throughout the postwar period. The behavior of the medical
schools in setting the number of places remains generally unex-
plored.[49] However, as Sloan (1971) has noted, the number of qualified
applicants may be an important determinant of the number of places
offered. Sloan studied aggregate time series for various subperiods
since 1934 and found that the number of applicants to medical school
was significantly responsive to economic incentives. The number of
applicants was decreased by a higher price of medical education
(tuition and fees net of student aid) and increased by a higher level of
physician income. In the postwar period the rising level of starting
salaries in business and the incomes of Ph.D.'s in the biological sci-
ences were also found to reduce the demand for medical education. A
special analysis of applicants with A averages in college (approximately the top 1 percent of college graduates) showed that in contrast to
other applicants, physicians' incomes and starting business salaries

47. See also R. Bailey (1970).
48. The total is also affected by the number of foreign-born doctors practicing in the
United States and, to a smaller extent, by Americans who go abroad for medical education and by foreign nationals who attend U.S. medical schools and then return to their
home countries. In 1967 approximately 11 percent of all doctors in the United States
were foreign educated. See Luft (1970) for an analysis of physician migration to the
United States.
49. See, however, Kessel (1958, 1970), Sloan (1968), and Fein and Weber (1971).

were not important for this group. Instead their demand for medical education was depressed by increases in the income of biological scientists. The effect on them of the price of medical education is uncertain, but it appears to have been unimportant.

The question whether there is an aggregate shortage of physicians has occupied public attention for a number of years. Official studies have generally been based on historical ratios of physicians to population, but this method has been criticized by Hansen (1964), Fein (1967), and others. Some economists have interpreted the rapid increase in doctors' incomes and the apparent excess demand by patients as evidence of a shortage. Hansen (1964) estimated that the internal rate of return to training as a physician (based on the cost of education and the lifetime income profile in comparison to that of a high school graduate with no further education) was about 13 percent; approximately the same value was obtained for 1939, 1949, and 1956. Sloan (1970) looked instead at the rate of return to college graduates who attended medical school for four years, had one year of internship, and no further specialty training. He found much higher rates of return, approximately 25 percent in 1955, 1959, and 1965. The difference from Hansen's results is presumably due primarily to the lower rates of return on college and specialty training than on medical education itself. If these rates of return are taken to be adequate indicators, the data support the view that the supply of medical education should be increased. The rates of return omit the nonpecuniary benefits and costs of medical practice and entail the assumption that an additional doctor could earn the average rate of return (that there is not a quality gradient with the current marginal doctor earning much less than the average). Still the existence of a substantial excess demand for medical education is itself evidence that there is a shortage in the sense that an unconstrained market equilibrium would occur at a larger quantity of physicians. This definition of shortage, however, ignores the significant distortions between private and social rates of return to medical education. The most significant of these are the substantial subsidies that make medical school tuition less than the cost of providing medical education and the widespread use of health insurance that inflates the demand for physicians' services. Any attempt to correct for these distortions would be very much complicated by the assumption that physicians' fees are not market-clearing prices.

Location. The substantial geographic variation in the number of physicians per capita has led to several studies of the location of physicians. These analyses have generally used a cross section of geographic areas to estimate the association between the doctor-population ratio and characteristics of the area. Benham, Maurizi, and Reder (1968) show that the relation of the physician-population ratio in a state to the level of per capita income and the number of medical school graduates has been rather stable since 1930.[50] An attempt to assess the restrictive effect of state licensure examinations by including the percentage of examinees who fail was unsuccessful; the coefficient always had the wrong sign (positive), presumably an indication of the inappropriateness of treating the variable as exogenous when the proportion of failures is probably a measure of the attractiveness of the state. Benham and his colleagues also estimate a structural supply equation that omits the level of per capita income but includes the average income of physicians in the state[51] and the extent of urbanization. The substantial income elasticity of supply (1.2) must be interpreted with caution because interstate differences in physician income may reflect differences in the proportion who are specialists. Fuchs and Kramer (1972) obtain similar results for 1966. More specifically, they find that doctors are more numerous in states where the price of physicians' services is higher, where there are more medical school graduates, and where there is more urbanization (or a population with higher incomes). They also find that the number of MDs originating in a state (born or previously resident) has no impact on the stock of physicians.

Static models like those of Benham, Maurizi, and Reder and of Fuchs and Kramer must be regarded as approximations to the actual dynamic process of stock adjustment. Since very few physicians move after entering private practice, the current pattern of physician location reflects the relative desirability of different locations during the past forty years and the subsequent deaths and retirements of doctors who established practices during those years. A static model is valid only if the interstate pattern of the explanatory variables has remained relatively constant over a long period of time. This is likely to be more true of some variables (relative per capita income) than of others (physicians' fees). Although dynamic stock adjustment models have not been specifically studied, Benham and his colleagues estimated equations for decade changes in the number of physicians in each state with a set of variables that could be interpreted as stock adjustment models. The equations generally had very low explanato-

---

50. Rimlinger and Steele (1963) and Steele and Rimlinger (1965) had examined these variables previously.

51. The specification is thus similar to the early work of Friedman and Kuznets (1945).

ry power and often had coefficients (including the lag adjustment parameter) of the wrong sign.

A more promising approach to dynamic specification is developed by Yett and Sloan (1971), who study the locational choices of individual recent medical school graduates. More specifically, they use data from a large national survey of physicians to study the location of doctors who were in private practice in 1966 but who had been in postgraduate training or military service in the previous year. Separate analyses were performed for specialists and general practitioners. In each case the doctor's locational choice was related to the characteristics of the state in which he was practicing. Both specialists and general practitioners were found to be attracted to states with above-average rates of growth of income and population and to be deterred from practicing in states where a high proportion of applicants failed the license examination. Specialists but not general practitioners are more likely to practice in states where a high proportion of the population lives in metropolitan areas. A most surprising and unsatisfactory result was that the coefficient of mean physician (specialist or general practitioners) income was significantly negative. The authors' suggestion that this may reflect the difference between current and permanent income is not very compelling. A more likely explanation is that there is a simultaneity bias: physicians' incomes are lower in attractive states because the supply of physicians is relatively large. An additional possibility is that the use of state averages may be misleading if there are substantial differences among areas within the state.

Yett and Sloan also examine the idea that a doctor is likely to practice in the state where he was born, educated, or received postgraduate training. Although their method of using conditional probabilities is interesting, the interpretation is unclear. While someone who chooses to do an internship and residency in a particular state is quite likely to practice there, it does not follow that the expansion of internship and residency programs will increase the state's supply of experienced physicians. The original decision to do an internship and residency in a particular state may only be an indication of the individual's preference for the state and his expectation of practicing there. A useful development of Yett and Sloan's general approach would be to recognize that the education and training variables are endogenous and to use a recursive model of the entire process.

The Choice of Specialty. Although specialists usually have higher incomes than general practitioners, the rate of return on specialty training is low and negative for some specialists. More specifically, Sloan (1970) notes that the very widespread and growing preference for specialty training cannot be reconciled with the traditional human capital analysis, since pediatrics and internal medicine have negative rates of return while the yield on training in psychiatry and general surgery is only about 6 percent. Nonpecuniary aspects of specialty practice presumably continue to attract doctors into these fields. There are also specialties with high rates of return (more than 10 percent in anesthesiology, radiology, and ophthalmology); since qualified MDs can generally obtain training in the specialty of their choice at some institution, the differential rates of return may reflect nonpecuniary differences among specialties.[52] To test this against the alternative hypothesis that yield differences merely reflect the slow adjustment of historically given stocks of physicians, Sloan estimated equations relating the number of residents in each specialty to the discounted lifetime earnings in that specialty, residency stipends, and the total number of available residences. While lifetime earnings had a statistically significant effect, the estimated impact of both lifetime earnings and residency stipends is extremely small. This evidence of a very small effect of economic incentives on specialty choice must, however, be regarded with caution, because of the inclusion in the equation of the number of available residencies. If hospitals adjust the number of residency positions to the supply of good applicants, the income and stipend coefficients would substantially underestimate the total effects of these variables. A complete model of the supply and demand for specialty residencies would be a useful next step.

The Economics of Health Insurance

More than 63 percent of the cost of personal health care was paid by private and government health insurance in 1971. The central role of insurance in the financing of health services and the growing public interest in some form of national health insurance have led to a number of related studies: econometric research on the demand for health insurance, studies of the effects of health insurance, including attempts to evaluate its welfare benefits and costs, and finally theoretical analyses of optimal insurance and related empirical research on national health insurance.

The Demand for Health Insurance

Analysis of the private demand for insurance in terms of expected utility maximization can be traced back at least as far as Friedman and

52. In particular, the amount of personal interaction with patients is generally very much less in specialties with high rates of return.

Savage (1948). The individual is assumed to choose among available insurance policies to maximize $E[U(W - P - Z)]$, the expected value of utility, where the argument of the utility function is wealth W minus the insurance premium P minus the random net loss Z. The net loss depends on the gross loss that would have occurred in the absence of insurance and the schedule relating insurance benefits to gross losses. This suggests that an econometric analysis of the quantity of insurance demanded or, more generally, the choice among insurance policies, should contain three types of variables: the parameters of the distribution of possible losses, the wealth or income of the household, and the price of the insurance service, that is, the difference between the premium and the expected benefits.

The special character of health insurance introduces additional complexities into this theory of demand. First, the gross expense is not a purely exogenous variable but depends on the extent of insurance coverage. Since the individual realizes that the marginal consumption of health services is therefore worth less than its actuarial value, while the premium must reflect that actuarial value, the demand for insurance is reduced. Closely related to this is the possibility that the preventive care that an individual exercises, and therefore the changes in his health status, may reflect his insurance for subsequent remedial treatment (Ehrlich and Becker 1972).

Second, the description of household choice in terms of maximizing the expected utility of net wealth may be an insufficient model of behavior. Health status as well as net wealth (or income) may be an argument of the utility function, and the marginal utility of net wealth may depend on health status. Since the payments by the insurer are likely to be negatively correlated with health status, generalization of the utility function would influence the choice of policy even if insurance did not affect the amount of care that the individual consumed. The fact that insurance coverage increases the consumption of services, which in turn increases health status, adds further complexity. Moreover, the use of expected utility maximization may itself be inappropriate; choices involving life and death are often cited as situations in which the continuity axiom of Von Neumann and Morgenstern or Savage may be unacceptable.

Third, most health insurance is bought by or for groups of employees rather than by individual families. The choice of a common coverage therefore reflects the group's rule for sharing the total cost of insurance and its process of balancing dissimilar preferences. Employers nominally pay a large fraction of the total cost of insurance. Although employees may actually bear the cost in the form of lower net wages, this may be imperfectly perceived, with the result that too much insurance is demanded. Even if employee perceptions are correct, the special tax treatment of health insurance (exclusion of employer payments and deduction of a part of individual payments) would increase the demand for this insurance.[53]

Despite these problems and complexities, useful empirical analysis of the demand for health insurance is beginning to accumulate. In a significant and innovative study Friedman (1971, 1974) used a modified form of expected utility analysis to explain individuals' choices among alternative insurance policies. More specifically, he studied how a large sample of federal employees chose among several different subsidized insurance policies. He assumed that they evaluated alternatives with a utility function in which an index of health and a constant absolute risk aversion function of wealth enter multiplicatively. Each employee's subjective perception of his own risk was assumed to correspond to a gamma distribution approximation of the objective experience of those with the same age and insurance coverage. For each age, sex, and family status combination, Friedman found the insurance option that would maximize expected utility. He also calculated the maximum premium that the employee could pay for each of the other insurance options and be as well off as he is paying the actual premium for the coverage that maximized expected utility. He then assumed that the logarithm of the odds that an employee chose one option rather than another was linearly related to (1) the difference in the maximum premiums for an employee in that age-income group, (2) the difference in the actual premiums, and (3) a taste variable that is specific to each policy but does not vary with the characteristics of the employee. Estimates of this log-odds regression showed that the difference in maximum premium was important and therefore established that the choice among policies is consistent with a tendency toward rational and informed evaluation of alternatives. The estimated coefficients also imply specific values for the risk aversion parameter; typical values were very high, 0.0026 for individuals and 0.0010–0.0035 for families. Although the specific form of the utility function, the implied relation between health services and health, and the particular way of mixing expected utility evaluation with stochastic choice imply that the parameter values should not be given undue weight, the study is important for its qualitative conclusion and methodological contribution.

---

53. M. Feldstein and Allison (1972) estimate that current tax laws imply a subsidy of at least 15 percent of total premiums. This exceeds the total profits and administrative costs of the insurance providers; that is, many families and their employers pay less for every dollar of health care purchased through insurance than they would have to pay to purchase that care directly.

Chapter 6 uses state aggregates for the period 1960–1965 to study the demand for hospital insurance. The primary interest is in a measure of the quantity of insurance defined as $\{(1 - ENR) + ENR \cdot COINS\}^{-1}$, where ENR is the proportion of the population enrolled in health insurance and $COINS$ is the average coinsurance rate paid by the insured; this variable, the inverse of the average coinsurance rate including those with no insurance, goes from one to infinity as the extent of insurance increases. The analysis uses the variables suggested by the general theory of demand for insurance: measures of the expenditure risk, the household income, and the price of insurance services. To reflect the lower price enjoyed by purchasers of group coverage, the study includes the proportion of employees in manufacturing industry or government to represent access to group insurance. Because of the endogenous character of health-care expenditure, the price and quantity aspects of the expenditure risk are separated.[54] Price is measured by average cost per patient-day; quantity is measured by the average per capita number of patient-days of care that would have been demanded if the price and insurance were the same in all states and all years in the sample. A stock adjustment model showed that the quantity of insurance responded quite slowly to differences between target and actual levels (an adjustment of 30 percent per year). The long-run elasticity of the quantity of insurance with respect to both the price and quantity variables was approximately 1.2 with standard errors of about 0.3 and 0.4; this implies that insurance adjusts, so that the average net expenditure on hospital care remains approximately unchanged as the gross price rises or the demand curve shifts.[55] The quantity of insurance also varies with the price of insurance; a higher ratio of premiums to benefits depresses demand (although not significantly), while a higher proportion of employees likely to obtain group coverage increases demand. The coefficient of per capita income is insignificant, possibly reflecting a balance of the decreased risk aversion and the increased health care consumption at higher incomes. The usual survey finding that higher-income families have more complete insurance coverage may reflect only the price effect of a greater likelihood of group coverage.

Fuchs and Kramer (1972) used state aggregates for 1966 to study the demand for insurance of expenses for physicians' services. They considered three alternative measures of demand: the percentage of

54. Using mean price and quantity variables implicitly treats the certainty equivalents of the distributions of risks faced by individuals in different states and years as scalar multiples of each other.

55. The insurance equation is obviously part of a simultaneous system and was estimated by a consistent instrumental variable procedure.

the population with insurance for physicians' services, the fraction of total expenditures paid by insurance, and the insurance benefits per capita. The qualitative results were generally the same for all three. The findings agreed in some respects with those obtained by Feldstein for hospital insurance but also conflicted in a number of ways. It is not clear whether this difference reflects actual contrasts between hospital and physician insurance or is due simply to differences in the definitions and methods used in the two studies. For example, Fuchs and Kramer report a significant positive income elasticity and a barely significant positive elasticity with respect to the ratio of union members to population. Since insurance for physician services is less common and generally less complete than hospital insurance, the income elasticity may in fact be greater. Alternatively, the union variable may be an inadequate measure of group coverage because large quantities of insurance are provided for nonunion workers in government and industry. The other variable measuring the price of insurance services, the ratio of premiums to benefits, was significantly negative as expected. The primary difference from the Friedman and Feldstein results is the absence of evidence that more insurance is purchased where expenditure is likely to be greater. The coefficient of the quantity variable[56] is negative but insignificant in the equation that measures the amount of insurance by the fraction of expenses paid by insurers and positive but insignificant in the equation measuring insurance by benefits per capita. Even more surprising, the coefficient of the average price variable is significantly negative in all the equations. Fuchs and Kramer suggest that this negative coefficient might reflect the fact that a higher price decreases the demand for care and therefore the amount of insurance measured in terms of benefits. This would seem to require an absolute price elasticity of demand greater than one, contrary to their findings. It also fails to explain why the desired fraction of costs paid by insurance would be substantially depressed. Although it would be useful to examine other specifications of this equation, it is likely that the ambiguities will be resolved only when better state data on physicians' services become available.

The Effects of Health Insurance

What effect does insurance have on the prevailing price and quantity of health services? What are the welfare gains and losses that result from insurance? The interpretation of these questions is ambiguous because insurance is itself endogenous in the health-care system. The

56. This is the actual quantity and not a measure of the location of the demand curve as in chapter 6; this quantity variable is treated as endogenous for estimation.

questions should therefore be interpreted as, what would happen to price, quantity, and aggregate welfare if the amount of insurance were constrained exogenously to assume some lower value?

Chapter 3 estimates the impact that the increase in insurance from 1958 through 1967 had on the equilibrium price of hospital care. This equilibrium price is defined as the gross price at which, given the stock of beds and the estimated desired utilization rate, the supply and demand for bed-days would be equal. During the decade being studied, the actual average gross price rose 91 percent. If the demand for hospital care is specified as a function of the net price of care (if the gross price and insurance variables are constrained to have the same elasticity), the increased insurance coverage contributes an 80 percent rise in the equilibrium price, about half of the total rise in the equilibrium price. If, however, separate demand elasticities are estimated for gross price and insurance, the increased insurance coverage is calculated to contribute only a 15 percent rise in the equilibrium price, which itself rises 90 percent.[57] Since expansion of the stock of beds lowers the equilibrium price and since increases in insurance induce additions to the bed stock, the estimates of 80 percent and 15 percent somewhat overstate the net inflationary impact of insurance within their respective models. However, even if the entire increase in beds were attributed to greater insurance coverage, the estimates of net inflationary impact would only be reduced to 75 percent and 10 percent.

The interdependence of price and insurance — more insurance raises the price of care while a higher price of care induces the purchase of more complete insurance — raises the question whether the combined market for hospital care and insurance is stable or whether the rapid increase in both insurance and prices is part of an explosive spiral.[58] Feldstein (chapter 6) has studied the dynamics of the two-equation model containing the price of hospital care and the quantity of hospital insurance. Even if the dampening effect of induced increases in the stock of beds is ignored, the hospital care and insurance markets are stable. The interdependence of price and insurance, however, implies that the effect on price of a change in any exogenous variable (the long-run multiplier) is substantially increased, probably between 35 percent and 100 percent.

The welfare effects of health insurance are difficult to assess. Five

57. Even if the gross price and insurance elasticities are unequal, 15 percent will understate the contribution of insurance if, because of characteristics of the basic data, the demand equations underestimate the elasticity of demand with respect to insurance.

58. The Fuchs-Kramer (1972) estimate of a negative effect of physicians' fees on the demand for insurance of physicians' services implies that that market is stable.

separate aspects can be distinguished. First, the insured gain from risk spreading, that is, from paying a fixed premium to reduce the risk of very large expenditures. Second, the insured also lose because insurance introduces a wedge between the gross cost of health services and the net price that they pay as patients and therefore distorts their consumption decisions. Third, an increase in insurance permits hospitals to sell a more sophisticated service and physicians to charge higher fees. These represent gains to the providers but losses to the consumers. Although the transfer of income from patients to physicians would traditionally be assumed to imply no net change in welfare, the same is not true for the increase in the cost and sophistication of hospital services. Physicians may prefer but place little value on the more sophisticated services, while patients will be induced by insurance and constrained by the limited alternatives to consume the more sophisticated services even though the value to them is less than the incremental cost. Fourth, there is a net welfare loss due to the use of resources in the sale and administration of insurance. Finally, there are those who remain uninsured and suffer a welfare loss because their risks are increased when prices rise and because they are now required to purchase a more sophisticated product than they would prefer.

Some of these effects have been studied. Although there is no estimate of the total welfare gain from risk spreading, Feldstein (chapter 6) has estimated the gross welfare loss that would result from increased risk bearing if the average coinsurance rate for hospital care were increased from 0.33 to 0.67. A Poisson model of the number of hospital spells and a gamma distribution of durations of stay are used with parameter values derived from national survey data and from previously estimated elasticities of demand. The welfare loss due to additional risk bearing is measured by the increase in the maximum premium that households would pay to avoid the uncertain expenditure minus the corresponding increase in actuarial value. Since a higher coinsurance rate for the population as a whole would lower the gross price and reduce the consumption of services, a higher coinsurance rate could under certain conditions actually lower the households' net risk bearing. The estimated welfare "loss" of increased risk bearing with a higher coinsurance rate therefore ranges from negative amounts to several billion dollars per year, depending on the choice of parameters.

Pauly (1968, 1969a, 1971) has emphasized the welfare cost that results from the distorting wedge that insurance places between the gross and the net price of care. Taking the gross price of care as exogenous, Pauly (1969a) used the traditional Hicks-Harberger triangle calculation to evaluate the welfare cost. For 1963 he obtained a loss of $450 million, approximately 10 percent of total benefits.[59] Feldstein (chapter 6) has extended this framework to the general equilibrium analysis, in which the price and perceived quality of health services are altered by insurance. This substantially increases the estimated welfare cost. Even with conservative estimates of the induced increase in gross price and of the sensitivity of demand to the level of resource inputs and to the price of care, the estimated welfare cost for 1969 was about $2.4 billion, or 30 percent of total insurance benefits and 20 percent of total private hospital expenditure. The corresponding welfare cost would have been only $600 million if the coinsurance rate had been 0.67 instead of 0.33. Feldstein combined these values with the estimated welfare gain from risk spreading to assess the net welfare effect of increasing the average coinsurance rate to 0.67. In the range of likely parameter values, this decrease in insurance coverage would yield an estimated net gain of $2 billion to $5 billion.

These studies leave a number of important questions for future research: the effects of differences among households in the extent and form of insurance; the implications of nonprice rationing and of the agency relationship; and the interdependence of private and public insurance.[60]

National Health Insurance

Arrow's (1963) paper emphasized the implications of uncertainty for the economics of medical care and launched a series of studies on the optimal form of health insurance. Arrow showed that if the cost of insuring (the insurance premium) depends only on the actuarial value of the risk, the optimal insurance coverage for any distribution of exogenous expenses and any utility function that is a concave function of net wealth provides complete insurance above some deductible. In the special case of an actuarially fair premium, the optimal insurance is complete, that is, the deductible is zero. Specific results about the optimal deductible and coinsurance features for particular

59. Pauly also used this analysis to assess the effects of increasing the comprehensiveness of coverage.

60. The two major programs of public insurance, Medicare (for the aged) and Medicaid (for the "medically indigent") have received very little quantitative economic analysis. M. Feldstein (1971a) estimated a model of the Medicare system that examined interstate variations in the use and cost of inpatient and outpatient services. The analysis suggests that Medicare has insulated older patients from the normal market forces so that their use of hospital services is less sensitive to total availability than that of the rest of the population. See also Russell (1973) and M. Feldstein (1973b).

cost structures and utility functions have been developed within Arrow's general framework by Pashigian, Schkade, and Menefee (1966), Mossin (1968), Smith (1968), and Gould (1969).

Pauly (1968) was the first to point out the significance of Arrow's assumption that health expenditures are exogenous random variables. When the consumption of medical services is price elastic, insurance distorts choices and the potential gains from risk spreading must be balanced against the losses due to consumption inefficiency. Zeckhauser and Spence (1971) developed this trade-off more formally, emphasizing the importance of the asymmetry of information between the insurer and the patient. Zeckhauser (1970) also considered the gains that could be achieved if different medical conditions could be unambiguously identified and the insurance benefits could be varied among the different conditions. In a quite different development of Pauly's analysis, Crew (1969) noted that the distortion in demand due to insurance could actually increase efficiency if, because of monopolistic behavior by providers, the quantity of care would otherwise be too small. Frech and Ginsburg (1972b) subsequently analyzed the implications of more general market imperfections and regulation for the design of optimal insurance. Although none of these studies has attempted to incorporate estimates of behavior or data on risk distributions, they provide a useful starting point for future econometric research.

The empirical studies of national health insurance have concentrated on forecasting the effects of alternative public policies. The most ambitious of these is an analysis by Yett et al. (1971) that used a 37-equation econometric model of the health-care sector to forecast time paths of response to different features of several prominent national health insurance proposals. Some of the coefficients of their model were estimated using data for a cross section of states, while others were obtained with aggregate national time series or were simply chosen to be consistent with recent data. The proposed plans contain specific institutional features (such as the use of special budgeting methods or review mechanisms) for which there is no date to estimate potential effects. Instead of ignoring these features, they were incorporated in a variety of ad hoc ways. Even quantitative provisions such as deductibles and coinsurance schedules had to be approximated very roughly to obtain policy variables that were compatible with the historically available data. The model is therefore preliminary (less than half of the coefficients are statistically significant), and the specific results of the simulations are only illustrative. Nevertheless, the analysis is an interesting exercise in the application of a complete sectoral model to the study of an important policy issue. The problems faced in the study also raise the question whether a traditional econometric model is capable of dealing with institutional innovations and of analyzing such detailed features as the structure of insurance benefits.

A microsimulation model was developed by Feldstein, Friedman and Luft (chapter 10) to study how different deductible and coinsurance schedules would affect the aggregate cost of national health insurance and the distribution of benefits among income and demographic groups. A large sample of insurance records and a model of price-elastic demand was used to take into account the probabilistic character of health expenditures and the joint importance of income and family characteristics. Although the analysis is therefore able to examine detailed differences in insurance coverage, it is limited to estimating the potential effects of insurance on demand and makes no allowance for changes in the price or supply of health services. A useful development of this approach would be to combine econometric evidence on the structure of demand and the response of providers with this method of stochastic simulation.

Wilensky and Holahan (1972) develop a different type of microsimulation analysis. They use the Health Interview Survey of the U.S. National Center for Health Statistics to estimate regression equations relating hospital and nonhospital expenditures to family demographic characteristics. To assess any proposed set of deductibles and coinsurance rates, they use the Current Population Survey data, assign a health expenditure to each family on the basis of the estimated equations, and then develop aggregate estimates for particular income and demographic groups. The Health Interview Survey is unfortunately an inaccurate source of expenditure information. Equally serious in the current context, the insurance coverage differs substantially among households, is generally incomplete, and is not described by the survey. The household expenditures, even if they were accurately known, would therefore not provide a good basis for estimating effects of alternative plans. The Wilensky-Holahan method also does not allow for the stochastic character of the health expenditures in the process of simulation since every family with the same set of demographic and income characteristics is assigned the same expenditure level.

Because national health insurance is likely to be one of the most significant public expenditure decisions of the eighties and would obviously have a major impact on the health-care sector, it is likely to be the focus of much economic analysis in the near future. One hopes that this work will use econometric studies to implement and extend the current theories of optimal insurance.

Some Problems of Econometric Method

Researchers have generally responded to the "nonstandard" character of the health-care sector by extending traditional theory and developing new models in an imaginative and sensible way. Some studies, however, have drifted either to the extreme of empirical estimation without theoretical analysis or to the opposite extreme of rigid attachment to constraints suggested by traditional theory. Estimation without theory is obviously an exaggeration; no one is guilty of selecting variables at random because they contribute to the explanatory power of an equation. But too many papers have included variables that are inappropriately defined for the model being studied, measured in units that are incompatible with the rest of the equation, or used in a linear relation when only an interactive specification would be sensible.

The inappropriate use of traditional economic theory is less common but no less misleading. An example illustrates the problem. In estimating the demand for two types of medical care (hospital care and physicians' services), should the Slutsky condition of equal cross-price effects be imposed? In addition to the usual problems of doing so, the special character of the demand for medical care implies several reasons for not imposing the constraint. To make the constraint appropriate, the "prices" of health services would have to be redefined to include the value of the patients' time as well as net money cost. Even then, the role of the physician and the possibilities of excess demand imply that the constraints applicable to standard theory will probably not be satisfied here. More generally, since every specification involves constraints, it is not possible to be dogmatic about the proper role for the restrictions implied by traditional theory. However, common sense suggests the value of examining more general specifications before choosing a final model.

The revolution in the teaching of econometric methods during the past decade is clearly reflected in the technical competence of the econometric studies of the health sector. The methodological shortcomings that persist are generally related to the specification of the model and to the interpretation of data rather than to the traditional statistical problems of estimation. Three such difficulties are common. First, there has been inadequate attention to the dynamics of behavior. Because of individuals' habits and institutional rigidities, short-run responses are often very different from long-run behavior. Static cross-sectional models estimated with data for periods of rapid change will yield coefficients that are between the correct long-run and short-run values.

Second, the special implications of the level of aggregation of the data are often ignored. Cross-sectional studies using state averages are appropriate if the variables are relatively homogeneous within states or if the structural relations are approximately linear. However, many variables that might be exogenous in a national model are endogenous when the unit of observation is a state or other geographical unit. Although simultaneous equations estimators have generally been used when they are appropriate, the list of endogenous variables has often been unduly restricted.

Microeconomic data for individual households, physicians, or hospitals offer the advantage of large samples with substantial variation in the exogenous variables. At the same time, however, the use of such data raises problems of interpretation whenever the behavior of individual units should not be considered in isolation. For example, the physicians' independent role in influencing households' consumption of health services (the incompleteness of the agency relationship) implies that the observed behavior of individual households depends on attributes of other households in the same area. Similarly, the prices charged by physicians and the quality level established by hospitals are influenced by the behavior of others in the same area. Studies that use microeconomic observations within a geographic area are needed.

The third type of estimation problem, the existence of measurement errors in the data, is particularly acute with microeconomic data. The substantial random error that is usually present in survey responses generally becomes unimportant when the data are aggregated. There is also more systematic error (due to respondents' forgetfulness or intentional distortion) that is not reduced by aggregation. In addition, while researchers often admit that a proxy is being used because more appropriate data are unavailable, there is usually no attempt to allow for this in the estimation.

These comments should not be interpreted as a general criticism of previous work. The econometric research in this area has generally been carefully and skillfully done. These remarks are offered to suggest ways in which future work can provide even more information. The number of good econometric studies of the health-care sector has been increasing. The past decade has seen a rapid development in the selection of worthwhile research problems and in the application of the skills of empirical analysis. The special character of health care has made this research a pioneering effort in the study of the public and nonprofit sector.

3 Hospital Cost Inflation: A Study of Nonprofit Price Dynamics

The empirical analysis of economic behavior has long remained the study of households and profit-making firms.[1] The growing importance of nonprofit enterprises, both as producers of goods and services and as objects of government policy, now compels us to extend the traditional area of analysis. This chapter presents an empirically estimable model of the nonprofit hospital industry and uses it to analyze the problem of hospital-cost inflation.[2]

The rapid rise of hospital costs has become a major problem of public policy. In 1970 hospital services cost the nation more than $20 billion. In the three years from mid 1967 to mid 1970, the cost per patient-day rose some 42 percent. Although this represents a significant acceleration, costs have been rising very rapidly for a much longer period: a day of hospital care cost five times as much in 1970 as it did in 1950. Although the nature and causes of this severe inflation are little understood, it has induced strong pressure for government action: national health insurance, expanded grants for hospital construction and modernization, manpower training programs, incentive reimbursement payments to encourage managerial efficiency. Unfortunately, without a better understanding of the mechanism of

Reprinted with permission from the *American Economic Review* 61, no. 5 (December 1971), pp. 853–872.

1. Quantitative research on the public sector has generally ignored the study of behavior and focused on establishing technical relations (cost and production functions), searching for empirical regularities in local government expenditure, and evaluating alternative programs (cost-benefit analyses and mathematical programming models). Some recent attempts to model optimizing behavior by local governments are a significant exception. See Gramlich (1969); Henderson (1968); Inman (1971).

2. This hospital industry model is part of a more general model of the health care sector that is currently being developed; for an early discussion of this project, see M. Feldstein (1968).

hospital-cost inflation, it is not possible to anticipate the impact of such policies.

Most discussions of hospital-cost inflation have focused on how inflation has occurred (more staff, higher wages, more equipment) rather than on why it has.[3] In contrast, the model developed here emphasizes the basic causes of hospital-cost inflation through time and of hospital-cost variation among different areas. The analysis suggests that despite the nonprofit nature of the hospital industry, hospital-cost inflation can be explained by a model of dynamic price adjustment to excess demand. Rapidly increasing wages and the expansion of hospital employment can be viewed primarily as the results rather than the fundamental causes of this inflation.

A Model of the Economic Behavior of Hospitals

This section presents an explicit dynamic model of the use, cost, and expansion of hospital inpatient services. It is convenient to describe the model by dividing the twelve equations into four groups: demand relations, price adjustment, components of cost, and expansion of capacity.

Demand Relations

The rate of hospital admissions *(ADM)* and the mean duration of stay per admission *(MS)* together constitute the per capita demand for hospital inpatient services. The same variables are likely to affect both *ADM* and *MS*: price, income, the availability of hospital facilities and alternative sources of care, the demographic composition of the population, and general attitudes about hospital care.[4] The rationale for

3. See, for example, *A Report to the President on Medical Care Prices* (U.S. Department of Health, Education, and Welfare 1967). Most empirical analyses of hospital costs have examined why costs differ among individual hospitals at a particular time rather than why the general level of costs has been rising through time. In a somewhat different type of study Lave and Lave (1970) identified variables that are associated with hospitals whose costs have recently increased faster than the average: teaching hospitals, hospitals in rural areas, and hospitals that had below-average costs in the beginning of their period of estimation. Salkever's related study (1970) found significant relations between cost increases and the number of interns, the local service industry wage rate, and the proportion of patients with insurance. My study (1971b) provides a general survey of why hospital costs have been rising but does not present a formal model or econometric estimates. For other discussions of the economics of hospitals, see Klarman (1964, 1965a, 1969), Newhouse (1970a), Reder (1965), and Weisbrod (1965).

4. It is assun.ed in this analysis that the patients' perception of the quality of care is independent of the actual services provided by individual institutions. Under reasonable assumptions, this does not change the qualitative conclusions of the analysis.

each of these variables and the methods of empirical implementation will be discussed in the next section. For the purpose of the general theoretical model, it is sufficient to consider the role of the price variable.

Hospital care is often described as a necessity and considered very insensitive to price. However, the substantial variation among areas in the rates of hospitalization and in mean durations of stay for different diagnoses and procedures shows that most treatment cannot be regarded as a technically determined necessity (M. Feldstein 1967; National Center for Health Statistics 1970). Although admission to a hospital for some diagnoses may be completely price inelastic, admission for other conditions and the mean stays for most case types are likely to be more price elastic.

The relevant price variable for studying demand is the cost to the patient net of insurance reimbursements[5] and relative to the price of other consumer goods and services. The problem of measuring this net relative price by a single variable will be discussed in the next section. For now, the gross price of a day of hospital care (P) is specified explicitly, while variables measuring the effect of insurance and of other consumer prices are included implicitly among the other explanatory variables of the demand equations.

Denote this set of explanatory variables by the vector $\mathbf{X}_t$; then the admission and mean stay equations are

$$ADM_t = ADM(P_t, \mathbf{X}_t), \tag{1}$$
$$MS_t = MS(P_t, \mathbf{X}_t). \tag{2}$$

The total hospital bed-days demanded (BDD) is defined by the identity

$$BDD_t = ADM_t \cdot MS_t. \tag{3}$$

Price Adjustment
The supply of patient-days can change only very slowly. An increase in a hospital's number of beds requires a relatively large "lumpy" investment. Such expansion of supply is also hampered by the nonprofit status of hospitals and their limited access to normal capital markets.[6] Although the percentage occupancy of available beds can be varied, hospitals generally have a desired occupancy rate that reflects both the need for excess capacity to deal with emergencies and the

5. The extent of hospital insurance is treated as predetermined in this model. Chapter 6 examines the feedback from higher hospital prices to the increased use of insurance.

6. Investment in hospital beds is discussed more fully later in this chapter.

relation between the occupancy rate, unit costs, and the quality of service; this desired occupancy rate *(R)* is treated as exogenous in this analysis. Equation (4) defines the effective or desired bed-days supplied *(BDS)* in the short run as the product of the number of beds *(BEDS)*, the desired occupancy rate *(R)*, and the number of days per year:

$$BDS_t = 365 \cdot R \cdot BEDS_t. \tag{4}$$

Given $\mathbf{X}_t$ and $BEDS_t$, equations (1)–(4) together imply an equilibrating price $(\overline{P}_t)$ at which there is no excess demand.[7]

$$ADM(\overline{P}_t, \mathbf{X}_t) \cdot MS(\overline{P}_t, \mathbf{X}_t) = 365 \cdot R \cdot BEDS_t \tag{5}$$

Hospitals respond to an increase in the equilibrating price by adjusting their actual price upward. Unlike ordinary business firms, hospitals do not raise prices in order to increase profits. Nor is there opportunity in the market for hospital services for patients to offer higher prices when there is excess demand. The mechanism that causes hospital prices to rise when the equilibrium price rises is quite different.

Every hospital's administration is under constant pressure to make changes that will raise costs per patient-day. The medical staff of the hospital wants more equipment, laboratory services, and professional staff with which to provide more sophisticated care to the hospital's patients. Patient comfort and satisfaction can be increased by enlarging the nursing staff. Other groups in the hospital bureaucracy — from the social work department to the dieticians — also want to increase the scope and quality of their services. There are in addition always demands for higher wage rates for current personnel. These pressures for higher cost per patient-day are contained by the hospital's need to cover costs with revenues.[8] If costs are to increase, the hospital's price must rise as well; with a constant demand function, this would cause the occupancy of hospital beds to fall below the desired level. How-

7. If $\mathbf{X}_t$ includes lagged values of *ADM* and *MS*, reflecting habit persistence in the demand for hospital services, $\overline{P}_t$ could alternatively be defined as the price that implies no long-run excess demand if only *ADM* and *MS* changed. However, defining P_t as equilibrating current demand and supply seems more consistent with the adjustment mechanism described later in this chapter.

8. Philanthropic contributions and income from endowment may permit small operating deficits for some institutions, while others try to earn small surpluses to be accumulated for future investment. The amounts involved are small enough to be neglected in this analysis. Local government hospitals may, of course, incur much larger deficits, and the analysis would have to be modified to describe their behavior specifically. In general, however, local governments prevent their public hospitals from spending more per patient-day than the cost in comparable voluntary hospitals in the same area.

ever, when the equilibrating price $(\overline{P})$ rises, both the price and the unit costs can be increased. In short, an increase in demand permits the hospital to yield to the internal pressure for higher-priced methods of care without reducing the percentage occupancy of beds. Prices rise toward the clearing price with a lag that reflects the hospital's uncertainty about $\overline{P}_t$ and its desire to moderate the speed of price increases. This price response can be approximated by the simple adjustment model:[9]

$$P_t - P_{t-1} = \lambda(\overline{P}_t - P_{t-1}). \tag{6}$$

The Components of Cost

Most discussions of hospital inflation stress the impact of the increasing cost of hospital inputs: more personnel, higher wages, more spending for equipment and supplies. The analysis of equations (1) – (6) shows that if the number of hospital beds is constant, rising hospital prices can be explained without reference to the course of input prices and quantities.[10] It is now time to consider explicitly the relation between the hospital price and the components of hospital cost.

Equation (7) is the basic budget constraint of the hospital:

$$P_t = C_t - D_t \tag{7}$$

where C_t is the average cost per patient-day and D_t is the deficit (or surplus) per patient-day. The deficit permitted by income from endowment and philanthropic donations is generally small and exogenous.[11]

The average cost per patient-day can be defined in terms of the number of employees per patient-day (N_t), the average wage rate (w_t), an index of the quantity of materials and supplies (J_t) and their price (π_t), and the interest and other fixed costs associated with previously acquired capital stock (k_t). The unit cost identity is

$$C_t = N_t \cdot w_t + J_t \cdot \pi_t + k_t. \tag{8}$$

9. In the empirical estimation, a logarithmic proportional adjustment model is used. Note that equation (5) is the usual simplification of employing a partial equilibrium adjustment in the context of a general equilibrium model. A more general adjustment assumption would relate the change in P to the disequilibrium in the stock of beds as well.

10. In fact, input prices can have an indirect effect on the price of hospital care through their effect on the number of hospital beds. This is considered in the discussion of investment in hospital capacity.

11. Even if the "deficit" is actually a desired surplus for future investment, I shall assume that it is exogenous. Although this could easily be modified by relating the desired surplus to the planned investment in beds, the link is probably too tenuous to be empirically important. Ginsburg's (1970) study of hospital investment supports this view.

I shall assume for now that hospitals treat w_t and π_t as exogenous and that they are in fact exogenous to the hospital industry as a whole.[12] Since equations (1)–(5) determine C_t while w_t, π_t, and k_t are predetermined, the hospital must choose the mix of labor and nonlabor inputs subject to the unit cost identity of equation (8). The actual process of bureaucratic choice is no doubt very complex. It can perhaps be summarized most efficiently by defining a variable that measures the quality of care as perceived by the hospital bureaucracy *(QH)* and assuming that N_t and J_t are chosen to maximize QH_t subject to the cost constraint of equation (8) and the prevailing production function[13]

$$QH_t = \phi_t(N_t, J_t). \tag{9}$$

The first-order conditions for such a constrained optimum can be solved (if the usual conditions defined by the implicit function theorem are satisfied) for N_t and J_t:[14]

$$N_t = N(C_t, w_t, \pi_t, k_t) \tag{10a}$$

and

$$J_t = J(C_t, w_t, \pi_t, k_t). \tag{10b}$$

Expansion of Capacity

Equations (1)–(10) describe how hospital use, price, and costs behave in the relatively short run. If the availability of hospital beds were exogenous, the model would be complete. However, in the long run hospitals affect the supply of beds by their investment behavior. Although the total capital budget of a hospital is generally constrained by the availability of government grants and private philanthropy, the institution has substantial scope for choosing between investment in

---

12. The empirical studies of this part of the model also consider a variety of more complex assumptions. It would be relatively easy to modify the analysis to allow some hospital wages to be endogenous to the hospital industry although exogenous to each individual hospital. The implications of assuming that individual hospitals have monopsony power is also investigated. For a more general discussion of hospital wage determination, including some aspects of the role of market imperfections and philanthropic wage policy, see M. Feldstein (1971b, sect. 5).

13. Since N_t and J_t are in intensive form (per patient-day), this analysis implicitly excludes the possibility of economies of scale.

14. Equations (10a) and (10b) are alternatives since, when one optimal input level is defined, the other is given by the constraint of equation (8). Although it need not concern us here that a hospital may be unable to reach the optimal levels of N_t and J_t within a single period, empirical estimates of this part of the model would have to make allowance for this.

more beds and other capital expenditures (new equipment, and the like).[15]

What determines how much a hospital invests in expanding the number of beds? Equations (1)–(10) define the trade-off that hospitals face between the number of beds *(BEDS)* and the quality of care as perceived by the hospital *(QH)*. All else equal, an increase in *BEDS* must decrease *QH:* an increased supply of bed-days lowers the equilibrating price *($\bar{P}$)* and therefore the actual price and the sustainable cost per patient-day. The lower cost per patient-day in turn restricts per day expenditure on labor and nonlabor inputs and therefore the hospital's perceived quality of care. The hospital administration must therefore choose between more patient-days and a more sophisticated service.

Figure 3.1 shows the basic relations of equations (1)–(10) and the implied quantity-quality trade-off.[16] The first quadrant shows, all other things being equal, the relation between the hospital's price *(P)* and the number of bed-days demanded *(BDD)*. The labeling of the horizontal axis implies the equality of *BDD* and bed-days supplied *(BDS)*. The linear relation between price and cost per patient-day, shown in quadrant II, corresponds to a hospital with an outside income that permits a small perpetual deficit. Quadrant III summarizes equations (8)–(10), showing the relation between the cost per patient-day and the maximum attainable level·of quality as perceived by the hospital. These three quadrants define the opportunity locus between the number of bed-days of care and quality of care that is drawn in quadrant IV. To emphasize the derived nature of the *Q-B* curve, the constructions of two of its points are explicitly shown.

The simplest assumption about the hospital's preferences is that they can be represented by a utility function whose arguments are the number of patient bed-days *(BDS)* and the quality of care as perceived by the hospital: $U = U(BDS, QH)$.[17] Figure 3.2 combines the implied indifference curves with the opportunity locus shown in quadrant IV of figure 3.1.[18] The point *BDS** indicates the number of bed-days de-

15. Ginsburg's (1970) study showed that one aspect of the very imperfect capital market faced by nonprofit hospitals is that the ability to borrow increases with the amount of funds obtained through philanthropy and government grants. He also showed the important extent to which investment in beds and other capital spending are directly competitive.

16. The figure represents a static model; it implicitly assumes that *P* adjusts to $\bar{P}$ immediately.

17. A similar utility function has previously been incorporated into formal models by M. Feldstein (1967), R. Evans (1970a) and Newhouse (1970a).

18. Although it is difficult to state the necessary conditions on equations (1)–(10) that

Figure 3.1

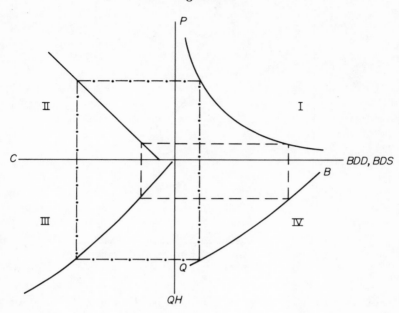

sired by the hospital and, given the constant proportionality relation
of equation (4), implies a desired stock of beds, *BEDS**. More formally, *BEDS** is defined as the stock of beds that maximizes the utility
function subject to the constraints of equations (1)–(10):[19]

$$BEDS_t^* = B^*(\mathbf{X}_t, w_t, \pi_t, k_t, D_t). \tag{11}$$

Equation (11) and figure 3.2 indicate the indirect way that the cost
of hospital inputs (w_t and π_t) can affect price. A rise in input prices
will, all else equal, lower the value of *QH* at each level of beds: the
price determined by that number of beds will purchase fewer inputs
and therefore yield a lower perceived quality. The *QB* curve of figure

would assure that the *Q-B* locus is quasi-concave from below, it is clear from the substance of the problem that an interior maximum must prevail.

19. This analysis assumes that the desired number of beds is independent of the interest and amortization ("user cost") per bed. Although this could easily be remedied by
treating k_t as endogenous in the long-run optimization problem, it would have very little effect since the correctly defined capital cost is a very small fraction of cost per patient-day (less than 10 percent). The simplifying assumption stresses that the indirect
effect on quality is the important determinant of the desired bed stock.

Figure 3.2

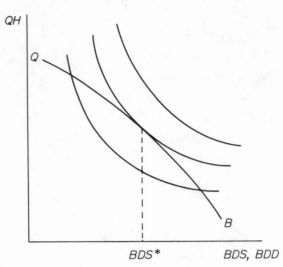

3.2 rotates downward in a counterclockwise direction. This is equivalent to changing the relative "price" of providing more bed-days of care in terms of the required reduction in QH. Like all uncompensated price changes, its effect is indeterminate. This leads to the surprising conclusion that a rise in input prices may actually lower the price of hospital care and induce hospitals to increase the number of bed-days of care provided, if the hospital's demand for inputs has greater than unit elasticity.[20]

The actual number of beds reflects a capital stock adjustment process toward $BEDS^*$, with the speed of adjustment depending on the availability of funds. Because this subject lies beyond the scope of this empirical study, a detailed discussion of the availability of funds and the way that they affect investment is not presented here. It is sufficient to write

$$BEDS_t = B(BEDS_t^*, BEDS_{t-1}, \text{availability of funds}). \quad (12)$$

This completes the system of twelve equations that simultaneously determine the availability, use, price, and cost structure of hospital inpatient care. Although this model, like all models, involves approxi-

---

20. In practice, of course, a reduction in QH is unlikely, but the input price effect may imply that QH and the price of hospital care grow more slowly than they otherwise would.

mations and simplifications, it is consistent with the general behavior of the hospital industry and provides a framework within which to make more specific tests and estimates.

The Demand Relations: Specification and Definitions

The variables that influence the demand for admissions and mean stay are price, income, the availability of hospital facilities and alternative sources of care, the demographic composition of the population, and general attitudes toward hospital care. Although the model described the behavior of individual patients and hospitals, data limitations require that the model be estimated for annual state aggregates. More specifically, the sample includes separate observations for each state and year in the decade 1958–1967, a total of 470 observations. The precise definitions used for the empirical estimation must reflect the theoretical relation, the level of aggregation, the availability of data, and the desirability of limiting the number of separate parameters to be estimated in any equation.

Price

The relative net price for each state and year was constructed using measures of the average gross price, the impact of insurance, and the general level of consumer prices. Each year the American Hospital Association publishes for every state the average cost per patient-day in short-term general hospitals.[21] These cost figures include interest and depreciation but exclude capital expenditures. Using average cost per patient-day as a measure of gross price is equivalent to ignoring the relatively small interstate differences in the average rate of surplus or deficit.[22]

The direct impact of insurance is to lower the net price paid by the patient at the time he decides how much care to consume. In practice, insurance does not pay merely a fixed proportion of hospital bills but some complex combination of proportional payments, fixed indemnities, and service benefits, subject to a variety of deductions, exclusions, and ceilings. However, treating insurance as a proportional reduction in price emphasizes its primary effect and provides a useful approxi-

21. The data are based on a survey of all hospitals and not a sample. The state average cost is a weighted average, weighting by the number of patient-days in each hospital.

22. The average daily service charge used as the hospital component of the consumer price index is both conceptually inferior (it omits all charges other than room and board, a large and growing part of the hospital bill) and not available for individual states.

mation for assessing its overall impact on demand.[23] More specifically, the insurance variable *(INS)* is defined as the ratio of the average net price paid by consumers *(NP)* to the average gross price (cost) of hospitals *(P)*.[24] Equivalently, it is the ratio of the aggregate net expenditure on short-term hospital services by consumers *(CONS)* to the aggregate total expenditure on short-term hospital services *(TEXP)* including net payments by consumers, insurance companies, and the government.[25] For state i and year t,

$$INS_{it} = \frac{NP_{it}}{P_{it}} = \frac{CONS_{it}}{TEXP_{it}}. \tag{13}$$

An explicit expression for the ratio NP to P is

$$INS_{it} = \frac{NP_{it}}{P_{it}} = \frac{H_{it}UI_{it}\mu_{it} + (1 - H_{it})\ UN_{it}\lambda_{it}}{H_{it}UI_{it} + (1 - H_{it})\ UN_{it}}, \tag{14}$$

where H is the proportion of the population with hospital insurance, UI is the utilization rate of the insured and UN of the uninsured, μ_{it} is the proportion of their hospital bills that the insured pay themselves, and λ_{it} is the ratio of the price paid by the uninsured to the gross price.

Although the expenditure data required to calculate *INS* are available for the nation as a whole for every year (see Reed 1969; Rice and

23. It is sometimes asserted that the effect of insurance is to lower the price elasticity of demand. There is no reason to believe that this is generally true; it depends on both the nature of the insurance and the structure of patients' preferences. If insurance paid 100 percent of hospital bills, patients would be completely insensitive to hospital price changes (a zero price elasticity). Other types of insurance may leave the price elasticity constant or even increase it. The approximation that insurance pays a proportion of the hospital bill illustrates this. It is perfectly possible that such insurance has no effect on the elasticity of demand; if, in the absence of insurance, the demand function has constant elasticity, this elasticity will not be changed by proportional insurance. It is also easy to see how insurance might actually increase the price elasticity of demand: at a very high price and in the absence of insurance, only medically urgent care would be purchased, with the result that a small rise or fall in price would have no effect on the quantity consumed while the introduction of proportional insurance that substantially lowers the net price induces patients to purchase many optional items, with the result that they might be quite sensitive to net price changes.

24. The inverse of this ratio was used as the definition of insurance in the previous study of physicians' fees (M. Feldstein 1970c).

25. The proportion of short-term hospital expenditure paid (or reimbursed) by insurance companies and the government rose from 68 percent in 1958 to 82 percent in 1967. If the national average total cost per patient-day had remained at its 1958 value of $28, the average net cost to be paid by patients would have fallen from $8.96 (32 percent of $28) to $5.04 (18 percent of $28) in 1967. In fact, average total cost per patient-day rose to $54, implying an 8.4 percent increase in net cost to $9.72.

Cooper 1970), the values for individual states had to be estimated for this study. Since the proportion of the population in each state and year who have hospital insurance is available (Health Insurance Institute 1968),[26] the required state values of INS_{it} can be estimated by using equation (14) if the comprehensiveness of the insurance (μ_{it}) is assumed to vary with time but not among the states in each year and if the relative price for the uninsured (λ) and the relative utilization rates (UI/UN) are assumed constant. Data from a 1963 national survey of 2,367 households indicated that the average values of λ and UI/UN were 0.42 and 1.2 (see Andersen and Anderson 1967). The national values of μ_t for each year were obtained from equation (14) by using the national values of H_t and INS_t. Although the resulting values of INS_t are a very imperfect measure of the extent of hospital insurance, this use of partial information to represent the impact of insurance as changing the net price of care seems preferable to using only the percentage of the population with hospital insurance (H_{it}) and ignoring the national data on the changing comprehensiveness of coverage (μ_t).

The composite relative net price variable (RNP_{it}) is defined as the product of the insurance variable and the gross price divided by the national consumer price index: $RNP_{it} = INS_{it}P_{it}/CPI_t$.

The introduction of Medicaid in 1966 provided state government insurance to millions of low-income families. By the end of 1966 twenty-five states had Medicaid programs; eleven more joined in 1967. The benefits, which include hospital, physician, and nursing home care, differ substantially among the states. Since many of the Medicaid eligibles previously had access to free hospital care but not to physicians and nursing homes, the expected net impact of Medicaid on hospital use by the poor is unclear. The states have not collected comparable data on the number of eligibles or the extent of use. The effect of Medicaid is therefore represented by a dummy variable that indicates a state's participation in Medicaid. More specifically, $MCAID_{it}$ equals 1/12 times the number of months that state i had a Medicaid program in year t. Because this measure is very crude, the estimated coefficient of the Medicaid variable should be regarded with great caution.

Income

Real per capita disposable income (INC_{it}) can be assumed to enter both the admission and mean stay demand functions in the usual

26. For 1966 and 1967 the number of persons with Medicare were included among the insured with prorating for the number of months of coverage in 1966. For a more specific discussion of the impact of Medicare, see M. Feldstein (1971a).

way.[27] It has been suggested that low income is likely to be associated with more disease, implying a negative association between income and admissions; this is considered when the actual estimates are presented.

Availability

Although measures of the availability of hospital beds and of alternatives to hospital care may seem to be inappropriate in demand equations, there are good reasons for including them in the list of possible variables. Consider the impact of hospital bed availability. The fact that the number of hospital beds per thousand population differs substantially among areas without any sizable effect on the occupancy rate has led some observers to comment that the supply of beds "creates its own demand."[28] This important statement is unfortunately ambiguous. Does it merely imply that an increase in the number of hospital beds will, all other things being equal, lead to an increase in the quantity demanded because it depresses the price of hospital care? Or does it imply that an increase in the number of hospital beds shifts the demand schedule? Such a "pure availability effect" could operate in several ways. A relative scarcity of hospital beds may increase the waiting time for admission for elective procedures, encouraging patients to obtain ambulatory care or to do without treatment.[29] Physicians may change their own criteria for deciding when a condition "requires" hospital care and how long a stay is "appropriate" for each type of care. This may be both a reaction (conscious or unconscious) to their perception of the shortage of hospital beds and a re-

27. The a priori argument that hospital care is a technical necessity and therefore completely income inelastic is wrong for the same reasons discussed in relation to price elasticity. Although the results of a 1963–64 national survey of hospital use (National Center for Health Statistics 1966b) showed no income elasticity of demand for admissions or patient-days, this evidence made no allowance for the association between income and other variables affecting hospital use. A similar 1962 national survey (National Center for Health Statistics 1966a) showed that higher-income families paid a higher price for hospital care, implying that if demand is price elastic it is also income elastic. For a further discussion of this survey data and somewhat different interpretation, see M. Feldstein (1971b).

28. Roemer and Shain were probably the first to point to this. For a review of this discussion, see Klarman (1965a, 1969a). Although the approximate equality of "effective supply" (about 80 percent of possible total bed-days) and bed use could in principle reflect a response of bed supply to the pattern of demand, there is substantial evidence from national experience in Britain (M. Feldstein 1967) and local area changes in the United States (Roemer 1961) to show that this is not so. See also the discussion of the relation between bed availability and utilization by Medicare patients in M. Feldstein (1971a).

29. The term "ambulatory" includes everything but inpatient care, that is, care in outpatient departments, doctors' offices, and patients' homes.

sponse to pressure from the hospitals themselves. By including both the price of hospital services and the per capita supply of short-term beds *(BEDS),* it is possible to test for the presence of a pure availability effect and to assess its magnitude.

Since many medical conditions can be treated on either an inpatient or an ambulatory basis, a greater availability of physicians in the area may induce relatively more ambulatory care. If the usual market mechanism were operating, a greater availability of physicians would tend to lower the price of physicians' services and therefore encourage a substitution of ambulatory for hospital care. However, a previous study (M. Feldstein 1971b) indicated that the market for physicians' services does not behave as traditional theory suggests; there appears to be a persistent excess demand for physicians' services, and price does not seem to vary systematically with changes in excess demand. For this reason, the availability of physicians and not their price is the appropriate variable to include in the hospital demand equations.

There is a different way in which local physician availability can affect hospital use. More physicians may not only encourage the substitution of ambulatory for inhospital care but may also increase the total amount of care, including inhospital care. More specifically, surgeons and other hospital-oriented doctors may induce increased demand for hospital care while general practitioners reduce that demand. For this reason, both the doctor-population ratio *(DOCS)* and the proportion of all doctors who are general practitioners *(GP)* are included in the regression.[30]

Population density *(DENS)* is another aspect of the availability of care. It is much easier to use ambulatory care in dense areas than in rural areas where patients live at substantial distances from hospitals and doctors. Increased density should therefore decrease the admission rate. Its effect on mean stay is unclear: patients can be discharged sooner in dense areas because ambulatory posthospital care is more easily provided in dense areas, but the lower admission rates may imply more serious cases requiring longer stays.[31]

Demographic Structure

The pattern of disease and the use of hospital services vary substantially by age and sex. Simple measures of the demographic structure like the proportion over age sixty-five and the proportion of males are too gross and ignore important interactions. The approach used here

30. Since these ratios change extremely slowly, they were treated as a constant for each state. The data for 1963 are derived from the American Medical Association.

31. Density may also be related to different patterns of disease incidence and therefore different admission and mean stay rates.

is to adjust each admission rate (ADM_{it}) by dividing it by a demographic index based on national admission rates in sixteen age-sex-color classes,[32] and the state's demographic structure. The demographically adjusted admission rate is denoted $ADMD_{it}$. A similar adjustment is applied to the mean stay variable using a demographic index based on national mean stays; the new variable is MSD_{it}.[33]

Time

A time trend *(TIME)* was included in both demand equations to represent technical progress and changing popular attitudes about hospital care. The actual improvements in medical science and the increasing general faith in scientific medicine should both contribute to increased admissions. The effect on mean stay is less certain; one form of technical progress has been the introduction of new methods of care that reduce the length of stay for many diagnoses.

Lagged Dependent Variables

The nature of hospital use is such that individual patients cannot develop any habitual behavior with respect to admissions and mean stays. However, to the extent that patients' behavior is influenced by community norms or by their physicians, customary standards may retard adjustment to changes in the exogenous variables that influence demand. The inclusion of a lagged dependent variable in each equation provides a proportional adjustment model for testing the importance of habit and estimating the speed with which demand responds to changes in its determinants.

Estimates of the Demand Equations

Estimates of several variants of the admission and mean stay equations serve three distinct purposes.[34] First, they establish the impor-

32. The variation by color is related less to disease incidence and more to attitude and discriminatory availability.

33. More specifically, the sixteen national admission rates are based on a 1963–64 survey by the National Center for Health Statistics (1966b). The demographic index for each state is obtained by weighting that state's age-sex-color composition in 1960 (U.S. Census of Population 1964) by the relative national admission rates. Although the relative use rates reflect any associations between demography and availability, price, and the like, the sampling and reweighting procedures make this unlikely to be a serious source of error. Although it would be desirable to allow each state's demographic index to vary through time, the data are available only for census years. However, the effect of this added detail is unlikely to be substantial; for the nation as a whole the demographic index changed less than 1 percent between 1950 and 1968.

34. For other estimates of aggregate hospital demand relations, see M. Feldstein (1968) and Rosenthal (1964).

tance of the traditional role for price as a determinant of the demand for hospital care. Second, they examine the effect on demand of the availability of physicians and hospitals beds. Third, they provide parameter values to test and estimate the price adjustment mechanism.

All the equations are specified as linear in the logarithms of the variables (except *TIME* and the *MCAID* dummy). The equations are estimated by an instrumental variable procedure that yields consistent parameter estimates.[35] Although a separate constant term for each state is not included, the lagged dependent variables are treated as endogenous to obtain consistent estimates even if the disturbances contain a systematic "state effect" or are otherwise serially correlated.[36]

Table 3.1 presents the basic demand equations without measures of bed or physician availability and without lagged dependent variables. Equation (15) shows a substantial and significant price elasticity of demand for admissions, −0.63. The income elasticity is statistically significant though very small, 0.078.[37] The positive independent growth rate (3 percent) and the negative effect of density are as expected. The coefficient of the *MCAID* dummy indicates that a state that had participated for an entire year in 1967 reduced its admission demand by about 8 percent of what it would otherwise have been. The corresponding mean stay parameters in equation (16) also show a significant and substantial price elasticity (−0.49) and a much larger income elasticity (0.465). The independent growth rate and the effect of density are both very small, reflecting the countervailing factors. The *MCAID* coefficient is insignificant and very small. Since the total demand for bed-days *(BDD)* is the product of the admission and mean

35. More specifically, the set of instruments includes all the exogenous variables in the two demand equations plus a number of other exogenous variables that would appear in other equations if a complete model of the health-care sector were being estimated. The method is thus similar in spirit to the technique suggested by F. Fisher but without the formal ordering and test procedure, which would, in any care, be impossible since a full model of the health sector has not been specified.

36. Even if the sample disturbances differ systematically among the states, the omission of separate constant terms does not bias the regression coefficients if the state effects are of the transitory type studied by Nerlove (1967) (see also Balestra and Nerlove 1966) or, more generally, if they are uncorrelated with the explanatory variables. Although a lagged dependent variable would be correlated with the disturbance if there is such a state effect, instrumental variable estimates are consistent. Balestra and Nerlove (1966) and Nerlove (1967) show that including separate constant terms may yield inferior estimates.

37. This very low value may reflect both the true income elasticity and a negative correlation between illness and income. Higher-income individuals may also consume higher-quality and higher-priced hospital services, a relation that is not considered in this model.

Table 3.1. Basic demand equations

	Dependent variable	Explanatory variables							Regression statistics	
Equation		RNP	RP	INS	INC	TIME	DENS	MCAID	RSS	SER
15	ADMD	−0.626			0.075	0.031	−0.071	−0.080	6.054	0.1142
		(0.048)			(0.030)	(0.003)	(0.005)	(0.024)		
16	MSD	−0.494			0.464	0.005	0.010	0.008	3.324	0.0846
		(0.035)			(0.022)	(0.002)	(0.003)	(0.018)		
17	ADMD		−0.550	−0.685	0.015	0.028	−0.075	−0.090	6.033	0.1142
			(0.106)	(0.088)	(0.081)	(0.004)	(0.007)	(0.027)		
18	MSD		−0.386	−0.580	0.378	0.000	0.004	0.006	3.474	0.0866
			(0.080)	(0.067)	(0.062)	(0.003)	(0.005)	(0.020)		

Note: Standard errors are shown in parentheses. All variables except *TIME* and *MCAID* are logarithms. The constant term for each equation is not shown. Observations are for individual states for 1958 through 1967. Estimation is by instrumental variables. The squared multiple correlation is therefore not shown. The final columns show the residual sum of squares and the standard error of the regression. Explanatory variables are: *RNP* relative net price; *RP* relative price; *INS* insurance; *INC* per capita disposable income; *DENS* population density; *MCAID* medicaid dummy.

stay demands, each total demand elasticity is the sum of the corresponding *ADM* and *MS* elasticities. The total price elasticity is therefore −1.12 and the total income elasticity is 0.54.

Because the relative net price variable is defined as the product of the relative price (*RP*, the gross price divided by the consumer price index) and the insurance variable *(INS)*, the specification of equations (15) and (16) is equivalent to constraining the elasticities with respect to *RP* and *INS* to be the same. The validity of this constraint depends on the assumption that treating insurance as a proportional price reduction is in fact a good approximation. Equations (17) and (18) drop the constraint and estimate separate elasticities with respect to *RP* and *INS*. In the admission equation (17) the two elasticities are quite close to each other (−0.55 and −0.68) and therefore to the original net price elasticity. The standard error of the estimate is unchanged; the other parameters are also essentially unchanged except that the income elasticity is decreased and insignificant. In the mean stay equation (18) the elasticities differ somewhat more (−0.39 and −0.58); the standard error of the estimate is slightly increased by dropping the constraint and the other parameters are essentially unchanged.

The equations in table 3.2 assess the effect on demand of the availability of physicians and hospital beds. Equation (19) adds the doctor-population ratio *(DOCS)* and the ratio of general practitioners to total physicians *(GP)* to the variables in the previous admission equation. Since the income elasticity is extremely small (0.01) and insignificant, the equation is reestimated without it as equation (20). The coefficients of the two physician variables reflect the opposite impacts of specialists and general practitioners. An increase in the doctor-population ratio causes a small increase in admissions, while an increase in the relative number of general practitioners reduces admissions.[38]

---

38. It is instructive to reinterpret the two physician coefficients of equation (20) to estimate the separate effects of general practitioners and other doctors. Let G be the ratio of general practitioners to the population and S the ratio of other doctors to the population Denoting the impact of the nonphysician variables by Z, equation (20) may be written

$$ADMD = (G + S)^{0.056} [G/(G + S)]^{-0.124}Z$$

or

$$ADMD = (G + S)^{0.180} G^{-0.124}Z.$$

The elasticities of *ADMD* with respect to G and S are therefore $0.180[G/(G + S)]$ -0.124 and $0.180 [S/(G + S)]$. In 1963 the national value of $G/(G + S)$ was 0.27. Calculated at this value, the elasticity of admissions with respect to G was −0.075 and the elasticity with respect to S was +0.131.

Table 3.2. Effect on demand of physician and hospital bed availability

Equation	Dependent variable	Explanatory variables										RSS	SER
		RNP	RP	INS	INC	TIME	DENS	MCAID	DOCS	GP	BEDS		
19	ADMD	−0.738 (0.057)			0.010 (0.036)	0.037 (0.003)	−0.091 (0.006)	−0.099 (0.026)	0.053 (0.029)	−0.124 (0.041)		7.004	0.1231
20	ADMD	−0.735 (0.056)				0.038 (0.003)	−0.090 (0.006)	−0.098 (0.026)	0.056 (0.026)	−0.124 (0.041)		6.973	0.1227
21	MSD	−0.593 (0.041)			0.418 (0.026)	0.010 (0.002)	−0.007 (0.005)	−0.007 (0.019)	0.025 (0.021)	−0.123 (0.029)		3.613	0.0884
22	MSD	−0.592 (0.041)			0.431 (0.024)	0.009 (0.002)	−0.006 (0.005)	−0.005 (0.019)		−0.140 (0.026)		3.622	0.0884
23	ADMD	−0.419 (0.68)				0.024 (0.003)	−0.064 (0.006)	−0.076 (0.019)	−0.011 (0.022)	−0.107 (0.029)	0.255 (0.044)	3.567	0.0879
24	ADMD	−0.435 (0.061)				0.025 (0.003)	−0.066 (0.006)	−0.078 (0.019)		−0.101 (0.027)	0.243 (0.038)	3.691	0.0893
25	MSD	−0.146 (0.072)			0.265 (0.030)	−0.0037 (0.0025)	0.029 (0.006)	0.031 (0.016)		−0.092 (0.021)	0.330 (0.047)	2.206	0.0691
26	MSD	−0.236 (0.041)			0.288 (0.026)		0.022 (0.004)	0.017 (0.013)		−0.108 (0.019)	0.277 (0.032)	2.200	0.0689
27	ADMD		−0.455 (0.051)	−0.043 (0.078)		0.031 (0.002)	−0.041 (0.006)	−0.026 (0.018)		−0.166 (0.025)	0.414 (0.041)	2.577	0.0747
28	MSD		−0.253 (0.041)	−0.127 (0.071)	0.327 (0.033)		0.028 (0.005)	0.037 (0.017)		−0.114 (0.019)	0.311 (0.036)	2.131	0.0679

Note: See note to table 3.1. Additional explanatory variables include *DOCS*, doctor-population ratio; *GP*, ratio of general practitioners to total physicians; *BEDS*, per capita bed availability.

The price elasticity (−0.74) is slightly greater than in equation (15); the other coefficients are unchanged. Equation (21) adds the two physician variables to the basic mean stay relation; *DOCS* is insignificant and the equation is therefore reestimated without it as equation (22). The zero elasticity with respect to *DOCS* and the negative elasticity with respect to *GP* implies that the elasticities with respect to the *GP*-population ratio and the specialist-population ratio are of equal absolute value (0.102 in 1963) and opposite sign.[39] An increase in the number of general practitioners reduces hospital stays while an increase in the number of specialists induces longer stays. The other coefficients are essentially unchanged from equation (16); the price elasticity is somewhat increased, and the very small elasticity with respect to density has become insignificant and has changed sign.

Equation (23) adds the per capita bed availability variable *(BEDS)* to equation (20); equation (24) reestimates this relation without the insignificant *DOCS* variable. The estimated admission elasticity with respect to *BEDS* (0.25) is highly significant, indicating the existence of a pure availability effect. With a constant price level, an increase in the per capita bed supply induces additional demand for hospital admissions. All the other coefficients are somewhat smaller than they were when the *BEDS* variable was not included. Similar results are obtained with the mean stay equation. Equation (25) adds *BEDS,* and equation (26) then omits the insignificant *TIME* variable. The pure availability effect elasticity of mean stay with respect to *BEDS* is 0.28. The price elasticity, which had been −0.59 in equation (22), is reduced to −0.24 but remains highly significant.

Considering equations (24) and (26) together shows that the elasticity of total demand for bed-days with respect to bed availability is 0.53. Since an increase in bed availability has almost no effect on percentage utilization,[40] it is a reasonable first approximation to say that half of an increased supply is absorbed by a pure availability effect (without a price decrease) and the other half by a fall in price.[41]

Finally, equations (27) and (28) repeat equations (24) and (26) with separate price elasticities for relative price *(RP)* and insurance *(INS)*. In both, the elasticity with respect to *INS* is less than the elasticity with respect to *RP*. In the admission equation (27) the elasticity with re-

39. This follows from the derivation of the separate elasticities.
40. The simple elasticity of total bed-day demand *(BDD)* with respect to bed availability *(BEDS)* is 0.92.
41. More beds in an area may also attract more specialist physicians, which would also increase demand.

spect to *INS* has become insignificant and the elasticities with respect to *GP* and *BEDS* have increased; the *RP* elasticity (−0.46) is essentially unchanged from equation (22). The reason for this difference between the *RP* and *INS* admission elasticities is not clear. It may be a statistical artifact, reflecting the approximations in defining *INS* or its collinearity with *GP* and *BEDS*. It may, however, reflect a greater concern in admission decisions with the gross price than with the net price, perhaps because patients are uncertain of their insurance coverage until after they have been hospitalized or even because physicians influence admissions more than mean stay and are more concerned with gross resource use than with the net cost to patients. Only further studies of a more disaggregated kind can clarify this. In the mean stay equation (28) the elasticity with respect to *INS* (−0.13) is statistically significant and the other coefficients are essentially unchanged from equation (26).

The basic specifications of equations (24) and (26) have been reestimated with lagged dependent variables to assess the speed with which demand adjusts to changes in the explanatory variables.[42] The results are presented in table 3.3. The coefficient of lagged admissions in equation (29) indicates that approximately half of the full long-run response of admission demand occurs in the first year and nearly 90 percent by the end of three years. The implied long-run elasticities (the coefficients divided by $1 - 0.472 = 0.528$) are very similar to the estimates of equation (24); these are reported in square brackets below the standard errors. The coefficient of the lagged mean stay in equation (30) shows a slower speed of adjustment, approximately 40 percent in the first year and 80 percent in three years. The long-run elasticities shows the same general results as equation (26) but a somewhat greater effect of bed availability and Medicaid and somewhat reduced elasticities with respect to price, income, and the *GP* variable. The lagged adjustment process may also contribute to the general impression of a very low price elasticity since the short-run price elasticity of total demand (−0.271) is less than half of the long-run elasticity (−0.553).

The important qualitative findings can be summarized briefly. First, there is a substantial price elasticity of demand for hospital beddays. Second, there is also an important pure availability effect; that is, an increase in the availability of beds increases quantity demanded by shifting the demand curve as well as by lowering the price. Third, a

---

42. This specification imposes the assumption that the speed of response is the same for all variables. With such short time series, it is unlikely that additional detail could be estimated by considering a more complex model.

Table 3.3. Demand equations with lagged adjustment

Equa-tion	Dependent variable	Explanatory variables								Regression statistics	
		RNP	INC	TIME	DENS	MCAID	GP	BEDS	LAG DEP VAR	RSS	SER
29	ADMD	-0.211 (0.054) [-0.400]		0.014 (0.003) [0.027]	-0.033 (0.007) [-0.062]	-0.058 (0.013) [-0.110]	-0.050 (0.020) [0.095]	0.139 (0.032) [0.263]	0.472 (0.093)	1.224	0.0543
30	MSD	-0.060 (0.035) [-0.153]	0.093 (0.037) [0.237]		0.012 (0.003) [0.031]	0.034 (0.008) [0.087]	-0.027 (0.018) [-0.069]	0.132 (0.036) [0.336]	0.607 (0.114)	0.625	0.0388

Note: Standard errors are shown in parentheses. Long-run elasticities are shown immediately below the standard errors in square brackets. All variables except TIME and MCAID are logarithms. The constant term for each equation is not shown. Observations are for individual states for 1959 through 1967. Estimation is by instrumental variables. The squared multiple correlation is therefore not shown. The last two columns show the residual sum of squares and the standard error of the regression.

high ratio of general practitioners to population lowers the demand for hospital care, while a high specialist-to-population ratio increases demand. Finally, there is a substantial lag in the adjustment of demand to the causal variables.

The Price Adjustment Mechanism

This section incorporates the parameter estimates of the previous section into the price adjustment mechanism of the first section. Rather than choose among the alternative parameter estimates on the basis of relatively small differences in the residual sums of squares, this section investigates three pairs of demand equations in assessing the price adjustment model: equations (24) and (26), which include physician and bed availability; equations (27) and (28), which have separate relative price *(RP)* and insurance (INS) elasticities; and equations (29) and (30), which add the lagged demand variables. The results for all three models provide very good explanations of the interstate and intertemporal variation in hospital prices.

Equation (4) described the desired short-run supply of bed days in the ith state at time t by

$$BDS_{it} = 365 \cdot R_i \cdot BEDS_{it}, \tag{31}$$

where R_i is the desired proportional occupancy rate of the available beds. The equilibrating gross price $(\bar{P}_{it})$, at which the bed-day demand equals BDS_{it}, is defined implicitly by

$$ADM(\bar{P}_{it}, \mathbf{X}_{it}) \cdot MS(\bar{P}_{it}, \mathbf{X}_{it}) = BDS_{it}. \tag{32}$$

The estimates of the third section of this chapter specified the admission and mean stay equations to be linear in the logarithms of the relevant variables. To implement the price adjustment model, we must rewrite the relative price variable *(RP)* as the ratio of the gross price to a CPI index variable $(RP_{it} = P_{it}/CPI_{it})$; the demographically adjusted admission and mean stay variables must also be rewritten explicitly in terms of the two demographic indexes:

$$ADMD_{it} = ADM_{it}/DEMADM_{it}$$

and

$$MSD_{it} = MS_{it}/DEMMS_{it}.$$

Then, letting lowercase letters denote the logarithm of the corresponding uppercase variable, we can write typical mean stay and admission equations as

$$adm_{it} = demadm_{it} + \alpha_0 + \alpha_1(p_{it} - cpi_{it}) + \alpha_2 ins_{it} + \sum_{j=3}^{k} \alpha_j x_{jit} \quad (33)$$

and

$$ms_{it} = demms_{it} + \beta_0 + \beta_1(p_{it} - cpi_{it}) + \beta_2 ins_{it} + \sum_{j=3}^{k} \beta_j x_{jit}. \quad (34)$$

where the x_{it} are the logarithms of the other variables in these demand equations. If the equations specify a composite RNP variable, then $\alpha_1 = \alpha_2$ and $\beta_1 = \beta_2$.

Equating the demand for bed-days ($bdd_{it} = adm_{it} + ms_{it}$) and the short-run supply at the equilibrating price ($\bar{P}_{it}$) implies

$$demadm_{it} + demms_{it} + \alpha_0 + \beta_0 + (\alpha_1 + \beta_1)(\bar{p}_{it} - cpi_{it}) + (\alpha_2 + \beta_2)ins_{it}$$
$$+ \sum_{j=3}^{k} (\alpha_j + \beta_j)x_{jit} = r_i + beds_{it} + log\, 365. \quad (35)$$

Solving for $\bar{p}_{it}$ and substituting into the proportional adjustment mechanism

$$p_{it} - p_{i,t-1} = \lambda(\bar{p}_{it} - p_{i,t-1}) \quad (36)$$

yields

$$p_{it} - p_{i,t-1} = \frac{\lambda}{\alpha_1 + \beta_1}[r_i + log\, 365 - \alpha_0 - \beta_0]$$
$$+ \frac{\lambda}{\alpha_1 - \beta_1}[beds_{it} - demadm_{it} - demms_{it}] + \lambda(cpi_{it} - p_{i,t-1})$$
$$- \frac{\lambda(\alpha_2 + \beta_2)}{\alpha_1 + \beta_1}ins_{it} - \lambda \sum_{j=3}^{k} \frac{\alpha_j + \beta_j}{\alpha_1 + \beta_1}x_{jit}. \quad (37)$$

Although equation (37) could be estimated directly, the substantial multicollinearity would make the directly estimated parameters quite unreliable. Moreover, it is unnecessary to do so since all the parameters except λ and r_i have already been obtained by estimating the demand equations. The estimation of λ and r_i can be achieved simply by using the previously estimated parameters to define the composite variable

$$Z_{it} = \frac{1}{\alpha_1 + \beta_1}\Bigg[beds_{it} - demadm_{it} - demms_{it} - (\alpha_2 + \beta_2)ins_i$$
$$- \sum_{j=3}^{k} (\alpha_j + \beta_j)x_{jit}\Bigg] + cpi_t - p_{i,t-1}, \quad (38)$$

which reduces the estimation equation to

$$p_{it} - p_{i,t-1} = \frac{\lambda}{\alpha_1 + \beta_1}[r_i + log\, 365 - \alpha_0 - \beta_0] + \lambda Z_{it}. \quad (39)$$

Equation (39) has been estimated by the same consistent instrumental variable procedure used for the demand equations. Since the r_i are presumed to differ, a separate constant term was estimated for each state. When Z_{it} is defined by the parameters of the demand equations (24) and (26), the estimated speed of adjustment (λ) is 0.250 with a standard error of 0.039. The price change in any year is approximately one-fourth of the difference between the equilibrating $(\bar{P}_{it})$ and the previous actual price $(P_{i,t-1})$. The values of $\bar{P}_{it}$ for each state and year were then calculated from equation (35) using the individual constant terms of equation (39) and the estimate of λ to calculate each r_i. Although the estimated speed of adjustment implies that the equilibrating price is generally not equal to the actual price, the values of $\bar{P}_{it}$ provide a very good explanation of the overall variation in actual price among states and years. More specifically, the simple correlation between P_{it} and $\bar{P}_{it}$ is 0.988. Since $\bar{P}_{it}$ is a function of variables such as insurance, income, and the availability of beds but not of the current or lagged values of P_{it}, this high correlation is evidence of the model's substantial explanatory power.

Very similar results were obtained when the parameters of equation (27) and (28) were used. The estimated adjustment speed is 0.280 with standard error 0.045. The simple correlation between P_{it} and $\bar{P}_{it}$ is also 0.988.

The parameters of the lagged adjustment demand equations (29) and (30) imply a much smaller short-run price elasticity of demand and therefore a much greater rise in the equilibrating price in response to a change in any of the other variables that affect demand. To be consistent with the actual price rise, the response speed in this equation is lower than in the previous equations (0.089 with a standard error of 0.017); the correlation is again very high (0.987). This model of slow adjustment to the price that equates short-run demand and supply therefore has the same empirical implications as the previous models of more rapid adjustment to the price that equates long-run demand and supply.

As the model of the first section of this chapter showed, the demand and price adjustment equations would provide a complete explanation of hospital-cost inflation if the supply of beds were fixed. During the decade 1958–1967, the per capita increase in beds was quite small (15 percent) in comparison with the increase in price (91 percent). This suggests that, as a first approximation, the demand and price adjustment analysis alone can provide useful estimates of the impact on hospital prices of rising income, more complete insurance, and the like. Such estimates must be interpreted with care; they represent the partial effect on price, assuming that the availability of bed-

Table 3.4. Contributions to hospital-cost inflation, 1958–1967

	CPI	INC	TIME	DENS	INS	MCAID	GP	BEDS
Percentage change[a]								
1958–1967	15.5	31.1	[9]	13.6	−44.5	[0.766]	−11.6	13.8
Equations								
(24) Elasticity and	1.000	0.429	0.037	−0.066	1.000	−0.091	−0.311	−0.715
(26) Contribution	15.5	12.3	35.8	−0.8	80.2	−6.7	3.9	−8.9
(27) Elasticity and	1.000	0.462	0.044	−0.018	0.241	0.016	−0.395	−0.388
(28) Contribution	15.5	13.3	48.3	−0.2	15.3	1.2	5.0	−4.9
(29) Elasticity and	1.000	0.429	0.049	−0.056	1.000	−0.042	−0.297	−0.725
(30) Contribution	15.5	12.3	55.1	−0.7	80.2	−3.1	3.7	−0.0

a. For *TIME* and *MCAID*, these are absolute changes. Since *INS* is defined as the ratio of net price to gross price, a fall in *INS* reflects an increase in the extent of insurance coverage.

days did not respond to shifts in demand. Similarly, the estimated effect of the actual increase in bed supply ignores the role of feedbacks through the price mechanism. A more complete analysis and a reduced form calculation cannot be done until the full model has been estimated.

Table 3.4 presents the current analysis of the contribution that each of the explanatory variables in the price adjustment equation made to the change in the equilibrating price for the nation as a whole. More specifically, the first row of the table shows the percentage change from 1958 to 1967 for the nation as a whole in each of the variables that influences the equilibrating price. Equation (37) was used to calculate the elasticity[43] of $\bar{P}$ with respect to each of these variables for the three sets of demand equations; these elasticities appear in the second, fourth, and sixth rows of the table. The rows marked "contribution" show the percentage increase in the equilibrium price implied by the elasticity and the percentage change of the corresponding variable. The sum of the contributions in any row is the total percentage change in $\bar{P}$ according to that model. Thus equations (24) and (26) imply that $\bar{P}$ rose 135 percent from 1958 to 1967. More than half of this increase is attributed to increased insurance coverage.[44] Since the actual price (average cost per patient-day) rose only 91 percent over

43. For *TIME* and *MCAID* the coefficients are not elasticities.
44. Note that since *INS* is defined as the ratio of net price to gross price, an increase in insurance coverage decreases *INS*.

this period, the estimate implies that even if there had been no further change in the explanatory variables, prices would have continued to rise substantially after 1967. The model of equations (27) and (28) offers a more optimistic prospect. The total increase in $\bar{P}$ was only 93.5 percent. This reflects the much smaller calculated impact of insurance. Finally, the results for equations (29) and (30) are quite similar to those for (24) and (26), with a total rise in $\bar{P}$ of 153 percent.

Hospital-cost inflation has become a significant national problem. Price increases averaging 12 percent a year from mid 1967 to mid 1970 have brought pressures for radical changes in the organization and financing of the health-care system. Economic advice about the problem has been hampered by the lack of previous empirical research and, more generally, of an analytic framework for describing the behavior of the hospital industry. This in turn reflects a general lack of attention to the problems of the nonprofit sector.

This chapter attempts to contribute to the general understanding of this important nonprofit industry and to provide specific information about the determinants of hospital-cost inflation. It has presented a theoretical model of the use, pricing, and expansion of hospital services. The demand and price adjustment equations were estimated using a mixed cross section of time-series sample of ten annual observations for each state.

The estimated demand equations showed substantial price elasticities for both per capita admission and mean stay per case and an important income elasticity for mean stay. A greater availability of general practitioners appears to reduce the demand for both admissions and for longer stay while a greater availability of other doctors has the opposite effect. The availability of beds was shown to increase admission and mean stay by a pure availability effect as well as through lower prices. The relatively slow response speeds in the demand and price adjustment equations suggest that substantial price increases may continue for some time, even if there is no additional stimulus to demand.

The model as a whole and the estimated equations in particular provide an alternative to the customary explanation of hospital-cost inflation. Increases in the components of cost are seen as primarily the result and not the cause of higher prices. The source of inflation is the pressure of the rising demand induced by increases in insurance coverage, personal incomes, the availability of hospital-oriented specialists, and so forth.

As insurance companies and the government pay a higher proportion of hospital bills, patients face a lower net price; from 1958 to 1967 this proportion rose from 68.1 percent to 82.3 percent. The estimates presented here suggest that this growth of insurance may account for as much as an 80 percent rise in the national equilibrating price. Moreover, the growth of insurance differs from the other causes of inflation in an important way. Insurance is bought to avoid the risk of unexpected expenditure; but because it provides a reduction in price at the time that care is purchased, it has the concomitant effect of artificially increasing the demand for care and its price.[45] Because hospital insurance is already so comprehensive, a further growth of the current type of insurance would lead to substantial price increases and might so limit price sensitivity that the system would become unstable and require direct controls.[46]

The opposite impacts of general practitioners and specialists on the demand for hospital care also has important implications. The estimates suggest that an increase in the number of general practitioners would induce a very large saving in hospital resources, on the order of $39,000 a year per general practitioner.[47] This estimate, if substantiated by more detailed studies, provides substantial support for a policy to increase the number of general practitioners or other providers of primary care. Conversely, the estimate of the increased use of hospital services induced by an additional specialist (again approximately $39,000 a year),[48] if verified by further studies, should be taken into account in any decisions to increase the number of hospital-oriented physicians.

This research is being extended in several directions. The two re-

45. For a very clear statement of this problem, sometimes pejoratively labeled "moral hazard," see Pauly (1968).

46. This study has of course assumed that the price elasticity has not been affected by increased insurance coverage. A separate study of this issue would undoubtedly be worthwhile.

47. This estimate is based on the following calculation. The estimated elasticity of bed-day use with respect to the ratio of general practitioners to total doctors is approximately −0.2. This implies that the elasticity of bed-day use with respect to the GP-to-population ratio is −0.2 times the ratio of "other doctors" to "total doctors." In 1967 this ratio was 0.78, implying an elasticity with respect to the GP-to-population ratio of −0.156. Thus a 10 percent increase in the GP-to-population ratio would reduce bed-days used by 1.56 percent. With ten general practitioners per 28,000 population in 1967 and 32,000 hospital-days for the same population, an increase of one general practitioner would reduce bed-day use by 505 days. Since the average cost per day in 1970 is some $77, the saving in hospital costs per additional general practitioner is approximately $39,000.

48. This follows from the fact that an increase or decrease in the total doctor-population ratio has no effect as long as the mix of doctors is unchanged.

maining sections of the hospital behavior model (the demand for current inputs and the expansion of capacity) will be estimated. The problem of quality change and its impact on consumer demand will be examined explicitly.[49] The growth of insurance and the behavior of physicians will also be made endogenous. If these related studies are successful, the research as a whole will provide the basis for a more complete behavioral model of the health-care sector.

49. See M. Feldstein (1971b, sect. 4) for a theoretical model of endogenous quality change in which patients' preferences determine the prevailing technology. (After this chapter was written, studies of input demand and capacity expansion were completed by Taylor (1975) and Ginsburg (1970). Chapter 4 deals with the effect of quality on consumer demand.)

4   Quality Change and the Demand for
Hospital Care

The cost of a day of hospital care in the United States has increased 600 percent in the past twenty years, an annual rate of more than 9 percent. During the same period the general consumer price index rose at only 3.5 percent per year. Although the rapid rise of the cost of hospital care is widely recognized, the nature of the increase and the reason for its explosive pace are little understood.

The rising cost of hospital care can be explained with the aid of an econometric model. The essence of the explanation is that the explosion of hospital costs reflects a rapid change in the quality and style of hospital care, not an increasing cost of providing the same product. The dramatic change in the quality of care is due primarily to the increased demand caused by the growth of private and public insurance.

A preliminary econometric model (Chapter 3) of the demand for hospital care made the strong and unwarranted assumption that the increasing quality of care has no effect on the demand for hospital services. However, a more expensive "quality" or style of hospital care increases the demand for those services. An increase in demand leads to a rise in the gross price of hospital care;[1] because of the nonprofit character of the hospital, this increase in revenue is used to provide a more expensive quality of care. This two-way relation between demand and quality makes the cost of a day of hospital care very sensitive to changes in insurance and is a potential source of explosive instability.

Reprinted with permission from *Econometrica* 45, no. 7 (October 1977), pp. 1681–1702.

1. The gross price of hospital care is average charge per patient-day. This must be distinguished from the net price, the charge minus the payments made by insurance companies and government insurance plans.

The first section of this paper presents an analytic model of the hospital "industry" in which quality affects the demand for hospital services and in which the purchase of private insurance is endogenous. Operational definitions and descriptions of the data sources for use in the econometric estimation are provided in the second section. Estimates of the model based on a cross section of time series for the individual states for the years 1958 through 1973 are presented in the third section. The fourth section discusses the price adjustment process and the dynamic multipliers of the model as a whole. A brief concluding section comments on some of the implications of this analysis.

A Model of Hospital-Cost Determination

This section presents a model of the demand and supply of hospital inpatient services. It is useful to describe the model by discussing the fifteen equations in five groups: demand for hospital care, demand for insurance, the determination of inputs and quality, price adjustment, and the expansion of capacity.

The Demand for Hospital Care

To avoid misunderstanding about the meaning of the demand function for hospital care, it is useful to begin by examining the role of the personal physician in determining the household's demand for hospital care. A common approach in previous studies has been to ignore the physician and discuss the demand for hospital services in the same way as the demand for other goods and services.[2] Prices, insurance, income, and the demographic characteristics of the household are then the basic determinants of demand. At the opposite extreme are those who argue that patients' preferences are irrelevant and that hospital use is determined by the physician. A patient who comes to a doctor lacks the technical information to evaluate alternative options and is acting under substantial stress. The physician determines the demand for hospital care on the basis of his perception of correct medical practice, or on the basis of his own convenience and self-interest, or by seeking to use available resources in a way that optimally balances their potential contribution to the health of his own patient against the use of those resources for other patients. Regardless of which of these is the correct description of the physician's criterion, the usual household demand variables of price, insurance, and income are irrelevant or, at most, influence the patient's decision to initiate care but do not affect the care that is then obtained.

2. For a survey of previous studies of the demand for hospital care, see chapter 2.

Neither of these extreme views is an adequate description of reality. Instead of considering the physician simply as a supplier of medical services, it is more appropriate to think of the relation between the patient and his physician as one of agency. Because the patient lacks the technical knowledge to make the detailed decisions, he delegates this authority to his physician with the hope that the physician will act for him as he would for himself if he had the appropriate expertise. This agency relationship develops because it is much easier for the patient to indicate his financial position, insurance coverage, and relevant preferences than it is for the physician to give the patient the information that he would require to make his own decisions.

If the agency relation is complete, that is, if the physician acts solely in the interest of the patient, then the observed demand equation is indistinguishable from the traditional model of demand by an informed consumer. Such a complete agency relation could be ignored in developing an empirical specification. Its role would be to reconcile the use of traditional demand analysis with the obvious fact that patients entrust many of their decisions about medical care to their physicians. If the agency relation is not complete — if the physician's decisions reflect not only the patient's situation and preferences but also his own self-interest the pressures from professional colleagues, a sense of medical ethics, and a concern to make good use of hospital resources — then there are variables that influence observed demand but do not enter the traditional household demand relations. These variables will be discussed in more detail in the next two sections.[3]

The rate of hospital admissions (ADM) and the mean duration of stay per admission (MS) are likely to be affected by the price per patient (P), the quality of care as perceived by the patient and his physician (Q), the extent of the patient's insurance (INS), and other variables including income, the demographic composition of the population, the availability of hospital facilities, and alternative sources of care. The method of empirically implementing each of these variables will be discussed in the next section.

The admission and mean stay equations can be written

$$ADM_1 = ADM\ (P_t,\ Q_t,\ INS_t,\ \mathbf{X}_t), \tag{1}$$
$$MS_t = MS(P_t,\ Q_t,\ INS_t,\ \mathbf{X}_t), \tag{2}$$

where $\mathbf{X}_t$ represents all the other explanatory variables in either of these equations. The total bed-days demanded (BDD) is defined by

$$BDD_t = ADM_t \cdot MS_t. \tag{3}$$

3. For a more general discussion of this agency relation, see chapter 2.

Demand for Hospital Insurance

A complete specification of the individual's demand for hospital services requires an analysis of the demand for hospital care insurance. By 1975, 88 percent of the cost of hospital inpatient care was paid by private and government insurance. For patients not financed by Medicare, Medicaid, or other public programs, private health insurance paid 79 percent of private hospital care. The demand for hospital care can usefully be analyzed as (1) a demand for insurance and then, conditional on that insurance and on the presence of some symptoms of illness, (2) a demand for hospital admission and duration of stay.

The general theory of the demand for insurance[4] implies that the extent of insurance coverage for hospital care will depend on the expenditure risk that the household faces (the price of hospital care and the quantity of hospital services that would be bought in the absence of insurance), the household income, and the price of insurance services.[5] The demand for private insurance $(PINS_t)$ can be specified as a function of the price of care (P_t) and other undefined variables $(\mathbf{Z}_t)$:

$$PINS_t = PINS(P_t, \mathbf{Z}_t). \tag{4}$$

The total insurance coverage of the populations (INS_t) depends on both the private insurance and the exogenous government insurance $(GINS_t)$:

$$INS_t = INS(PINS_t, GINS_t). \tag{5}$$

Specific definitions of the insurance variables will be provided later in this chapter.

The Determination of Inputs and Quality

I turn now to the behavior of the hospital. Although all the variables controlled by the hospital are determined as part of a simultaneous system, it is helpful to look at the hospital's decisions as conditional on the price per patient-day. The impact of these decisions on the price can then be examined.

Conditional on the gross price per patient day, P_t, the budget constraint of the hospital is

$$C_t = P_t + D_t, \tag{6}$$

4. See, in particular, Ehrlich and Becker (1972), Mossin (1968), and Smith (1968). For special features of the demand for health insurance, see chapters 6 and 8, Arrow (1963), M. Feldstein (1973c), Friedman (1971), Pauly (1968, 1974), Rosett and Huang (1973), Zeckhauser (1970), and Zeckhauser and Spence (1971).

5. An explicit empirical specification is presented in chapter 6.

where C_t is the average cost per patient-day and D_t is the deficit per patient-day. The deficit permitted by income from endowment and philanthropic donation is generally both small and exogenous.[6]

The average cost per patient-day is allocated among personnel, materials, and the interest and other fixed costs associated with previously acquired capital:

$$C_t = W_t N_t + \pi_t J_t + k_t, \tag{7}$$

where N_t is the number of employees per patient-day, W_t is the average wage rate, J_t is an index of the quantity of materials and supplies, π_t is their price, and k_t is the interest and fixed costs. I shall assume that hospitals treat W_t and π_t as exogenous and that they are in fact exogenous to the hospital industry as a whole.[7]

The hospital chooses the labor and nonlabor inputs subject to the constraint implied by equation (7). The process and criterion of bureaucratic choice within the hospital have been the subject of substantial controversy.[8] The process of choice can, however, be summarized efficiently by defining an unobservable variable that measures the quality of care as perceived by the hospital bureaucracy (QH_t) and assuming that N_t and J_t are chosen to maximize QH_t subject to the constraint of equation (7) and the prevailing production function

$$QH_t = \phi(N_t, J_t). \tag{8}$$

The optimum inputs implied by the first-order conditions for a maximum of (8) subject to (7) can be written

$$N_t = N(C_t, W_t, \pi_t, k_t) \tag{9a}$$

and

$$J_t = J(C_t, W_t, \pi_t, k_t). \tag{9b}$$

6. Davis (1972b) has suggested that the "deficit" is actually a desired surplus for future investment. Although the model could be extended in his way, I think the effect is empirically too small to warrant the extra complication of the model. Ginsburg's (1970) study of hospital investment supports this view.

7. There is no difficulty with the assumption that the prices of materials and supplies do not depend on the hospitals' demands. Most hospital personnel have skills that are not restricted to the hospital industry and therefore have wages that are probably determined independently of hospital demand; Fuchs (1975) shows that after adjustment for differences in education and other variables associated with labor quality, there has been little overall change in the relative wage of these nonspecific hospital personnel. The supply of nurses and technicians may be more inelastic (A. Taylor 1975b) but the relative increase in their wages may instead represent a shift of their supply curve (as other occupations become more accessible or attractive to women) or what I have described elsewhere as a philanthropic wage policy (M. Feldstein 1971b; chapter 3).

8. See Davis (1972b, 1973), Newhouse (1970a), and Pauly and Redisch (1973).

One of these equations is redundant because the corresponding input can be determined from the budget constraint (7) and the other input quantity.

The quality of care as perceived by the patient (and his own physician) need not be the same as the quality of care perceived by the hospital bureaucracy. To emphasize this potential difference, the quality of care perceived by the patient is denoted Q and is related to the inputs by a different function:

$$Q_t = \psi(N_t, J_t). \tag{10a}$$

The input equations imply that this can instead be written as

$$Q_t = Q(C_t, W_t, \pi_t, k_t). \tag{10b}$$

Price Adjustment

The ten demand and supply equations can now be used to calculate the excess demand for bed-days in the short run when the number of beds $(BEDS_t)$ is fixed. Equations (1)–(3) imply that the number of bed-days demanded satisfies[9]

$$BDD_t = BDD(P_t, Q_t, INS_t, \mathbf{X}_t). \tag{11}$$

The desired short-run supply of bed-days (BDS_t) is proportional to the product of the stock of beds and the desired occupancy rate (R):

$$BDS_t = 365 \cdot R \cdot BEDS_t. \tag{12}$$

Although the percentage occupancy of beds can be varied, hospitals generally have a desired occupancy rate that reflects both the need for excess capacity to deal with emergencies and the relation between the occupancy rate, unit costs, and the quality of services; this desired occupancy rate will be treated as exogenous.

Hospitals respond to an increase in the difference between demand (BDD) and desired short-run supply by increasing their price. Although this response to excess demand is the same that we would expect in a competitive industry, the reason for the price increase is different. Hospitals do not raise prices in order to increase profits. Because of the hospital's nonprofit character, the higher price is translated into more resource inputs. Every hospital's administration is under constant pressure to make changes that will raise costs per patient-day. The medical staff want more equipment, laboratory services, and professional aides with which to provide more sophisticated

---

9. Equations (4) and (5) could be used to substitute for insurance (INS_t) and equations (7), (9), and (10) to substitute for quality (Q_t). Equation (11), however, is most appropriate for the current purpose.

care to the hospital's patients.[10] Enlarging the nursing staff would increase patient comfort and satisfaction while easing the burdens on the original staff. Good reasons can be found for a myriad of expenditures. These pressures are contained by the hospital's need to cover costs with revenues. With constant demand, an increase in price would cause the occupancy of hospital beds to fall below the desired level. However, when the demand increases, the price and the cost per day can both rise without lowering occupancy.

This adjustment can be approximated by the proportional response model:[11]

$$\ln P_t - \ln P_{t-1} = \lambda \ (\ln BDD_t - \ln BDS_t). \tag{13}$$

This completes the model of the hospital's behavior in the short run when the number of beds is predetermined.[12] Figure 4.1 presents the equilibrium system for a fixed number of beds and constant insurance coverage.[13] The *DD* line in the first quadrant indicates the combinations of gross price per day and quality that induce a bed-day demand equal to the desired bed-day supply (equations (11) and (12)). With a constant price, an increase in quality should unambiguously increase the demand for hospital admissions. However, the effect of quality on the mean duration of stay per admission is ambiguous: a higher quality of care increases the desirability of an additional day for a patient in a given condition but reduces the desired stay if the patient is healthier at each length of stay because of the greater intensity of care.[14] The empirical evidence indicates that the net effect of an increase in quality (with price fixed) is to increase the demand for bed-days. To maintain a constant bed-day demand, an increase in price must be offset by an increase in quality; the *DD* line therefore slopes upward. The *D'D'* line corresponds to a different level of the exogenous variables and will be discussed later in this chapter. The construction of the *QP* line will now be described.

10. Pauly and Redisch (1973) develop a theory in which physicians want these inputs because they increase their own incomes.

11. Alternative Marshallian models of price adjustment were also considered. The statistical estimates of the demand equations presented later imply that (with fixed beds and input prices) no equilibrium price per patient-day existed in the early part of the sample period; a Marshallian adjustment process is therefore not possible for this period.

12. This is also a useful description of the hospital's behavior when the stock of beds is controlled by a regulatory authority. Such control is becoming increasingly common under so-called certificate of need legislation.

13. In figure 3.1 the diagram in the axes are different.

14. The mean duration per spell will also be affected by changes in the mix of patients that accompanies any change in the admission rate. A higher quality of care may also increase mean duration by prolonging the life of patients.

Figure 4.1

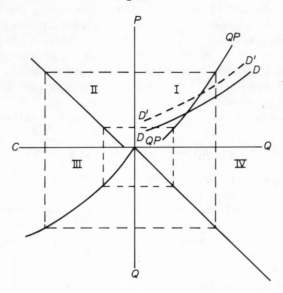

The linear relation between price and cost per patient-day (equation (6)) is shown in quadrant II. The positive intersection with the C axis implies that the hospital has endowment and gift income that permits a small deficit per patient-day. Quadrant III summarizes the relationship between cost per day and quality (equations (7)–(10)). An increase in cost per day permits an increase in inputs and therefore an increase in the quality as perceived by the patients and their physicians. The fourth quadrant is an identity relation that brings quality to the horizontal axis of quadrant I.

Quadrants II, III, and IV define a locus of quality-price points (line QP is quadrant I) that satisfy the hospital's budget and production relations. To emphasize the derived nature of the QP line, the construction of two of its points is shown explicitly. The intersection of the QP line and the DD line shows the combination of price and quality that satisfies the production-cost constraint (QP) and induces the required demand for bed-days (DD).

Before turning to the hospital's choice of a quantity of beds, it is interesting to examine the comparative statics of this fixed-bed equilibrium. Note first that an increase in insurance coverage shifts the DD line up, that is, insurance increases the number of bed-days demanded at the initial price with a given quality. The upward shift of the DD curve increases both price and quality. The induced increase in quality makes the rise in price greater than it would be with fixed quality.

The curves are drawn to imply a stable equilibrium. If demand responds sufficiently strongly to an increase in quality, the interaction of price and quality can be explosively unstable. To examine this possibility and to indicate the specific stability conditions in a way that can be checked empirically, consider a constant elasticity representation of the model. Equations (11) and (12) can be combined to write

$$BEDS = k_1 P^{-\alpha} INS^\beta Q^\gamma \tag{14}$$

where the constant k_1 reflects the occupancy rate and all the exogenous variables of the demand equations. With fixed input prices, equation (10b) can be written

$$Q = k_2 P^\rho. \tag{15}$$

Combining these two equations yields

$$BEDS = k_3 P^{\gamma\rho-\alpha} INS^\beta. \tag{16}$$

If the direct effect of price on demand (elasticity α) is equal to the indirect effect through quality (elasticity $\gamma\rho$), demand is independent of price; the hospital can set any price and still maintain the desired demand for bed-days. More generally, if $\gamma\rho - \alpha > 0$, demand is an increasing function of price and again there is no limit to the price and quality that the hospital can choose. The stability of the equilibrium in figure 4.1 thus implies $\gamma\rho < \alpha$, a condition that is now satisfied, as will be shown in the third section.

An upward shift in the *DD* curve can also be caused by increasing income and by the changing tastes of physicians and patients that lead to a growing demand for sophisticated care. Historically, increasing insurance and income and changing tastes have all led to rising price and quality.

Consider next the effect of an exogenous improvement in technology. This increases the quality that can be achieved for any level of cost; it shifts down the cost-quality curve in quadrant III. This in turn shifts the *QP* line in quadrant I to the right: a higher quality becomes available at every price. The intersection of quality and price then magnifies this effect: the higher quality allows a higher price along the *DD* line, which permits higher cost and thus yet higher quality, and so on. The result is an increase in price and a greater increase in quality than would have followed from the technological change with fixed average cost. Thus, while technological change generally results in lower unit costs in most industries, technological change in hospitals leads to an increase in quality and a higher unit cost.

An exogenous increase in the cost of hospital inputs (W_t and π_t) has the surprising effect of reducing the price and unit cost of hospital care. An increase in input costs reduces the quality achievable at any cost level and thus shifts the QP line to the left in quadrant I. More explicitly, (1) higher input costs lower quality for given price; (2) to maintain demand the hospital must lower its price; and (3) this further reduces quality and thus lowers demand even further. The equilibrium levels of price and quality are thus both reduced. This conclusion depends of course on the assumption that the stock of beds is fixed. An increase in input prices could raise the equilibrium price and quality if it resulted in a sufficient reduction in the stock of beds.[15]

The Choice of Bed Capacity

It is now time to drop the assumption that the stock of beds is fixed and examine the hospital's long-run adjustment of capacity. Recall that the hospital's choice of labor and nonlabor inputs is determined to maximize quality as perceived by the hospital decision makers (QH in equation (8)). More generally, the hospital's preferences can be represented most simply by a utility function whose arguments are the quantity of care (the number of bed-days, BDS) and the quality of care:

$$U = U(BDS, QH). \tag{17}$$

A change in the number of beds shifts the DD curve in quadrant I. The curve $D'D'$ represents a smaller number of beds than the DD curve because the desired capacity utilization can be achieved at a higher level of price for each level of quality. An increase in the number of beds thus decreases the equilibrium price and the corresponding quality QH. This is shown as the $B - QH$ line in figure 4.2.[16] An indifference curve representing the utility function of equation (17) identifies the desired number of bed-days, BDS^*. Given the proportionality of BDS and $BEDS$ (see equation (11)), this point also implies a desired stock of beds, $BEDS^*$.

The desired stock of beds can be expressed as a reduced-form function of the variables that influence the DD and QP lines:

15. The conclusion with a fixed stock of beds depends also on the assumption that the equilibrium is stable. If the DD locus cuts the QP locus from below, the conclusion is reversed but the equilibrium is unstable. In practice, increases in input prices have occurred at the same time as increases in demand and changes in technology that, all other things being equal, would increase the equilibrium price.

16. Line QP of figure 4.1 shows the positive relation between price and quality as perceived by the patient (Q). But equation (8) is analogous to equation (10a) and shows that a similar positive relation exists between price and quality as perceived by the hospital.

Figure 4.2

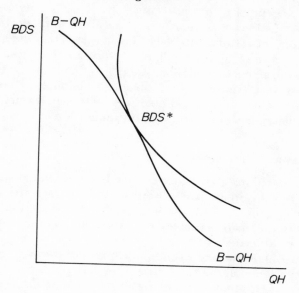

$$BEDS_t^* = BDS^*(INS_t, \mathbf{X}_t, W_t, \pi_t, k_t). \qquad (18)$$

The actual stock of beds reflects a capital stock adjustment toward $BEDS_t^*$. The speed of adjustment depends on the availability of funds and the extent of regulatory limits on expansion. Since this is not developed further in this chapter, it is sufficient to write

$$BEDS_t = BEDS\ (BEDS_t^*, BEDS_{t-1},$$
availability of funds, regulatory limits). $\qquad (19)$

Anything that limits the expansion of the stock of beds increases the average cost per patient-day. If the net price elasticity of demand after allowing for the indirect quality effect ($\alpha - \gamma\rho$ in equation (16)) is less then one, an exogenously determined increase in the number of beds will decrease *total* expenditure on inpatient care.[17]

This model could be extended to deal explicitly with the effect of

---

17. Equation (16) implies that P is proportional to $B^{1/(\gamma\rho - \alpha)}$. Therefore expenditure, BP, is proportional to $B^{1 + 1/(\gamma\rho - \alpha)} = B^{(\alpha - \gamma\rho - 1)/(\alpha - \gamma\rho)}$. Since $\alpha - \gamma\rho > 0$, expenditure varies inversely with the number of beds if $\alpha - \gamma\rho - 1 < 0$. In practice, an increase in the number of beds is generally accompanied by an increase in gross price (and therefore in total spending) because both are reflections of greater demand; the test deals with an exogenously determined shift in the number of beds, not a change of the endogenous equilibrium.

technical change along the lines suggested in Feldstein (1971b, chap. 4). Such exogenous technical change alters the quality production functions (equations (8) and (10)) and therefore shifts downward the curve in quarant III of figure 4.1. This in turn alters the location of the $B - QH$ locus of figure 4.2. The effect of an exogenous technical change on the actual level of quality depends finally on the point on B $- QH$ chosen by the hospital. Such an analysis of quality change shows that an exogenous shift in technology is neither necessary nor sufficient to achieve an actual increase in the quality level.

Definitions and Data Sources

The basic equations of the model have been estimated with a cross section of individual state observations for each of the years 1958–1973. This section describes briefly the definition and measurement of the major variables. Other variables are explained when they are introduced.[18]

The rate of hospital admissions per capita and the average duration of stay per admission are calculated from data published annually by the American Hospital Association (for example, 1974). Because hospital use varies substantially by age and sex, the admission rate is transformed into an index number that measures the rate of admissions relative to the rate that would be expected on the basis of the age-sex-color composition of the state in that year.[19] The mean stay per case is transformed in a similar way. The demographically transformed variables are denoted $ADMD_{it}$ and MSD_{it}.

The gross price of hospital care (P_{it}) was measured by the average cost per patient-day in short-term general hospitals, a figure published annually for each state by the American Hospital Association. Using average cost to measure gross price ignores the very small interstate differences in the average rate of surplus or deficit. Although the gross price determines the hospital's budget constraint, it is the price net of insurance (NP_{it}) that the patient faces when he (with his physician) decides how much care to buy. The admission and mean

18. A detailed list of exact data sources is presented in the appendix.

19. The expected admission rate for each state and year is a weighted average of sixteen age-sex-color admission rates obtained in a 1963–64 survey by the National Center for Health Statistics (1966b). The weights are the relative age-sex-color populations in the state and year. Population proportions were estimated for each year on the basis of census information. Although the relative use rates by age-sex-color reflect any associations between demography and price, and so on, the sampling and reweighting procedure used by the National Center for Health Statistics makes this unlikely to be a serious source of error.

stay demand equations are therefore specified as a function of the net price relative to the cost of other goods and services as measured by the consumer price index: $RNP_{it} = NP_{it}/CPI_t$.

Measuring the net price faced by the patient is extremely difficult. The full complexity of actual insurance coverage — proportional payments, fixed indemnities, and service benefits subject to a variety of deductions, exclusions, and ceilings — cannot be summarized by the available data. For the purpose of this chapter the impact of insurance is summarized by a single parameter, the fraction of hospital costs that the patients must pay out of pocket. More specifically,

$$INS_{it} = PENR_{it} \cdot PCOINS_{it} + (1 - PENR_{it}) \cdot GCOINS_{it}, \quad (20)$$

where $PENR_{it}$ is the proportion of the population enrolled in private health insurance, $PCOINS_{it}$ is the average coinsurance rate of such persons (the fraction of private hospital costs that they pay out of pocket), and $GCOINS_{it}$ is the proportion of the hospital costs of those without private health insurance that are not paid by government programs but must be paid by the uninsured themselves.[20] This definition implies that an increase in INS_{it} raises the net cost of hospital care to the patient; more precisely, $NP_{it} = P_{it} \cdot INS_{it}$.

An explicit measure of INS_{it} was estimated for each state and year on the basis of the proportion of the population enrolled in private insurance in that state and year $(PENR_{it})$ and of national data for each year on payments for hospital care by private insurance, government programs, and consumers.[21] The adequacy of this estimate is limited by the extent to which the effective coinsurance rate for private insurance and the comprehensiveness of government hospital insurance for the poor differ among the states.

The measurement of quality (Q_{it}) is based on equation (10b), relating quality to average cost per day and the prices of labor and nonlabor inputs. More specifically, quality is assumed to be a function of the real resources consumed by the hospital per patient-day; this makes the simplifying assumption that a change in relative input prices that leaves a fixed-weight input price index unchanged does not alter quality. The input price index for hospital services is a weighted average of (1) the average wage per full-time equivalent employee in

20. This definition is an extension of the one used in chapter 3. Medicare is actually classified as a private insurance program for applying this definition.

21. The enrollment data are published annually by Health Insurance Institute (see, for example, 1973–1974) while the annual national expenditure data are derived from the *Social Security Bulletin,* February 1975 ("National Health Expenditures"). The general method is described in chapter 3. The national time series for the inverse of *INS* is presented in chapter 1.

short-term general hospitals (W_{it}) as published by the American Hospital Association (see, for example, 1974) and an index of the price of nonlabor hospital inputs (π_t) described in chapter 5. The nonlabor price index uses the most detailed input-output coefficients to measure the relative importance of different hospital inputs and then uses these weights to combine specific components of the wholesale price index and consumer price index. The overall input price index for each state is a weighted average of the labor and nonlabor prices with the state-specific quantities of labor and nonlabor inputs in 1963 used as weights:

$$INP_{it} = k\{N_{i.} \, W_{it} + J_{i.} \, \pi_{it}\}, \qquad (21)$$

where $N_{i.}$ is the number of full-time equivalent hospital employees per patient-day in state i in 1963 and $J_{i.}$ is an index of nonlabor inputs per patient-day in state i in 1963. The scalar k is an arbitrary constant.

With this measure of the price of hospital inputs, quality can be defined as a function of average cost per patient-day (P_{it}) divided by INP_{it}. In the application this function is assumed to have constant elasticity:

$$Q_{it} = Q_0 \, e^{vt} \, (P_{it}/INP_{it})^\rho. \qquad (22)$$

Of course, some of the variation in real resources per patient-day (P_{it}/INP_{it}) over time and across states reflects differences in efficiency, in economies of scale, capacity utilization, and the like. Equation (22) should therefore be written as a stochastic function. The estimated coefficient of the quality variable in any of the equations estimated in this chapter should be regarded as subject to the resulting errors in variables bias and therefore probably biased downward. But the extent of such bias is likely to be small because most of the observed range of variation across states and years in such things as occupancy rate and size distribution can be responsible for very little of the variation in real resource inputs.[22]

The other variables in the analysis will be described when they are introduced.

Estimated Demand Equations

The estimates of the basic demand equations for hospital care are based on annual observations for each state for the period from 1958 through 1973. Separate estimates are presented for the periods be-

22. On the importance of quality change relative to other sources of the changed real resource cost per patient-day, see chapters 3 and 6 and M. Feldstein (1971b, 1973c).

fore and after the great expansion of government health insurance with the introduction of Medicare and Medicaid in 1966.

The equations are specified to be linear in the logarithms of the variables. A lagged dependent variable is included in each equation to reflect the fact that the admission rate and the mean duration of stay do not respond fully within one year to changes in the causal variables.

The equations are estimated by an instrumental variable procedure that yields consistent estimates.[23] The lagged dependent variables are treated as endogenous to obtain consistent estimates even if the disturbances contain systematic state effects or are otherwise serially correlated (Balestra and Nerlove 1966).

Consider first the effects of price on the admission rate and mean stay over the entire period from 1958 to 1973.[24] Equation 1 of table 4.1 shows that the elasticity of admission demand with respect to the price of hospital care net of insurance and relative to all other prices *(RNP)* is −0.10 in the short run and −0.21 in the long run. With a 52 percent adjustment speed per year, nearly 90 percent of the long-run response is achieved in three years. The price elasticity of the mean stay is insignificant and very small, 0.03 in the short run and 0.08 in the long run. Because the number of bed-days demanded is the product of the admission rate and the mean duration of stay, the price elasticity of bed-day demand is the sum of the two component elasticities, or −0.13 in the long run.

The long-run elasticity of hospital admissions with respect to quality[25] is 0.44; an increase in the resources used per patient-day causes a substantial increase in the demand for admissions. In contrast, the greater resource intensity decreases the mean stay per case; the impact of resources in speeding the recovery of the patient outweighs the increase in the attractiveness of a longer stay at any given stage of recovery. The net effect of these offsetting influences is that

23. The procedure is not equivalent to two-stage least squares only because some of the exogenous variables in the complete model have been excluded.

24. The dependent variables are actually the demographically adjusted admission rate and mean stay.

25. Recall that quality is defined as a constant elasticity function of the real inputs per patient day; see equation (22). The estimated demand coefficient is actually the product of the elasticity of demand with respect to quality and the elasticity of quality with respect to real inputs per patient-day; in the notation of equations (14) and (15), the estimated demand coefficient is $\gamma\rho$. Because the nonlabor price index (π_t of equation (21)) is not adjusted for interstate differences in the prices of such things as heat, food, and services, and because the labor input wage index (W_{it}) is not adjusted for differences in the quality of hospital workers, the input prices index (INP_{it}) used to define Q_{it} is normalized to reflect only intrastate variations.

Table 4.1. Quality and the demand for hospital care

Equa-tion	Dependent variable	Period	Explanatory variables									S.E.E.[a]
			RNP	Q	TIME	INC	GP	BEDS	DENSITY	MCAID	CONST	
1	ADMD	1959–1973	-0.099 (0.024) [-0.208]	0.209 (0.059) [0.438]	-0.006 (0.026) [-0.013]		0.009 (0.011) [0.019]	0.154 (0.025) [0.323]	-0.019 (0.004) [-0.040]	-0.027 (0.007) [-0.057]	0.523 (0.065)	0.047
2	MSD	1959–1973	0.028 (0.023) [0.077]	-0.172 (0.034) [-0.470]		0.059 (0.028) [0.161]	-0.017 (0.012) [-0.046]	0.182 (0.041) [0.497]	0.019 (0.004) [0.052]	0.019 (0.006) [0.052]	0.634 (0.097)	0.042
3	ADMD	1959–1965	-0.042 (0.044) [-0.134]	0.543 (0.158) [1.734]	-0.009 (0.005) [-0.029]		0.026 (0.014) [0.083]	0.094 (0.038) [0.300]	-0.011 (0.006) [-0.035]	–	0.687 (0.105)	0.044
4	MSD	1959–1965	-0.080 (0.040) [-0.444]	0.022 (0.063) [0.122]		0.053 (0.050) [0.294]	-0.002 (0.013) [-0.011]	0.022 (0.057) [0.122]	0.004 (0.006) [0.022]	–	0.820 (0.159)	0.032
5	ADMD	1966–1973	-0.236 (0.076) [-0.292]	0.642 (0.250) [0.796]	-0.023 (0.012) [-0.029]		0.014 (0.028) [0.017]	0.198 (0.059) [0.245]	-0.039 (0.011) [-0.048]	-0.006 (0.016) [-0.007]	0.193 (0.187)	0.086
6	MSD	1966–1973	0.005 (0.029) [0.002]	-0.200 (0.032) [-0.870]		0.038 (0.028) [0.165]	-0.023 (0.015) [-0.100]	0.114 (0.041) [0.496]	0.012 (0.004) [0.052]	-0.006 (0.007) [-0.026]	0.770 (0.083)	0.041

Note: Standard errors are shown in parentheses and long-run coefficients in square brackets. All variables are in logarithms except *MCAID* and *TIME*. The 1959–1973 sample contains 705 observations. See the text for information about the sample, the estimation method, and the definitions of the variables.

a. Standard error of estimate.

the long-run elasticity of the demand for bed-days with respect to quality is −0.03.

Before examining the estimates for the two subperiods, I will comment briefly on the other explanatory variables. The *TIME* variable, an annual time trend, reflects both the technical progress that increases quality for given resource inputs (v of equation (21)) and the gradual changes in other factors that influence hospital admissions: changing attitudes about hospital care, improved methods of ambulatory care, and so on. Income *(INC)* never had a significant effect, a result that is consistent with survey data on hospital admissions by income class.[26] The association of higher income with better health and a higher opportunity cost of time may offset the otherwise normal positive income elasticity of demand.

Traditional demand theory suggests that the prices of complements and substitutes should also be included in the demand equations. For hospital care these are the fees (net of insurance) charged by specialists who practice in the hospital and by general practitioners. There is, however, substantial evidence that these fees are not market-clearing prices. Because of the persistence of excess demand for physicians' services (Feldstein 1970c) the availability of physicians per capita is a more appropriate variable than their price. Even the demand for the services of surgeons, whose time is greatly underutilized, appears to be determined by their availability rather than by their fees (Hughes et al. 1972). These availability effects are examples of the incomplete agency relation.

Although the availability of surgeons and other hospital-based specialists should increase the demand for hospital admissions, the availability of general practitioners has an ambiguous effect. General practitioners can provide an alternative to hospital care for some conditions; however, general practitioners also act to diagnose ambulatory patients and prescribe hospital care. I have studied the effects of the numbers of general practitioners per capita and of the number of other physicians per capita. While total doctors per capita does not have any effect, the ratio of general practitioners to all doctors appears to increase slightly the admission rate and to decrease the mean duration of stay.

An increase in the supply of beds per capita raises the admission rate and the mean duration of stay per case. The coefficients of the *BEDS* variable show that there is a direct availability effect in addition to the usual effect through price. This direct availability effect also

26. See National Center for Health Statistics (1966b), Anderson and Benham (1970), and Davis and Russell (1972).

reflects the physician's role and the incompleteness of the agency relationship. Where beds are scarce, the physician is under pressure from other physicians and hospital administrators to share capacity with others; where beds are plentiful, this pressure is gone and administrators encourage the full utilization of capacity. A physician's concern with the use of hospital facilities for the general welfare of the community would also make his use of beds sensitive to availability.

Since the net price variable measures the effect of public as well as private insurance, the small negative coefficient of the Medicaid admission variable implies that Medicaid does not increase the admission rate by as much as an equal amount of private insurance would. This may reflect the reluctance of hospitals to admit Medicaid patients because they are generally paid less per patient-day by Medicaid than by other patients.

Finally, population density has a small but significant effect, decreasing admission rates and increasing mean stay. Where population is more dense, patients can more conveniently be treated on an outpatient basis, and fewer short-stay admissions occur.

The separate equations for the two subperiods suggest that there may be a changing pattern of response to price and quality and possibly a change in the speed with which the admissions rate responds to its determinants. The very high positive short-run and long-run elasticities with respect to quality for the years 1959–1965 imply that an increase in price and equiproportional increase in real resource inputs (Q) would then increase demand. Except for any resulting changes in hospital wage rates or an expansion of the number of beds, the system was clearly unstable during this period. For the more recent subperiod the situation is more complex. In the short run the positive quality effect outweighs the direct price effect, but the long-run price and quality elasticities are both negative.

There is also some evidence that the availability of beds is a more important determinant of use in the later period when the price elasticity is lower. The coefficients of the other variables are generally similar in the two periods.

Estimated Price Adjustment and the Dynamic Multiplier

The price of hospital care rises when the demand for bed-days (BDD_t) exceeds the number of bed-days that the hospital wishes to supply (BDS_t). Since the number of beds is fixed in the short run, the supply of bed-days depends on the hospital's desired occupancy rate (R). Although I have not tried to model the reasons for differences among states in this desired occupancy rate, the estimates permit the value of R to differ among states.

The introduction of federal price controls in August 1971 limited the hospitals' ability to adjust prices. Controls on hospitals were continued after they were ended for other industries and remained beyond the end of the 1973 terminal year of the current sample. The form of the controls was changed every year in an attempt to eliminate the price increases that were possible under previous rules.[27] Perhaps only in 1973 did controls become effective because only then were increases in average patient costs controlled rather than the unit costs for particular services. Separate binary variables are included for each of the three control years ($V71$, $V72$, and $V73$).

Combining equations (11)–(13) provides the desired estimation equation:

$$\ln P_{i,t} - \ln P_{i,t-1} = -\lambda \ln R_i + \lambda(BDD_{i,t} - BEDS_{i,t}) \\ + \alpha_{71}V71_t + \alpha_{72}V72_t + \alpha_{73}V73_t. \tag{23}$$

The equation is estimated by a consistent instrumental variables procedure in a way that allows a separate constant term ($-\lambda \ln R_i$) for each state. The results are presented in table 4.2.

The price adjustment coefficient (λ) has apparently increased substantially during the sample period. The estimate of $\lambda = 0.12$ for the early part of the sample is significantly less than the more recent $\lambda = 1.05$. It is fortunate that the response was so slow in the period when the equilibrium was unstable. If prices had adjusted faster to the moving target of no excess demand, the rate of hospital-cost inflation would have been even greater. The more recent coefficient implies that a given increase in demand (with constant supply) leads to an immediate equiproportional increase in price.

The price control variables do not provide any clear evidence that controls kept hospital price increases lower than they would otherwise have been. The only significant coefficient is for 1971; it is positive, implying that in 1971 hospital prices rose more rapidly than the model otherwise predicts even though controls were in effect for five months. The coefficients for the other years are insignificant. The only positive thing that can be said about controls is that the abnormally high price increase of 1971 did not continue into 1972 and 1973.

The price adjustment equation can be used in conjunction with the other equations of the model to quantify the effect of changes in the exogenous variables. More specifically, I shall use a very simplified version of the model that was developed in the first section to examine the effect on the price per patient-day of an exogenous change in in-

27. See Cost of Living Council (1974) and Ginsburg (1974) for analyses of the form and effects of controls.

surance. Although insurance is one of the endogenous variables of a more complete model, its role is so important in increasing the price and quality of hospital care that it is worthwhile to examine the effect of a change in insurance by treating it as if it were exogenous.[28] The analysis is also substantially simplified by treating as exogenous the prices and wages paid for hospital inputs and the number of hospital beds per capita.[29] The simplified model is thus denied two important stabilizing influences that limit the actual response of price to insurance: the induced rise in input prices reduces the quality increase that is made possible by a gross price increase, while the induced increase in the number of beds absorbs some of the increase in demand. In spite of these simplifications the estimated system for the entire period (equations 1 and 2 of table 4.1 and equation 1 of table 4.2) is dynamically stable.[30]

Equations (1)–(3), (12), (13), and (22) are linear in the logarithms and can be solved for the effect of insurance on price. The parameter estimates based on the full sample imply that the one-year impact multiplier is only 0.072; that is, a 10 percent increase in *INS* raises the real gross price by only 0.72 percent in the first year. But the long-run multiplier is 0.81, and the convergence is quite rapid; the four-year multiplier is 0.38, and 75 percent of the equilibrium response occurs within seven years.

The multiplier values are large enough to imply that insurance can account for most of the increase in the real price of hospital care during the past decade. The average cost per day rose from $48 in 1966 to $152 in 1975. If we normalize the general level of consumer prices at 1.0 in 1975, this is equivalent to a rise from $81 in 1966 to $152 in 1975, an increase of 88 percent.

Recall that *INS* is the inverse of the average coinsurance rate of the

28. The model is estimated with insurance as an endogenous variable, but it is then solved with insurance treated as exogenous. On the demand for insurance, see chapters 6 and 8 and M. Feldstein (1973c).

29. The number of short-term general beds only increased from 3.9 per thousand population in 1966 to 4.5 per thousand in 1975. Moreover, the supply of beds is now generally controlled by local regulatory agencies under certificate-of-need legislation.

30. It is clear from the coefficients of the demand equation for the earlier subperiod that the simplified subsystem is unstable; an increase in price is self-sustaining because of the greater demand stimulus of an equiproportionate increase in *Q*. The simplified system for the second subperiod is also dynamically unstable, essentially because of the short-run stimulative effects of increases in quality and the particular time patterns of changes in admissions, mean stay, and price. This instability should not be given much weight in evaluating the model since it is based on the simplified subsystem with important "dampers" deleted and because it depends on the rather inaccurate estimates of the speeds of demand and adjustment.

Table 4.2. The adjustment of price to excess demand

			Explanatory variables			
			Annual price control variable			
Equation	Period	Excess demand	$V71$	$V72$	$V73$	S.E.E.[a]
1	1959–	1.044	0.054	0.030	0.002	0.081
	1973	(0.149)	(0.014)	(0.014)	(0.012)	
2	1959–	0.121	–	–	–	0.040
	1965	(0.145)				
3	1966–	1.052	0.046	0.022	−0.006	0.107
	1973	(0.513)	(0.018)	(0.023)	(0.021)	

Note: Standard errors are shown in parentheses.
a. Standard error of estimate.

population, including both private and government insurance. In 1966 insurance paid 76.9 percent of hospital costs; *INS* was thus 4.3.[31] By 1971 government and private insurance paid 86.3 percent of hospital costs, an *INS* value of 7.3. The value of *INS* rose only slightly during the next five years, to 8.4. This rise in insurance from 4.3 to 8.4 would eventually increase the real price by 70 percent. The assumption that two-thirds of this adjustment occurred by 1975 implies a 47 percent increase in the real price, from \$81 to \$119, more than half of the observed increase during the past decade. Of course, the earlier increases in insurance (*INS* rose from 3.5 in 1960 to 4.3 in 1966) also contributed to the price rise during the past decade.

The price of care will continue to increase throughout the 1970s because of insurance changes that have already occurred. Moreover, if insurance coverage increases from the current 88 percent to 92 percent, *INS* would rise from 8.4 to 12.5. This alone would increase the equilibrium price of care by 37 percent.

Hospital costs have risen rapidly because insurance has increased the demand for hospital care. Hospitals have responded to this increased demand by raising prices and providing a more expensive style of care. This change in the apparent quality has further increased demand, setting off another round of price and quality increases.

In the period from 1958 through 1965 this process was explosively unstable. As quality increased, however, the sensitivity of demand to quality diminished. The system as a whole became stable after 1966,

31. See table 1.6 for the data on insurance.

but prices continued to rise at a rapid rate. The primary force propelling this increase in the real cost of insurance has been the growth of insurance.

The rapid increase in hospital costs creates financial hardship for many of those who require hospital care but whose insurance is less complete than the average. The desire to eliminate these financial burdens was the impetus of Medicare and Medicaid and remains a powerful force in favor of increased public insurance. The rapid increase in hospital costs has also raised greatly the cost of insurance premiums; today they are a significant drain on disposable income. These higher costs for almost everyone have stimulated political action to limit the increase in hospital costs. More complete insurance and a limit to the price of hospital care are incompatible with the current private nonprofit system of hospital care. If hospital costs are to be restrained, the government must either control hospital care or stop increasing hospital insurance.

Appendix: Data Sources

ADM   Admission rate per capita, published annually for each state in American Hospital Association, *Hospital Statistics*.

ADMD   *ADM* divided by expected admission per capita. The expected admission rate is a weighted average of sixteen age-sex-color specific rates published in National Center for Health Statistics (1966b) with the weights for each state and year based on interpolation and extrapolation of the 1960 and 1970 census population statistics.

MS   Mean stay per admission, published annually for each state in American Hospital Association, *Hospital Statistics*.

MSD   *MS* divided by expected mean stay. Same method used as for *ADMD*.

RNP   Real net price equals *PRICE* multiplied by *INS* and divided by *CPI*.

PRICE   Average cost per patient-day, published annually for each state in American Hospital Association, *Hospital Statistics*.

INS   Insurance. An estimate of the fraction of hospital costs paid directly out of pocket by patients. The formula and sources used to calculate *INS* are discussed in chapter 3. The only changes are in the treatment of Medicare and Medicaid. Data on national health expenditures are from the February 1975 *Social Security Bulletin*; the fiscal year figures presented there have been interpolated to calender years. Data on health insurance coverage of the population are published by the Health Insurance Institute for each state annually in *Source Book of Health Insurance Data*. The estimates of *INS* used in this paper are based on table 1.6.

CPI	Consumer Price Index. Only a single national figure is used. Published in *Economic Report of the President*.
Q	Quality defined as *PRICE* divided by an input price index, *INP*.
INP	See equation (21). $N_{i.}$ is the number of full-time equivalent hospital employees per patient-day in 1963 and is published in *Hospital Statistics* for that year. W_{it} is the average payroll per full-time employee, published annually for each state in *Hospital Statistics*. The nonlabor input price index π_{it} is a weighted average of detailed components of the wholesale price index and consumer price index; the method of constructing π_{it} is $J_{i.}$ is described in detail in chapter 5.
TIME	An annual time trend.
INC	Per capita income in constant dollars, published in *Annual Abstract*.
GP	The ratio of the number of general practitioners to the total number of physicians. Data are published by the American Medical Association (*Distribution of Physicians in the United States*) for 1958, 1963, 1966, 1969, and 1972. The other years have been interpolated.
BEDS	The number of "short-term general and other special" beds per capita, published annually for each state and year in *Hospital Statistics*.
DENSITY	Population per square mile. Based on the *Statistical Abstract* annual population estimates.
MCAID	A binary variable equal to one for a year in which a state participated in the Medicaid program.

5   The Quality of Hospital Services: An Analysis of Geographic Variation and Intertemporal Change

Economists are generally accustomed to discussing the prices and quantities of goods and services while saying rather little about their quality. At a formal level, different qualities of the same product may be treated as a set of different products. As a substantive matter, however, the determinants of product quality and the dynamics of product change are significant problems that have been unduly neglected.

For health services in particular, the quality is an important issue to which economists have given too little attention. This has been particularly true in empirical research.[1] In studying the operation of any nation's health-care system, it is useful to have an economic measure of the quality of care provided at different times and places. Such a measure is important not only for monitoring the general performance of the health-care system but also for analyzing the demand for care, forecasting the effects of changes in the method of financing, and assessing the welfare implications of policies that would alter the expenditure on health services.

A good measure depends on its purpose. For a regulatory agency charged with evaluating the quality of care or for a cost-benefit analyst examining the desirability of a particular program, the only suitable measure of quality is an assessment of the effects of care on the health of the relevant population. This chapter is less ambitious. I

This chapter was published in *The Economics of Health and Medical Care*, ed. Mark Perlman (London: Macmillan, 1974), pp. 402–419. Reprinted by permission of the International Economic Association and Macmillan, London and Basingstoke.

1. The quality of health services has been discussed in a number of studies, including Arrow (1963), M. Feldstein (1967, 1971b, chapter 6), Grossman (1972a), Newhouse (1970a), Pauly and Redisch (1973), and Reder (1969), but none of these incorporates a quality measure into an empirical analysis.

want a measure that is useful for aggregative analyses of the quality of hospital services. I shall consider a measure useful if it permits us to assess the extent and change of geographic variation in the quality of care, and if it can be used as an index of quality in an econometric model of the health-care sector. I have no doubt that the measure presented here is a crude one, but I believe that by the standards that I have defined, it is also a useful one. I hope that by directing attention to this issue and providing an operational measure of quality, I shall succeed in encouraging others to deal with this important subject.

The next section will discuss the conceptual problems of defining an aggregate quality index and will develop the formulas required to make this operational. A key variable used in calculating the quality measure is a price index for hospitals' nonlabor inputs. Such an index was constructed using input weights based on the 1963 United States input-output study; the method and results are described in the third section. The fourth section analyzes the substantial and persistent geographic variation in the overall price of inputs. The fifth section then examines the intertemporal change and geographic variations in the quality of hospital services. The last section indicates a number of directions for future research.

The Measurement of Quality

My original interest in developing an aggregate quality measure was motivated by work that I was doing on the demand for hospital services (chapter 3). Using a pooled cross-sectional sample of time series for each of the individual states of the United States for 1958 through 1967, I estimated equations relating the demand for hospital admissions and for mean durations of stay per case to the price of care net of insurance and to other explanatory variables including income, population density, and the availability of physicians. The dependent variables were adjusted for interstate differences in the demographic composition of the population. A typical equation could be summarized as

$$ADM_{it} = k_0 \, NP_{it}^{\alpha} \, e^{\gamma_0 t} \, (\prod_j X_{jit}^{\beta j}) \, U_{it}, \tag{1}$$

where ADM_{it} is the demographically adjusted admission rate. NP_{it} is the price net of insurance deflated by the consumer price index, t is a time trend, the X_{jit} are other explanatory variables, and U_{it} is a disturbance term. The subscripts i and t refer to the state and the year. The equation was estimated by a consistent instrumental variable procedure after a logarithmic transformation. The time trend reflects both technical progress and the changing popular attitudes about hospital care.

The specification of equation (1) implicitly assumes that other variations in quality, through time or between states, do not affect demand. I accepted this as a basis for analysis on the assumption that patients were not likely to be able to discern and respond to actual variations in the quality of services provided. Nevertheless, I was concerned about the lack of specific testing of this assumption. Moreover, when I later analyzed the role of the physician in the demand for hospital services, I recognized that the patient may often act as he would if he had the expertise to perceive quality differences.[2] If a more appropriate specification includes the quality of care Q_{it}, that is, if

$$ADM_{it} = k_0 \, NP_{it}^{\alpha} \, e^{\gamma_0 t} \, (\prod_j X_{jit}^{\beta_j}) \, Q_{it}^{\eta} \, U_{it}, \qquad (2)$$

the omission of Q_{it} leads to incorrect inferences about the other demand parameters and, perhaps, about the qualitative behavior and efficiency of the health-care system in general. If quality and price are positively correlated, the price elasticity estimated in equation (1) would be biased toward zero.[3]

More generally, my analysis of hospital-cost inflation (M. Feldstein 1971a,b) rested largely on changes in the quality or style of hospital care. In *The Rising Cost of Hospital Care,* I developed a theoretical model of quality change in a context in which individual demand for care does reflect the quality of services. To test this model and to integrate it with the earlier empirical work requires an operational measure of the quality of hospital services in each state. Finally, the analysis of the welfare economics of health insurance depends on the effect of quality on demand. More specifically, the welfare gain or loss that results from changes in the level of health insurance depends on the effect of changes in the resource input per patient-day on the quantity of care demanded at each price (chapter 6).

The constant elasticity specification of equation (2) suggests a simple "constant elasticity" model of the relation of quality to resource inputs:

$$Q_{it} = k_1 \, e^{\gamma_1 t} \, R_{it}^{\rho}, \qquad (3)$$

where R_{it} is a measure of the resource inputs per patient-day. The

2. The theory of a generalized agency relation between the patient and his physician is developed in chapter 2.

3. While a strong correlation might be assumed to exist, the correlation would actually be attenuated by differences in local costs and, more important, by the use of price net of insurance. Whether the price elasticity is biased toward zero actually depends on a positive partial correlation between quality and price, given all the other variables in the equation.

constant k_1 is an arbitrary choice of units, but γ_1 and ρ are unknown parameters. If this relation is substituted into equation (2), it is clear that the parameters k_1 and γ_1 are not identified. The constant term of equation (2) becomes $k_0 k_1{}^\eta$ and the time term becomes $\gamma_0 + \gamma_1 \eta$. Similarly, the coefficient of T_{it} is $\rho\eta$. The estimation therefore provides neither the parameters of the quality function (equation (3)) nor the elasticity of demand with respect to quality (η). Nevertheless, this estimate of equation (2) may provide all the information required for practical analysis. The estimated price elasticity of demand (α) would no longer be biased by the omission of Q_{it}. Moreover, the analysis of hospital-cost inflation and the welfare economics of insurance depend only on the effect of additional resource inputs on the demand for care, that is, on the combined parameter $\rho\eta$.[4]

The simple specification of equation (3) implies strong assumptions. The technical progress that occurs with time is neutral in that it raises the quality in the same proportion at all levels of resource inputs.[5] The efficiency with which resources are turned into the quality of service is assumed constant or is subsumed into the time term. For this reason, the specification is more useful for the analysis of a large group of hospitals than for comparing individual hospitals. No distinction is made among the different types of quality increase that may be produced with additional resource inputs. In chapter 3 I assumed that a relation like equation (3) exists between inputs and quality as perceived by the providers, that is, quality in terms of the providers' preferences. For demand analysis the relevant aspect is quality as perceived by the patients and their physicians. More generally, hospitals may differ in the way in which they allocate additional resource inputs per patient-day to increase the several different dimensions of the quality of service: the efficacy of treatment, the intensity of treatment (reduction in duration of stay with given overall efficacy), the level of patient amenities, and the extent of facilities and services that appeal primarily to the providers. The particular mix of the quality facets that is chosen depends on the market conditions faced by each hospital. In short, using resource inputs to measure quality is only a first approximation more suitable for some purposes than for others.

The resource input per patient-day (R_{it}) can be measured as the ra-

4. Equation (3) specifies a nonstochastic relation. Introducing a multiplicative random error poses no special problem. Since R_{it} must be treated as an endogenous variable in estimating equation (2), some form of instrumental variable procedure will be used. This is sufficient to permit consistent estimation even if Q_{it} contains an unobserved random error.

5. See M. Feldstein (1971b, chap. 4) for an analysis of nonneutral technical change in this context. Even such neutral technical progress can be either cost increasing or cost reducing, depending on perferences and market structure.

tio of an index of average cost per patient-day $(JACPPD_{it})$ to an index of hospital input prices $(PRIN_{it})$:

$$R_{it} = JACPPD_{it}/PRIN_{it}. \qquad (4)$$

Data on average cost per patient-day are published annually for individual hospitals and as state averages.[6] The index of average cost per patient $(JACPPD_{it})$ is defined as the ratio of average cost per patient-day in state i and year t $(ACPPD_{it})$ to the national average in a base year:

$$JACPPD_{it} = ACPPD_{it}/ACPPD_{a0}. \qquad (5)$$

The subscript a denotes a national average and the subscript 0 denotes the base year. Equation (5) implies that the national average of *JACPPD* in the base year is one. No index of input prices $(PRIN_{it})$ exists on a state or even on a national basis. An important aspect of this study has been the development of such an index. This input price index is also scaled so that it has a national average of one in the base year.

Two types of inputs may be distinguished. Labor inputs are purchased in a relatively local market. Substantial interstate differences in wage rates can therefore persist. It is important to have a separate wage index value for every state and year. Nonlabor inputs are generally available in a national market. A single price index for nonlabor inputs is therefore sufficient.[7]

The basic input price index is a Laspeyres index of wages and nonlabor input:

$$PRIN_{it} = w_{it}N_{a0} + \pi_t J_{a0}/w_{a0}N_{a0} + \pi_0 J_{a0}, \qquad (6)$$

where w_{it} is an index of hospital wages for state i; π_t is national price index for nonlabor inputs, N_{a0} is the national average quantity of labor inputs in the base year, and J_{a0} is the national average quantity of nonlabor inputs in the base year.

---

6. See, for example, American Hospital Association (1967). The data used in the current study refer only to nonfederal short-term general and other special hospitals. They specifically exclude mental hospitals and other long-stay facilities. The definition of cost also excludes capital costs; this is likely to result in an underestimate of costs by only about 10 percent but may also introduce some differential bias between observations.

7. A national price index for hospital inputs was previously developed in National Advisory Commission on Health Manpower (1967), V. Taylor (1969), and M. Feldstein (1971b). No geographical disaggregation was attempted. More important, each of these studies used the general wholesale price index to measure the price of hospital nonlabor costs.

The average hospital wage in state i and year t is measured by the ratio of total hospital payroll to the number of full-time equivalent employees.[8] This procedure fails to make specific allowance for local differences or changes in the job mix and quality of employees. This is probably not a serious deficiency. A previous analysis showed no evidence of substantial overall change in the average job level of hospital employees in the decade 1956–1966 (Feltstein 1971b, pp. 57–58). The job mix and quality of employees may, however, differ across states. Further disaggregation of the labor input would be desirable. The average payroll per full-time equalivalent employee was then converted to an index number with a national average of one in 1958. A corresponding measure of the quantity of labor inputs in each state and year was defined by dividing the payroll costs per patient-day by the wage index. N_{a0} is the national average of these quantities for the base year, 1963.[9]

The national price index for nonlabor costs (π_t) is defined as a weighted average of the separate price indexes for all the products purchased by the hospitals. The construction of this index is the subject of the next section. There is obviously no physical measure of the average base-year quantity of nonlabor inputs (J_{a0}). Instead, J_{a0} is defined by analogy with N_{a0} as the ratio of nonlabor costs to the price index of nonlabor inputs:

$$J_{a0} = ACPPD_{a0} - w_{a0}N_{a0}/\pi_0. \tag{7}$$

The resource input measure (P_{it}), defined by equations (4)–(7). reflects variation among states and through time. Although this is important for monitoring the extent and change in the inequality of resource use, it may be inappropriate for demand analysis. The demand for hospital care may respond to changes in the quality of services that are produced locally but may not reflect interstate differences in the quality of care. Stated somewhat differently, patients may perceive and respond to the relative quality of services but may not know, be able to judge or respond to the absolute level of the quality of services. An increase in the quality of services in a particular market may increase the demand for those services, but the initial level of

8. The data, published by the American Hospital Association, exclude most physicians.

9. The wage and nonlabor price indexes, w_{it} and π_t, are scaled to be one in 1958, the first year for which data are analyzed here. This choice of scale obviously does not affect the analysis. The weights in the index number of equation (6) are the 1963 national quantities. The choice of a base year does, of course, affect the behavior of the index. The year 1963 was chosen because of the availability of the detailed input-output data. This base year is also conveniently in the middle of the current period of analysis.

services may not affect the initial level of demand. To explore the implications of this hypothesis requires a resource input index that reflects changes through time but not across states. This could be accomplished by dividing each value of R_{it} by R_{io}, the value of R_{it} in the base year. An alternative and more appropriate index would permit the weights on w_{it} and π_t to differ among states. To do so it is only necessary to replace N_{a0}, J_{a0}, and w_{a0} in equations (6) and (7) by N_{io}, J_{io}, and w_{io}. The state-specific indexes constructed in this way are denoted RS_{it}. They are all equal to one in the base year. All interstate variance in other years reflects differences in the rates of change of resource inputs.

Input-Output Technology and a Price Index for Hospital Nonlabor Inputs

This construction of a new price index for hospital nonlabor inputs is based on technological information developed for input-output analysis and on detailed price indexes provided by the Office of Business Economics of the U.S. Department of commerce and by the Bureau of Labor Statistics of the U.S. Department of Labor. The new index will also be compared with the general wholesale price index that has previously been used as a proxy for nonlabor hospital costs.

The hospital nonlabor price index is defined by the equation

$$\pi_t = \sum_k a_{k0}\, q_{kt}, \tag{8}$$

where a_{k0} is the quantity of input k used by hospitals in the base year, and, q_{kt} is the value of the price index in year t for inputs of type k. This price index is scaled so that $q_{k,\,1958} = 1$ for all k.

The 1963 U.S. input-output table of order 367 contains information on the purchases of the hospital industry (industry number 77.02) from each of the other industries.[10] These data were then aggregated to the two-digit ISP level, since price indexes are generally not available on a more detailed basis.[11] Thirty-five of the eighty-six two-digit industries are sources of hospital inputs. These are listed with their 1963 sales to the hospital industry in table 5.1. Twelve of the

10. The input-output table and a discussion of methods is published in U.S. Department of Commerce (1969). The hospital industry (77.02) corresponds to SIC industry 8061. It includes all forms of hospitals (but not convalescent homes, rest homes, and the like) and is therefore broader than the average cost per patient-day data that exclude long-term institutions.

11. The two-digit input-output industry (ISP) level is not the same as the two-digit SIC (Standard Industrial Classification). For an analysis of the SIC categories corresponding to ISP industries, see *Survey of Current Business* (Sept. 1965) p. 33.

Table 5.1. Components of a price index for hospital nonlabor inputs

Source industry	Industry title	Hospital purchases, 1963 ($m)
1	Livestock and livestock products	5.0
2	Other agricultural products	29.9
7	Coal mining	4.2
12	Maintenance and repair construction	143.3
14	Food and kindred products	218.2
19	Miscellaneous fabricated textile products	12.8
24	Paper and allied products, except containers and boxes	21.7
26	Paperboard containers and boxes	4.2
27	Chemicals and selected chemical products	23.0
29	Drugs, cleaning and toilet preparations	317.1
31	Petroleum refining and related industries	19.4
32	Rubber and miscellaneous plastics products	27.4
35	Glass and glass products	1.8
36	Stone and clay products	2.4
41	Screw machine products, bolts, nuts, etc., and metal stampings	0.8
55	Electric lighting and wiring equipment	0.1
58	Miscellaneous electrical machinery, equipment and supplies	0.5
59	Motor vehicles and equipment	0.6
62	Professional, scientific, and controlling instruments and supplies	95.9
63	Optical, ophthalmic, and photographic equipment and supplies	50.0
64	Miscellaneous manufacturing	3.2
65	Transportation and warehousing	42.8
66	Communications, except radio and television broadcasting	50.1
68	Electric, gas, water, and sanitary services	192.4
69	Wholesale and retail trade	187.5
70	Finance and insurance	44.3
71	Real estate and rental	450.3
72	Hotels and lodging places; personal and repair services, except automobile repair	58.0
73	Business services	91.9
75	Automobile repair and services	20.0
77	Medical, educational services, and nonprofit organizations	5.1
78	Federal government enterprises	32.3
79	State and local government enterprises	5.3
81	Business travel, entertainment, and gifts	159.1
82	Office supplies	25.6

thirty-five industries supplied extremely small quantities, less that $6 million each in 1963 and, collectively, less than 1.5 percent of total hospital nonlabor purchases. These small industries were therefore ignored in constructing the price index. Deflating the remaining twenty-three values of sales to 1958 dollars (by the individual price indexes described later) provided the values of the a_{k0}'s required by equation (8).

The twenty-three price indexes for the industries (the q_{kt}'s) were derived from several sources. The Office of Business Economics (OBE) of the U.S. Department of Commerce provided unpublished time series of implicit deflators for the value of production of each two-digit ISP manufacturing industry. This relates to industries 13–64 inclusive. The published OBE composite index of construction costs[12] was used for industry 12, maintenance and repair construction. The wholesale price index (WPI) component for processed foods was used for the purchases of agricultural products (industry 2), and the WPI component for producers' finished goods was used for industries 81 and 82.[13] The remaining industries are classified as services in the ISP system. Because there are no wholesale price indexes for the purchases of services by business firms, components of the consumer price index were used for these industries.[14] Although a more detailed matching of price indexes with the specific categories of hospital inputs might be pursued, it is unlikely that the extra work would repay the effort.

Table 5.2 presents the price index for hospital nonlabor costs derived according to equation (8) and the corresponding annual values of the wholesale price index. From 1958 through 1967 hospital nonlabor costs rose 13.1 percent, compared with 5.7 percent for the wholesale price index and 15.5 percent for the consumer price index.

The wholesale price index is not a very satisfactory measure of the price of hospital nonlabor inputs. It substantially understates the overall rise in hospital nonlabor prices. Although the correlation between the two series is 0.88, this is largely due to the common trend. This is shown by equation (9):

$$\pi_t = 0.34 + 0.57\ WPI_t + 0.0106\ TIME, \qquad R^2 = 0.993. \qquad (9)$$
$$\quad\ \ (0.08) \qquad\ \ (0.0006)$$

---

12. See U.S. Department of Commerce, *Business Statistics,* 1967 ed., p. 51.

13. These are treated as dummy industries in the construction of the input-output table. They are best considered as a residual for otherwise unallocated purchases.

14. More specifically, the following CPI components were used: ISP 66, nondurables less food and apparel; ISP 68, fuel and utilities; ISP 71, rent; ISP 75, transportation services; for the remaining six industries, "other services."

Table 5.2. Price index for hospital nonlabor costs

Year	Hospital nonlabor price index (π_t)	Wholesale price index[a] (WPI_t)	Consumer price index[a] (CPI_t)
1958	1.000	1.000	1.000
1959	1.009	1.002	1.007
1960	1.023	1.003	1.024
1961	1.034	0.999	1.035
1962	1.044	1.002	1.047
1963	1.052	0.999	1.060
1964	1.064	1.001	1.073
1965	1.081	1.021	1.091
1966	1.109	1.055	1.123
1967	1.131	1.057	1.155

a. The published WPI and CPI indexes have 1967 = 100; they have been rescaled for convenience in comparison with π_t. The numbers in the table have also been rounded.

The relative standard errors imply that the partial correlation of π_t and *TIME* is substantially greater than the partial correlation of π_t and WPI_t.

The consumer price index is actually a better proxy for the hospital nonlabor price index during the period 1958–1967. The simple correlation between CPI_t and π_t is 0.999, and a regression analogous to equation (9) shows that the coefficient of CPI_t (0.90, s.e. 0.07) is much more important than the coefficient of *TIME* (0.001, s.e. 0.001). It would, of course, be necessary to compare substantially longer series of π_t and CPI_t before deciding whether the consumer price index could generally be used as a proxy for hospital nonlabor input prices.

Geographic Variation in Input Prices

Before examining the variation and change in the quality of services, it is worthwhile to look briefly at the behavior of input costs. The input price index $(PRIN_{it})$ defined by equation (6) has been evaluated for each state and year. Table 5.3 summarizes the distribution among states for each of the years from 1958 through 1967; the index is scaled so that the average value of $PRIN_{it}$ for 1963 is equal to 1.0.

The average input price rose 35 percent, from 0.85 in 1958 to 1.15 in 1967. If this is compared with the 13 percent increase in the price of nonlabor inputs (shown in table 5.2), it is clear that average wages have risen very much faster than the price of nonlabor inputs. The 35 percent increase in the price of inputs can also be compared with the

Table 5.3. Geographic variation in input prices

Year (1)	National average (2)	Input price index ($PRIN_{it}$)			
		Standard deviation (3)	Coefficient of variation (4)	Maximum (5)	Minimum (6)
1958	0.851	0.061	0.072	1.012	0.756
1959	0.884	0.066	0.075	1.044	0.771
1960	0.914	0.075	0.082	1.092	0.788
1961	0.937	0.074	0.079	1.122	0.807
1962	0.963	0.078	0.080	1.156	0.837
1963	1.000	0.106	0.106	1.433	0.843
1964	1.023	0.089	0.087	1.241	0.881
1965	1.061	0.088	0.083	1.272	0.934
1966	1.079	0.087	0.081	1.292	0.938
1967	1.150	0.096	0.083	1.396	1.009

85 percent rise in average cost per patient-day during the same period. The higher cost of inputs can, by itself, account for only two-fifths of the higher cost per patient-day.

The variation in input prices among the states is significant. The average input price in the highest-cost state (column (5)) has generally been about 35 percent to 40 percent higher than the average price in the lowest-cost state (column (6)). This range reflects a symmetric distribution with a coefficient of variation of about 0.08, as shown in column (4). It is clear that there has been no tendency for the relative inequality of input prices to increase or decrease during the decade.

The average increase in input prices during the decade was approximately as large as the 1958 interstate range of input prices. Moreover, the rate of price increase varied rather substantially, from 26 percent in Wyoming to 50 percent in New York. Despite this relatively rapid and varied increase and the importance of the local wage component, the specific interstate pattern of input prices has remained quite stable. The correlation between $PRIN_{it}$ in 1958 and 1967 is 0.91. The relation between the two sets of prices is also very close to proportional. Equation (10) shows that the elasticity of $PRIN_{i,\ 1967}$ with respect to $PRIN_{i,\ 1958}$ is approximately one:

$$\log PRIN_{i,\ 1967} = 0.110 + 1.055 \log PRIN_{i,\ 1958}, \quad R^2 = 0.83. \quad (10)$$
$$(0.070)$$

This equation indicates that there has been no tendency for lower input prices to "catch up" with the national average or for states with higher input prices to be brought back into line. This is also shown by the absence of a significant correlation between the relative increase in the input price $(PRIN_{i,\ 1967}/PRIN_{i,\ 1958})$ and the input price level in 1958; the actual correlation (0.12) is positive and insignificant.

The persistence of substantial interstate variation in input prices and the stability of the pattern of differentials reflect the general absence of a single national market for labor and, more specifically, the special characteristics of the labor market for hospital employees. The preponderance of low-skilled workers and the substantial number of married women both weaken the tendency for wages to equalize across areas. But this is just the supply side of the labor market. A full explanation of the interstate differences in wages and of their variation through time also requires an analysis of hospitals' demand for labor services and their wage policies. Although an attempt to explain these changes lies beyond the scope of this chapter,[15] the stable interstate variations indicate that a cross section of states should be a useful data base for developing such an analysis.

The pattern of input prices implies that residents of different states must pay quite different prices to purchase the same level of quality.[16] This implies that any federal program of health care or health insurance that tries to provide the same quality of services in all states will distribute quite unequal dollar benefits. Similarly a program that provides the same dollar benefits per patient-day will distribute quite unequal real benefits.[17]

Geographic Variation and Intertemporal Change in Quality

The index of resource use per patient-day (R_{it}) has been evaluated using the definition of equations (4)–(7). To emphasize the relation between resource use and quality, I shall refer to R_{it} in the following analysis as an index of quality. A comparison with the definition in equation (3) shows that this ignores the role of time and implies that quality increases proportionately with resource inputs $(\rho = 1)$. Ignor-

---

15. See Altman (1971) and Benham (1971) for interesting attempts to develop econometric models of the labor market for hospital nurses. In M. Feldstein (1971b) I discuss why the nonprofit nature of the hospital may make the usual supply and demand analysis inadequate for explaining the wages of hospital employees.

16. It is worth emphasizing the caveat that some of the wage differentials may actually reflect quality differences in personnel.

17. The persistent interstate differences in wages may also have an important implication for any possible future national wage policy for the health industry. Any attempt to set national wages would conflict with the natural forces that have led to the current differentials. The result might be shortages of some areas and excess supply in others.

Table 5.4. Geographic variation in hospital quality

| Year (1) | National average (2) | Hospital quality index (R_{it}) | | | |
		Standard deviation (3)	Coefficient of variation (4)	Maximum (5)	Minimum (6)
1958	0.868	0.075	0.086	0.706	1.052
1959	0.888	0.078	0.088	0.693	1.033
1960	0.912	0.087	0.095	0.729	1.075
1961	0.967	0.086	0.089	0.770	0.123
1962	0.982	0.092	0.094	0.790	1.167
1963	1.000	0.102	0.102	0.743	1.204
1964	1.037	0.093	0.090	0.840	1.233
1965	1.078	0.096	0.089	0.867	1.292
1966	1.139	0.103	0.090	0.952	1.355
1967	1.185	0.123	0.104	0.966	1.454

ing time has no effect on relative interstate variation but does understate the amount of quality increase during the decade. If quality is a convex function of resource inputs ($\rho < 1$), the following analysis overstates the relative variation in hospital quality. The general qualitative conclusions, particularly about the stability of that variation and of its geographic pattern, would be unaffected.

Table 5.4 summarizes the interstate distribution of quality for each year in the decade. The interstate variation is substantial and persistent. The coefficient of variation remains between 8.5 and 10.5 percent and indicates no clear trend in relative inequality. The quality index is generally 50 percent higher in the maximum state than in the minimum. The pattern of quality differences also remained relatively stable from the beginning to the end of the decade; the correlation of $R_{i,\ 1967}$ and $R_{i,\ 1958}$ is 0.81.

Although the rate of quality increase for some states departed substantially from the mean — the increases ranged from 17 percent to 57 percent, with a mean of 37 percent — there was no overall tendency for the low-quality states to move upward more rapidly. The elasticity between the quality levels at the beginning and end of the decade is approximately one:[18]

18. This equation also yields the elasticity of $Q_{i,\ 1967}$ with respect to $Q_{i,\ 1958}$. This elasticity is independent of the value of ρ and, of course, of the time term: $\log Q_{it} = \log k_1 + \rho_1 t + \rho \log R_{it}$. The first two terms are constants while ρ multiplies both the dependent and independent variables.

$$\log R_{i,\ 1967} = 0.305 + 0.966 \log \overline{R}_{i,\ 1958}, \qquad R^2 = 0.653. \qquad (10)$$
$$(0.105)$$

This is also confirmed by the low and insignificant correlation of the growth of quality $(R_{i,\ 1967}/R_{i,\ 1958})$ and its 1958 level: $r = 0.045$.

The persistence and stability of the pattern of quality differences requires further explanation. A simple hypothesis is that quality is high where the price of quality is low, that is, that there is an inverse relation between R_{it} and $PRIN_{it}$ across states for each year. Data for 1967 clearly contradict this. The correlation between $R_{i,\ 1967}$ and $PRIN_{i,\ 1967}$ is actually positive and significant $(r = +0.71)$.[19] One possible explanation of this is that the input price index is higher in states where other factors that increase the quality of care are also above average. Equation (11) relates the logarithm of quality to the logarithm of real per capita income *(INC)*, a measure of insurance coverage *(INS)*, and the input price index.[20]

$$\log R_{it} = -3.83 - 0.175 \log (INC) + 0.043 \log INS \qquad (11)$$
$$(0.132) \qquad\qquad (0.071)$$

$$+ 1.24 \log PRIN_{it}, \qquad \overline{R}^2_{\ 1967} = 0.52.$$
$$(0.25)$$

Neither of the two demand variables is significant, while the price elasticity is large and of the wrong sign. Similar results are obtained for other years.[21]

The implication of equation (11) is clear. The local price of hospital inputs is not exogenous but is jointly determined with the quality and quantity of hospital care. The forces that raise the local quality of care also increase the price of hospital inputs. This may operate through the usual forces of supply and demand for hospital labor. States with higher quality per day are also likely to have more patient-days per capita. Both factors raise the demand for hospital personnel and therefore the local wage. Moreover, because of the special nonprofit character of the hospital, the positive correlation of wages and hospital quality may also reflect a deliberate philanthropic wage policy on the part of hospitals. Hospitals that are insulated from the usual pres-

19. The usual errors-in-variables problem would tend to bias the coefficient toward zero. Moreover, since R_{it} is defined as the ratio of a cost index to $PRIN_{it}$, errors of measurement in $PRIN_{it}$ would be expected to introduce a negative bias.

20. *INS* is defined as the proportion of hospital charges paid directly by patients; see the second section of chapter 3. The use of log R_{it} rather than log Q_{it} changes the scale of the coefficients but not their relative magnitudes or *t*-statistics.

21. The simple correlation of quality and income is, however, positive; the 1967 elasticity is 0.30 (s.e. = 0.08).

sures of the competitive market may choose to use their discretionary market power to raise both the quality of services and the wages of hospital employees.[22]

The emphasis on geographic differences in the quality of hospital services should not obscure the fact that the rapid growth of individual quality levels is at least as significant as the inequalities that exist at any time. The state with the lowest quality level in 1965 had already achieved the national average of 1958. Since this measure ignores the effect of the passage of time on scientific progress and general innovation, it understates the extent to which changes in the absolute level of quality may dominate relative differences. In assessing the overall performance of the health-care sector, it is important to remember that dynamic adjustments may be more important than static inequality or inefficiency.

To conclude this section, I shall return to the issue of the role of quality in the demand for care and, more specifically, to the problem of the bias in the estimated price elasticity when a measure of quality is not included in the demand equation. The discussion of the second section showed that the price elasticity of demand is biased toward zero if there is a positive partial correlation between the logarithm of the net price variable (NP_{it}) and the logarithm of the resource input variable (R_{it}).[23] The parameter ρ that relates resource input to quality affects the magnitude of the bias but not its existence or sign. Although a full analysis of this question lies beyond the scope of this chapter, it is interesting to examine the simple correlation between price and quality. Since the demand equation is specified to be linear in the logarithms of the variables, I shall consider the correlation between the logarithms of price and the logarithms of the quality or resource input variable.

For the entire ten-year sample the correlation between $\log R_{it}$ and the logarithm of the real price per patient-day is, as would be expected, very high: $r = +0.943$.[24] The correlation is almost the same when attention is limited to a single year; for 1967 it is +0.940. The price variable in these correlations is the gross price charged by the hospital and not the price net of insurance that is actually paid by the patient.

22. A model of the hospital choosing the quality of services is presented in chapter 3. The notion of a philanthropic wage policy is developed in M. Feldstein (1971b, chap. 5)

23. If the equation is estimated by two-stage least squares or some other instrumental variable procedure, the bias is more complicated and depends on the correlation of the omitted variable with the instruments. If the first stage has a low residual variance, this will not differ appreciably from the ordinary least-squares bias.

24. The price variable is defined as the average cost per patient-day deflated by the annual consumer price index.

The correlation of resource input and net price is substantially lower, 0.633 for the entire period and 0.607 for 1967. Finally, if we assume that demand depends only on the intrastate changes in quality and not on the differences among states, we must look at the relation be-tween $\log (NP_{it})$ and $\log (RS_{it})$.[25] For the entire decade, this correlation is only 0.327. All these correlations suggest that omitting a measure of quality from the demand equation is likely to result in a downward bias of the estimated price elasticity. Since only simple correlations have been examined and the problem of simultaneity has been ignored, this must be regarded as a plausible hypothesis and a reason for more work rather than as a definite conclusion.

Questions for Future Research

Several research problems are suggested by the current study: the role of quality in the demand for care and the extent of philanthropic wage setting in nonprofit hospitals. Closely related is the question how input prices affect the level of quality and the rate of product innova-tion.

The period since 1967 has seen an extremely rapid increase in hos-pital costs. It would be valuable to extend the current study to more recent years. Of particular interest would be the effect of the very sub-stantial growth of federal health-care funds for the poor and the aged on the interstate distribution of quality.

An international comparison of the extent of interregional varia-tion in the quality of services would shed light on the effect of health-sector organization and financing on the equality of care. I suspect that such differences in quality variation between national health ser-vices, like the British, and private nonprofit systems, like that in the United States, are relatively small. It would be of further interest to examine the relation in different national settings between local qual-ity and variables such as income and urbanization.

Finally, a quite different economic measure of quality should be examined and related to the current analysis. Hedonic quality indexes assess quality by the market's willingness to pay for attributes of a product (Griliches 1971). If the agency relationship between patients and physicians is relatively complete, a hedonic quality index (with adjustment for insurance) would be an appropriate normative mea-sure of quality.[26] The relation between the hedonic index and the cur-

25 Recall that RS_{it} is constructed so that it equals 1.0 in every state in 1963 and there-fore reflects only intertemporal change.

26. See chapter 2 for a discussion of a complete and incomplete agency model of the physician's role in the demand for hospital care.

rent real input measure of quality could be investigated. Such an analysis would help us understand the way in which the local market structure affects how hospitals allocate additional resource imputs between the services and facilities valued by patients and those valued by the providers.

The quality of care and the process of product change are central to any analysis of the health-care sector. Although the measurement problems here are potentially enormous, quite simple measures may be useful in a number of areas of aggregate analysis.

Part Two

Tax Subsidies and Excess
Health Insurance

The amount of health insurance that is optimal for an individual depends on balancing the advantage of risk reduction against the disadvantage of demand distortion. The current U.S. tax system subsidizes the purchase of excessive health insurance by excluding the employer's premiums from the employee's income subject to income and Social Security taxes. The chapters in Part Two develop this idea more fully, quantifying the extent of the tax subsidy, the amount of overinsurance, and the resulting loss in economic welfare.

Chapter 6 begins by specifying and estimating a structural equation for the demand for health insurance. The parameter estimates indicate that an increase in the price of hospital care causes a substantial increase in the demand for insurance. There is thus a mutually reinforcing behavior between the purchase of insurance and the demand for and supply of hospital care: more insurance increases the price of care, and a higher price of care increases the demand for insurance. Although the system is dynamically stable, the interdependence between insurance and the price of care implies that there is more insurance and a higher price of care than would otherwise prevail. This interdependence also magnifies that effect of changes in any exogenous variable on both the price of care and the level of insurance.

The second part of chapter 6 estimates the welfare gains that would result from decreasing insurance by raising the average private coinsurance rate from 0.33 to 0.50 or 0.67. The gross welfare gain from reduced price distortion and the gross welfare loss from increased risk bearing are calculated separately and compared. Estimates are provided for a wide range of parameter values; the most likely values imply a gain equal to nearly one-third of private hospital care expenditure. Only if the demand for care is quite sensitive to the level of resource inputs per day and to the price of care while the price of care is quite unresponsive to the average level of insurance would the welfare loss of additional risk bearing due to an increase in the coinsurance rate outweigh the welfare gains of reduced price distortion.

Chapter 7 examines the magnitude of the tax subsidy that results from excluding employer health insurance premiums from taxable income and from allowing a deduction for some of the individual payments for health insurance. The analysis uses data on the average employer contribution for health insurance in thirty-two separate industries, on the distribution of earnings by industry, and on new estimates of the relation of family taxable income to the earnings of the primary earner in the family. The calculations imply a 1969 tax subsidy of $2.0 billion on insurance premiums of $15.7 billion. Most of this tax saving accrues to middle- and upper-income families, with the saving per family rising rapidly with income because of higher marginal tax rates and greater average employer payments to health insurance. More recent estimates indicate that the tax subsidy for 1978 is likely to exceed $10 billion on insurance premiums of approximately $42 billion.

Chapter 8 examines how the tax subsidy distorts the demand for health insurance. Although the analysis is more complex than in other chapters, the underlying idea is simple. A formal model of household demand for insurance — reflecting the protection provided, the distortion in demand, and the net premium — is used to simulate the effect of tax subsidies on a typical individual's chosen insurance coverage. The analysis shows, for example, that with no tax subsidy a family with moderate risk aversion and moderate price elasticity would choose to pay 80 percent of its bills while a marginal tax rate of 40 percent would cut that family's optimal coinsurance rate in half. Calculations are presented for a variety of tax rates, and aggregate effects are derived. A further analysis compares four alternative insurance plans (with different deductibles and coinsurance rates) and shows how quite small tax subsidies can shift the family's preferred insurance from relatively high deductibles and coinsurance rates to the low deductible and low copayment policies that are now most common. Since the marginal tax rates for 1970 used in these calculations are low in comparison to current rates, the analysis of this chapter is likely to understate the effect of the tax subsidy on the demand for insurance.

6   The Welfare Loss of Excess
Health Insurance

This chapter will show that American families are in general overinsured against health expenses. If insurance coverage were reduced, the utility loss from increased risk would be more than outweighed by the gain due to lower costs and the reduced purchase of excess care. Moreover, the estimated net gain from even a one-third reduction in insurance is quite large, probably exceeding several billion dollars per year.

The economics of health insurance is of particular importance today. Health insurance has become a major issue of public policy. Some form of national health insurance is very likely to be enacted within the next few years. Government health insurance payments under Medicare and Medicaid already exceed $8 billion. Private health insurance, encouraged by favorable tax treatment, has increased rapidly; premiums in 1970 exceeded $17 billion. Private insurance and government programs together accounted for over 59 percent of personal health expenditures and nearly 87 percent of hospital bills.

Too much health insurance can actually reduce welfare. At first this seems contrary to much of the recent literature on the economics of insurance.[1] It is well known that if certain conditions are satisfied, it is optimal for individuals to insure completely against all uncertain expenses. Moreover, these personally optimal decisions are also Pareto optimal for the community as a whole by extension of the usual welfare analysis to Arrow-Debreu contingent commodities (Arrow 1964).

Reprinted from the *Journal of Political Economy* 81, no. 2 (March-April 1973), pp. 251–280, by permission of the University of Chicago Press. Copyright © 1973 by the University of Chicago.

1. See, for example, Arrow (1963, 1965), Pashigian, Schkade, and Menefee (1966), Borch (1968), Mossin (1968), Smith (1968), and Gould (1969).

For health care, however, the usually assumed conditions are not satisfied. In particular, the level of expenditure on health care is not a purely exogenous random variable. Even if the occurrence of illness is beyond the individual's control, his demand for care (given any illness) is to some extent a discretionary decision. Insurance against expenditure for health services therefore increases the consumption of those services unless demand is completely price inelastic. This destroys the optimality of complete insurance. The welfare loss due to the distortion of demand must be balanced against the welfare gain of risk spreading. The individual's optimal insurance policy therefore involves some degree of risk sharing or "coinsurance."[2]

Health insurance also introduces a quite different distortion because of the special character of the health-care market. The price and type of health services available to any individual reflect the extent of health insurance among other members of the community. Physicians raise their fees (and may improve their services) when insurance becomes more extensive (M. Feldstein 1970c). Nonprofit hospitals also respond to the growth of insurance by increasing the sophistication and price of their product (chapter 3). Thus even the uninsured individual will find that his expenditure on health services is affected by the insurance of others. Moreover, the higher price of physician and hospital services encourages more extensive use of insurance. For the community as a whole, therefore, the spread of insurance causes higher prices and more sophisticated services, which in turn cause a further increase in insurance. People spend more on health because they are insured and buy more insurance because of the high cost of health care.[3]

The purpose of this chapter is to analyze the economics of health insurance in greater detail and to provide estimates of the relevant magnitudes. The first two sections develop a more specific analysis of the demand for health insurance and its dependence on the price of health services; the third shows how insurance raises the price of hospital care; and the fourth, derives specific estimates of the potential

2. This point was made by Pauly (1968) in a comment on Arrow (1963). The basic problem has long been referred to in the insurance literature as "moral hazard." The welfare loss due to price distortion has received extensive analysis in relation to taxes and public pricing (for example, Hotelling 1938; Harberger 1964). This reason for a deductible or coinsurance is of course quite different from the case considered by Arrow (1963), Pashigian, Schkade, and Menefee (1966), and Smith (1968) in which risk is truly random but the insurance company does not sell actuarially fair policies.

3. Richard Rosett has called my attention to the similarity of this situation to the prisoners' dilemma problem.

welfare gain from reduced price distortion and the potential welfare loss from reduced risk avoidance. The last section summarizes the analysis and suggests a way out of the current dilemma.

The Demand for Health Insurance

The demand for insurance is not like the demand for most goods and services. Health insurance is purchased not as a final consumption good but as a means of paying for the future stochastic purchases of health services. The influences of both price and income are therefore different from their usual roles in demand analysis. A number of special institutional features must also be taken into account in analyzing the demand for health insurance.

Before one can discuss the determinants of demand in detail, a measure of the quantity of insurance that an individual purchases must be provided. Actual insurance policies are characterized by a complex mixture of coinsurance rates, deductibles, exclusions, ceilings, and special schedules. To reduce this to a single parametric measure of the quantity of insurance, I shall assume that an insured person pays a fixed fraction of all health expenditures with that fraction depending on the insurance policy chosen. In insurance terminology this is equal to the coinsurance rate. A useful simple measure of the quantity of insurance is the inverse of the average coinsurance rate in the population; this varies from one in the absence of insurance to infinity when there is complete insurance.

Consider now the role of price in determining the demand for insurance. The premium for a given quantity of insurance actually reflects two different prices: the price of insurance per se and the price of health services. The price of insurance per se can be measured by the ratio of the premium charged to the expected benefits. It reflects the administrative costs and profits of the insurance companies. The higher the ratio of premiums to benefits, the smaller the family's optimal quantity of insurance.[4] Over the past twenty years changes in the premium-benefit ratio have been small relative to changes in the total premium cost for a given quantity of insurance and have, to a substantial extent, been a reflection of the growth of group coverage. Moreover, because of the relatively high variance in family health expenditures, the insurance buyer's uncertainty about the expected

4. See Arrow (1963), Pashigian, Schkade, and Menefee (1966), Smith (1968), and Friedman (1971) for a formal analysis of this type of problem. This of course assumes that the substitution effect dominates the income effect.

benefits probably outweighs the relatively small changes in the premium-benefit ratio.

The effect of changes in the price of health services on the demand for insurance is both more important and more complex. In the likely case in which the elasticity of demand for services is between zero and minus one, an increase in the price of health services increases the total expenditure on them. This, in effect, increases the expenditure risk against which the individual insures and therefore raises the demand for insurance.[5]

Income also affects the demand for health insurance in unusual ways. For a given probability distribution of health expenses, higher income tends to make families more willing to assume risk, which in turn reduces their demand for insurance.[6] Against this must be balanced three ways in which higher income tends to raise the demand for insurance. First, families with higher incomes are likely to spend more for health services at any net price. In a sense, therefore, they have greater expenditure risk against which to insure. Moreover, insurance premiums are generally not higher for families with higher incomes. This effectively lowers the ratio of premiums to expected benefits and may even make it less than one. Second, higher-income families can benefit more from the tax rule that excludes employer payments for health insurance from taxable income. This tax treatment is often sufficient to make the net cost of the premium less than the expected value of benefits (M. Feldstein and Allison 1972). Third, low-income families have generally been eligible for medical care at public expense, even before the introduction of Medicaid. For them, the value of private insurance is substantially reduced. The net effect of income on the demand for insurance is therefore indeterminate.

Other factors influence the demand for health services and, there-

5. It is interesting to compare this relation with the usual concept of complementarity. Health insurance might be called an "expenditure complement" of health services because its demand falls when a rise in the price of health services reduces the expenditure and not merely the quantity purchased. An increase in the price of insurance per se lowers the demand for health services, not because of the usual complementarity effect, but because the resulting decrease in the quantity of insurance raises the effective price of health services at the time of illness. Alternatively, if one ignores the two facets of premium and treats the premium as the price of insurance, health insurance may behave like a Giffen good.

6. This need not be true if the utility function is not characterized by decreasing absolute risk aversion (Pratt 1964; Arrow 1965). Moreover, even this substantially simplifies the problem by considering a utility function whose only argument is net wealth. A satisfactory theory would include a measure of health as well. The effect of wealth on insurance would then depend on the way in which the two arguments of the utility function were interrelated. For an analysis of these problems and an explicit model of the choice among insurance options, see Friedman (1971). For a discussion of further complexities, see Schelling (1968).

fore, for health insurance. As chapter 3 showed, a great local availability of hospital beds increases the quantity of hospital services demanded directly as well as through a lower price. More general practitioners in an area reduce the demand for hospital care while more specialists increase it. Population density and other demographic factors also influence the demand for care.[7] Factors that raise the demand for services increase the expenditure risk and thus increase the demand for insurance. At the same time the factors that increase the use of services also have an effect that tends to reduce the demand for insurance. Recall that the households' optimal quantity of insurance reflects a balancing of the gain from additional risk spreading against the loss of consuming additional care whose value is less than its actuarial cost. Factors that increase the use of services for example, the availability of hospital beds, lower the value of the marginal unit of care and thus reduce the optimal quantity of insurance.

The most important institutional feature of the health insurance market is that most insurance is purchased by groups rather than by individuals. The most common type of group is the employees of a firm or the associated labor union. Such groups are much more common in manufacturing and government services than in industries such as agriculture, retail distribution, and construction. The purchase of health insurance is often compulsory or highly subsidized for members of such groups. An individual's type of employment is therefore likely to have a substantial effect on his probability of being insured. Moreover, for several reasons the quantity of insurance per insured person is also likely to be greater in group policies than in policies purchased by individuals. Groups enjoy much lower premium-benefit ratios; this reflects both economies of scale in administration and a general absence of adverse selection. The tax rule that excludes employer payments for health insurance from taxable income encourages employees to forego money income for more comprehensive insurance. It is also likely that employees assume that employer payments for health insurance do not result in a corresponding decrease in money income. This encourages the tendency of both unions and employers to provide relatively comprehensive benefits.[8]

Finally, an empirical analysis of the demand for health insurance should recognize the habitual character of the demand for insurance

7. Much less is known about the demand for physicians' services. M. Feldstein (1970c) concludes that excess demand prevails in the market for physicians' services and that the parameters of a demand function cannot be estimated. The empirical analysis of the following sections deals primarily with insurance for hospital services.

8. Their desire that these benefits be clearly visible to employees may explain the tendency to insure against relatively small expenses (including drugs and physicians' fees) while "castastrophic" expenses of very low probability are left uninsured.

services. The importance of group purchases of insurance reinforces this tendency for the frequency and quantity of insurance coverage to change slowly.[9]

Estimated Demand Equations

The previous section provides a basis for specifying an empirical demand function for hospital insurance and, in particular, for estimating the effect of the price of hospital services on the demand for insurance. The data used in the study are a cross section of time series for individual states for the years 1959–1965.[10] Comparable data on insurance coverage are not available before 1959. The introduction of Medicare and Medicaid in 1966 creates problems of the substitution of public for private insurance that cannot be studied until more disaggregated data become available.

Measurement and Specification

Two measures of the demand for hospital insurance will be used. ENR_{it} is the proportion of the population in state i in year t that is enrolled for health insurance.[11] $QINS_{it}$ is a measure of the quantity of insurance. More specifically, if the average coinsurance rate among those who are insured is denoted $COINS$,[12] the quantity of insurance is measured by

$$QINS = [(1 - ENR) + ENR \cdot COINS]^{-1} \qquad (1)$$

9. I received a copy of the interesting paper by Ehrlich and Becker (1972) too late to incorporate their insights on "self-insurance" and "self-protection" into this analysis. The extensive use of health insurance, its provision by employers and the government, and the fact that the individual's premium is generally independent of his own behavior may tend to reduce self-protection (preventive care and good health habits) and self-insurance (early treatment and the reduction of work activities that exacerbate an illness). The effect is unclear, however, because some of the self-protection and self-insurance activities in relation to expensive serious illness are actually insured (preventive care and early treatment) while others are not (good diet and reduction of work activities). A full analysis would require an extension of the Ehrlich-Becker binary event model to multiple conditional risks.

10. Because of the special character of the Washington, D.C., area, a composite unit of Washington, Virginia, and Maryland was created.

11. Each enrollment proportion was actually adjusted for the age-sex composition of the state's population by dividing the raw enrollment proportion by an age index number. This index number is a weighted average of the proportions of the state population in eight age-sex groups, weighting by the relative national insurance coverage rates in those groups.

12. This variable is thus different from *INS* as used in M. Feldstein (1970c) and chapter 3; it does not reflect the price paid by uninsured patients.

This implies that if the entire population were insured $(ENR = 1)$, the value of $QINS$ would equal the inverse of the coinsurance rate. More generally, $\partial QINS/\partial ENR > 0$ and $\partial QINS/\partial COINS < 0$.

Although the proportions of the population in each state and year who have insurance are available (Health Insurance Institute 1959–1968), the corresponding values of $COINS$ are not. Because of the data limitations, it was necessary to assume that $COINS$ varied from year to year but not from state to state. The annual values of $COINS$ were calculated by a method similar to that described in chapter 3.[13]

The price of insurance services *(PINS)* was estimated for each state and year as the ratio of total health insurance premiums to benefits. Because the premium-benefit ratio is lower for hospital insurance than for other forms of health insurance, $PINS$ overestimates the true value in a way that varies among observations depending on their mix of insurance coverage. Separate state data for hospital insurance benefits and premiums are not available. A regression of $PINS$ on the mix of health insurance proportions (hospital, medical, and surgical) was therefore used to derive an adjusted premium-benefit ratio *(PINSA)*.

The price of hospital care *(PCARE)* was measured by the average cost per patient-day in short-term general hospitals (American Hospital Association 1959–1965) deflated by the consumer price index for that year.

Two measures of the state's income distribution were studied. The first is the mean per capita income deflated by the annual value of the consumer price index; this is denoted *INC*. The second measure is an attempt to derive a single variable summary of the state's income distribution that is more relevant to the demand for insurance. It is essentially a weighted average of the household incomes in the state, weighting each income by an estimate of the national proportion of persons with that income who are insured. A more specific description of this variable, denoted *INSINC*, is given in the appendix to this chapter.

The impact of other factors that affect hospital use was taken into account in a way that utilizes the information found in chapter 3. It was shown there that the number of patient-days demanded *(PDD)* can be represented by a function of the form[14]

$$PDD = k\ PCARE^{\eta 1}\ INS^{-\eta 1}\ INC^{\eta 2} \prod_{j>2} X_j^{\eta j}, \qquad (2)$$

13. The current estimates represent a slight improvement because three years of survey data were employed, and relative utilization rates were related to the changing relative prices. The survey data are from Andersen and Anderson (1967).

14. See 12.

where *INS* measures the effect of both private insurance and other programs that reduce the price of care to uninsured persons and the X_j's include demographic factors, availability, and the like.

The constraint that the coefficients of *PCARE* and *INS* are of equal absolute value implies that patients' demand responds to the net price that they pay. The effect on demand of the X_j's is therefore proportional to $PDD \cdot (PCARE/INS)^{-\eta_1} INC^{-\eta_2}$. This composite term, calculated using the estimated values $\hat{\eta}_1 = -0.67$ and $\hat{\eta}_2 = 0.29$ from the previous demand study, will be referred to as *USEX*.

The employment variable used to represent the effect of group purchase was defined as the proportion of employees in the state who worked in manufacturing or government services. It will be denoted *GROUP*.

Finally, the habitual nature of insurance demand has been represented by a proportional adjustment model. For the enrollment equation this specification is

$$\frac{ENR_{it}}{ENR_{i,t-1}} = \left(\frac{ENR_{it}^*}{ENR_{i,t-1}}\right)^\lambda, \tag{3}$$

where ENR_{it}^*, the long-run equilibirum enrollment proportion corresponding to the current values of the explanatory variables, is defined by the relation (using lowercase symbols to represent the logarithms of the corresponding uppercase variables):

$$enr^* = \beta_0 + \beta_1(pins) + \beta_2(pcare) + \beta_3(inc) \\ + \beta_4(usex) + \beta_5 \, group. \tag{4}$$

Although it would in principle have been desirable to examine more general lag structures to represent habitual behavior,[15] the short time series available for each state contains too little information to be useful for this.

The final estimation equations for *ENR* and *QINS* are thus of the form

$$enr_{it} = \lambda\beta_0 + \lambda\beta_1(pins_{it}) + \lambda\beta_2(pcare_{it}) + \lambda\beta_3(inc_{it}) \\ + \lambda\beta_4(usex_{it}) + \lambda\beta_5(group_{it}) + (1-\lambda)enr_{i,t-1} \tag{5}$$

Estimation

Equation (5) is part of a complete model of the health-care sector.[16] The explanatory variables *pins*, *pcare*, and *usex* are endogenous. The

---

15. See Houthakker and Taylor (1966) for a variety of habit-adjustment equations.

16. For an earlier discussion of this project and estimates of other parts of the model, see M. Feldstein (1968, 1971a) and chapter 3.

equation was estimated by an instrumental variable procedure that yields consistent parameter estimates. More specifically, the set of instruments contains the current and lagged exogenous variables of the equation (*group* and *inc*) as well as exogenous variables from other equations of the model. A full two-stage least-squares estimator could not be used because the complete model has not yet been fully specified.

Although a separate constant term for each state is not included, the lagged dependent variable is treated as endogenous; that is, it is not included in the instrument set. This maintains the consistency of the parameter estimates even if the disturbances contain a systematic "state effect" or are otherwise serially correlated.[17]

Parameter Estimates

Table 6.1 presents parameter estimates for both the proportional enrollment *(ENR)* and quantity of insurance *(QINS)* equations. The estimates show that despite the offsetting factors that influence the effect of each variable, most of the variables identified in the previous section have a determinate impact.

The most important of the coefficients for this general analysis is the elasticity with respect to the price of care. The estimated values indicate a substantial and significant positive elasticity of both *QINS* and *ENR* with respect to *PCARE*. A rise in the price of hospital services causes an increase in the proportion enrolled and in the total quantity of insurance. The effect of increased expenditure risk thus more than outweighs the tendency to purchase less care (and therefore less insurance) as price rises.

The coefficients of *USEX,* the variable that measures the "location of the demand curve" (the total effect of the factors other than *PCARE* and insurance that influence the quantity of hospital care demanded), are significantly positive and, in the *QINS* equation, approximately equal to the coefficients of *PCARE*. This supports the hypothesis that the demand for insurance reflects the expenditure risk, that is, that *QINS* responds to changes in the product of price and quantity.[18] More generally, this positive elasticity indicates that a rise in any of the factors that increases the demand for hospital care (for example, the relative number of medical specialists in the area)

---

17. See Balestra and Nerlove (1966).

18. Exact equality is not to be expected because higher price would reduce the demand for care (and therefore insurance) and higher *USEX* would, by reducing the marginal value of additional care, reduce the demand for insurance. It is a coincidence that both of these reductions are approximately equal.

Table 6.1. Insurance demand equations

Equation	Dependent variable	PCARE	USEX	PINSA	GROUP	INC	INSINC	Lagged dependent variable	R^2	SE
1	QINS	0.388	0.383	-0.093	0.265	-0.021	–	0.680	0.867	0.076
		(0.094)	(0.146)	(0.202)	(0.113)	(0.077)		(0.167)		
		[1.213]	[1.197]	[-0.291]	[0.828]	[-0.066]				
2	QINS	0.353	0.359	-0.100	0.250	–	-0.015	0.699	0.877	0.073
		(0.088)	(0.140)	(0.200)	(0.110)		(0.129)	(0.164)		
		[1.173]	[1.193]	[-0.332]	[0.831]		[-0.049]			
3	ENR	0.062	0.073	-0.057	0.060	-0.011	–	0.870	0.96	0.034
		(0.035)	(0.049)	(0.085)	(0.041)	(0.034)		(0.063)		
		[0.477]	[0.561]	[-0.438]	[0.462]	[-0.085]				
4	ENR	0.062	0.071	-0.055	0.058	–	-0.020	0.873	0.96	0.034
		(0.035)	(0.051)	(0.084)	(0.045)		(0.067)	(0.070)		
		[0.488]	[0.559]	[-0.433]	[0.620]		[-0.157]			

Note: Standard errors are shown in parentheses. Long-run elasticities are shown immediately below the standard errors in square brackets. All variables are logarithms. The constant term for each equation is not shown. Estimates are for 1960–1965. Estimation is by instrumental variables. The R^2 must therefore be interpreted with caution. The final column presents the estimated standard error of the regression.

causes an increase in insurance and thus in the price of care.[19]

The coefficients of the adjusted price of insurance *(PINSA)* have the expected sign but are insignificant. Using the unadjusted variable *(PINS)* also yields insignificant coefficients. The reason for this is not clear. It may well be that most of the variation in the ratio of premiums to benefits is due to differences in the extent of group coverage and to differences in the relative importance of service benefit contracts (the Blue Cross type) and indemnity contracts (offered by commercial insurers).

The *GROUP* variable is significantly positive, showing that the premium and tax advantages associated with group coverage do increase the demand for insurance. Both measures of the income effect are insignificant in the *ENR* and *QINS* equations. This probably reflects the balancing of positive and negative income effects. It is not incompatible with the survey evidence[20] that higher-income families are more likely to be insured since the *INC* and *INSINC* coefficients show the net effect of income after the effect of the type of employment *(GROUP)* and the local price and use of care are taken into account; all three of these variables are positively correlated with income.

The lagged dependent variables show that the demand for insurance adjusts quite slowly to changes in the explanatory variables. As might be expected, enrollment adjusts even more slowly than the quantity of insurance. The long-run elasticities are approximately six times the short-run elasticities in the *ENR* equations and three times the short-run elasticities in the *QINS* equations.

The Interdependence between Insurance and the Price of Care

The previous section established the important impact of the price of care on the demand for insurance. We continue our analysis of this interdependent relation by examining the effect of insurance on the price of care.

The effect of insurance on the price of hospital care has been studied in some detail in chapter 3.[21] The mechanism by which increased insurance raises the price of hospital care is summarized briefly by figure 6.1.

---

19. This is in addition to its direct effect (through increasing the equilibrating price with a fixed quantity of insurance) as discussed in chapter 3.

20. See the appendix to this chapter.

21. Although this section discusses only hospital prices and insurance, the same general point applies to physicians' services. M. Feldstein (1970c) discusses the effect of insurance on the price of physicians' services.

Figure 6.1

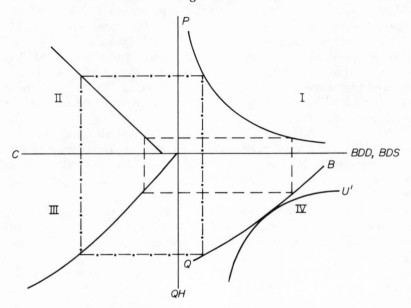

Quadrant I shows the number of bed-days of care demanded *(BDD)* as a function of the price per patient-day charged by the hospital *(P)* when the quantity of insurance is fixed. Since the hospital is a nonprofit organization,[22] this price is equal to the average cost per patient-day *(C)* minus whatever deficit the hospital can incur because of charitable contributions and income from endowments.[23] This is shown in the second quadrant. The cost that a hospital can incur per patient-day determines the staff and facilities that it can employ. The hospital's decision makers select the input mix that maximizes the quality of care as they perceive it.[24] This relation between cost and quality as perceived by the hospital *(QH)* is shown in the third quadrant. Finally, quadrant IV shows the set of feasible combinations of patient-days *(BDD)* and quality *(QH)*. The curve *QB* that bounds this set is, in effect, an opportunity locus or "budget constraint" for the

22. The analysis would have to be modified to deal with municipal hospitals and the small number of proprietary hospitals. The market is dominated, however, by the nonprofit institutions.

23. Deficits (and surpluses) are generally small and are here considered exogenous except in the very short run.

24. This is the quality of care *as perceived by the hospital*. It need not have a comparable effect on patients' health or their perception of quality.

hospital's long-run planning. The hospital selects its quantity and quality of services subject to this constraint. The chosen point on the opportunity locus reflects the particular preferences of the hospital decision makers, represented here by the indifference curve U'.[25]

An increase in insurance raises the demand curve for hospital services to a curve such as $D'D'$ in figure 6.2. At every price charged by the hospital, the net price paid by the patient is lowered by the increase in insurance, and the quantity demanded is therefore increased. This shift of the demand curve has the effect of shifting the QB opportunity locus further away from the origin (to $Q'B'$), permitting an increase in both quantity and quality. If both quantity and quality are "normal goods" in the preferences of the hospital, an increase in insurance raises both the price of care and the quantity provided. Note that this response does not depend on the usual mechanism by which increased demand raises price through higher profits and higher input costs. It is primarily by inducing a change in the hospital's product that insurance raises its price.[26]

Figure 6.2

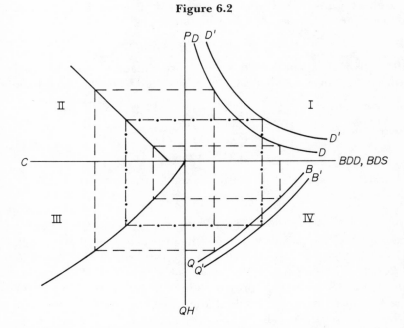

25. See chapter 3 for a number of clarifications and qualifications of this analysis. See also Klarman (1969b) and M. Feldstein (1971b).

26. See M. Feldstein (1971b) for a discussion of the effect on the wages of hospital employees.

Figures 6.3a and 6.3b combine this relation of price as a function of insurance (the *PP* curve) with the relation of insurance as a function of price (the *II* curve) discussed in the previous two sections. Recall that the measure of the quantity of insurance, *QINS* as defined by equation (1), can range between one for no insurance and infinity for complete insurance. In figure 6.3a the equilibrium elasticity of price with respect to insurance is less than the inverse of the elasticity of insurance with respect to price. The opposite is true in figure 6.3b. In both cases the level of price that prevails in equilibrium exceeds the price that would have prevailed if there had been no insurance.

Other properties of the system, including its dynamic stability and the qualitative effects on *P* and *I* of shifts in either of the functions, depend on a more precise specification. The dynamic version of the *II* curve that was estimated in the last section can be summarized as (ignoring the state subscript and using *x* to denote all the other variables)

$$quins_t = \lambda\epsilon_1 x_t + \lambda\epsilon_2\, pcare_t + (1 - \lambda)\, quins_{t-1}. \qquad (6)$$

The effect of insurance on price, described by figure 6.2 and estimated in chapter 3, can be similarly summarized as[27]

$$pcare_t = \mu\epsilon_3 z_t + \mu\epsilon_4 quins_t + (1 - \mu)\, pcare_{t-1}. \qquad (7)$$

After this pair of simultaneous difference equations has been solved, the dynamics of this system can be represented by the reduced form

$$
\begin{bmatrix} qins \\ pcare \end{bmatrix}_t = \frac{1}{(1 - \lambda\mu\epsilon_2\epsilon_4)}\begin{bmatrix} (1 - \lambda) & (1 - \mu)\lambda\epsilon_2 \\ (1 - \lambda)\mu\epsilon_4 & (1 - \mu) \end{bmatrix}\begin{bmatrix} qins \\ pcare \end{bmatrix}_{t-1}
$$
$$
+ \frac{1}{1 - \lambda\mu\epsilon_2\epsilon_4}\begin{bmatrix} \lambda\epsilon_1 & \lambda\mu\epsilon_2\epsilon_3 \\ \mu\epsilon_3 & \lambda\mu\epsilon_1\epsilon_4 \end{bmatrix}\begin{bmatrix} x \\ z \end{bmatrix}_t. \qquad (8)
$$

It is easy to prove that this system is stable if and only if

$$(1 - \lambda\mu\epsilon_2\epsilon_4)\,(1 - \lambda\mu) < 1.$$

Since the adjustment rate coefficients (λ and μ) are both between zero and one, this inequality is satisfied if the product of the short-run elasticity of *QINS* with respect to *PCARE* ($\lambda\epsilon_2$) and the shortrun elasticity of *PCARE* with respect to *QINS* ($\mu\epsilon_4$) is less than one. The estimated values of the former ($\lambda\epsilon_2$), presented in table 6.1, were 0.35 and 0.39. The system is therefore stable if the short-run elasticity of *PCARE* with respect to *QINS* is also less than one. To see that this inequality is satisfied, consider first the long-run elasticity of *PCARE* with respect

27. This simplifies the relation by combining all other variables in z_t and by ignoring the difference between *INS* and *QINS*. See note 12 and chapter 3.

Figure 6.3

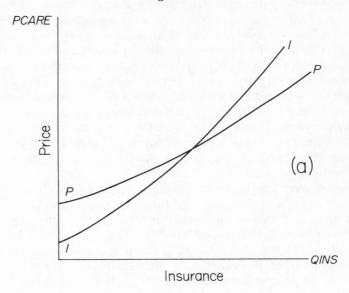

(a)

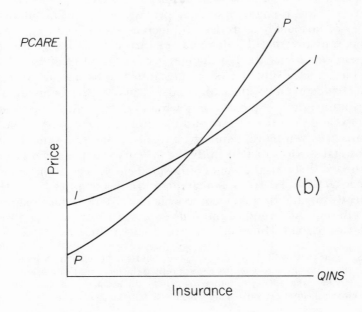

(b)

to $QINS$. This reflects both the elasticity of demand with respect to insurance and the extent to which hospitals increase the number of beds when the opportunity locus (QB in figure 6.1) shifts. The maximum value of the elasticity occurs when (1) the demand for hospital care depends only on the net price paid by patients (which is the product of $PCARE$ and the coinsurance rate for insured persons), (2) all persons are insured, and (3) hospitals do not increase the bed supply in response to an increase in insurance. In this case the elasticity of $PCARE$ with respect to $QINS$ is one; such a price increase keeps the net price constant and therefore prevents any excess demand or supply with the constant number of beds. Dropping any of the three assumptions implies a lower elasticity. Moreover, this is a long-run elasticity; the relevant short-run elasticity ($\mu\epsilon^4$) is necessarily lower. The system is therefore stable.

The qualitative properties of the response of equilibrium $PCARE$ and $QINS$ to shifts of the II and PP functions depend on the relative magnitudes of the long-run elasticities of $QINS$ with respect to $PCARE$ and $PCARE$ with respect to $QINS$. Equations (6) and (7) imply that figure 6.3a is relevant if $\epsilon_2\epsilon_4 < 1$, that is, if the long-run elasticity of $QINS$ with respect to $PCARE$ is less than the inverse of the long-run elasticity of $PCARE$ with respect to $QINS$. Table 6.1 shows that the estimated value of the former (ϵ_2) is approximately 1.2.[28] The maximum value of ϵ_4 is one, but the most likely value is substantially less. For example, since not all persons are insured, a decrease in the coinsurance rate raises demand less than proportionately. The increased number of hospital beds as demand increases also lowers ϵ_4. Finally, there is evidence that the demand for care may be less sensitive to changes in insurance than to changes in the gross price of care. These three factors are likely to make ϵ_4 substantially less than one. In figure 6.3a a change in any of the exogenous factors that raises the demand for insurance shifts the II curve down and to the right. The effect of this is to raise the price of care and therefore to increase the quantity of insurance even more. Similarly, any factor that raises the demand for hospital services or that shifts the PP curve up for any other reason (such as a rise in the wages of hospital employees) induces an increase in $QINS$ and therefore magnifies the effect on price.

Precise estimates of the extent to which interdependence magnifies these effects would require the full reduced-form equations for the health-care system. However, a useful approximation can be obtained

28. Since the stability of the system actually depends on the relation between $PCARE$ and INS (the ratio of price to net price which reflects the fact that the uninsured generally pay less than the full price) rather than $QINS$, the estimated value of ϵ_2 exceeds the relevant elasticity. This makes it more likely that figure 6.3a is appropriate.

on the basis of this analysis. Equation (8) implies that the equilibrium reduced-form *PCARE* equation is

$$pcare = \frac{\epsilon_3}{1 - \epsilon_2\epsilon_4}z + \frac{\epsilon_1\epsilon_4}{1 - \epsilon_2\epsilon_4}x. \tag{9}$$

If a rise in *PCARE* did not induce an increase in insurance ($\epsilon_2 = 0$), then a 1 percent increase in z would cause *PCARE* to rise ϵ_3 percent. The interdependence of price and insurance causes *PCARE* to rise by $\epsilon_3/(1 - \epsilon_2\epsilon_4)$ percent. Even an estimate of $\epsilon_2\epsilon_4$ as low as 0.25 implies that the interdependence increases the price "multipliers," (the equilibrium reduced-form coefficients of the price equation) by more than 30 percent. A more likely value of $\epsilon_2\epsilon_4 > 0.5$ implies that these multipliers are more than doubled.

Finally note that equation (9) implies that the interdependence of price and insurance raises the level of hospital prices directly (by way of the term $\epsilon_4\epsilon_1 x > 0$) as well as by increasing the price multipliers.

The Welfare Effects of Reducing Insurance

This section derives a number of alternative estimates of the net welfare effect of reductions in the general level of health insurance. The welfare of a typical household would be lowered by its increased risk bearing, but it would also be raised by the reduced distortion of prices (the artifically low price to patients and the inflated gross cost of care). To simplify the calculation of the net welfare effect, the gross gain from reduced price distortion is calculated first without regard to the uncertainty of expenditure, and then the gross loss of increased risk bearing is calculated. The analysis shows that the net effect of reduced insurance would most probably be a substantial gain.

The Gross Gain from Reduced Price Distortion
It is clearest to begin by deriving an explicit measure of the welfare loss due to price distortion at the current level of health insurance. The gain from partial reductions of the insurance can then be calculated.[29]

---

29. See Harberger (1964, 1971) for an explanation and defense of the types of assumption implicit in this analysis. It is assumed in particular that the demand curves, which reflect the individual's preferences and his physician's advice, are appropriate valuations of hospital care. Although health care has often been referred to as a merit good, with the implication that demand curves undervalue care, there is evidence that, even in the absence of insurance, patients would demand too much medical care because of a combination of uncertainty, fear, faith in science, and the advice of self-interested physicians. See Dubos (1959) for some important insights on this issue.

Figure 6.4

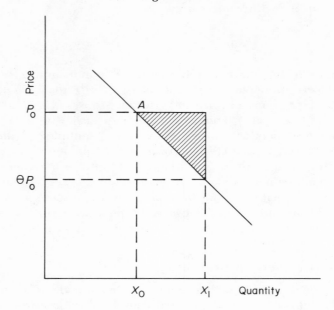

The welfare loss due to price distortion is similar to the excess burden of an excise tax. However, the effect of insurance on the price and quality of care makes the analysis more complex. If we ignore these complexities, the calculation of the welfare loss is illustrated by figure 6.4. Point A identifies the equilibrium in the absence of insurance. Price P_0 is charged by hospitals and paid by patients; the quantity (patient-days) consumed is X_0. Insurance lowers the net price to ΘP_0 and increases the quantity to X_1.[30] The welfare loss is the shaded area, $\frac{1}{2}(P_0 - \Theta P_0)(X_1 - X_0)$, representing the difference between the cost of the additional care $[P_0(X_1 - X_0)]$ and its value to consumers $[\frac{1}{2}(X_1 - X_0)(P_0 + \Theta P_0)]$. A simple expression for the loss in terms of the elasticity of demand with respect to net price (η) and the total cost in the absence of insurance (P_0X_0) can be derived as[31]

$$L = -\frac{1}{2}P_0(1 - \Theta)\frac{dX}{d\Theta P}P_0(1 - \Theta) = \frac{1}{2}\eta(1 - \Theta)^2 P_0X_0. \quad (10)$$

30. Thus θ is the coinsurance rate and $QINS = \theta^{-1}$.

31. Pauly has called my attention to an earlier paper of his (pauly 1969a) in which an equation similar to (10) was used to estimate the gross welfare cost of health insurance. That analysis did not consider either the effects of insurance on the price of care or the risk-reduction value of the insurance.

This analysis exaggerates the loss due to the increased quantity of patient-days of care consumed. Because insurance raises the gross price per patient-day, the demand does not increase as much as it would if the gross price remained P_0. The resulting change in the quality of care may, however, shift the demand curve and partly offset the higher price. Moreover, the increased quality in itself also reduces the welfare loss. This more general analysis is shown in figure 6.5.

Figure 6.5

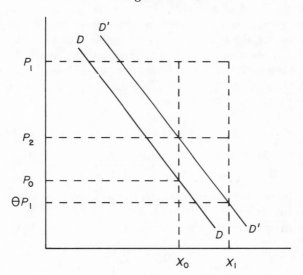

Before the introduction of insurance the price is P_0 and the quantity is X_0. The introduction of insurance raises the equilibrium gross price to P_1 while the net price falls to ΘP_1. The increased gross price (cost) per patient-day provides a service that is of higher quality as perceived by the hospital. If it is also of higher quality as perceived by the patients, the demand curve shifts upward. In figure 6.5 the demand curve shifts from DD to $D'D'$. The price that patients would pay for the original number of patient-days (X_0) of the new and higher-quality product is P_2. At the price ΘP_1 the equilibrium quantity is X_1.

The shift to the postinsurance equilibrium implies an extra cost of $(P_1 - P_0)X_0 + P_1(X_1 - X_0)$. The extra benefit of this shift is

$$(P_2 - P_0)X_0 + [\Theta P_1 + \frac{1}{2}(P_2 - \Theta P_1)](X_1 - X_0).$$

The welfare loss is therefore[32]

$$L = (P_1 - P_2)X_0 + [P_1(1 - \Theta) - \tfrac{1}{2}(P_2 - \Theta P_1)](X_1 - X_0). \quad (11)$$

To derive a parametric expression suitable for calculating the welfare loss associated with different values of Θ, we introduce the following notation: let $\Pi = P_1/P_0$ measure the gross price change resulting from the introduction of insurance and let $\alpha = (P_2 - P_0)/(P_1 - P_0)$ reflect the increase in quality as perceived by patients and as measured by the change in their willingness to pay for the original quantity of patient-days relative to the change in cost. It is clear from the analysis of the third section that $\Pi > 1$ and $\alpha \gtreqless 1$. Moreover, the small increase in patient-days that has accompanied the great growth of insurance during the last two decades implies that the relevant values of Π and α are such that the change in quantity is relatively small even when Θ becomes relatively low. Using the price elasticity $\eta = (dX/d\Theta P)$ $(\Theta P/X)$ evaluated at P_2 and the fact that $(X_1 - X_0) = -(P_2 - \Theta P_1)$ $(\partial X/\partial \Theta P)$, we can rewrite equation (11)

$$L = \left\{ (1 - \alpha)(\Pi - 1) + \frac{\tfrac{1}{2}|\eta|}{2}[\Pi(1 - \Theta) + (1 - \alpha)(\Pi - 1)] \right.$$
$$\left. \times \left[\frac{1 + \alpha(\Pi - 1) - \Theta\Pi}{1 + \alpha(\Pi - 1)} \right] \right\} P_0 X_0. \quad (12)$$

This expresses the loss in terms of the unknown expenditure in the absence of insurance $P_0 X_0$. It will be convenient to replace $P_0 X_0$ by an expression in terms of the current actual expenditure, $P_a X_a$:

$$P_a X_a = \Pi_a \left[1 - \eta + \frac{\Theta_a \Pi_a \eta}{1 + \alpha(\Pi_a - 1)} \right] P_0 X_0, \quad (13)$$

where the subscript a on Π and Θ indicates that these are the current actual values. Although Π_a is uncertain, using equations (12) and (13) permits making a consistent assumption about the relation of Π and Θ.

To evaluate the potential gain from reduced insurance coverage, we now compare the loss associated with the current value of $\Theta = 0.33$ to the losses with higher coinsurance rates of $\Theta = 0.50$ and 0.67.[33] To assess the sensitivity of these estimates to the assumption about the

32. This calculation assumes that the demand function is linear.

33. In 1969 private insurance paid 70 percent of the private expenditure for hospital care. Raising the coinsurance rate is probably a suboptimal way of reducing insurance coverage. A greater net welfare gain could be achieved by the use of deductibles, varying coinsurance rates, and payments that are disease specific (see Zeckhauser 1970, Pauly 1971, and chapter 9).

behavioral parameters (η, α, and Π), the calculations are presented for several values of each of these parameters. The price elasticity of demand takes the conservative values $|\eta| = 0.4$ and $|\eta| = 0.8$.[34] The demand shift parameter, α, is assigned values over the very wide range: 0, 0.33, and 0.67. The value of Π, that is, the ratio of gross price with insurance to gross price without insurance, exceeds one and varies inversely with the coinsurance rate Θ. In the special case in which gross price varies so as to keep net price constant,[35] $\Pi = \Theta^{-1}$. A more conservative estimate of the sensitivity of the welfare loss to the extent of insurance is also calculated by using $\Pi = \Theta^{-1/2}$. If the value of Π is written $\Theta^{-\beta}$, there are twelve combinations of η, α, and β for which the welfare comparisons have been calculated.

The results are presented in table 6.2. The dollar losses are based on 1969 private expenditure for hospital services $(P_a X_a)$ of $12.6 billion.[36] There is a substantial gross welfare loss, between $2.4 billion and $3.7 billion, even if $\alpha = 0.67$. For $\alpha = 0.33$ the loss is larger: between $4 billion and $6 billion, depending on the particular values of η and β.

The final columns of table 6.2 show the gain from raising Θ from its current value of 0.33 to values of 0.50 and 0.67. Using moderate and relatively conservative values of α between 0.33 and 0.67 implies that raising the coinsurance rate to 0.50 produces a gain of between $1.2 billion and $3.4 billion. If the coinsurance is raised to 0.67, the gain is between $1.9 billion and $4.8 billion.

The Gross Loss from Increased Risk Bearing

An increase in the coinsurance rate has two effects on the household's risk. For a given probability distribution of expenditure, the risk is obviously increased. But the higher average coinsurance rate implies a lower gross price and a smaller quantity of services purchased. These reduce the risk. Although the net effect is likely to be an in-

34. The hospital demand study in chapter 3 estimated $|\eta| = 0.67$. This may be an underestimate because the higher net price observations probably correspond to higher gross price and therefore higher quality.

35. This has in fact been approximately true for the past twenty years. If net price is expressed in constant dollars, it rose by 4 percent between 1950 and 1968, from $12.20 to $12.64.

36. Total hospital expenditures in 1969 were approximately $24 billion. Federal, state, and local governments pay approximately half of these costs. Although some of this is for mental hospitals and other special long-stay programs, a substantial amount is for general hospital care. The calculations therefore understate the welfare loss by ignoring the excess cost of government programs. Moreover, only the distortive effects of private insurance are taken into account.

crease in risk bearing, this need not be so. The analysis estimates the effect on risk bearing for the different parameter combinations of η, α, and β that were considered in the preceding section. The estimated effect on risk bearing is therefore directly comparable with the price distortion effects of table 6.2.

Table 6.2. Welfare gains from reduced price distortion

$|\eta|$	α	β	Loss for θ equal to			Gain[a] from raising θ to	
			0.33	0.50 ($ millions)	0.67	0.50 ($ millions)	0.67
0.4	0.00	1.0	8,442	4,158	2,048	4,284	6,394
0.8	0.00	1.0	8,442	4,158	2,048	4,284	6,394
0.4	0.00	0.5	5,586	2,968	1,512	2,617	4,074
0.8	0.00	0.5	5,753	2,946	1,442	2,806	4,311
0.4	0.33	1.0	5,824	2,685	1,258	3,139	4,565
0.8	0.33	1.0	5,971	2,619	1,178	3,352	4,794
0.4	0.33	0.5	4,006	2,087	1,036	1,919	2,970
0.8	0.33	0.5	4,308	2,149	1,012	2,159	3,296
0.4	0.67	1.0	3,340	1,487	665	1,853	2,676
0.8	0.67	1.0	3,701	1,557	652	2,144	3,048
0.4	0.67	0.5	2,445	1,240	588	1,205	1,856
0.8	0.67	0.5	2,885	1,401	624	1,484	2,261

a. Based on 1969 private hospital expenditure of $12.6 billion.

The difference in a household's risk bearing between two different coinsurance rates can be expressed in terms of the maximum premiums that they would pay to avoid this risk. More specifically, let the expected utility of a household with income[37] Y and uncertain medical expenditure X be $E[U(Y - \tilde{X})]$.[38] An insurance policy with premium q_i and coinsurance rate Θ_i raises the expected utility to $E[U(Y - q_i - \Theta_i\tilde{X_i})]$.

The cost of risk bearing with coinsurance rate Θ_i may be defined as

37. It would in principle be preferable to use wealth (including current income) or to use a multiperiod framework. This would reduce the value of insurance for any utility function with decreasing risk aversion.

38. This ignores the problem that the utility of income may be a function of the state of health. See note 6.

the maximum premium $(q_i{}^*)$ that the household would pay to avoid the uncertain expenditure. That is, $q_i{}^*$ is defined by

$$U(Y - q_i - q_i{}^*) = E[U(Y - q_i - \Theta \tilde{X}_i)]. \tag{14}$$

In the definition of $q_i{}^*$ the uncertain expenditure is assumed to be X_i; that is, the hypothetical complete insurance is a mental experiment and does not change the actual gross expenditure. The net cost of risk bearing with coinsurance rate Θ_i may then be defined as $q_i{}^* - E(\Theta_i \tilde{X}_i)$, that is, the excess of the maximum premium over the actuarial value. The value of the loss from increased risk bearing when the coinsurance rate rises from Θ_i to Θ_j is the difference between net cost of risk bearing with Θ_j and the net cost of risk bearing with Θ_i.

$$V = q_j{}^* - q_i{}^* - E\Theta_j \tilde{X}_j + E\Theta_i \tilde{X}_i. \tag{15}$$

The utility function with constant absolute risk aversion,[39] $U(Y) = e^{-RY}$, is convenient for analyzing this problem. Substituting into equation (14) implies that $q_i{}^*$ is defined by

$$\exp\{-R(Y - q_i - q_i{}^*)\} = E[\exp\{-R(Y - q_i - \Theta_i \tilde{X}_i\}], \tag{16}$$

or

$$\exp\{Rq_i{}^*\} = E\exp\{R\Theta X_i{}^*\}. \tag{17}$$

The household's gross welfare loss (V) due to increasing the coinsurance rate from Θ_i to Θ_j therefore satisfies

$$\begin{aligned}
\exp\{RV\} &= \exp\{R(q_j{}^* - q_i{}^* - E\Theta_j \tilde{X}_j + E\Theta_i \tilde{X}_i\} \\
&= \frac{E(\exp\{R\Theta_j \tilde{X}_j\})}{E(\exp\{R\Theta_i \tilde{X}_i\})} \cdot \frac{\exp\{R\Theta_i E \tilde{X}_i\}}{\exp\{R\Theta_j E \tilde{X}_j\}}.
\end{aligned} \tag{18}$$

To calculate these expected values requires a model of the stochastic behavior of annual household expenditure for hospital care, conditional on each of the two values of the coinsurance rate. It was suggested before that the relation between the price of care, the coinsurance rate, and the price in the absence of insurance (P_0) be represented by

$$P_i = P_0(\Theta_i)^{-\beta}, \tag{19}$$

where the maximum value of β is 1 and the most likely values lie

39. The parameter R is a measure of the absolute risk aversion (Pratt 1964; Arrow 1965).

between 0.5 and 1.0. The average quantity of care, that is, the average number of patient-days per family *(D)*, is

$$E(\tilde{D}_i) = E(\tilde{D}_0)\left\{1 - \frac{\eta}{\Theta_i}[\alpha + (1-\alpha)\Theta_i^\beta - \Theta_i]\right\}, \qquad (20)$$

where D_0 is the average days of care in the absence of insurance.[40] The average expenditure is therefore

$$E(\tilde{X}_i) = [E(\tilde{D}_0)]P_0(\Theta_i)^{-\beta}\left\{1 - \frac{\eta}{\Theta_i}[\alpha + (1-\alpha)\Theta_i^\beta - \Theta_i]\right\}. \qquad (21)$$

The actual number of patient-days in a family depends on the number of times that household members are hospitalized and the duration of stay on each of these occasions. The Poisson process provides a reasonable model for the number of hospitalizations, $\tilde{N}_i$.[41] The durations of stay on these occasions, $\tilde{S}_n$, will be assumed to follow independent gamma distributions.[42]

Together these assumptions imply that

$$E(e^{R\Theta_i\tilde{X}_i}) = \sum_{N=0}^{\infty} \Pi_N \cdot Ee^{RP_i\Theta_i} \sum_{n=0}^{N} \tilde{S}_n. \qquad (22)$$

The probability of N hospitalizations is given by $\Pi_N = e^{-M_i} M_i^N/N!$ where M_i is the mean number of hospitalizations per household with coinsurance rate Θ_i. Since the durations of stay are independent,[43]

$$Ee^{RP_i\Theta_i} \sum_{n=0}^{N} \tilde{S}_n = [E(e^{RP_i\Theta_i\tilde{S}})]^N. \qquad (23)$$

The expectation on the right-hand side of equation (23) is the moment-generating function of the gamma variable $\tilde{S}$ and may therefore be written

$$E(e^{RP_i\Theta_i\tilde{S}}) = (1 - RP_i\Theta_i\gamma_i)^{\delta_i}, \qquad (24)$$

where the mean of $\tilde{S}$ equals $\gamma_i\delta_i$ and the variance of $\tilde{S}$ equals $\gamma_i^2\delta_i$. If changes in insurance alter the mean and variance but not the relative variance of the distribution (if stays are increased proportionately as they would with constant elasticity), the value of δ is not a function

40. Neither P_0 nor D_0 is actually required in the calculations that follow.

41. For previous applications of the Poisson process to hospital admissions, see N. Bailey (1957) and Rosenthal (1964). Its use in the current context ignores intrafamily and intertemporal correlations. Both are unlikely to have more than a small effect when the time interval is a year.

42. The γ distribution can provide a good approximation to the highly skewed distribution of stays. The assumption of independence is obviously reasonable for stays of different individuals. For the same individual on different occasions, independence is more likely for unrelated illness than for related illnesses.

43. Equation (22) also reflects the fact that S_0 is identically zero.

of the coinsurance rate. This assumption will be used in the analysis that follows.

Equations (24) and (22) yield

$$E(e^{RP_i\Theta_iX_i}) = \sum_{N=0}^{\infty} \frac{e^{M_i}M_i^N(1 - RP_i\Theta_i\gamma_i)^{-\delta N}}{N!} \tag{25}$$
$$= \exp\{M_i[(1 - RP_i\Theta_i\gamma_i)^{-\delta} - 1]\}.$$

The expected expenditure can be written in terms of the parameters of the stochastic process as

$$E(X_i) = P_iM_i\gamma_i\delta. \tag{26}$$

Substituting (25) and (26) into (18) and taking logarithms yields an expression for the welfare loss of increased risk bearing:[44]

$$V = R^{-1}\{M_j[(1 - RP_j\Theta_j\gamma_j)^{-\delta} - 1] - M_i[(1 - RP_i\Theta_i\gamma_i)^{-\delta} - 1]\} \tag{27}$$
$$+ \Theta_iP_iM_i\gamma_i\delta - \Theta_jP_jM_j\gamma_j\delta.$$

We need to evaluate equation (27) for Θ_i equal to the current value (0.33) and Θ_j equal to 0.50 and 0.67. The current values of P_i, M_i, γ_i, and δ can be estimated from available data. The value of P_j can be calculated from P_i with equation (19). Equation (20) permits the calculation of the product $M_j\gamma_j\delta$ (the mean number of days of hospital care if $\Theta = \Theta_j$) from the observed $M_i\gamma_i$ but does not provide separate estimates of M_j and γ_j. The elasticity of the admissions rate with respect to price is approximately twice the elasticity of the mean stay per admission with respect to price (chapter 3). The values of M_j and γ_j are therefore calculated by assuming that the proportional change in M_j is twice the proportional change in γ_j and that the product $M_j\gamma_j$ is related to $M_i\gamma_i$ in the way indicated by equation (20).[45]

Data collected by the National Center for Health Statistics (1971) indicate that the mean duration of stay in 1969 was 8.4 days.[46] An earlier survey (National Center for Health Statistics 1966b) provides the data with which to calculate the skewness parameter of the gamma distribution of stays per admission; $\delta = 0.42$.[47] The mean stay of 8.4 days then implies that $\gamma_i = 20$. The average annual number of hospi-

---

44. Recall that the risk bearing may actually decrease, making the welfare change a welfare gain.

45. More specifically, $\ln(M_j/M_i) = 2\ln(\gamma_j/\gamma_i)$.

46. This excludes persons sixty-five years old and over (who are covered by Medicare) as well as persons who died in the hospital or were patients in special long-stay institutions.

47. Recall that δ is the inverse of the relative variance of the duration of stay and is assumed to be unaffected by the coinsurance rate.

talizations depends on the family size; for a family of four persons less than sixty-five years old, $M_i = 0.47$ (National Center for Health Statistics 1971). Since there were 180 million persons under age sixty-five in 1969, the total welfare effects of increasing the coinsurance rate will be calculated by multiplying the value per family (V) by 45 million.[48] The average hospital cost per patient-day was $71 in 1969. The total cost of $12.6 billion is the product of this price ($71), the admission rate (0.47), the mean stay (8.4), and the total number of families (45 million).[49]

The only remaining parameter needed to calculate V in equation (27) is R, the coefficient of risk aversion. It is perhaps easiest to derive reasonable values of R by considering a simple bet. A man who is willing to participate in a fair bet in which there is an even chance of winning and of losing $1,000 has $R = 0$ and would place no value on insurance. If he requires a side payment of $50 to make such a bet (if he requires odds of $1,050 to $950), his risk aversion is 0.0001.[50] If he requires a side payment of $150 (if he is just indifferent between no bet and an even chance of winning $1,150 and of losing $850), his risk aversion is $R = 0.0003$. A very risk-averse individual who requires 2:1 odds in order to make the bet (a side payment of $333 so that there is an even chance of winning $1,333 and of losing $667) has a risk aversion of $R = .0007$. The calculations of the welfare loss of increased risk bearing have been done for these values of R.[51]

Table 6.3 presents the estimated welfare losses associated with increased risk bearing when Θ goes from 0.33 to 0.50 and 0.67. Separate estimates are shown for the twelve combinations of η, α, and β and for the three values of R.

For $\alpha = 0$, that is, when the change in inputs associated with higher costs per patient-day does not cause the demand curve to shift, an increase in the coinsurance rate actually decreases average expendi-

---

48. The average family actually contains fewer than four persons. The assumption of 45 million four-person families increases the risk per family and therefore the loss from increasing the coinsurance rate.

49. The $12.6 billion is very close to the estimate of $12.1 billion prepared by the Social Security Administration.

50. The value of R is found by solving the equation $U(y_0) = \frac{1}{2}U(y_0 - 1,000 + 50) + \frac{1}{2}U(y_0 + 1,000 + 50)$ or, more specifically, $\exp[-Ry_0] = \frac{1}{2} \exp[-R(y_0 - 1,000 + 50)] + \frac{1}{2} \exp[-R(y_0 + 1,000 + 50)]$. The assumption of constant absolute risk aversion implies that the initial income y_0 does not affect the value of R.

51. Perhaps intuition is aided if these absolute risk-aversion parameters are related to proportional risk-aversion parameters $(r = yu''/u')$ at a family income of $10,000. Since $r = yR$, the three values of R correspond to proportional risk aversion parameters of 1, 3, and 7. These are the implied local elasticities of the marginal utility function. This suggests that 1 and 3 are likely to be more reasonable than 7.

Table 6.3. Welfare loss from increased risk bearing

			Loss from raising θ to 0.50 ($ millions)			Loss from raising θ to 0.67 ($ millions)		
$\lvert\eta\rvert$	α	β	$R = .0001$	$R = .0003$	$R = 0.0007$	$R = .0001$	$R = .0003$	$R = .0007$
0.4	0.00	1.0	−930	−1,027	−1,346	−1,714	−1,905	−2,552
0.8	0.00	1.0	0	0	0	0	0	0
0.4	0.00	0.5	−260	−306	−459	−488	−563	−852
0.8	0.00	0.5	0	0	0	0	0	0
0.4	0.33	1.0	−378	−433	−614	−807	−919	−1,298
0.8	0.33	1.0	925	985	1,161	1,380	1,468	1,721
0.4	0.33	0.5	457	463	470	674	678	670
0.8	0.33	0.5	−1,525	1,620	1,897	2,273	2,410	2,802
0.4	0.67	1.0	57	35	−45	−135	−146	−336
0.8	0.67	1.0	1,525	1,620	1,897	2,273	2,410	2,802
0.4	0.67	0.5	956	997	1,106	1,476	1,535	1,697
0.8	0.67	0.5	2,255	2,391	2,780	3,360	3,551	4,086

Note: Based on 1969 private hospital expenditure of $12.6 billion. Negative values indicate welfare gains.

tures sufficiently to decrease overall risk bearing. A decrease in risk bearing also occurs with $\alpha = 0.33$ if the price is sufficiently sensitive to Θ (for a high value of β) and the demand is sufficiently insensitive to the lowering of price (a low value of $\lvert\eta\rvert$). Even if $\alpha = 0.67$, a sufficient increase in Θ can reduce the risk bearing.

The most likely values of $\lvert\eta\rvert$, α, and β are a low elasticity of demand with respect to both price and inputs and a high sensitivity of price with respect to Θ. These conditions tend to make an increase in Θ actually lower the amount of risk bearing. The remainder of table 6.3 shows how much risk bearing increases if these conditions are not satisfied. For risk-aversion coefficients less than $R = 0.0003$, raising Θ to 0.50 increases risk bearing by a maximum value of $2.4 billion. Raising Θ to 0.67 yields a maximum increased risk of $3.6 billion. With the much more risk-average coefficient of $R = 0.0007$, the increases reach $2.8 billion and $4.1 billion. To interpret these numbers it is necessary to compare them with the gains from reduced price distortion that were reported in table 6.2.

The Net Welfare Gain from Reducing Insurance
Table 6.4 shows the difference between the welfare gains from reduced price distortion and the welfare loss from increased risk bearing. For the more plausible values (low $\lvert\eta\rvert$ and α, high β and $R \leq$ 0.0003), the estimates indicate very large gains from reducing insur-

Table 6.4. Net welfare gain from reducing insurance

$\lvert\eta\rvert$	α	β	Loss from raising θ to 0.50 ($ millions)			Loss from raising θ to 0.67 ($ millions)		
			$R = .0001$	$R = .0003$	$R = .0007$	$R = .0001$	$R = .0003$	$R = .0007$
0.4	0.00	1.0	5,214	5,311	5,630	8,108	8,299	8,946
0.8	0.00	1.0	4,284	4,284	4,284	6,394	6,394	6,394
0.4	0.00	0.5	2,877	2,923	3,076	4,562	4,637	4,926
0.8	0.00	0.5	2,806	2,806	2,806	4,311	4,311	4,311
0.4	0.33	1.0	3,517	3,572	3,753	5,372	5,484	5,863
0.8	0.33	1.0	2,427	2,367	2,191	3,414	3,326	3,073
0.4	0.33	0.5	1,462	1,456	1,449	2,296	2,292	2,300
0.8	0.33	0.5	634	539	262	1,023	886	494
0.4	0.67	1.0	1,796	1,818	1,898	2,811	2,822	3,012
0.8	0.67	1.0	619	524	247	775	638	246
0.4	0.67	0.5	249	208	99	380	321	159
0.8	0.67	0.5	−771	−907	−1,296	−1,099	−1,290	−1,825

Note: Based on 1969 private hospital expenditure of $12.6 billion. Negative values indicate welfare losses.

ance. For $\alpha = 0$ the gains range between $4.3 billion and $8.9 billion. For $\alpha = 0.33$ the gains range between $0.5 billion and $5.9 billion, with an average value of $3.0 billion. Only with a high value of α, a high price elasticity ($\lvert\eta\rvert = 0.8$), and a low sensitivity of price to insurance ($\beta = 0.5$) do the estimates indicate a welfare loss from reduced insurance. These estimates are relatively insensitive to changes in the risk-aversion coefficient. In short, the overall analysis suggests that the current excess use of health insurance produces a very substantial welfare loss.[52]

These calculations have, of course, used the assumption that insurance pays a fixed proportion of all expenses. Although this is a convenient simplification for this analysis, it is not a fully accurate description of the typical insurance coverage. Health insurance provides virtually complete reimbursement for relatively small and moderate hospital bills but is generally quite inadequate for the small proportion of families that have very large expenses.[53] This implies that the

52. For a variety of reasons, for example, the exclusion of public insurance and non-hospital care, these values are likely to understate the true welfare loss.

53. A 1963 national survey (Andersen and Anderson 1967) found that among *insured* families with medical expenditures in the top 20 percent of the national distribution, only one-third received insurance benefits exceeding half of their expenditures while another third received benefits of less than one-fifth of their expenditures.

values of table 6.4 are underestimates of the potential welfare gains since they are based on underestimates of the current price distortion and overestimates of the current protection against risk.

The analysis and conclusions of this chapter can be summarized briefly. The first two sections specified and estimated a structural equation for the demand for health insurance. The parameter estimates indicate that an increase in the price of hospital care causes a substantial increase in the demand for insurance. The following section then examined the interrelation between the purchase of insurance and the demand and supply of hospital care. There is mutually reinforcing behavior: more insurance increases the price of care, and a higher price of care increases the demand for insurance. Although the system is dynamically stable (nonexplosive), the interdependence between insurance and the price of care implies that there is more insurance and a higher price of care than would otherwise prevail. This interdependence also increases the effect of changes in any exogenous variable on both the price of care and the level of insurance.

The final section estimates the welfare gains that would result from decreasing insurance by raising the average coinsurance rate from 0.33 to 0.50 or 0.67. The gross welfare gain from reduced price distortion and the gross welfare loss from increased risk bearing are calculated spearately and compared. Estimates are provided for a wide range of parameter values. The most likely values imply net gains in excess of $4 billion per year.[54] Even a rather conservative selection of parameter values implies net gains of approximately $2 billion to $3 billion. Only if the demand for care is quite sensitive to the level of resource inputs per day and to the price of care while the price of care is quite unresponsive to the average level of insurance would the welfare loss of additional risk bearing due to an increase in the coinsurance rate outweigh the welfare gains of reduced price distortion.

It seems reasonable to conclude that an increase in the average coinsurance rate would increase welfare and that the net gain would probably be quite substantial. Moreover, a more general restructuring of the form of health insurance, reducing its role as a method of prepaying small and moderate hospital bills, and increasing its role in protecting against the major financial risks of very large health expenses, could produce even greater gains.[55]

54. These are based on 1969 private hospital care expenditure of $12.6 billion.

55. See chapters 9 and 10 for the analysis of such a proposal to restructure health insurance.

Appendix: Measurement of State Income Distribution

This appendix describes the use of survey data to derive a single variable measure of the state's income distribution that is particularly relevant to the demand for health insurance. This variable was referred to in the text as *INSINC*.

Let the function $h(y)$ represent the probability that a household with income y is insured, and let $f(y)$ be the relative frequency distribution of incomes in a particular state. The effect of this income distribution on the proportion of households in the state that are insured may be represented by the integral $\int h(y) f(y) \, dy$, that is, the weighted average of the insurance probabilities with the income density as weights.

Values of $h(y)$, the proportions of households at each income level that are insured, were estimated in a national survey of approximately 42,000 households (National Center for Health Statistics 1967). This survey data can be well represented by a function of the form $h(y) = 1 - k e^{-ay}$; that is, as income rises, the probability of being insured tends to one. The parameters k and a can be estimated with the regression equation

$$\log[1 - h(y)] = \log k - a \, \log y, \qquad (A1)$$

using the income classes in the survey as observations The estimated values are $k = 7{,}956$ and $a = 0.6192$.

Substituting this form of $h(y)$ into the income-insurance integral yields

$$INSINC = \int (1 - k \, e^{-ay}) f(y) dy = 1 - k \int e^{-ay} f(y) \mathrm{dy}. \qquad (A2)$$

The final integral is the moment-generating function for the income distribution $f(y)$ with "dummy" parameter $-a$. Using the log-normal distribution to approximate $f(y)$ implies

$$INSINC = 1 - k(1 + \rho)^{a(a+1)/2} \bar{y}^{-a} \qquad (A3)$$

where $\bar{y}$ is the mean income in the state and ρ is the relative variance of income (the ratio of its variance to $\bar{y}^2$).

The value of ρ for the nation as a whole has, like other measures of income inequality, remained nearly constant for the period 1959–1965. As a further approximation, the value of $\rho = 0.55$ was used in practice. This implies that *INSINC* for each year and state is a function of $\bar{y}$ and the parameters k and a. The values of this variable derived from equation (A3) were used in the estimates presented in the second section of the text.

7   Tax Subsidies of Private Health Insurance: Distribution, Revenue Loss, and Effects

Nearly all of the $17.2 billion of private payments for health insurance is subsidized by special tax advantage.[1] Employer contributions for health insurance benefits are excluded from both the corporate and the personal income tax base. Individual payments for health insurance can be partly deducted from personal taxable income. Together, these involve a substantial loss of tax revenue and a significant subsidy for the purchase of insurance. The distribution of this subsidy among income classes is very unequal, with significantly greater subsidies going to higher-income families.

The current study provides a detailed analysis for 1968 and 1969, the most recent years for which data are available. The first section considers the employer contribution for health insurance benefits. A method is developed for estimating the total of employer contributions and allocating this total among income groups. The tax loss and its distribution are then estimated. The second section deals with the deduction of individual insurance premiums in the calculation of personal taxable income. The total cost of this subsidy and its distribution are estimated. The last section discusses the effect of this tax subsidy on the demand for health insurance and the market for health services.

This chapter was written with Elisabeth Allison and published in *The Economics of Federal Subsidy Programs*, pt. 8, A Compendium of Papers Submitted to the Subcommittee on Priorities and Economy in Government of the Joint Economic Committee, 93rd Congress, 2d sess. (Washington, D.C.: U.S. Government Printing Office, July 1974), pp. 977–994.

1. The $17.2 billion refers to Mueller (1972, pp. 3–19). The recent annual rate of growth suggests that by 1972 this would exceed $21 billion.

The Exclusion of Employer Premium Payments

In 1969 employers paid approximately $7.3 billion in health insurance premiums. These premiums are excluded in defining taxable income for both the personal income tax and the Social Security payroll tax. If these premiums had instead been paid to the same workers in the form of wages and salaries, the additional tax revenues would have been at least $1.63 billion. The distribution of this $1.63 billion tax saving among income classes was substantially regressive.

These conclusions are based on an estimated distribution of employers' contributions by family income.[2] This is turn depends on two separate estimates: (1) the distribution of employers' contributions by employees' earnings and (2) the distribution, within each earnings class, of total family income including spouse's earnings and other family income (interest, dividends, and rent).

Consider first the distribution of employer's contributions by employees' earnings. In estimating this distribution we have tried to avoid any assumptions that would increase the estimated total tax cost or the estimated regressivity of the premium payments. In particular, we have assumed that within each industry all employees receive the same employer contribution. The estimated differences between earnings classes in the employer contribution is therefore due solely to interindustry differences in average employer contributions and in the distribution of earnings. The effect of this is to bias the estimates toward a smaller tax loss and a less regressive distribution.[3]

Estimation of the distribution of employers' contributions by employees' income begins with a distribution of the average 1969 employer contribution in each of thirty-two industries. This is shown in table 7.1.[4] Information on the distribution of earnings in each industry[5] and the assumption that all employees in each industry receive the same benefit permit the calculation of the employers'

2. This section outlines the basic estimation method; additional detail is available in the appendix to this chapter.

3. A 1963 survey (Bureau of Labor Statistics, 1965c) showed that employer contributions were generally higher for white-collar employees. Rice (1966, p. 585) found no difference in employer contributions by size of firm within individual industries.

4. Because we assume that married women are effectively covered by their husbands' insurance, the employer contributions per employee are adjusted by the calculation to exclude married women employees. No attempt is made in the analysis to allow for the lower value of benefits to single men and women. Since they have lower than average earnings, this further underestimates both the tax cost and the regressivity.

5. The sources for this data are Bureau of Labor Statistics (1970b) and Bureau of the Census (1971).

Table 7.1. Average employer contributions for health insurance by industry

Industry	Average contribution per employee	Industry	Average contribution per employee
Mining	$328	Apparel	$ 59
Construction	170	Paper	175
Ordinances	274	Printing	151
Lumber	175	Chemicals	222
Furniture	175	Petroleum	233
Stone, glass, clay	227	Rubber	197
Primary metals	322	Leather	197
Fabricated metals	199	Wholesale trade	96
Machinery, except electrical	199	Retail trade	62
Electrical machinery	253	Finance, insurance, real estate	101
Transportation equipment	189	Transportation	171
Instruments	178	Utilities	172
Miscellaneous manufacturing	168	Communication	172
Food	205	Services	31
Tobacco	205	Federal government	96
Textiles	86	State and local government	155

contribution by employees' earnings for the economy as a whole.[6] This distribution by employees' earnings is converted to a distribution by family income with the aid of a joint distribution of husbands' and wives' earnings in 1969 calculated from the *Current Population Survey*, and a distribution of "other income" (interest, dividend, rent) by family income based primarily on the Federal Reserve Board Survey of Financial Characteristics.[7]

The distribution of employers' contributions by family income is shown in column 3 of table 7.2.[8] It rises from a low of $96 in the lowest income brackets to approximately $170 above $10,000. This very

Table 7.2. Estimates of tax reduction by family income class, 1969

Family income (1)	Number (thousands) (2)	Employer contribution per family (3)	Marginal tax rate (4)	Tax reduction per family (5)	Total tax reduction (6)
Less than $1,000	2,377	$ 96	.126	$12.10	$ 28,761
$1,000–1,999	2,052	96	.204	19.58	40,178
$2,000–2,999	2,055	113	.187	21.13	43,422
$3,000–3,999	2,045	122	.199	24.28	49,653
$4,000–4,999	2,466	138	.192	26.50	65,349
$5,000–5,999	2,915	145	.203	29.44	85,818
$6,000–6,999	3,424	154	.251	38.65	132,338
$7,000–7,999	3,812	145	.260	37.70	143,712
$8,000–9,999	7,230	159	.186	29.57	213,791
$10,000–14,999	12,016	169	.220	37.18	446,755
$15,000–24,999	6,863	174	.270	46.98	322,424
$25,000 and over[a]	972	162	.363	58.81	57,165
All income classes	48,227	—	—	—	1,629,364

a. Tax rates and reduction based on $40,000.

6. More specifically, if P_i is the average employer payment per employee (excluding married women) in industry i and n_{ij} is the number of employees (again excluding married women) in income class j and industry i, we calculate the average employer payment for employees in income class j as $P_j = \Sigma\, n_{ij} P_i / \Sigma\, n_{ij}$.

7. Projector and Weiss (1966). Implicit in this conversion is the assumption that when both husband and wife are employed, only the husband's insurance is of value to the family. Details on the method of estimating 1969 "other income" on the basis of the Federal Reserve Board survey are presented in the appendix.

8. These incomes refer only to the earnings of husbands and wives and their income from property (rent, interest, dividends). Specifically excluded are all transfer payments and earnings of other persons in the same family. This is appropriate for our tax calculation but overstates the number of low-income families.

substantial rise has been found even though the method tends to underestimate the relation between earnings and employers' payments for insurance.[9]

The marginal tax rates by income class, calculated from Pechman's estimates of the average effective tax rates, are shown in column 4.[10] The relevant marginal tax rates include the personal income tax and Social Security tax payments. Since we assume that an employer who did not pay the insurance premium would have paid an equal amount in gross wages, the relevant Social Security tax is the sum of the employer and employee taxes, or 9.6 percent in 1969. This is, of course, relevant only if the husbands' earnings did not exceed the 1969 limit of $8,000 on taxable payroll income.[11]

The tax saving per family by income class is shown in column 5. It increases much more rapidly than the employer contributions, from a low of $12.10 in the lowest category to more than $35 for incomes over $10,000. At an income of $40,000 (used to calculate tax rates in the $25,000+ class), the tax reduction is $58.81.[12] Although the tax reduction tends to rise continually over the full range of incomes, the rise is fastest up to an income of $6,000. The families with incomes below $6,000 receive very much smaller subsidies than the rest of the population.[13]

Column 6 shows the total tax reduction for all families in each income class. The sum of these tax reductions, that is, the total revenue loss due to excluding employer contribution in defining income, is

9. The estimates in this table indicate that the total of these employer contributions was $10.1 billion.

10. The effective marginal income tax rate in income class j is defined by the formula

$$mt_j = \frac{(at_{j+1})(INC_{j+1}) - (at_j)(INC_j)}{INC_{j+1} - INC_j}$$

where at_j is the average tax rate in income class j and INC_j is the average income in income class j. Estimates of the average effective tax rates are presented in Pechman (1966).

11. Within each income class above $8,000, some families have two earners and the husbands' income is below the $8,000 limit. Information from the distribution of husbands' and wives' earnings was used to obtain the appropriate average Social Security tax rate in each income class.

12. The marginal tax rates of column 4 are also probably a conservative estimate of actual marginal rates and therefore of the regressivity of the tax reductions.

13. This analysis makes no allowance for Medicaid or Medicare. The families eligible for these programs are treated as if they actually receive employer benefits. This also reduces the apparent inequality between income classes, although the effect is likely to be small in almost all states.

$1.63 billion. Our assumptions would tend to produce an underestimate of the actual revenus loss.[14]

An alternative way to assess regressivity of the tax reduction is to compare the cumulative percentages of tax reductions and families by income class. This is shown in table 7.3. The regressivity is greatest in

Table 7.3. Distributional implications of tax reductions due to employer contribution exclusion, 1969

Family income	Tax savings per family	Cumulative percentage of tax reduction	Cumulative percentage of families
Less than $1,000	$12.10	1.8	4.9
$1,000–1,999	19.58	4.2	9.2
$2,000–2,999	21.13	6.9	13.4
$3,000–3,999	24.28	10.0	17.7
$4,000–4,999	26.50	14.0	22.8
$5,000–5,999	29.44	19.2	28.8
$6,000–6,999	38.65	27.3	35.9
$7,000–7,999	37.70	36.2	43.8
$8,000–9,999	29.57	49.3	58.8
$10,000–14,999	37.18	76.7	83.7
$15,000–24,999	46.98	96.5	97.9
$25,000 and over	58.81	100.0	100.0

the lower income classes. Twenty-nine percent of families had incomes below $6,000 but received only 19 percent of the tax reductions. The top 16 percent of families received 23 percent of the tax reductions.

The Deduction of Individual Premium Payments

The current tax law provides that a taxpayer can deduct 50 percent of his health insurance premium, up to a maximum deduction of $150, in calculating his taxable income. Unlike other medical expense deductions, this deduction does not require that expenditures exceed a minimum amount.

In 1968 a deduction for health insurance premiums was taken on

14. Although this estimate is substantially higher than the value for fiscal year 1968 of $1.1 billion, in the Annual Report of the Secretary of the Treasury for 1968 (1969) the $1.1 billion excluded the Social Security tax.

19,562,860 taxable returns.[15] This was 41 percent of the taxable returns with itemized deduction and 27 percent of all returns.

The total of all such deductions was $1.75 billion, implying an average deduction of $89.40 per return on which an insurance deduction was taken. Table 7.4 shows the distribution of deduction by income class. To put this information in perspective, the table also shows the number of returns and the total income in each income class.

The amount by which the insurance deductions reduce taxes in each income class is the product of the total insurance deduction (column 5 of table 4) and the appropriate marginal rate in that income class. There are two ways to estimate the marginal tax rate by

Table 7.4. Distribution of health insurance deductions by income class, 1968

Adjusted gross income (1)	Number of returns[a] (2)	Total adjusted gross income (thousands) (3)	Number with insurance deduction[b] (4)	Total insurance deductions[b] (thousands) (5)
Under $1,000	7,735,280	$203,841	c	c
$1,000–1,999	7,467,095	11,062,792	149,200	9,221
$2,000–2,999	5,896,399	14,653,921	476,347	32,905
$3,000–3,999	5,565,323	19,456,758	778,781	58,475
$4,000–4,999	5,279,417	23,717,836	1,040,306	85,518
$5,000–5,999	4,998,207	27,484,220	1,278,862	101,498
$6,000–6,999	4,955,627	32,206,627	1,525,918	131,774
$7,000–7,999	4,743,142	35,572,227	1,580,827	138,801
$8,000–8,999	4,613,452	39,160,955	1,705,248	151,834
$9,000–9,999	4,023,579	38,178,720	1,566,147	141,874
$10,000–14,999	11,985,301	144,542,748	5,647,347	513,535
$15,000–19,999	3,660,989	62,117,475	2,086,158	200,192
$20,000–24,999	1,181,010	26,075,927	724,408	73,746
$25,000–49,999	1,239,870	41,194,949	700,113	83,541
$50,000 and over	384,017	36,951,491	231,751	26,197
All income classes	73,728,708	554,420,487	19,562,860	1,749,125

a. All returns, including those with no tax liability.
b. Data here relates to taxable returns only.
c. No value given by Internal Revenue Service because of high sampling variability.

15. The Internal Revenue Service publishes the distribution of deductions for insurance premiums only every other year. Data for 1970 are not yet available. (Internal Revenue Service 1970, p. 317).

adjusted gross income class. The "statutory tax rate method" takes the average taxable income in each adjusted gross income class and uses the marginal statutory tax rate for that income class.[16] The "effective tax rate method", used in the first section, is calculated by relating the difference in average taxes between income classes to the differences in the average adjusted gross income.

Table 7.5 presents the two estimates of the relevant marginal tax

Table 7.5. Alternative estimates of marginal tax rates and total tax reduction by adjusted gross income class, 1968

Adjusted gross income (1)	Estimated marginal tax rate		Estimated total tax reduction ($ thousands)	
	Statutory rate method (2)	Effective rate method (3)	Statutory rate method (4)	Effective rate method (5)
Under $1,000	.151	.123	0	0
$1,000–1,999	.151	.117	1,392	1,079
$2,000–2,999	.151	.109	4,969	3,587
$3,000–3,999	.161	.111	9,414	6,491
$4,000–4,999	.172	.116	14,709	9,920
$5,000–5,999	.172	.120	17,458	12,180
$6,000–6,999	.182	.140	23,983	18,448
$7,000–7,999	.204	.130	28,315	18,044
$8,000–8,999	.204	.154	30,974	23,382
$9,000–9,999	.204	.178	28,942	25,253
$10,000–14,999	.204	.222	104,761	114,004
$15,000–19,999	.269	.219	53,852	43,842
$20,000–24,999	.301	.265	22,198	19,543
$25,000–49,999	.388	.384	22,397	32,125
$50,000 and over	.063	.433	15,797	11,343
All income classes			389,162	339,244

rates and of the corresponding reduction in tax by income class. In general, the marginal rates based on the statutory tax rate method are higher than the marginal rates derived with the effective tax rate method. The total tax reduction implied by the statutory tax rate method is $389 million. For the effective tax rate method the total tax reduction is $339 million. Since the total of individual payments for

16. Assuming all taxpayers use income splitting provides a conservative estimate of these rates, particularly in high-income brackets.

Table 7.6. Distributional implications of tax reductions due to personal deductions, 1968[a]

Adjusted gross income (1)	Tax reduction per taxpayer[b] (2)	Cumulative percentage of total tax reduction[b,c] (3)	Cumulative percentage of total adjusted gross income[b,c] (4)	Cumulative percentage of total taxes[b,c] (5)	Cumulative percentage of returns[b,c] (6)
Under $1,000	$ 0	0	0.9	0.0	10.5
$1,000 – 1,999	0	0.3	2.7	0.5	20.6
$2,000 – 2,999	0.61	1.4	5.3	1.6	28.6
$3,000 – 3,999	1.17	3.3	8.8	3.5	36.2
$4,000 – 4,999	1.88	6.2	13.1	6.2	43.3
$5,000 – 5,999	2.44	9.8	18.0	9.5	50.1
$6,000 – 6,999	3.72	15.2	23.8	13.6	56.8
$7,000 – 7,999	3.80	20.6	30.2	18.4	63.3
$8,000 – 8,999	5.07	27.5	37.3	23.9	69.5
$9,000 – 9,999	6.28	34.9	44.1	29.5	75.0
$10,000 – 14,999	9.51	68.5	70.1	53.4	91.2
$15,000 – 15,999	11.98	81.4	81.3	65.5	96.2
$20,000 – 24,999	16.55	87.2	86.0	71.3	97.8
$25,000 – 49,999	25.91	96.7	93.4	82.7	98.5
$50,000 and over	29.54	100.0	100.0	100.0	100.0

a. Based on the effective tax rate method.
b. All taxpayers, including those who did not claim the insurance deduction and those not liable for tax.
c. Cumulative percentage to top income in income class.

health insurance was approximately $6.6 billion in 1968,[17] these tax reductions are a subsidy of about 5 percent of individual premiums. However, since a significant part of these individual payments were the employee's share of premiums financed primarily by employers, this greatly understates the effective rate of subsidy. We return to this in the third section.

The distributional implications of these tax subsidies can be best understood if the tax reductions of table 7.5 are expressed on a per taxpayer basis and if the share of the total tax reductions going to each income class is related to its share of total taxes and of total income. This is done in table 7.6 using the tax reduction estimates based on the more conservative effective marginal rate method.

The regressivity of the tax reductions is striking. Half of the tax returns are for incomes of less than $6,000. The average tax reduction from the insurance deduction is about $3 at this income level. For incomes of $10,000 to $15,000 the tax reduction is still less than $10 per taxpayer. At $20,000, however, it is about $17; above $50,000 it is over $30. The cumulative percentages show that families with incomes of less than $6,000 account for half of the tax returns but only about 10 percent of the tax reduction. Nearly two-thirds of the tax reduction goes to the 25 percent of taxpayers with incomes above $10,000. A third of the tax reduction goes to the 10 percent of taxpayers with incomes above $15,000.

A comparison of the distribution of tax reductions with the distributions of incomes and of taxes paid shows that for incomes below $9,000 the share of tax reductions is approximately proportional to taxes paid and therefore less than proportional to adjusted gross income. Between $15,000 and $25,000, the tax reductions are approximately proportional to income. Only above that level do the reductions become progressive.

Effects on the Demand for Insurance and Health Services

The annual tax subsidy of nearly $2 billion encourages an excessive use of health insurance and inflates the demand for hospital and medical care.[18] The current section provides a brief description of these distortions.

The tax subsidy means that for many insured persons the net cost of the insurance premiums is less than the average benefits paid by

17. The estimate of $6.6 billion is 51 percent of total premium of $12.9 billion. In 1969 the employer payments of $7.3 billion were 49 percent of total premiums of $14.7 billion (Mueller 1972).

18. For further discussion, see M. Feldstein (1971b) and chapters 3 and 6.

health insurers. If the $2.0 billion subsidy is subtracted from total 1969 premiums of $14.7 billion, the net cost of the premiums is $12.7 billion.[19] This is actually 3 percent less than the $13.1 billion of insurance benefits paid by insurers in 1969.

Many families (and their employers) therefore pay less for every dollar of health care that they purchase through insurance than they would have to pay to buy that same care directly. Since premiums do not increase in proportion to the actuarial value of the policy because of a fixed component in the cost of administration, the marginal rate of subsidy on additional insurance is likely to be greater than the average rate of subsidy. Moreover, since administrative costs are much higher for individual policies and small groups than for large groups, the net cost of premiums is actually very much less than the average benefits for many persons who are insured as members of large groups. Finally, since premium income is collected some time before benefits are paid, the companies' premiums and benefits for the same calendar year (1969) may cause a substantial understatement of the net rate of subsidy.

The net subsidy of insurance and the fact that for most families it is actually cheaper to purchase care through insurance than to buy it directly obviously encourages the purchase of more insurance than the household would choose to purchase just for the advantage of risk spreading. This subsidy may also explain why so much shallow-coverage insurance (coverage for small and moderate health expenses but not very large or catastrophic expenses) is purchased when more serious risks are still uninsured. Households that choose not to insure against major risks may nevertheless take advantage of the tax subsidy that is available for prepaying small health expenses.[20]

The effect of this artificially expanded use of insurance is an increase in the demand for health care and a resulting rise in its price. More explicitly, insurance lowers the price of health services to the patient at the time that he purchases care. The lower net price encourages him to purchase more expensive care than he would if he had to pay the full price.[21] It is important to recognize that insurance

19. The 1969 subsidy due to excluding employer payments was $1.63 billion. The 1968 estimates of $339 million and $389 million understate the corresponding figure for 1969.

20. It is also likely that employees assume that employer payments for health insurance do not result in a corresponding decrease in money income. This encourages the tendency of both unions and employers to provide relatively comprehensive benefits.

21. A number of studies indicate that the demand for care is sensitive to price and therefore rises when insurance lowers the net price of care; see, for example, chapter 3 and Rossett and Huang (1973).

increases demand by distorting the price and not merely by making cash available at the time of illness. Insurance can increase demand as much for high-income families with substantial liquid assests as for low-income families with small savings. Hospitals respond to this increase in demand by raising the general sophistication of their care and therefore the average cost per day.[22] Physicians also appear to raise their average fee when their patients have more insurance.[23] This increase in health-care prices increases the risk of families and therefore encourages the purchase of even more insurance. The tax subsidy thus accelerates the unfortunate cycle by which more insurance causes prices to rise, increasing the demand for insurance and thus raising prices further.

In short, the special tax treatment of personal and employer payments for health insurance causes a substantial revenue loss, distributes these tax reductions very regressively, encourages an excessive purchase of insurance, distorts the demand for health services, and thus inflates the prices of these services. Removing these special tax advantages would be a useful part of any program to reform the system of health insurance, increase the efficiency of the health-care system, and reduce the rate of inflation of health-care prices.[24]

Appendix: Estimation of Employer Contributions by Income Class

The estimates of employer contributions by industry are based on three sources: the biannual survey of employee benefits conducted by the Chamber of Commerce, the Bureau of Labor Statistics surveys of compensation practices and payroll hours, and the compensation data published in July issues of *Survey of Current Business*.

1. The data for all manufacturing industries,[25] wholesale and retail trade, finance, insurance, and real estate, utilities and communication is taken from *Employee Benefits 1969*.

22. For an analysis and specific estimates of this response, see M. Feldstein (1971b) and chapter 3.

23. See M. Feldstein (1970c, pp. 121–133).

24. Appendix A of the original paper provides a brief and nontechnical description of the way that insurance increases the cost of hospital care. This description overlaps and is superseded by part of chapter 1 of this volume.

25. The Chamber of Commerce tabulation does not provide separate estimates for "ordnance and accessories" and for miscellaneous manufacturing. Contributions for these two relatively small industries were estimated by fitting an equation relating average annual earnings and annual benefits, using the Chamber of Commerce data for all other manufacturing industries.

The published survey presents the average cost of insurance benefits (as a percentage of payroll, cents per payroll hour, and dollars per year per employee) by industry for a composite item including life insurance premiums as well as health insurance. A special tabulation separating the two on an industry basis[26] was prepared for this survey: the figures for health insurance are presented in table 7.1.

The Chamber of Commerce sample is biased in that large firms are overrepresented. Inasmuch as most forms of supplementary compensation (like wage and salary levels) are correlated with firm size, users of this data have generally adjusted benefit payments downward.[27] However, Rice (1966), using 1959 and 1962 data, found no significant relationship between employer contributions to health insurance and the firm size and wage level. Therefore, no adjustments were made before using the results of the special tabulation as industry benefit data.

2. Data for contract construction, mining, transportation, and federal employment is based on Bureau of Labor Statistics studies of employee compensation and payroll hours.[28] This series of studies reports employer contribution as "life, accident and health insurance" as "cents per paid hour" and "per cent of total expenditures" for selected years. In order to make the Bureau of Labor Statistics data comparable to the 1969 manufacturing data, three adjustments were made.

First, an average percentage derived from the Chamber of Commerce tabulation was used to apportion the employer contributions between health and life insurance payments; the Chamber of Commerce data showed that about 82 percent of employer contributions to life and health insurance go to health in manufacturing industries and about 67 percent does in nonmanufacturing industries. Second, to arrive at an annual contribution, the adjusted cents per paid hour

26. The two items are not separated in the published report because a number of employers contract with one carrier to provide both life and health insurance for their employees and consequently were unable to furnish cost data for each item separately. The special tabulation indicated that 10 percent of the 1,115 reporting companies had such dual coverage and that their average costs (as a percent of payroll) for the combined life and health package of 3.7 percent was equal to the summed average for companies reporting separately. Consequently, it has been assumed that the pattern for companies reporting separately is representative of all companies.

27. See, for example, Livernash (1970, pp. 79–144).

28. Studies used were Bureau of Labor Statistics (1960, 1964a,b,c,d, 1965a,b, 1971). The 1971 study provided comparative data on federal and private supplementary compensation practices. The annual contribution figure used for federal government employees is based on the reported number of employees in U.S. Civil Service Commission Bureau of Retirement and Insurance (1970).

was multiplied by 52 times the average work week for that industry.[29] The resulting annual contribution figure was then updated to 1969 by multiplying a factor of 11 percent per year elapsed between the year in which the study was made and 1969. The adjustment figure was derived from Bureau of Labor Statistics studies of compensation in the private, nonmanufacturing sector.[30]

3. Comprehensive surveys of supplementary compensation practices for the service industries and for state and local government are not available.[31] In its absence, an indirect method of estimating employer contributions was devised. The Commerce Department publishes annual data on supplements to wages and salaries by industry division,[32] including the service industry and state and local government. Multiplying this by the ratio for all nonmanufacturing industries of health contributions to total supplementary compensation provides an estimate of total employer contribution for an industry.

The estimate of total contributions for all employers if $7.3 billion. This is the Social Security estimate of $11.5 billion, including employee contribution.[33] Some discrepancy may result from the rule used for apportioning contribution between health and life insurance. Alternatively, if low-wage employees typically receive health insurance first among supplementary benefits, the estimate for the service sector may be too low.

Employer Contributions for Married Women
Women make up over one-third of the labor force. Almost 65 percent of these employed women are married.[34] Working wives require two modifications in the estimation of the distribution of health-care supplement. First, with a working wife family income will be considerably higher than husband's income and the appropriate marginal tax rate will be higher. Second, and less obvious, is the effect on the distribution of health insurance subsidies. The problem arises as follows: A married woman who requires some variety of covered health care presumably can claim under the health insurance plan at her place of

29. Bureau of Labor Statistics (1970a, p. 149).

30. Percentage computed on basis of data contained in Bureau of Labor Statistics (1963, 1966, 1968). See also Kolodrubetz (1971a, pp. 21–36).

31. The most comprehensive data available on supplementary compensation practices are contained in U.S. Bureau of Census (1967). Data on health insurance coverage for state and local government employees are presented; however, the variance in plans is so great that contributions cannot be plausibly inferred from coverage data.

32. U.S. Department of Commerce (1970), table 6.7; 1969, table 3.3).

33. Kilodrubetz (1971).

34. Woman's Bureau (1970, p. 112).

employment or submit a claim as a dependent under her husband's health plan. If employed wives generally apply under their own plan, families with more than one wage earner receive double subsidies. If they generally claim under their husbands' plans, the average contribution per employee understates the true subsidy being given to men employed in the industry.

We have assumed that women typically collect under their husbands' plans. There are three reasons for this assumption. First, about one-quarter of the women in the work force are part-time employees and as such not included under most group health plans.[35] Second, the somewhat fragmentary evidence on turnover rates indicates that women's turnover rates are substantially higher. Thus, if there is some lag in coverage (as is typical, for example, in the service industry), a woman frequently may not have the option of presenting a claim at her place of employment. Finally, the health plan offered at a husband's place of employment is generally superior in terms of both breadth and depth of coverage. Across industries, health benefit payments are positively correlated with earnings, and male employment is concentrated in the relatively high-paying durable goods, manufacturing, mining, construction, and utilities industries, while the majority of female jobs are found in nondurable goods, manufacturing, services, and retail trade, all low-wage industries.

To adjust for this assumed claims behavior of married women, in industries in which more than 10 percent of employees are women the average benefit level used in intermediate calculations has been adjusted upward. We assume that married women are distributed in the same way among industries as all other women; thus 65 percent of the women employees in each industry are assumed to be married. Then the adjustment for the industry is given by

$$B_i = \frac{B_i'N_i}{N_i - 0.65N_{wi}}$$

where B_i = estimated average benefit in industry$_i$, B_i' = reported average benefit in industry$_i$, N_i = total employment in industry$_i$ and N_{wi} = employment of women in industry$_i$.[36]

To obtain the relevant income distribution of beneficiaries by income class within an industry, the industry income distribution for married woman was subtracted from the overall industry income dis-

35. Woman's Bureau (1970. p. 12).

36. Data on women's employment by industry is taken from Bureau of Labor Statistics (1970c, pp. 52–58).

tribution.[37] What remained was an income distribution by industry for married men and unattached individuals.

Relationship of Earned Income to Family Income

The relevant tax rate for a household depends not on the annual earnings of the head of the household, but on total income, the sum of husband's and wife's income (for married workers), and any unearned income. An estimate of total income was derived from the earnings of the head or the hosehold in a two-step process. In the first step, the earnings of married men were matched with earnings of their wives on the basis of the joint distribution of husband-wife earnings presented in *Current Population Survey*.[38]

The second step was to move from earned income for both families and unrelated individuals to total income. Data from a Federal Reserve Survey[39] was used to compute an average unearned income for each husband-wife income combination, some 120 different groups. No attempt was made to construct a similar table for unmarried individuals. Instead, it was assumed that the unearned income received by an unmarried employee was equal to that received by a married employee of the same earnings class with a nonworking spouse.

37. The income distribution for all women on an industry basis was obtained from U.S. Bureau of Census, (1971d).

38. U.S. Bureau of Censis (1971a).

39. Projector and Weiss (1966).

8 Tax Subsidies, the Rational Demand for Insurance, and the Health-Care Crisis

Because insurance affects behavior, it is best to be less than fully insured. The consumer's optimal purchase of actuarially fair insurance depends on balancing his gain through avoiding risk against his loss through the distortion of his behavior. For health insurance the optimal coverage reflects the individual's risk aversion and the price elasticity of his demand for care. If the available insurance is not actuarially fair, that is, if the expected benefits are not equal to the premium, the consumer's purchase of insurance would, of course, diverge from the optimum.[1]

The U.S. tax system now provides a major subsidy for the purchase of health insurance. This subsidy is likely to have increased substantially the demand for such insurance. Since much of the extremely rapid rise in health-care costs can be attributed to the growth of insurance coverage during the past twenty-five years, this tax subsidy is responsible for much of what is widely perceived as a health-care crisis.[2] Moreover, recent estimates indicate that the current total extent

This chapter was written with Bernard Friedman. Reprinted with permission from the *Journal of Public Economics* 7, no. 2 (April 1977), pp. 155–178. The basic model and computer programs described in this chapter are an extension of work done for the Department of Health, Education, and Welfare and described in an unpublished technical report, "The Demand for Supplementary Private Insurance" (1972). A more complete version of the current chapter was presented with the same title in Harvard Institute of Economic Research Discussion Paper no. 382 (1974).

1. The theory of the demand for insurance has been discussed by Arrow (1963, 1974, 1976), Ehrlich and Becker (1972), M. Feldstein (chapter 6), Pauly (1968, 1974), Phelps (1973), Rosett and Huang (1973), Smith (1968), Spence and Zeckhauser (1971), and Zeckhauser (1970).

2. For evidence of the impact of health insurance on the cost of health services, see M. Feldstein (1970c, 1971b) and chapter 3.

of insurance coverage is substantially beyond the optimal level and may induce a welfare loss of several billion dollars per year.[3]

Most health insurance in the United States is provided through employer groups. Employer payments for health insurance premiums are a deductible business expense for the employer but are not part of taxable income to the employee. The value of these premiums is also excluded in calculating the base for the Social Security payroll tax. Excluding health insurance premiums from taxable wages and salaries provides a very substantial subsidy for even relatively low paid workers. A dollar of additional wages paid to a married worker with $8,000 of taxable income is subject to federal income tax of 22 percent and a Social Security tax of 11.7 percent; the effective marginal rate is thus 33.7 percent. If the dollar is instead spent by the employer on health insurance, no tax need be paid. The current tax system therefore permits health insurance to be purchased by such an individual at a discount of 33.7 percent.[4]

The tax system also subsidizes consumers' direct payments for health insurance. In calculating taxable income, an individual may deduct 50 percent of health insurance premiums up to a maximum deduction of $150 and then may deduct the remainder of the premium if he itemizes medical expenses. The individual deduction is much less important than the exclusion of employer payments.[5]

The marginal federal tax rate of the typical employee has risen rapidly in the past twenty-five years. In 1948 a married worker with two children who earned the private nonagricultural wage typically paid no federal income tax and a Social Security tax of only 2 percent (including the employer's share). By 1973 a similar worker would pay a marginal income tax rate of 15 percent, a Social Security tax of 11 percent, and often a state income tax. The purpose of this paper is to assess the likely magnitude of the effect of the tax subsidy of health insurance premiums and to examine the general equilibrium results of the increased demand for health insurance. The second section develops an explicit computable model of the household's demand for health insurance when insurance affects the demand for care. This model is used in the third section to simulate the effect of tax subsidies on a typical individual's demand for insurance. The fourth section extends this microsimulation model to the entire population to

3. See Rosett and Huang (1973) and chapter 6.

4. The effective subsidy is usually even greater than this because most states have state income taxes and exclude employer payments from taxable income. (chapter 7).

5. Health Insurance Institute (1976–74). M. Feldstein and Allison estimated that 81 percent of the federal tax subsidy is due to the exclusion of employer payments.

estimate the impact of the tax subsidy on the aggregate demand for insurance in 1970. The relation between the growth of insurance and the rise of health care prices is analyzed in the fifth section. There is a brief section final that considers the welfare loss of the tax subsidy and some of the more general implications of the current analysis.

Moral Hazard and the Demand for Health Insurance

A risk-averse individual facing the possibility of an exogenously given random loss would choose to be fully insured if actuarially fair insurance were available. When the extent of insurance coverage affects the magnitude of the random loss, the choice of insurance is more complex. This section presents an explicit model of the optimal demand for insurance when such moral hazard exists. Within this model it is easy to compute how departures from actuarially fair premiums alter the demand for insurance.[6]

The basic purpose of insurance is to lower the net cost of health services at the time that the patient purchases care.[7] More specifically, the net cost (N) to the patient of an additional unit of care depends on the gross price (P) charged by the provider, the coinsurance rate (C), and the nonmonetary cost per unit of care (λ):[8]

$$N \times C \cdot P + \lambda. \tag{1}$$

It is convenient to describe the individual's basic illness experience by a random variable X, defined as the quantity of care that he would consume at $P = 1$ if he were uninsured $(C = 1)$, that is, at net price $N = 1 + \lambda$. If the individual "draws" value X_0, his demand conditional on X_0 depends on the net cost per unit of care. More specifically, with a constant elasticity demand function, the individual would consume

$$Q_0 \times X_0 \left(\frac{C \cdot P + \lambda}{1 + \lambda} \right)^{\eta}, \tag{2}$$

where $\eta < 0$ is the price elasticity of demand.

6. The model assumes that the individual buys only one health insurance policy, thus avoiding the problem raised by Pauly (1968). Although some individuals do have more than one policy, the vast majority have one policy provided by their employer. The purchase of insurance in employment groups also generally avoids the self-selection problem of asymmetric information discussed by Rothschild and Stiglitz (1976).

7. Health insurance benefits are generally a fraction of the patient's health-care expenditure or a fixed amount conditional on the consumption of a particular service.

8. See Acton (1972) and Phelps and Newhouse (1972b) for a discussion of the importance of time in the cost of acquiring medical care. Nonmonetery cost also includes anxiety and pain. The specification of equation (1) reflects the suggestions of Chiswick (1976) for improving our earlier specification (chapter 8).

By lowering the net cost of health services at the time of care, insurance affects both the volume of care consumed and the financial risk that the individual faces. For any given basic illness experience (X) the patient consumes more care. The gross cost of the care increases, but if the price elasticity is less than one, the net cost of care at the time of illness is reduced[9] and the individual faces a smaller financial risk. If the individual must pay the actuarial (expected) value of the insurance benefits, the effect of the insurance is to increase the individual's expected total health expenditure. This greater cost is offset by the larger volume of services that are obtained and by the reduced risk that results if the price elasticity is less than one.

The optimal insurance coverage depends on balancing these countervailing effects. It is best to analyze this problem by considering first the effect of insurance on the consumption of care and the value to the individual of the additional care. The effect on financial risk can then be evaluated. Combining these effects provides a measure of the relative desirability of difference insurance coverages and therefore a criterion for selecting a particular insurance coverage.[10]

Figure 8.1 shows the demand curve (dd) for health services conditional on the random event X_0. In the absence of insurance, the net price is $P + \lambda$ and the quantity consumed is $X_0[(P + \lambda)/(1 + \lambda)]^\eta$. If insurance lowers the net price to $C \cdot P + \lambda$, the individual consumes $X_0[(C \cdot P + \lambda)/(1 + \lambda)]^\eta$. The light shaded area represents the value to the consumer of the incremental consumption. This is the sum of the additional net cost $\{X_0[(CP + \lambda)/(1 + \lambda)]^\eta - X_0[(P + \lambda)/(1 + \lambda)]^\eta\}$ $(CP + \lambda)$ and the traditional consumer surplus triangle.[11] To derive an analytic expression for this, we use the inverse demand function relating price to quantity; to avoid ambiguity, we denote this price function by $\phi(Z|X_0)$, where Z is simply the variable of integration and the conditioning on X_0 is made explicit. This yields the consumer value.

---

9. This will be true even if the elasticity is greater than one if the nonmonetary cost is positive. The precise condition is $C(CP + \lambda)^\eta < (P + \lambda)^\eta$.

10. This approach implicitly assumes that the marginal utility of wealth depends only on wealth and is not a function of the state of health. See Arrow (1974, 1976) for an analysis of insurance demand when the marginal utility of wealth is a function of the individual's health status.

11. Since the representative individual actually pays the full actuarial cost

$$(P + \lambda)X_0[(CP + \lambda)/(1 + \lambda)]^\eta,$$

insurance induces a welfare loss indicated by the black triangle. This measure of the welfare loss ignores the general equilibrium effects on the health-care system and is therefore likely to understate the actual loss (chapter 6). Since this analysis is concerned with individual choice rather than welfare analysis, there is no harm in ignoring this.

Figure 8.1

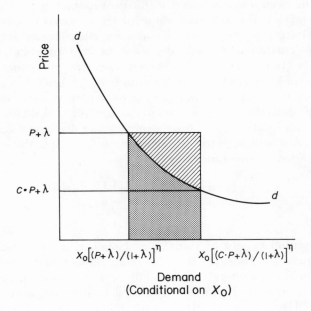

Demand
(Conditional on X_0)

$$V_0 = \int_{X_0[(P+\lambda)/(1+\lambda)]^{\eta}}^{X_0[(CP+\lambda)/(1+\lambda)]^{\eta}} \phi(Z|X_0)\,dZ. \tag{3}$$

In the specific constant elasticity demand case of equation (2), this value is

$$V_0 = \int_{X_0[(P+\lambda)/(1+\lambda)]^{\eta}}^{X_0[(CP+\lambda)/(1+\lambda)]^{\eta}} \left[\frac{Z(1+\lambda)^{\eta}}{X_0}\right]^{1/\eta} dZ, \tag{4}$$

or

$$V_0 = \frac{\eta(1+\lambda)^{-\eta}X_0}{\eta+1}\{(CP+\lambda)^{1+\eta} - (P+\lambda)^{1+\eta}\}. \tag{5}$$

Consider now the financial effect of the insurance on an individual with initial wealth W. With no insurance a random illness of level X_0 would involve an expenditure of $PX_0[(P+\lambda)/(1+\lambda)]^{\eta}$ and would reduce wealth to $W - PX_0[(P+\lambda)/(1+\lambda)]^{\eta}$. With insurance characterized by a coinsurance rate C, the patient's net out-of-pocket expenditure becomes

$$E_0(C) = CPX_0[(CP+\lambda)/(1+\lambda)]^{\eta}. \tag{6}$$

The individual's wealth therefore becomes $W - E_0(C) - \pi(C)$, where $\pi(C)$ is the premium associated with coinsurance rate C. The premium depends on the actuarial value of the insurance benefits, the markup charged by the insurance company, and the subsidy provided by the tax system. More specifically, since the insurance company pays $(1 - C)PX_0[(CP + \lambda)/(1 + \lambda)]^n$ when X_0 occurs, an actuarially fair premium is $(1 - C)P[(CP + \lambda)/(1 + \lambda)]^n \int_0^\infty Xf(X)dX$, where $f(X)$ is the probability density function for the basic illness experience. If the insurance company applies a markup at rate M in calculating its premium change, and the government provides a subsidy at the rate S on the gross premium, then the actual net premium cost to the individual for a policy with coinsurance rate C is

$$\pi(C) = (1 - S)\ (1 + M)\ (1 - C)P$$
$$[(CP + \lambda)/(1 + \lambda)]^n \int_0^\infty Xf(X)dX. \tag{7}$$

The essential benefit of insurance arises because the individual's utility function is concave. It is therefore important to convert the financial effect to a utility measure. For now, the utility of net wealth conditional on event X_0 for an individual with coinsurance rate C is denoted $U[W - E_0(C) - \pi(C)]$. The utility "gain" of the *change in financial position* is[12]

$$U[W - E_0(C) - \pi(C)] - U[W - PX_0[(P + \lambda)/(1 + \lambda)]^n].$$

The utility gain of the *incremental health care* can be evaluated by converting the value of care (V_0) to a utility value by multiplying the dollar amount (equation (5)) by the appropriate marginal utility of money. For computational convenience later, we use a marginal utility evaluated at an average of the insured and uninsured expenditures:

$$U'\left[W - \frac{\pi(C) + E_0(C) + PX_0[(P + \lambda)/(1 + \lambda)]^n}{2}\right].$$

The *net* utility gain of insurance with coinsurance rate C, conditional on X_0, is thus[13]

---

12. This "gain" will be negative for some valuess of X_0.

13. The utility value of health care is measured indirectly by the individual's willingness to pay, and health status as such does not enter the utility function. See Arrow (1974) for a discussion of the implied separability and a discussion of an alternative approach.

$$g(C|X_0) = U[W - E_0(C) - \pi(C)] - U[W - PX_0((P + \lambda)/(1 + \lambda))^\eta]$$

$$+ U'\left[W - \frac{\pi(C) + E_0(C) + PX_0[(P + \lambda)/(1 + \lambda)]^\eta}{2}\right] \cdot V_0. \quad (8)$$

The expected utility gain associated with coinsurance rate C is thus

$$G(C) = \int_0^\infty g(C|X) \cdot f(X)dX, \quad (9)$$

where $f(X)$ is again the probability density function of the random illness event X. The individual ranks the alternative insurance options by calculating G for each and then chooses the insurance policy with the highest value of G. Although this optimization has been described in terms of insurance policies with a single parameter (the coinsurance rate), the same procedure can be applied to describe the choice among policies characterized by coinsurance rates, deductibles, and upper limits.

Two issues are raised by this analysis. First, how is the demand function for health-care posited in equation (2) consistent with the underlying utility function? Second, is it appropriate to use the uninsured demand curve as a basis for evaluating changes in care induced by changes in insurance? Both issues are closely related to the form of the utility function. We shall approximate the utility of wealth function by $U(W) = -e^{-RW}$. Tony Atkinson has pointed out to us that the constant elasticity demand function of equation (2) (with $\lambda = 0$) can be derived by extending this utility function to include health expenditure conditional on the X_0 value as $U(W, E_0|X_0) = -\exp\{-RW\}\exp\{R\psi(E_0 X_0)\}$, where $\psi(E_0, X_0) = [1/(1 - U)]E_0^{1-U}X_0^U$ where $U > 1$. We ignore this interdependence between the utility of wealth and the utility of health in calculating the consumer surplus area under the demand curve.

We base our estimate of the welfare loss of nonoptimal consumption of health care on the demand function of equation (2). This should be regarded as a compensated demand function in the sense that there is compensation for any change in price to offset the income effect that would otherwise result. In addition, the estimated welfare loss (V_0) conditional on X_0 is converted to a utility value by using a marginal utility that is also conditional on X_0 and increases with the increasing severity of the disease as measured by X_0. We do not, however, make any allowance for the fact that very large expenditures in the absence of insurance have an income effect that causes too little consumption of health services in comparison to the insured situation even with zero price elasticity. Our analysis therefore overstates the optimal coinsurance rate for very large values of X_0. This should be dealt with more fully in any analysis of the optimal overall insurance policy with variable coinsurance rates, but we believe that the issue is not very important in the single coinsurance rate analysis. Moreover, we are concerned with explaining the rather complete insurance of small expenses that now exists and not with the insurance of catastrophic expenses. All the empirical evidence shows a negligible or zero income elasticity of the demand for health care (M. Feldstein 1974b).

Tax Subsidies and the Choice of Coinsurance Rate

The process of choice can be made operational by specifying the appropriate distribution of the basic illness experience $[f(X)]$ and selecting a particular form for the utility function. The effect of different rates of government subsidy (S) on the individual's choice of coinsurance rate can then be studied.

A detailed study of the individual insurance claims for more than three hundred thousand federal government employees and their dependents indicates that the distribution of insured health expenditures can be well approximated by a gamma distribution (Friedman 1971, pp. 66–70). The gamma distribution is convenient in a number of ways. If each individual's experience follows an independent gamma distribution, a family's experience distribution is easily derived. Moreover, the constant elasticity form of the demand function in equation (2) implies that a gamma distribution for actual expenditure corresponds to a gamma distribution for the basic illness experience. The parameters α and β of the gamma distribution

$$f(X) = k_0 X^\alpha e^{-X/\beta} \tag{10}$$

can be inferred directly from the parameters of the actual expenditure distribution, the coinsurance rate of the federal employees' plan, and the assumed price elasticity.[14] For the actual expenditures in 1970 families with two adults and two children, $\alpha = -0.61$ and $\beta = 1573$. From equation (7) it follows that the premium for coinsurance rate C is

$$\pi(C) = (1 - S)(1 + M)(1 - C)P(CP + \lambda)^\eta(1 + \lambda)^{-\eta}(\alpha + 1)\beta, \tag{11}$$

since the mean of the X distribution is $(\alpha + 1)\beta$.

The utility function with constant absolute risk aversion, $U(\cdot) = -e^{-R(\cdot)}$, is particularly convenient for analyzing this problem. The

---

14. The value of k_0 is selected for each pair of α and β to make the integral of the density equal to one.

expected utility gain of coinsurance rate C can be evaluated as the sum of three integrals:

$$
\begin{aligned}
G(C) = &\int_0^\infty U\left[W - CPX\left(\frac{CP + \lambda}{1 + \lambda}\right)^\eta - \pi(C)\right] \cdot f(X)\,dX \\
&- \int_0^\infty U\left[W - PX\left(\frac{P + \lambda}{1 + \lambda}\right)^\eta\right] f(X)\,dX \\
&+ \int_0^\infty U'\left[W - \tfrac{1}{2}CPX\left(\frac{CP + \lambda}{1 + \lambda}\right)^\eta + \pi(C) + PX\left(\frac{P + \lambda}{1 + \lambda}\right)^\eta\right] \\
&\times \frac{\eta(1 + \lambda)^{-\eta}X}{\eta + 1}\left[(CP + \lambda)^{1+\eta} - (P + \lambda)^{1+\eta}\right]f(X)\,dX.
\end{aligned}
\tag{12}
$$

The first two integrals represent the expected utility "gain" of the change in the financial position due to being insured. The third integral is the value of the additional care that is consumed.[15] With constant absolute risk aversion the first integral may be written

$$
\begin{aligned}
&-\int_0^\infty \exp\{-R[W - CPX(CP + \lambda)^\eta(1 + \lambda)^{-\eta} - \pi(C)]\}f(X)\,dX \\
&= -e^{-R[W-\pi(C)]}\int_0^\infty \exp[RCP(CP + \lambda)^\eta(1 + \lambda)^{-\eta}X]f(X)\,dX.
\end{aligned}
\tag{13}
$$

The right-hand side integral is simply the moment-generating function for the variable X with a generating parameter of $RCP(CP + \lambda)^\eta$ $(1 + \lambda)^{-\eta}$. With $f(X)$ a gamma distribution, we obtain

$$
\begin{aligned}
&-e^{-R[W-\pi(C)]}\int_0^\infty \exp[RCP(CP + \lambda)^\eta(1 + \lambda)^{-\eta}X]f(X)\,dX \\
&= -e^{-R[W-\pi(C)]}[1 - RCP(CP + \lambda)^\eta(1 + \lambda)^{-\eta}\beta]^{-(\alpha+1)}.
\end{aligned}
\tag{14}
$$

The second integral can be evaluated in the same way to obtain

$$
\begin{aligned}
&\int_0^\infty U[W - PX(P + \lambda)^\eta(1 + \lambda)^{-\eta}] \cdot f(X)\,dX \\
&= -e^{-RW}[1 - RP(P + \lambda)^\eta(1 + \lambda)^{-\eta}\beta]^{-(\alpha+1)}.
\end{aligned}
\tag{15}
$$

The third integral is a bit more complex to evaluate. The form of the utility function implies that $U'(\cdot) = -RU(\cdot)$. The third integral is therefore equal to

$$
\begin{aligned}
&\frac{Re^{-R[W-0.5\,\pi(C)]}\eta(1 + \lambda)^{-\eta}[(CP + \lambda)^{1+\eta} - (P + \lambda)^{1+\eta}]}{(1 + \eta)} \\
&\times \int_0^\infty X \cdot e^{\xi X}k_0 X^\alpha e^{-X'\beta}\,dX,
\end{aligned}
\tag{16}
$$

where $\xi = 0.5RP(1 + \lambda)^{-\eta}[C(CP + \lambda)^\eta + (P + \lambda)^\eta]$.

15. The marginal utility of money used to evaluate the additional care is itself a function of the expenditure level and therefore of X.

It is clear that although the integral in equation (16) differs from the moment-generating function by the presence of an additional X term, this integral is equivalent (except for a constant) to a moment-generating function for a gamma distribution with parameters $\alpha + 1$ and β. It can be shown that

$$\int_0^\infty e^{\xi X} k_0 X^{\alpha+1} e^{-X'\beta} dX = (1 - \xi\beta)^{\alpha+2}\beta(\alpha - 1). \tag{17}$$

Substituting these values into equation (12) and multiplying both sides of the equation by e^{RW} yields

$$
\begin{aligned}
e^{RW}&G(C) \\
=&-e^{R\pi(C)}[1 - RCP(CP + \lambda)^\eta(1 + \lambda)^{-\eta}\beta]^{-(\alpha+1)} \\
&+ [1 - RP(P + \lambda)^\eta(1 + \lambda)^{-\eta}\beta]^{-(\alpha+1)} \\
&+ \frac{Re^{R\cdot\pi(C)'2}\eta(1 + \lambda)^{-\eta}[(CP + \lambda)^{1+\eta} - (P + \lambda)^{1+\eta}]\beta(\alpha - 1)}{1 + \eta} \\
&\times (1 - \xi\beta)^{\alpha+2},
\end{aligned} \tag{18}
$$

where again $\xi = 0.5\,RP\cdot(1 + \lambda)^{-\eta}[C(CP + \lambda)^\eta + (P + \lambda)^\eta]$.

Since e^{RW} is a constant for each individual, maximizing $e^{RW}G(C)$ with respect to C is equivalent to maximizing $G(C)$, the expected gain itself.[16]

Although a simple analytic expression for the optimal coinsurance rate cannot be obtained, the value of $e^{RW}G(C)$ can easily be calculated from equation (18) for any $0 \leq C \leq 1$ and the optimal value can be selected by a search procedure.[17] For these calculations we measure the unit of care so that $P = 1$. The premium is calculated from equation (11) with the insurance company's markup $M = 0.09$, the average excess of premium over benefits for private insurance in 1970 (Cooper et al. 1973). Three parameters describe individual preferences: the price elasticity of demand for medical care (η), the relative non-monetary cost per unit of care (λ), and the measure of risk aversion (R). Although these parameters significantly affect the desired coinsurance rate, the relative impact of the tax subsidy is similar under different assumptions. Results are presented for several values of each parameter.

Empirical evidence on the demand for medical care indicates an absolute price elasticity substantially greater than zero but almost

16. The constant absolute risk aversion utility function thus implies that the optimal insurance does not depend on the individual's wealth. This also implies that it is not necessary to select an appropriate measure of wealth (as income) in order to evaluate the individual's optimal behavior.

17. The search procedure locates the optimal C to the nearest 0.02.

certainly less than one.[18] Results are presented for $\eta = -0.3, -0.5$, and -0.7. The appropriate value of η is of course the individual's perception of his demand elasticity and not necessarily his actual demand elasticity. The frequency of popular statements about the price insensitivity of the demand for medical care suggests that perceived values are less than actual values. Since most individuals have relatively little experience with serious illness, they have little opportunity to study their own behavior and to develop a correct estimate of their own demand elasticity.

Since the money price per unit of care has been normalized at one, the value of λ measures the ratio of nonmoney cost to gross money price per unit of care. Although there is no firm evidence on which to base a choice of λ, it is reassuring that the results are not sensitive to the choice of different values of λ between 0.1 and 0.5.[19]

It is easiest to derive possible values of the coefficient of risk aversion (R) by considering a simple bet. A man who is willing to participate in a fair bet in which there is an even chance of winning and losing $1,000 has $R = 0$ and would want a coinsurance of $C = 1$, that is, no insurance. If he requires a side payment of $50 to make such a bet (if he requires odds of $1,050 to $950), his risk aversion is 0.0001.[20] If he requires a side payment of $150 (if he is just indifferent between no bet and an even chance of winning $1,150 and losing $850), his risk aversion is 0.003. A very risk averse individual who requires a side payment of $240 (so that there is an even chance of winning $1,240 and losing $760) has a risk aversion of 0.005. The calculations of the optimal coinsurance rate have been done for these three values.[21]

Table 8.1 presents the optimal coinsurance rate at different mar-

---

18. See chapter 2 for a critical survey of this evidence.

19. The use of a constant λ is clearly a great simplification. See Chiswick (1976) for a discussion of how our measure of the nonmonetary cost might be extended.

20. The value of R is found by solving the equation

$$U(W_0) = 0.5\, U(W_0 - 1000 + 50) + 0.5\, U(W_0 + 1000 + 50),$$

or, more specifically,

$$\exp(-RW_0) = (0.5)\exp[-R(W_0 - 1000 + 50)] + (0.5)\exp[-R(W_0 + 1000 + 50)].$$

The assumption of constant absolute risk aversion implies that the initial wealth W_0 does not affect the value of R.

21. Perhaps intuition is aided if these absolute risk-aversion parameters are related to proportional risk-aversion parameters $(r = WU''/U')$ at an initial wealth of $10,000. Since $r = WR$, the three values of R correspond to proportional risk-aversion parameters of 1, 3, and 5. These are the implied local elasticity of the marginal utility function. This suggests that 1 and 3 are likely to be more reasonable than 5.

Table 8.1. Optimal coinsurance rates with different tax subsidies

Adjusted family income	Marginal tax rate[a]	R = 0.0001 Price elasticity			R = 0.0003 Price elasticity			R = 0.0005 Price elasticity		
		−0.3	−0.5	−0.7	−0.3	−0.5	−0.7	−0.3	−0.5	−0.7
<$6,000	0.21	0.56	0.70	0.78	0.44	0.58	0.68	0.36	0.48	0.60
$6,000−$7,999	0.22	0.54	0.68	0.76	0.42	0.56	0.68	0.36	0.48	0.60
$8,000−$9,999	0.17	0.62	0.74	0.82	0.48	0.62	0.72	0.38	0.52	0.64
$10,000−$11,999	0.18	0.60	0.74	0.82	0.46	0.60	0.72	0.38	0.50	0.64
$12,000−$14,999	0.19	0.58	0.72	0.80	0.46	0.60	0.70	0.38	0.50	0.62
$15,000−$24,999	0.23	0.52	0.66	0.76	0.42	0.56	0.66	0.36	0.48	0.60
$25,000 and over	0.29	0.46	0.58	0.68	0.38	0.50	0.60	0.32	0.44	0.54
All families with two adults, two children		0.57	0.70	0.79	0.44	0.58	0.69	0.37	0.49	0.61
No tax subsidy		0.94	1.00	1.00	0.64	0.80	0.90	0.50	0.64	0.78

a. Based on 1970 tax rates (includes only employee's share of Social Security tax and no state income tax).

ginal tax rates and the corresponding optimum if there were no tax subsidy. This analysis represents a conservative estimate of the potential effect of the tax subsidies. The marginal tax rate in each income class is the sum of the estimated marginal federal income tax rate for married taxpayers in that income class and the employee's share of the Social Security tax.[22] No state tax rate is included. The results are based on a value of $\lambda + 0.1$.

The dramatic effect of the tax subsidy can be illustrated well by examining the optimal coinsurance rates corresponding to moderate risk aversion ($R = 0.0003$) and a moderate price elasticity (-0.50). With no tax, such a family would want a coinsurance rate of 0.80, that is, the family would pay 80 percent of its bills while the insurance company would pay 20 percent. Even in the lowest income bracket (less than $6,000), with a marginal tax rate of 21 percent, the tax subsidy greatly increases the desired amount of insurance. The optimal coinsurance rate becomes 0.58, representing a more than doubling of the insured proportion. Because the Social Security tax ceases to contribute to the marginal rate for incomes above $8,000, the overall marginal rate temporarily decreases in spite of the progressivity of the income tax schedule.[23] But even with a marginal rate of 17 percent, the optimal coinsurance rate is 0.62. At a high marginal rate of 40 percent (not shown in the table), the optimal coinsurance rate drops to only 0.40. The weighted average of the optimal coinsurance rates, weighting by the relative numbers of families with two adults and two children in each of the income classes, is 0.58.

An increase in the price elasticity of demand has two effects on the optimal coinsurance rate. The primary effect of a greater demand elasticity is that insurance induces a greater loss through the distorted demand for care; this reduces the optimal amount of insurance, that

22. The income class is based on a broad definition of adjusted family income that corresponds to the usual definition of economic income: consumption (including imputed rents) plus taxes paid plus the net increase in the value of assets. The marginal federal income tax rate is an average of the marginal rates for all families in the income class. These distributions of taxable income within adjusted family income class are computed with the 1970 MERGE File prepared by the Brookings Institution from the 1967 Survey of Economic Opportunity and the corresponding Treasury Tax File. A conservative feature of this calculation is that the tax rate for the open-ended category of taxable income above $20,000 was based on a taxable income of only $20,000. See Okner (1972) and M. Feldstein (1974a) for a description of the data and the method of calculation.

Including the employer's share would increase all marginal rates by 4.8 percent. Including only half of the total Social Security tax is intended to reflect the weak association between future benefits and the level of taxable earnings under Social Security.

23. An example of this is shown in table 8.3.

is, it increases the optimal coinsurance rate. A greater demand elasticity also implies a greater financial risk and therefore a greater demand for insurance. Only with extremely high risk aversion could the second effect dominate. With $R = 0.0003$ an increase in the price elasticity from -0.3 to -0.7 raises the optimal coinsurance rate in the absence of a tax subsidy from 0.64 to 0.90. The optimal coinsurance rate is also higher at each marginal tax rate, but the relative increase in insurance coverage is essentially unchanged. The average coinsurance rate for all families rises from 0.44 to 0.69.

Greater risk aversion implies lower optimal coinsurance rates and a smaller tax effect. With $R = 0.0003$ and a price elasticity of -0.5, the optimal coinsurance rate with no tax is 0.80 and falls to an average of 0.58 when tax subsidies are introduced. The share paid by insurance therefore more than doubles, from 20 percent with no subsidy to more than 40 percent. With the very high risk aversion of R 0.0005,[24]

Figure 8.2

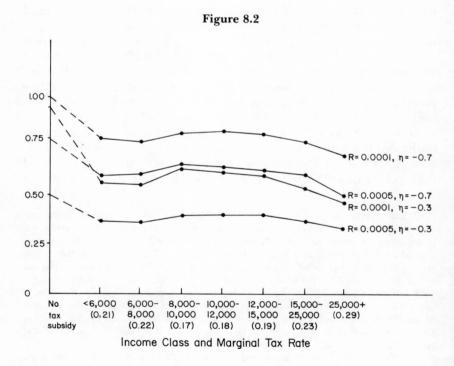

Income Class and Marginal Tax Rate

24. Recall that this implies that the marginal utility function of a family with $10,000 has a local elasticity of 5.

the optimal coinsurance rate is only decreased a small amount, from 0.64 to 0.49.

Figure 8.2 summarizes the effect of the tax subsidy on the optimal coinsurance rate for two values of R and for the low and high price elasticities. Within this framework the optimal coinsurance rate is quite sensitive to the tax subsidy. Actual insurance policies are of course more complex, generally involving deductibles as well as co-insurance payments[25] and providing different coverage for hospital and nonhospital expenditures. The next section extends the analysis to a more realistic description of insurance options and examines the impact of the tax subsidy on actual coverage of the U.S. population in 1970.

The Aggregate Impact of the Tax Subsidy on the Demand for Insurance

The analysis of the actual impact of the tax subsidy on the demand for insurance in the United States requires three modifications of the methods used in the preceding two sections. We have enriched the description of the insurance options to include deductibles as well as coinsurance and to allow for different coverage for hospital and non-hospital care. The specification of this enlarged model is a natural extension of the one-dimensional model.[26] This section discusses the required bivariate specifications of the parameter of the stochastic illness experience and examines the consistency of the parameter values with the actual insurance coverage. It then shows that the U.S. tax subsidy has had a substantial effect on aggregate insurance coverage.

Parameter Values and Tests of Consistency

The family or unrelated individual is the basic unit of analysis. The entire population under the age of sixty-five is divided into sixteen types of demographic unit (husband and wife and two children; single female; and so forth) and twelve income classes. The analysis finds the optimal insurance coverage for each of the 192 family types with and without the current tax subsidy.

The bivariate basic illness distribution $f(X_H, X_M)$ is not constrained to a particular parametric form. Instead, empirical distributions using 24 classes of expenditure for each type of care (576 expenditure cells)

---

25. A deductible in an insurance policy is the amount that must be paid by the insured before the insurance company begins to share any of the costs.

26. The enlarged model is presented in Feldstein and Friedman (1972).

were estimated on the basis of the actuarial experience of the 200,000 federal employees using the data described in the preceding section. More specifically, for each assumed set of demand elasticities, separate bivariate basic illness distributions for an employed adult, a dependent spouse, and a child were inferred from the observed actuarial distributions. Family basic illness distributions were then obtained for the 16 demographic types by convoluting the 24 by 24 matrices of frequencies.[27]

In order to aggregate the simulation results for the 192 different income and demographic categories, population frequencies were computed from the Current Population Survey for 1971.[28] For each family category classified by demographic type and income, an estimated marginal tax rate in 1970 was computed from an Internal Revenue Service tabulation of tax returns.[29]

The demand for insurance depends on the demand elasticities and the degree of risk aversion. An important step in the analysis was to narrow the region in the "parameter space" to values that are roughly consistent with the observed 1970 experience. More specifically, we examined three sets of price elasticities (high, $\eta_{HH} = -0.7$ and $\eta_{MM} = -0.6$; moderate, $\eta_{HH} = -0.5$ and $\eta_{MM} = -0.4$; low, $\eta_{HH} = -0.25$ and $\eta_{MM} = -0.20$) and values of R between 0.0001 and 0.0006.[30] Families were assumed to choose among five insurance options:

Option	Deductibles		Coinsurance	
	D_H	D_M	C_H	C_M
1	$500	$500	0.5	0.5
2	100	150	0.5	0.5
3	50	100	0.3	0.3
4	50	50	0.2	0.2
No insurance	0	0	1.0	1.0

27. This convolution assumes independent illness experience within families. Some evidence to support this was obtained by comparing the actual distribution for three-person families with the convoluted distribution.

28. The 1971 Current Population Survey contains income information for 1970.

29. The tabulation gives the numbers of returns cross-classified by taxable income and adjusted gross income. An average of the statutory marginal rates was computed for each income class. For all families with earnings below $8,000, an additional 5 percent was added to the marginal rate to represent the marginal employee Social Security contribution.

30. A zero cross-price elasticity was assumed to reduce the number of required calculations. Davis and Russell (1972) provide some evidence of a positive cross-price elasticity, but medical services in their study were limited to hospital outpatient care.

Option 3 represents typical 1970 coverage for a family with an employed head.[31] Feasible values of R for each set of demand parameters are those that for the given tax laws imply aggregate 1970 experience resembling the actual experience. In addition, combinations of R and the demand elasticities are eliminated if they do not satisfy the following criteria: (1) All families would choose some insurance option rather than no coverage, even when there is no tax subsidy. (2) More extensive coverage is chosen by those with the highest marginal tax rate (0.34 in our calculations) than by those with the lowest marginal tax rate (0.17).

The resulting subset of feasible values of R was a subset of those considered in the third section. An intuitively clear pattern of results is that higher demand elasticities require higher assumed risk aversion to fit the observed experience. For families of two adults and two children, the moderate demand elasticities and $R = 0.0003$ imply that option 3 was selected for incomes below \$8,000 and for incomes above \$12,000; in the interval between \$8,000 and \$12,000 option 2 was preferred.[32] For $R = 0.0005$ option 3 is chosen for incomes below \$15,000 and option 4 for higher incomes. With the low price elasticities similar insurance results are obtained with lower values of R. An increase in λ from 0.1 to 0.5 increases the demand for insurance and therefore makes lower values of R consistent with each set of demand elasticities.

Effects of the Tax Subsidy
We have examined the effect of the tax subsidy for a variety of feasible combinations of R, λ, and the price elasticities. To do this, we have compared the insurance options chosen with the current tax subsidy to the options that would be chosen with no tax subsidy. The results generally indicate that the tax subsidy causes a substantial increase in the extent of insurance.[33]

31. See Reed and Carr (1968). In 1970 aggregate private health-care expenses for the population under age sixty-five were \$12.9 billion for hospital care and \$10.4 billion for medical services. Consumers paid directly 27 percent of hospital expenses and 52 percent of medical expenses. This difference in average effective coinsurance rates is consistent with option 3 because of the larger medical deductible and because the distribution of medical expenses is much less skewed than the distribution of hospital expenses.

32. This result reflects the drop in the marginal rate due to the upper limit of \$8,000 on the Social Security tax. In practice, because of the group coverage, option 3 would be chosen by the entire group.

33. We have assumed that the tax subsidy is the only source of variation in net premium cost among income classes. This ignores the difference among income classes in the access to group coverage and the systematic variation in the ratio of premiums to benefits; see Mitchell and Vogel (1974).

For example the families of two adults and two children with moderate price elasticities and $R = 0.0003$ who chose option 3 with the current tax subsidy would chose option 1 if the subsidy were removed. This implies that the coinsurance rates nearly double from 0.3 to 0.5 and that the deductibles rise from $D_H = 50$ to $D_H = 500$ and from $D_M = 100$ to $D_M = 500$. Their average effective coinsurance rate (the ratio of consumer payments to gross expenditure) therefore increases from 0.45 with option 3 to 0.87 with option 1. Removing the tax subsidy also makes all families with $R = 0.0005$ choose option 2 even if they would choose option 3 with the tax subsidy.

The simplest way to assess the overall impact of the tax subsidy is by comparing the average effective coinsurance rate for the entire population with and without the subsidy. For this purpose it is important to recognize that the actuarial experience of the federal employees does not provide a representative sample of all U.S. families, particularly in regard to geographic distribution, employment status, and occupation. For each set of demand parameters (η_{11}, η_{22}, and λ) the basic illness distributions were calibrated to give the actual 1970 private expenditures on hospital and medical care on the assumption that all families had the same typical (option 3) insurance coverage.[34] Given these basic illness distributions, the optimal insurance coverage was then calculated for each type of family both with and without the tax subsidy.[35]

Table 8.2 compares the average effective coinsurance rates for three different parameter assumptions. The first column shows that with no tax subsidy the average optimal coinsurance rate would be between 55 percent and 60 percent. The effect of the tax subsidy is to reduce the optimal coinsurance rate to about 40 percent. This represents an increase of about 50 percent in the share paid by insurance, from about 40 percent to about 60 percent. The next four columns show that the effect is greater for medical expenses than for hospital expenses. Hospital expenses are much more skewed, and a greater

34. For this calculation, the option 3 insurance coverage is used for a preliminary simulation to estimate the national aggregate expenditures corresponding to each set of demand parameters. Suppose that the estimated expenditures for some set of demand parameters are E_H^* and E_M^* and that the actual 1970 expenditures are E_H^0 and E_M^0. The ratios E_H^*/E_H^0 and E_M^0/E_M^0 are then used to deflate the expenditure units of the corresponding baseline distributions.

35. Since the optimal insurance with the subsidy does not correspond to option 3 for all family types, the implied values of the expenditures are not exactly equal to the actual values. The agreement is always within 10 percent and usually much closer. Because the insurance depends on the distribution, there is no simple way of extending the method described in footnote 34 to yield an exact calculation.

Table 8.2. Effects of the tax subsidy on the aggregate demand for insurance

	Average effective coinsurance rates					
	Total		Hospital		Medical	
Parameter values	No subsidy	Subsidy	No subsidy	Subsidy	No subsidy	Subsidy
Low price elasticities ($R = 0.0003$)	0.58	0.37	0.44	0.32	0.76	0.43
Moderate price elasticities ($R = 0.0003$)	0.59	0.46	0.44	0.37	0.79	0.56
Moderate price elasticities ($R = 0.0005$)	0.55	0.39	0.42	0.33	0.76	0.46

Note: All calculations use $\lambda = 0.1$. Low price elasticities are $\eta_{11} = -0.25$ (hospital) and $\eta_{22} = -0.20$ (medical); moderate elasticities are $\eta_{11} = -0.50$ and $\eta_{22} = -0.40$.

rate of insurance is therefore appropriate both with and without the tax subsidy. The tax subsidy reduces the optimal hospital coinsurance rate from 44 percent to 32 percent with the low price elasticities and $R = 0.0003$. By contrast, in this case the optimal medical coinsurance falls from 0.76 to 0.43.

The substantial effect of the tax subsidy implied by these calculations probably understates the true effect. The four insurance options are likely to force individuals to buy more insurance in the absence of the tax subsidy than they would if more alternatives were available. Although option 2 is chosen frequently, option 1 is rare. An alternative coverage, relating the size of the deductible to income, would probably be preferred to option 2 in the absence of a tax subsidy and would raise the effective coinsurance rate even more.

The Growth of Insurance and the Rise in the Price of Care

The growth of insurance increases the demand for health care and causes the price of health services to rise. From 1950 to 1972 the cost of hospital care rose at an annual rate of 8.3 percent while all consumer prices increased at only 2.5 percent. The cost of physicians' services also outpaced the CPI, rising at an annual rate of 4.1 percent. Because the growth of insurance has been the primary cause of the exceptional rise in health-care prices, it can be said that the tax subsidy has been responsible for much of the health-care crisis of the past decade. This section examines the interdependence of price and insurance.

The nature of the price rise is particularly important. The primary reason that health-care prices rise in response to an increase in insurance is not the greater unit cost of providing more of the same type of care (a rising supply curve in the traditional sense) but that hospitals and physicians are induced to produce a different and more expensive product. This change in the "style" or sophistication of care has been particularly important for hospitals. From 1958 to 1967 the cost per day of hospital care rose 117 percent. During the same period a price index of hospitals' inputs rose only 35 percent. Almost all the increase in the cost of hospital care in excess of the general rise in prices is due to the increase in resource inputs per patient-day associated with the changing style of care.[36] Although a large fraction of the increase in physicians' fees has been absorbed in higher physicians' incomes, the growth of insurance has also induced an increased sophistication of ambulatory care.[37]

It is not clear how the changing character of care has influenced the patients' demand for health services.[38] The greater sophistication of facilities and services may please physicians who enjoy the practice of modern scientific medicine without increasing the demand for services by patients.[39] But to the extent that patients perceive and appreciate the higher quality of care that accompanies a higher gross price,[40] they will reduce their demand by less in response to any given increase in net price induced by a rise in gross price than to an equal increase in net price induced by a rise in the coinsurance rate. This may be expressed by generalizing the conditional demand function of equation (2) to

$$Q_0 = X_0 P^\gamma \left(\frac{CP + \lambda}{1 + \lambda}\right)^\eta. \tag{19}$$

The new term, P^γ, with $\gamma > 0$, reflects the way in which an increase in the gross price (P) stimulates demand while an increase in the net price $(CP + \lambda)$ reduces demand. The analysis of this section com-

36. For an analysis of the composition of cost increases, see M. Feldstein (1974b). More generally, the effects of insurance on the costs and quality of hospital care are discussed in M. Feldstein (1971b) and in chapter 3.

37. See M. Feldstein (1970c) and Fuchs and Kramer (1972).

38. The emphasis on the patient's demand for services oversimplifies the process by which the patient and physician together determine the demand for care. For a description of this agency relation see chapter 2.

39. Although this may seem implausible, in the more familiar setting of the university it is clear that adding facilities and personnel that please the faculty may have little or no effect on the demand for admission by potential undergraduates.

40. Econometric evidence that a greater resource input per patient-day increases the demand for hospital care is presented in chapter 4.

pares the conventional demand specification ($\gamma = 0$) with the specification of equation (19) in the case $\gamma = -0.5\,\eta$.

An increase in the price of care has a complicated impact on the optimal coinsurance rate. One effect of a higher price is an increase in financial risk and therefore a lower optimal coinsurance rate. But a higher price also increases the welfare loss that results from price distortion at each coinsurance rate; the partial effect of this is to raise the optimal coinsurance rate. The net response of the optimal coinsurance rate to the gross price of care is therefore indeterminate and can change sign as price changes.[41] The greater the individual's risk aversion (R), the more likely it is that a higher price will increase the demand for insurance. Similarly, the greater the individual's absolute price elasticity ($|\,\eta\,|$), the more likely it is that a higher price will reduce the demand for insurance.

To analyze the relation of optimal coinsurance to gross price, we have generalized the expected gain function of the third section to incorporate the demand function of equation (19). We then take the price of care in 1970 as 1 and analyze the optimal coinsurance rates that would prevail at earlier prices. More specifically, we find the optimal coinsurance rates corresponding to 1.0, 0.8, 0.6, 0.4, and 0.2. Table 8.3 shows the average optimal coinsurance rates at these price levels for different combinations of risk aversion (R), net price elasticity (η), and gross price elasticity (γ). The results clearly demonstrate the countervailing effects of risk aversion and price elasticity. With $R = 0.0003$, $\eta = -0.50$, and $\gamma = 0.25$, the demand for insurance decreases until $P = 0.80$ and then stops falling. Increasing the risk aversion (to $R = 0.0005$) implies that the demand for insurance begins to rise at $P = 0.8$, while decreasing the price elasticity implies that the demand for insurance rises over the entire price range.

When a higher price increases the demand for insurance, the interdependence enlarges the effect of any exogenous increase in price or in the demand for insurance. But even in this case the results of table 8.3 indicate that the elasticity of the coinsurance rate with respect to the price level is low enough to keep the markets for care and for insurance stable in spite of the interdependence.[42]

---

41. This is contrary to the simplifying assumption of a constant elasticity function relating coinsurance to price that was used in chapter 6 to estimate the response of insurance to gross price in an econometric study using aggregate data.

42. This confirms the conclusion in chapter 6; see the discussion there for the specific stability conditions. The more basic requirement for stability $\partial Q/\partial P < 0$ is assumed to be satisfied. It follows from equation (19) that this will be true if $|\eta|\gamma > (CP + \lambda)|CP$; as C decreases, the likelihood of instability increases.

Table 8.3. Effect of the price of care on the optimal coinsurance rate

	$R = 0.0001$				$R = 0.0003$				$R = 0.0005$			
Price η	−0.50	−0.30	−0.50	−0.70	−0.50	−0.30	−0.50	−0.70	−0.50	−0.30	−0.50	−0.70
of care γ	0.00	0.15	0.25	0.35	0.00	0.15	0.25	0.35	0.00	0.15	0.25	0.35
0.20	0.482	0.507	0.483	0.432	0.471	0.492	0.480	0.428	0.458	0.469	0.467	0.428
0.40	0.553	0.545	0.564	0.531	0.525	0.495	0.530	0.518	0.494	0.457	0.506	0.504
0.60	0.612	0.561	0.619	0.625	0.554	0.484	0.565	0.594	0.506	0.426	0.522	0.563
0.80	0.662	0.565	0.662	0.709	0.570	0.464	0.584	0.650	0.503	0.398	0.514	0.597
1.00	0.701	0.565	0.701	0.786	0.584	0.445	0.584	0.689	0.491	0.368	0.491	0.614
0.20[a]	0.640	0.840	0.640	0.540	0.620	0.870	0.640	0.520	0.600	0.740	0.620	0.520

Note: Optimal coinsurance rates (except for the final row) reflect tax subsidies based on marginal tax rates shown in table 8.1. Average coinsurance rates are weighted averages for all families with two adults and two children. All calculations use $\lambda = 0.1$.

[a] With no tax subsidy.

This chapter has focused on the effect that the tax subsidy of health insurance premiums has had on the demand for health insurance. There has been no discussion of the welfare effects of the subsidy or of the implications of our analysis for future tax policy. We therefore conclude with some brief remarks on these subjects.

Because the special tax treatment of health insurance is in effect the subsidy of a subsidy, the welfare loss is very large in relation to the tax subsidy itself. Although the welfare loss of a tax subsidy is usually a function of the tax rate and tax base, in the current case the subsidy reflects the average insurance rate and the magnitude of the insured health expenditure. Chapter 6 estimated the welfare loss of excess insurance for hospital care. Although the methods and assumptions of chapter 6 differ somewhat from those used in this chapter, the earlier results are useful for indicating the substantial magnitude of the welfare loss that results from the tax subsidy. In chapter 6 it was found that increasing the average coinsurance rate from 0.33 to 0.50 may yield a welfare gain in 1969 of about $3 billion. This gain should be compared with total 1969 private hospital spending of $12.9 billion. By 1972 private hospital expenditure increased to $17.0 billion; an equal proportional increase in the welfare change would imply a welfare gain of $4 billion.

The preceding analysis indicated tax subsidy induces an even greater distortion in the demand for medical insurance. Since private expenditure for physicians' services ($14 billion in 1972) is only a little less than private expenditure for hospital services, the welfare loss that results from the tax subsidy is likely to be large.

A further important welfare cost results from the loss of revenue due to the tax subsidy. More specifically, to keep the same total tax revenue the government must increase the marginal tax rates to offset the fall in the tax base. Based on estimates of the 1970 fall in tax revenue of approximately $3.8 billion (chapter 7; Mitchell and Vogel 1974), a labor supply elasticity of $\epsilon = 1$ implies a welfare loss of $1.10 billion, while $\epsilon = 0.5$ implies a welfare loss of $0.55 billion.

Although none of these estimated welfare losses is very precise, it is clear that combining the losses due to excess insurance with the loss due to a higher marginal tax rate implies that the welfare cost of the tax subsidy is very large, approximately $8 billion in 1970. Since the total subsidy is only some $4 billion, the relative inefficiency is extremely large.

The distribution of the tax subsidy among income classes is quite unequal, with significantly greater subsidies going to higher-income families. In 1969 average annual employer insurance payments per family rose from less than $100 in the lowest income families to more than $160 in families with incomes over $10,000 (chapter 7). The tax saving is more than twice as great for the higher-income families than for those with the lowest incomes: an average of about $25 for families with less than $5,000 of income and more than $50 for families with income greater than $25,000. The top 16 percent of families receive more than 23 percent of the tax subsidy, while the bottom 16 percent receive less than 10 percent of the subsidy.[43]

Eliminating the special tax subsidies of health insurance premiums should be a high priority subject for tax reform. The current law encourages an excessive purchase of insurance, distorts the demand for health services, and thus inflates the prices of these services. Because the current provisions involve a subsidy of a subsidy, the welfare loss is particularly large. Moreover, the revenue loss is substantial and the tax reductions are distributed very regressively.

It now seems likely that some form of national health insurance will be introduced within a few years. It is to be hoped that the benefit structure will use substantial deductibles and coinsurance in a design that balances the advantages of reducing risk against the disadvantages of distorting demand. If individuals are free to purchase additional private insurance to supplement the public program, the current tax rules will encourage the purchase of excessive supplementary coverage. Eliminating the current deduction and exclusion are therefore important even if national health insurance is enacted.[44]

43. The benefits of the personal deduction for health insurance premiums are even more regressive. The tax saving is less than $5 for taxpayers and adjusted gross incomes below $7,500 but more than $25 for taxpayers with adjusted gross incomes over $25,000. The bottom 50 percent of taxpayers receive 10 percent of the subsidy while the top 10 percent of taxpayers receive more than one-third of the subsidy.

44. With national health insurance the problem of excessive coverage is even more complex. Supplementary private insurance that reduces the effective deductibles and coinsurance rates will increase the family's expected benefits of the public policy without any increase in the family's cost of the public policy. Thus, even without the tax subsidy, there would be an incentive for excessive supplementary insurance coverage unless the national health insurance deductibles and coinsurance payments are required to be paid in cash and are not reinsurable.

Part Three

Issues in National Health Insurance

The first chapter in this part is quite different from all the other chapters in this volume. Instead of a scientific investigation of some aspect of the health-care system, chapter 9 presents a normative policy analysis and a proposal for national health insurance. The chapter begins by suggesting six objectives by which any national health insurance proposal should be judged. The analysis then criticizes the existing insurance coverage for its lack of protection against very large expenses but reject the prevailing national health insurance proposals because of their distortionary effects and high cost. An alternative major-risk insurance proposal, with copayments and maximum out-of-pocket liabilities related to income, is then described and analyzed.

Chapter 10 provides a detailed analysis of the costs and distributional consequences of a variety of major-risk insurance proposals. The analysis uses a microsimulation model based on the national expense of more than three hundred thousand federal employees. Microsimulation of this type is required because of the extreme nonlinearities introduced by deductibles and upper limits. Because of the income-related copayments, the expected net benefits decline sharply with income while the mean and maximum payments for health care rise significantly with income.

The last chapter extends this type of microsimulation analysis by incorporating an explicit model of the supply and price responses in the markets for hospital care and physicians' services. Although there are no explicit aggregate demand equations in this analysis, the microsimulation model can be solved for prices that equate supply and demand. An alternative model is also developed in which hospital prices rise because hospitals change the nature of their product while physicians increase their prices in response to greater demand or increased insurance without setting a market-clearing price. The analysis uses these models to calculate the costs and other consequences of alternative national health insurance plans. While much of the debate about the effects of national health insurance has focused on the uncertainty about the responsiveness of household demand, this chapter shows that uncertainty about supply response may be even more important.

9 A New Approach to National Health Insurance

A new approach to national health insurance is urgently needed. The present system of financing health care provides inadequate protection, encourages inefficient use of resources, and accelerates the inflation of medical costs. Unfortunately, the proposals for national health insurance now being discussed will not remedy this situation. A different approach to national health insurance would avoid the major shortcomings in the present system and in the previously suggested alternatives.

Any proposed system for financing health care should be judged by the following six objectives.

1. *Prevent deprivation of care.* No individual should be deprived of medical care because of inability to pay, just as no individual should go hungry or lack adequate housing because of low income. Moreover, no one should be encouraged to delay care because his insurance will not pay for preventive or ambulatory care but only for hospitalized treatment of the more serious illness that may ensue.

2. *Prevent financial hardship.* No family should suffer substantial financial hardship because of the expense of unpredictable illness or accident.

3. *Keep costs down.* A financing system should encourage efficient use of resources and discourage medical-care price inflation. Whenever possible, patients should use relatively low cost ambulatory facilities rather than high-cost in-hospital care. Hospitals should be induced to moderate the forces that raise the cost of care: increased personnel, unnecessary pay raises, and a proliferation of technical facilities and services. Physicians should not be encouraged to increase their fees by the knowledge that, because of insurance, the cost to their own pa-

Reprinted with permission from *The Public Interest,* no. 23 (Spring 1971), pp. 93–105.

tients will rise little if at all. In short, the financing method should encourage cost consciousness in the decisions of patients, doctors, and hospital administrators.

4. *Avoid a large tax increase.* High taxes distort the supply of work effort and cause inefficient use of resources in the economy as a whole. Therefore, a national health insurance program that raises substantial funds from taxpayers and returns it in the form of health insurance has a large hidden cost in lower national income. The magnitude of total spending on health care makes this an important consideration. In fiscal year 1968–69 government spent nearly $19 billion on personal health care; private expenditures then approached $34 billion. Transferring this private spending to the public sector would require a very large increase in tax rates. For example, if it were to be financed by an increase in the individual income tax, collections would have to rise more than 30 percent. If the Social Security payroll tax were used, its rate would have to be doubled.

5. *Be easily administered.* The administration of a health-care system should not require complex procedures, which are costly and inconvenient, or arbitrary decisions, which imply that resources are not used appropriately.

6. *Be generally acceptable.* Any new method of financing should be acceptable to physicians and to hospitals as well as to the general public. A system that is disliked by either would encounter substantial political opposition and, if instituted, would be hampered by lack of cooperation and an inadequate supply of new personnel in the long run.

The Current System

Although almost every American is enrolled for some form of health insurance, the current coverage is typically shallow. That is, families incurring large medical bills often find that their insurance pays only a relatively small portion. A 1963 National Opinion Research Center survey found that the average annual expenditure for medical care among survey families was $370 and that approximately one-fifth had expenses exceeding $500.[1] Among the *insured* families that spent more than $500, only one-third received benefits exceeding half of their expenditures while another third received benefits of less than one-fifth of their expenditures. Today, as in 1963, most hospital insurance pays a relatively high proportion of small and moderate bills

1. This survey of 2,367 families containing 7,803 individuals is reported in Andersen and Anderson (1967).

but imposes a variety of ceilings on use and an effective overall ceiling on benefits; the less restrictive major medical insurance policies cover less than half of the population under sixty-five.

The absence of deep coverage leaves a large residue of financial hardship and may also prevent many people from seeking potentially expensive care. Moreover, the fact that hospitalization (including surgical) insurance is much more complete than insurance for non-surgical physician care discourages patients from seeking preventive care and induces them to gamble with their health in the knowledge that, should untreated minor symptoms become severe, a short stay in hospital is likely to be relatively costless.

The current system of financing medical care has also contributed to the high and rapidly increasing costs of such care. A substantial body of research has shown that because of the structure of insurance coverage, patients obtain expensive (but covered) in-hospital care when much less expensive (but uncovered) ambulatory care would have been as effective. Insurance has also accelerated the rising cost of in-hospital care. Ironically, although the hospital patient with a large bill often finds his insurance grossly inadequate, the *average* patient stays a relatively short time (the 1968 mean stay in community hospitals was 8.4 days) and has almost his entire hospital bill paid for by insurance. For most days of care, therefore, the hospital does not sell its sevices to individual patients but collects its costs from an insurance company or Blue Cross plan. Of the approximately $9.9 billion of private expenditure on hospital care in 1968, more than 73 percent was covered by insurance. Since 1966, the problem has been exacerbated by Medicare and Medicaid; government now purchases nearly half the total hospital care. Because hospitals are able to pass almost all cost increases on to insurance companies and the government, there is neither internal incentive nor external pressure from patients to moderate cost increases. Finally, the growth of medical insurance has accelerated physician fee inflation not only by increasing demand but also by allowing the physician to raise his fee without imposing an equal extra burden on his own patient.

Subsidy-Credit Plans

Thus our current system of financing health care provides inadequate coverage while inducing substantial cost inflation. Judged by the first three criteria, this system has failed badly.

The combination of inadequate coverage and rapidly rising costs has stimulated a variety of proposals for national health insurance. All plans are of two basic types: one involves direct subsidies or tax credits for the purchase of the current type of health insurance from private insurance companies; the other is universal comprehensive public health insurance.

The proposals to give subsidies and tax credits to purchasers of voluntary insurance differ only in detail. Each provides a maximum level of tax credit or subsidy that would be paid to purchasers of insurance in the lowest income group and a schedule of lower subsidies to higher-income groups. The proponents of these schemes have concentrated their attention on the method of government finance for the program (general tax revenue and payroll taxes) and the costs of the particular schedules of subsidies. The maximum premium subsidies have varied between $200 per family and $500 per family in the different proposals; these numbers should be compared with an estimate[2] of $850 per family of four for a fully comprehensive health insurance in 1968 (including dental care and drugs as well as hospitalization and physicians' services) and the actual 1968 average premium per family of four of $304.[3]

These subsidy proposals have two major objectives: to encourage the purchase of more health insurance and to replace Medicaid. However, a subsidy would have no effect on the purchase of insurance by families that already spend as much as their maximum subsidy for insurance. As the estimte of $304 for the average actual premium indicates, proposed subsidies of $200 or $300 are likely to have little effect on the total purchase of insurance, except perhaps among relatively low income groups. (Surprisingly, there has been no estimate of the extent to which subsidies or credits would exceed current expenditures on insurance by families at different income levels.) As for the second objective—the replacement of Medicaid—it is true that these plans might remove a substantial burden from state and local governments. But it would also replace the current relatively comprehensive insurance coverage that Medicaid provides in many states for low-income families with more limited coverage. The major effect of the subsidy-credit plans would be an income transfer, generally in the form of tax reduction, from higher-income groups to middle-income and lower-middle-income groups. For many such families there would be no incentive to purchase more health insurance—their current policies cost as much as the maximum subsidy that they would be entitled to receive—but only a welcome reduction in taxes.

Because the subsidy-credit plans rely on current forms of health insurance, they perpetuate all the weaknesses of the present system.

2. Waldman (1969).
3. Reed (1969).

Some individuals would still be deprived of care because of prohibitive costs. The danger of financial hardship would remain. The forces that encourage medical-care price inflation would not only remain but would be intensified to the extent that insurance coverage grows. Moreover, the program would require a substantial tax increase, estimated at between $10 billion and more than $15 billion; expenditure increases resulting from such a program would probably make the actual tax increases much greater.

Because a large proportion of the government expenditure on these programs would simply redistribute income without increasing health insurance, they should be compared to the negative income tax and other programs for welfare reform. In terms of its ability to alleviate real poverty, the subsidy-credit health insurance schemes are much less effective per dollar of tax increase than more direct redistributive programs.

There is, in short, little to recommend these proposals as a way of improving the health-care system, or of containing costs, or of increasing protection. They are an inefficient way of redistributing income and an inappropriate way of assisting state governments currently burdened with Medicaid expenditures.

Uniform Comprehensive Health Insurance

The proposals for uniform comprehensive health insurance generally advocate something like an extension of Medicare to the entire population. More comprehensive programs would abolish the small deductible and coinsurance features of Medicare, eliminate its limit on the length of covered hospitalization, and extend coverage to drugs and dental care.

There is no doubt that under comprehensive insurance no one would be deprived of needed care because of inability to pay or suffer any financial hardship because of unpredictable illness. In terms of the other criteria, however, such plans must be judged unacceptable.

Although comprehensive insurance would remove the current incentive for patients to use inpatient rather than ambulatory care, it would not introduce any positive incentives for the efficient use of resources. Whatever cost consciousness still exists among patients, doctors, and administrators would be removed. There would be no incentive to limit the rising cost of hospital care, to use paramedical personnel more widely, or to produce physicians' services more efficiently. With all bills paid by the government, nothing would limit the rise in hospital wage rates and physicians' incomes. In such a situation the government would be forced to introduce direct controls and producer incentives in an attempt to contain costs.

Detailed controls, fee schedules, and limits on hospital charges might, of course, prevent rising costs, but the experience of Canada, Britain, and Sweden suggests that health costs rise very rapidly even in government health programs with extensive direct controls. Such controls would not achieve, and might actually work against, an efficient use of health resources. They would certainly require a large number of arbitrary policy decisions and engender the hostility of the basic providers. Such arbitrary decisions pose a more serious problem than may be generally recognized: What is a "reasonable" level of hospital daily cost? At what rate should hospitals improve facilities, add staff, raise the level of amenities? How many beds should there be per thousand population? How much should different medical specialists earn? These are not technical questions that could be answered "objectively" if only enough research were done—they involve tastes and value judgments about the relative desirability of different goods and services.

Finally, even if expenditures were not to rise, the provision of comprehensive insurance would require a substantial tax increase: over $20.5 billion to replace current private expenditure on physician and hospital services and an additional $13.3 billion, if drugs and personal health care were to be included.

Comprehensive insurance would thus shift the problem of the health-care sector to a conflict between cost inflation and controls. No matter where the balance between these was struck, there would be no natural incentive to efficiency and a large government expenditure to be paid for by higher taxes.

A New Approach

My proposal is extremely simple: major-risk insurance (MRI) and government-guaranteed postpayment loans. Every family would receive a comprehensive insurance policy with an annual direct expense limit (deductible) that increased with family income. A $500 "direct-expense limit" means that the family is responsible for the first $500 of medical expenses per year but pays no more than $500 no matter how large the year's total medical bills. Different relations between family income and the direct expense limit are possible. For example, the expense limit might start at $300 per year for a family with income below $3000, be equal to 10 percent of family income between $3000 and $8000, and be $800 for incomes above that level. The details of the schedule are unimportant at this point. The key feature is an expense limit that is large in comparison with average family spending on health care but low relative to family income. The availability in addition of government-guaranteed loans for the postpayment of medical bills would allow families to spread expenditures below the expense limit over a period of a year or even more.[4]

Major-risk insurance is the most important type of health care insurance for the government to provide. It concentrates government effort on those families for whom medical expenses would create financial hardship or prevent appropriate care. Because relatively few families have such large expenditures in any year, MRI need not be a very costly program. Moreover, as explained later in this chapter, MRI is likely to help limit the inflation of medical costs. In terms of our six criteria, these are the advantages of the MRI plan:

1. *Deprivation of care.* If the maximum annual expenditure on health were limited to 10 percent or less of family income, no family would be deprived of care because of inability to pay. (If it is believed that certain preventive care and early diagnostic tests would not be done as much as is desirable, the MRI policy could be supplemented by specific coverage for these activities at relatively little additional cost.)

2. *Financial hardship.* MRI would also prevent financial hardship by limiting the financial risk to 10 percent or less of annual income. The availability of government-guaranteed postpayment loans would permit bills to be spread more comfortably over the year.

3. *Cost inflation.* An increase in insurance coverage generally exacerbates the inflation of hospital costs. However, the universal provision of MRI might reduce hospital-cost inflation by eliminating or at least decreasing the current use of shallow-coverage insurance. Families would have little to gain from such insurance when MRI had removed the risk of major expense. The cost of an insurance policy would be high relative to the upper limit on expenses guaranteed by the MRI. The ensuing reduction in ordinary insurance would help check inflation by reintroducing cost consciousness and incentives to efficient resource use.

Some figures and an example will clarify these ideas. Table 9.1, which is based on a 1963 survey updated to 1968–69 prices, shows the distribution of family expenses for medical care. The average family spending was $600, but half the families spent less than $320. This uneven distribution — with a high percentage of the costs falling on a relatively small proportion of the families — suggests why MRI would reduce the use of ordinary shallow coverage. An $800 MRI policy would lower the average uncovered expenditure to approxi-

4. For a detailed discussion of postpayment, see Eilers (1969).

Table 9.1. Distribution of family expenses for medical care

Expense	Percentage of families	Cumulative percentage
$ 0–79	17.8	17.8
80–159	11.7	29.5
160–319	18.7	48.2
320–479	12.8	61.0
480–639	9.5	70.5
640–799	6.3	76.8
800–1199	10.0	86.8
1200–1599	5.1	91.9
1600–3199	6.5	98.4
3200+	1.6	100.0

mately $400. Although a family could, therefore, buy comprehensive insurance for somewhat more than $400, why should they pay for insurance protection when the *maximum* difference between the benefits and the premiums is a relatively small amount—less than $400?

The effect is even stronger for families with a lower MRI limit. An MRI policy with a $320 limit would reduce average uncovered expenditure to $230. There would be little for a family to gain by paying a premium of at least $230 for an insurance policy against a maximum risk of only $320, especially if postpayment loans are available to spread the expense.

The primary virtue that makes health insurance attractive today is its protection against the risk of larger expenses; when this feature is preempted by the MRI policy, additional coverage should cease to be attractive. The demand for additional insurance would therefore come only from families that expected to have higher than average medical bills—by the families for which the expected benefits were larger than the premium. But such a process of self-selection would raise premiums, further limiting the demand for insurance. The result would be to reduce and perhaps eventually eliminate the current shallow coverage.

This reduction implies that although individuals would be protected by MRI against major expenses for health care, the vast majority of payments for physician and hospital services would not be covered by insurance. Because most physician and hospital care would be paid for directly by the patient, the inflationary forces inherent in the current insurance system would be checked. The current tendency to use insured hospital care instead of relatively less expensive ambulatory services would be replaced by an incentive to choose the most efficient combination of resources to obtain care: ambulatory care, paramedical personnel, and so on. Although patients often do not have the technical information to make such choices, the prospect of substantial cost differences would induce them to seek their physician's advice.

The potential impact on hospital costs is substantial. In 1968 the average daily cost in short-term voluntary hospitals was approximately $70 and the average stay was about eight days, implying a total cost of $560. Under MRI most families would find a high proportion of their bill not covered by insurance. Patients and doctors would, therefore, become more careful in selecting a hospital. Hospital administrators would become more cost conscious in order to maintain demand for their beds and to reduce the burden on their patients. The doctors affiliated with a hospital would become less interested in cost-increasing acquisitions with little impact on patient health and more concerned to keep costs down and obtain high value for money spent on new equipment; high costs would encourage patients to seek a physician who could provide care in another hospital and in addition would impose an extra burden on the patients who remain with them.

Patients' desire to substitute ambulatory care for the more expensive hospital services would increase the demand for physicians' services and therefore tend to raise their fees. This would be somewhat offset by a second shift in demand — from physician care to care by supervised paramedical personnel. Moreover, to the extent that physicians have been raising fees not merely in response to the pressure of demand but because doing so imposes little or no burden on insured patients, future fee inflation could be expected to decrease.

For families that exceed their expense limit MRI would be equivalent to comprehensive insurance. They would therfore have no incentive to limit their spending for medical care.[5] But the basic cost per day in hospitals would be determined not by the willingness of those relatively few families to spend but rather by the preferences of the far larger number of patients who would not be reimbursed. MRI insurance carriers could prevent excesses in physicians' fees and hospital durations of stay by requiring that the same care be given and fees be charged to these patients as to those who are paying for their care. Because most medical services would be paid for directly, the

5. The next section describes a way of modifying the MRI principle to include a coinsurance feature that would substantially reduce the number of families that exceed their expenditure limit without increasing the maximum financial burden for each family.

standard of customary charge and customary care would provide a meaningful reference standard, as they currently do not.

In short, MRI would introduce a cost consciousness and a basis for cost comparison that could improve efficiency and contain medical care inflation.

4. *Tax burden.* The cost to taxpayers for an MRI program would not be large relative to the benefits conferred. The exact amount would depend on the particular schedule of deductibles and the overall impact of the program on utilization and unit costs. I estimate that the cost per family with an $800 limit MRI policy would be $186; with a $300 policy limit, the cost would be $355. By 1968–69 more than half the households had incomes over $8,000 and would therefore receive $800 limit MRI policies. If we assume that 55 percent of households receive $800 limit policies and that the remaining 45 percent are distrubuted evenly among $640, $480, and $320 limit policies, the total cost of MRI for the population below sixty-five years of age would be $13 billion. Against this figure would have to be offset savings from Medicare and Medicaid. Moreover the universal provision of MRI would suggest ending the income tax deduction for medical expenses, further reducing the net cost of MRI.

5. *Administrative simplicity.* The MRI insurance would be relatively simple and inexpensive to administer. Survey data indicate that less than 25 percent of the families with $800 limit policies would make any claim. Even among families with $300 limit policies, only 52 percent would make claims. Each family that exceeds its MRI limit would submit only one claim in a year. Additional families could, of course, apply for postpayment loans.

Reduction in the use of shallow insurance plans with their vast number of small claims would permit a substantial saving in administrative costs. In 1968–69 private expenses for prepayment and administration exceeded $1.7 billion. Because MRI would act to contain cost inflation and to increase efficiency, there would be no need for detailed controls or essentially arbitrary policy decisions. Planning efforts could be concentrated on problems that cannot be solved by the natural forces of supply and demand.

6. *General acceptability.* An MRI scheme should be acceptable to physicians, hospitals, and the general public. It would have the virtue of providing full protection against serious financial hardship without the controls or fee schedule that would accompany other forms of insurance. The current freedom of physicians and hospitals would be preserved. If MRI were administered by the same insurance companies that currently provide health insurance, the net effect would be a small increase in their total premium.

Coinsurance

MRI could be improved by introducing a coinsurance feature above a basic deductible. This would make consumers cost sensitive over a wider range of expenditures without increasing the maximum risk to which they are exposed.

For example, the annual direct expense limit of 10 percent of income could be replaced by a basic deductible of 5 percent of income followed by 50 percent coinsurance for an additional 10 percent of income. A family with a $6,000 income would thus be fully responsible for the first $300 of medical expenses and half of the next $600, implying a maximum total payment of $600. The maximum total expenditure is thus the same as for the MRI plan.

Although the family's maximum payment would be unchanged, the coinsurance would make families cost conscious over a much wider range of expenditures. With an income of $8,000 or more, the family pays half of the bills for expenditures from $400 to $1,200. Fewer than one family in seven has expenses exceeding this amount. For lower-income families the effect is equally great: although a family with an income of $4,800 would have a 40 percent chance of exceeding a $480 expense limit, there is only one chance in four of exceeding the $720 limit implied by the 50 percent coinsurance plan.

The coinsurance variant of MRI would have the advantage of increasing cost consciousness without raising the maximum risk; it would also reduce the chance that the family would be required to spend the maximum amount. For families with incomes of $8,000 or over, the risk of incurring net costs of $800 is reduced from one chance in four to one chance in seven. For families with incomes of $4,800 the risk of spending $480 is reduced from 40 percent to 25 percent.

There is only a slight extra cost to the government for this extra protection and the added cost consciousness of coinsurance. The average cost per family of MRI with coinsurance is $249 compared with $233 without it. There would be a small increase in the cost of administering additional claims, but these extra costs would be more than justified by the much greater cost consciousness that would be obtained.

The MRI and postpayment proposal raises a number of questions. What would happen to Medicaid and Medicare? How would group practice, the increased use of paramedical personnel and other improvements in efficiency be encouraged? Would preventive care be neglected? What would be the role of areawide planning?

MRI would make Medicaid unnecessary. "Medical indigency" for families above the poverty line ($3,300 in 1969 for a family of four) would be eliminated by the provision that health-care spending not exceed 10 percent of income. Families below the poverty line who are currently covered by Medicaid could be given in addition to the MRI policy a cash grant equal to their expected health spending; with a $320 deductible this would be approximately $230. This would leave the family with little risk of unsubsidized and uncovered expenditure (a maximum of about $90 per year for the family), would remove the distinction between welfare patients and others, and would encourage these families to have the same cost consciousness in health spending as the rest of the population. This method of replacing Medicaid is consistent, both in spirit and in adminstrative machinery, with the new approaches to welfare policy such as the Family Allowance Plan and Negative Income Tax, advocated by members of both political parties. It could alternatively be administered within the framework of the current welfare system but without the complex details of the Medicaid program.

Because of the special economic and health problems of the retired aged, it would probably be best to continue Medicare in its current general form as part of the Social Security program. In the spirit of the MRI proposal, the deductibles in parts A and B of Medicare could be increased and compensating amounts added to the Social Security retirement benefits. Even if Medicare is left essentially unchanged, its future cost levels would be restrained by the cost-conscious environment that MRI would create.

A related issue is raised by conditions, such as total chronic kidney failure, in which treatment costs several thousand dollars per year and tens of thousands of dollars during a single illness. MRI might either include these or, by imposing a ceiling, leave their financing to special public programs and private health insurance as at the present. The appropriate solution to this delicate social problem lies outside the scope of this chapter.

Organizational changes that might increase the efficiency with which medical care is produced, such as group practice and the use of paramedical personnel, would be encouraged under MRI by the natural pressure from patients to obtain care at lower cost. A specially trained pediatric nurse or other paramedical worker, capable of providing the same quality of care currently rendered by physicians but at lower cost, would be easier to incorporate into the system of medical care if patients have an incentive to keep costs down than if, because of comprehensive insurance, they can request the more expensive physician care at little or no cost to themselves. Similarly, if group practice is a more efficient way to produce medical care, demand for this type of service would grow as lower costs are passed on to patients in the form of lower fees. Comprehensive prepaid group practice could easily be incorporated into an MRI system by allowing families to apply the actuarial value of their MRI policies against the annual charge of the prepaid group.

The increased reliance on individual preferences and the market mechanism made possible by MRI would not completely eliminate the need for areawide planning. A variety of decisions—the location of expensive diagnostic and treatment equipment, the investment in long-lived hospital facilities, the training of specialized personnel— might still be improved by such coordination. But the behavior of patients who are paying for a large portion of their medical care would help to guide these planning decisions and would act as a long-run check on their appropriateness. Moreover, the MRI system would leave to the market those decisions that planners would have to make if a high proportion of expenses were reimbursed by insurance: What is the "right" level of hospital cost per patient-day? What is the "appropriate" charge for different doctors' services? How much "should" doctors in different specialties earn? In short, areawide planning would be able to concentrate on the problems that cannot be solved by the natural forces of supply and demand.

10 Distributional Aspects of National Health Insurance Benefits and Finance

National health insurance is likely to be one of the most significant public expenditure decisions of the next decade. Personal health expenditures in 1971 exceed $60 billion and are rising rapidly. A national program that increases this total, redistributes the benefits, and reallocates the financing would have a significant distributional impact.

The program design options that will influence this distributional impact include (1) the way that the structure of the insurance coverage (deductibles, coinsurance rates)[1] is related to income and family composition and (2) the mix of revenue sources (income-related premiums, payroll tax, general tax revenue) used to finance the program. An economic analysis of the distributional aspects of alternative national health insurance programs therefore involves not only the usual issues of tax incidence but also two special complexities peculiar to health insurance. First, because insurance coverage is defined in terms of deductibles, coinsurance rates, and the like, the value of the benefits to any family depends on the underlying probability distribution of expenditures. Second, the characteristics of this distribution depend on the random events of illness and the price elasticity of demand.

In this study of the distributional impact of alternative health insurance options, a special method of simulating the distribution of health

This chapter was written with Bernard Friedman and Harold Luft. Reprinted with permission from the *National Tax Journal* 25, no. 4 (December 1972), pp. 497–510.

1. The "deductible" of an insurance policy is the amount that must be paid by the insured family before the insurer begins to pay any share of the expenses. The deductible here is defined on an annual and per family basis. The "coinsurance rate" is the fraction of each dollar of expense in excess of the deductible that the family itself must pay.

expenses with different insurance coverages and price elasticities is developed. A new set of data on health spending is employed in this simulation. The estimation of the distribution of financing uses an original analysis of the sources of household income by the demographic characteristics of the family. We hope that this study will aid the discussion of national health insurance and serve as an example of the analysis of income distribution considerations in public expenditure planning.[2]

The first section of the chapter describes the method of simulating the actuarial value of the benefits and total expenditures under alternative insurance coverage options. The second section discusses the data analysis and alternative incidence assumptions used in assessing the impact of different financing options on families with different income levels and demographic characteristics. The third section suggests several measures that are useful for evaluating the distributional impact of alternative programs. In the third section a "standard plan" of coverage and financing options is analyzed. The fifth section then shows the effects of several incremental program changes in both the insurance coverage and financing. There is a brief final summary section.

Calculating the Value of Alternative Insurance Options

The alternative insurance coverage options can be described in terms of three main parameters: the deductible, the basic coinsurance rate, and the upper limit beyond which the coinsurance rate falls to zero or to some nominal level.[3] In practice, we have generally fixed the upper limit at $1,400 and assumed a zero coinsurance rate for expenditures above that level.[4] The analysis developed here allows the deductible and the coinsurance rate to vary with family income and with the numbers of adults and children. This permits the actuarial value of the coverage, the expected out-of-pocket expenditure, and the maxi-

2. The study differs from general analyses of the incidence of taxes and the benefits of government programs (for example, Musgrave et al. 1951, Gillespie 1965) in focusing on the *marginal* effects of a new program, analyzing the allocation of benefits with much greater accuracy, and allowing for the relation between demographic and income variables. The special data analysis used in assessing the distribution of taxes also permits particular improvements.

3. A number of other specific features, including deductibles for specific expenditures, such as the first day of hospital care, could in principle be analyzed.

4. The purpose of such an upper limit is to set a ceiling on the family's maximum out-of-pocket expenditure; see the third section of this chapter and also chapter 9. Even with very comprehensive insurance, less than 10 percent of all families exceed this level.

mum out-of-pocket expenditure to depend on family income and composition.[5]

Calculations of the actuarial value of the coverage and the expected out-of-pocket expenditure under different insurance options utilize data on the national experience of 335,000 federal employees and their families in 1968.[6] All these persons were covered by the federal employees Aetna High-Option policy, a very comprehensive coverage with a low deductible ($50 per individual except that the first $1,000 of room and board is fully reimbursed) and a low coinsurance rate (20 percent).[7] This implies that the basic expenditure distribution is not distorted by differences among families in insurance coverage or by low levels of insurance coverage that discourage expenditure.[8]

The observed expenditure distributions are adjusted to 1969 levels and used to derive the distributions of expenditures for different insurance coverages and different price sensitivities of demand. The basic model of price sensitivity implies a constant price elasticity: three alternative price elasticities ($\beta = 0, 0.33, 0.67$) were studied.[9] Table 10.1 shows the simulated insurance benefits in 1969 for a family of two adults and two children. The deductible and coinsurance rate varies with family income and composition according to the formula adopted for the standard plan in the fourth section. The deductible is $50 per adult plus $25 for each child plus $50 for each thousand dollars of income up to a maximum of $600 at an income of $12,000 and a coinsurance rate of 8 percent plus 4 percent for each thousand dollars of income up to a maximum of 0.56 percent.[10] Alternative estimates are provided for the three price elasticities. In each case the benefits decline as income increases. The benefits decline more rapidly with income when demand is price sensitive than when it is not.[11]

5. We assume that the Medicare program continues to finance the care of those over sixty-five and analyze only the additional financing for those under sixty-five.

6. We are grateful to Joseph Zisman of the U.S. Civil Service Commission for providing these data.

7. Certain expenses are excluded from coverage, principally routine physical exams, routine dental care, well-baby care, eyeglasses, and custodial care. See Friedman (1971) for more information on the basic sample.

8. Both of these have been problems in the previous use of survey data (Andersen and Anderson 1967) to derive potential expenditure distribution. See chapter 9.

9. See the appendix to this chapter for a detailed description of the method used.

10. A consequence of this coverage is that the maximum out-of-pocket risk rises from $400 at an income of $3,000 to $1,048 at an income of $12,000.

11. The apparent anomaly that benefits decline more rapidly with the low price elasticity ($\beta = -0.33$) than with the high ($\beta = -0.67$) may reflect the fact that changing the elasticity alters the underlying expenditure distribution as well as the relation between this and the observed distribution.

Table 10.1. Simulated insurance benefits of standard plan,[a] family of two adults and two children

Price elasticity (β)	Family income							
	Under $3,000	$3,000–$4,000	$4,000–$5,000	$5,000–$6,000	$6,000–$7,000	$7,000–$8,000	$8,000–$10,000	$10,000+[b]
0	$498	422	391	363	338	317	288	258
−0.33	504	408	366	317	290	270	235	216
−0.67	494	368	309	274	254	244	227	216

a. See text for description of standard plan.
b. There is no change in the insurance coverage and therefore the benefits above $12,000.

Table 10.2. Simulated direct expense of standard plan, family of two adults and two children

Price elasticity (β)	Family income							
	Under $3,000	$3,000– $4,000	$4,000– $5,000	$5,000– $6,000	$6,000– $7,000	$7,000– $8,000	$8,000– $10,000	$10,000+[a]
0	$113	189	220	248	273	294	323	354
−0.33	107	163	180	198	213	226	237	251
−0.67	94	127	126	135	139	145	149	158

a. There is no change in the insurance coverage and therefore the direct expense above $12,000.

Table 10.2 shows the corresponding simulated average direct expenses (out-of-pocket payments) at different income levels and with different price elasticities. The direct expense rises with income. As would be expected from the relation between income and the deductible and coinsurance rate, the rate at which direct expense rises with income is inversely related to the price elasticity of demand.

Estimating the Incidence of Alternative Financing Plans

We have considered three basic methods of financing a national health insurance program: premiums, a Social Security – type payroll tax, and an increase in the personal income tax. This section describes these options in detail, explains the shifting assumptions, and discusses the data and methods used to estimate the actual incidence by family composition and income class.

The premium[12] can be a function of the number of adults and children as well as of family income. It is assumed that the entire premium is borne by the family, that is, that it is not shifted in any way.[13] A premium paid by an employer is not dealt with specifically. It could be treated as equivalent to a premium paid by the family.[14]

In analyzing the use of a proportional payroll tax, we consider three different upper limits to the range of taxable earnings: $9,000, $12,000 and $15,000. Alternative assumptions about the extent of forward shifting are also considered.[15] All tax not borne by the worker on whose wage it is levied is assumed to be shifted forward and to be borne in proportion to family income.[16]

The revenue raised through the personal income tax is assumed to be derived from a proportional increase in the average tax rate in each income bracket; that is, the ratio of the taxes paid by any two taxpayers is unchanged. This chapter also follows the tradition of as-

---

12. It is assumed that the premiums are compulsory. A voluntary plan in which the value of benefits was sufficiently greater than the premium for each family would be effectively equivalent.

13. This is consistent with our treatment of the income tax. See footnote 17, however. We have also assumed that the benefits, although income related, are not shifted.

14. This ignores special problems of two-earner families if employers must pay separately for both. An income-related employer contribution might alternatively be treated as a payroll tax.

15. The incidence of this tax should not depend on the proportion nominally levied on the employer. A reader who maintains that the degree of shifting depends on the nominal source of the tax can of course interpret the proportion shifted as an average of the two separate shifting proportions.

16. Varying the extent of forward shifting implicitly allows any combination of incidence on capital and labor.

suming that income taxes are not shifted.[17] The incidence of the income tax by income class is based on average tax rates for each income class derived from Pechman (1966) and adjusted so that the yield from multiplying all such income tax liabilities by 0.01 is $780 million.[18]

To estimate the distributional impact of alternative methods of financing, we need to know the number of families of each demographic type by income class and the average earnings subject to payroll tax of each such family for the three different maximum payroll tax limits.[19] In order to integrate the distributional aspects of financing and benefits, we classify the families by the number of adults, whether or not they are sixty-five years old or over, and the number of children.[20]

The 1967 Survey of Economic Opportunity (SEO) data file was chosen to estimate the necessary data.[21] The data collection for the SEO was done by the Bureau of Census for the Office of Economic Opportunitv. The 1967 SEO included detailed questions on family structure and income by type. Wage and salary and self-employment income were collected individually for each person fourteen years old and over. Other forms of income (interest, rent, dividends, welfare payments) are reported only on an interview unit (which corresponds to a census family) basis. When an interview unit was encountered that included two or more families, we allocated the interest, rent, and dividend income in proportion to the number of adults in each family. All other income (primarily welfare and other transfer payments) are allocated on a per capita basis.

17. It is in principle wrong to assume that the Social Security–type tax is shifted and the income tax is not. Indeed, the current Social Security tax has an income effect but not a substitution effect for a large proportion of workers, while the income tax has both effects for all workers. An income tax is therefore more likely than a social security tax to reduce labor supply and therefore to cause the tax to be shifted.

18. This is based on personal income tax receipts of $78 billion in calendar year 1969.

19. This is complicated by the existence of two-earner families. If the payroll tax is on the first $9,000 of income, a family with one worker with earnings of $12,000 only pays tax on $9,000 while a two earner family in which each earns $6,000 pays on $12,000.

20. Those over sixty five would contribute to the financing if they are taxpayers but would not receive additional benefits.

21. Published census materials do not provide enough detail to meet these data requirements. Census data are also inadequate because of differences in the definition of a family. The census includes in a family all persons living in the same household who are related by blood or marriage. Thus extended families in which elderly parents are living with their children or in which young adults live with their parents are counted as single families. For this study we need to define the family unit in the terms that would be used in defining insurance coverage.

The survey reports the number of families in 1967 by 1966 income. We adjusted these data to a 1969 basis by separately inflating each of the components of income of each family on the basis of the average national per family growth in that component.[22] These components were then combined to determine estimated 1969 family incomes and estimates of the family's taxable payroll income for the three individual maxima.[23]

Criteria for Program Evaluation

Three types of criteria are relevant in assessing the distributional impact of any set of national health insurance options: (1) the progressivity of benefits and costs, (2) the implied marginal "net tax" rates, (3) the extent of protection against the risks of relatively large medical expenses.[24] In the next two sections a "standard plan" national health insurance option will be evaluated in terms of these criteria. A number of incremental changes in that plan will then be considered in the fifth section. It is useful therefore to consider the general criteria at this time.

The progressivity of the insurance benefits is assessed by calculating the actuarial value of the payments by the insurer for each income class. The difference in benefits between income classes reflects both the differences in family composition and the income-related character of the deductible and coinsurance rate. There are several possible definitions of the *costs* of the program to a family. The most appropriate in this context is the sum of the premiums, the taxes paid (both payroll and income), and the additional burden of shifted taxes. The *net benefits* (the benefits minus the costs) will also be examined.

Another measure of progressivity of some interest is the *average total payment* for medical care by families in each income class. This includes the *cost* plus the direct out-of-pocket payment for care. If the price elasticity of demand for care is zero, the sum of the benefits and the direct payment is a constant for each family composition, uninfluenced by changes in the deductible and coinsurance. When demand is

22. The inflators were derived from the Current Population Reports (1970, 1969, 1967).

23. The number of families in each adjusted income class was then increased proportionately to allow for the growth in the total number of families from 1967 to 1969.

24. This analysis ignores the indirect distributional impact of the end of Medicaid and of employer contributions for health insurance that could be expected to accompany the introduction of national health insurance. See, however, M. Feldstein and Allison (1972).

price elastic, however, this sum depends on the features of the insurance coverage. When the price elasticity is zero, an increase in *average total payment* is an increased financial burden with no additional care being received. More generally, however, there is no unambiguous interpretation of variations in this variable. If a higher *average total payment* is accompanied by an increase in the care received, the additional payment may represent either a gain or loss. The measure of *average total payment* should therefore be considered an index of average financial burden but not a measure that varies with family welfare.

In addition to examining gross benefits and net benefits by income class, it is useful to have a summary measure of the distributional impact. This is particularly convenient when a change in the plan does not affect different income classes in any simple systematic way. The uniformly distributed dollar (UDD) measure of benefit distribution is used in the next two sections for this purpose. The basic purpose of the UDD measure is to combine the benefits to families in different income classes into a single measure in a way that reflects a consistent value judgment about distributional equity. More specifically, the UDD measure of benefits is a weighted sum of the benefits per family in each income class:

$$\text{UDD} = \sum_i B_i W_i N_i / \sum_i W_i N_i, \tag{2}$$

where B_i is the benefit per family in income class i, W_i is the weight given to a marginal dollar to a family in that income class,[25] and N_i is the number of families in class i. If B_i is equal to one, UDD is also equal to one. Thus one UDD unit is the social value of a dollar given to each family, that is, the social value of a uniformly distributed dollar.

In principle, a separate analysis could be done for any particular set of W_i's. More practically, it is convenient to relate the W_i's to income by a simple functional relation. The constant elasticity function, $W_i = Y^{-\alpha}$, is both familiar and convenient. For $\alpha = 1$, it implies that the weight given to a marginal dollar of income varies inversely with the income of the recipient family; for example, a dollar to a family with $5,000 receives twice as much weight as a dollar to a family with $10,000. Values of α greater than one imply a more egalitarian value judgment, that is, the relative weight to benefits in higher-income

25. More formally, W_i would be described as the marginal social utility of a dollar given to a family in that income class.

families falls more rapidly. The converse is obviously true for values of α less than one.[26]

An important facet of the distributional aspect of a large public expenditure program is the set of marginal "tax" rates implied by the reduction of benefits and increase of costs as income rises. Recent experience with programs designed to concentrate benefits on low-income families has shown that if care is not taken, the implied marginal rates can reach or even exceed 100 percent. High marginal rates, especially for low- and middle-income families, may have important disincentive and distortionary effects. Two measures of the marginal rate are worth considering. The first is similar to the change in net benefits but excludes the shifted portion of the tax; that is, the marginal *net* tax rate in income class i is defined as

$$\frac{(P_{i+1} + T_{i+1} - B_{i+1})}{\overline{Y}_{i+1} - \overline{Y}_i} - \frac{(P_i + T_i - B_i)}{\overline{Y}_{i+1} - \overline{Y}_i},$$

that is, the increase in premiums P and taxes T minus the decrease in benefits B, all divided by the change in average income Y. This is likely to overstate the marginal rate perceived by families. The family knows how deductibles and coinsurance rates change with income but may not be aware (or respond to) changes in the actuarial value of the benefits. A second measure, equal to the marginal gross tax rate, therefore reflects only the change in premiums and taxes:

$$\frac{(P_{i+1} + T_{i+1}) - (P_i + T_i)}{\overline{Y}_{i+1} - \overline{Y}_i}.$$

Just as the previous definition tends to overstate the effect, this definition understates it.[27]

The third distributional criterion for evaluating a national health insurance option is its effectiveness in reducing the financial risk of abnormally high health expenditures. The best single definition of this is the *maximum out-of-pocket expense* that the family could incur in a year. For example, a policy with a $300 deductible and a 50

---

26. For a further discussion of the uniformly distributed dollar measure, see M. Feldstein (1972). It would be interesting to extend the UDD measure to reflect differences in family size; Bridges (1971) suggests a possible approach.

27. Two other measures might be worth examining. First, if families assume that the employer actually bears the payroll tax, the taxes might be redefined in this way. Second, the marginal rate might be defined in terms of average total payments, although this raises the problems discussed in that connection in the text.

percent coinsurance rate from $300 to $1,400 would have a maximum out-of-pocket expenditure of

$$\$300 + 0.50(\$1,400 - \$300) = \$850.$$

Of course, the probability of reaching this maximum of $1,400 is relatively low,[28] but the very purpose of insurance is to prevent financial losses of very small probability but very serious consequence.[29] A maximum out-of-pocket expenditure of $850 may of course be reasonable for a family with an income above $7,000 or $8,000 but much too great a burden for families with incomes of $4,000 or $5,000. Moreover, even if high-income families could accommodate themselves to maximum out-of-pocket expenses as high as $1,500 or $2,000, the high variance at this level would probably induce them to purchase additional insurance. If part of the purpose of the national health insurance program is to provide a type of insurance that increases cost consciousness and the efficiency of resource use, the maximum out-of-pocket expenses should be low enough to discourage the purchase of additional insurance.[30]

Evaluation of a "Standard Plan"

The insurance coverage and financing option described here performs well by the criteria of the previous section. The sensitivity of the evaluation to family composition and to the assumption about tax shifting is examined. This "standard" plan is offered not as a "best" plan but as a starting point for possible modifications.[31]

The standard plan provides for a deductible with a basic amount of $50 per adult plus $25 per child and an income-related amount that increases at the rate of $50 per $1,000 of family income in excess of $3,000 to a maximum of $450 at an income of $12,000. The coinsurance rate equals 8 percent plus 4 percent per $1,000 of family income to a maximum of 56 percent at $12,000. The coinsurance rate is payable by the family on all expenses between the deductible and $1,400; there is no coinsurance above $1,400.

28. Only 11 percent of families with two adults and two children would have gross spending of $1,400 per year even with very comprehensive insurance. If demand is price elastic, this deductible and coinsurance rate implies that a smaller fraction of families would reach $1,400.

29. This shows the disadvantage of an insurance coverage with even a small coinsurance rate for all levels of expenditure unless its purpose is to prevent the consumption of care for extremely expensive diseases.

30. For a discussion of this range of issues, see chapter 6 and M. Feldstein (1971b).

31. See M. Feldstein and Luft (1973) for a discussion of the use of linear programming to design optimal expenditure programs subject to distributional constraints.

The total cost of benefits under this plan is $15.1 billion. This leaves an estimated $12.2 billion to be paid as direct out-of-pocket expenses by the families.[32] The $15.1 billion cost is financed by a combination of premiums, payroll tax, and increased income tax. The premium is $50 per family plus 1 percent of the income between $3,000 and $12,000. The maximum premium is thus $140. This collects $5.6 billion, leaving $9.5 billion to be raised by taxes.

A payroll tax of 1 percent on both wage and salary earnings and self-employment income to a maximum of $9,000 yields revenues of $3.9 billion. Although the basic calculation assumes no shifting of this tax, the significance of this assumption is examined later. The remaining deficit, $5.6 billion, is raised by increasing income tax rates by 7.1 percent, that is, by multiplying the 1969 rates in each bracket by 1.071.

Table 10.3 shows the distribution of benefits by income class and by family composition. For each type of family composition benefits fall significantly as income rises. The relative difference is greatest in small families, but the absolute difference is greatest in large families.

Table 10.4 shows the corresponding distribution of average direct out-of-pocket expenditures. For each family composition the total of benefits and direct expenses is a constant; this total rises from $248 for a single adult to $927 for two adults and five or more children. The structure of the insurance coverage implies that average expenditure also rises rapidly with income. Even for very large families, however, it remains a very small fraction of family income.

The full distributional impact of the program depends, of course, on the allocation of the taxes as well as the benefits. This is analyzed in table 10.5 for all families combined. The distribution of benefits by income class (column 2) shows a very surprising result: average benefits are approximately constant for all families with incomes above $5,000, and this benefit level actually exceeds the levels for lower-income families. This seems to contradict the strongly progressive character of the benefits shown in table 10.3. The explanation of this apparent anomaly is that the lower-income groups contain more aged families (who receive no additional benefit from national health insurance) and more small families. The relatively greater number of small families also reflects the relation between age and income, with low incomes being concentrated among the young and the old. Because of the importance of demographic features in understanding distribu-

32. These calculations are based on an assumed zero price elasticity of demand, implying that total expenditure is fixed. This total of $27.3 billion for 1969 is 76 percent of the private health expenditures of $36.0 billion in that year. The difference is due to various forms of uncovered health expenditures (dental care, ophthalmic services, and the like).

Table 10.3. Distribution of benefits by income class, all families combined

Adults	Children	Under $3,000	$3,000–$4,000	$4,000–$5,000	$5,000–$6,000	$6,000–$7,000	$7,000–$8,000	$8,000–$10,000	$10,000+
					Family income				
1	0	$245	$175	$160	$147	$137	$128	$117	$105
1	1	292	227	208	191	177	164	149	132
1	2	342	279	255	235	217	201	182	161
1	3+	438	364	335	308	284	264	237	210
2	0	382	321	296	277	259	243	223	201
2	1	427	361	334	311	290	273	249	224
2	2	477	404	376	350	326	306	279	252
2	3	533	455	424	394	369	347	318	286
2	4	585	502	467	436	409	384	353	319
2	5+	711	620	579	545	513	485	449	409

Note: Calculations are based on a zero price elasticity of demand.

Table 10.4. Distribution of direct expense by income class, all families combined

Adults	Chil-dren	Under $3,000	$3,000–$4,000	$4,000–$5,000	$5,000–$6,000	$6,000–$7,000	$7,000–$8,000	$8,000–$10,000	$10,000+
					Family income				
1	0	$ 3	$ 73	$ 88	$101	$111	$120	$131	$143
1	1	33	98	117	135	148	161	177	193
1	2	63	125	150	169	187	203	222	243
1	3+	111	185	214	241	265	285	312	339
2	0	64	125	150	170	188	204	224	246
2	1	87	152	180	202	223	241	264	289
2	2	110	183	211	237	261	281	307	335
2	3	134	212	244	273	298	320	350	381
2	4	160	243	278	309	336	361	392	426
2	5+	215	307	348	381	413	441	478	518

tional impact, we shall examine a separate analysis for a homogenous demographic type. Before doing so, however, we continue to examine the implications of table 10.5.

Column 3 of table 10.5 shows the average contribution of families in each income class to the financing of the program, including premiums, payroll tax, and income tax.[33] The result is a very progressive financing structure: families with incomes between $6,000 and $7,000 pay twice as much as those between $3,000 and $4,000 but only half as much as families with incomes between $12,000 and $15,000. Payments then continue to rise, reflecting the progressivity of the personal income tax. As a result, the net benefits (shown in column 4) decline rapidly with income. The break-even point occurs between $8,000 and $10,000.

Another measure of progressivity, shown in column 5, is the relation between income and average total payment for health care (the sum of average out-of-pocket expense, premiums, and taxes).[34] This rises continuously from a low of $46 in the lowest income class to a high of $1,498 in the highest income class.

Table 10.5. Distribution of benefits and financing, standard plan, all families combined

Income bracket (1)	Benefits (2)	Cost to family (3)	Net benefit (4)	Average total payment (5)	Additional marginal gross tax rate (percent) (6)	Additional marginal net tax rate (percent) (7)
Less than $2,000	$157	$ 33	$124	$ 46	1.6	−1.4
$2,000–$2,999	202	57	145	82	2.5	3.3
$3,000–$3,999	194	82	112	167	3.3	1.3
$4,000–$4,999	214	115	99	235	3.4	1.0
$5,000–$5,999	239	150	89	311	3.0	2.5
$6,000–$6,999	244	179	64	372	3.3	3.5
$7,000–$7,999	241	212	29	431	3.4	3.1
$8,000–$9,999	246	264	−18	529	3.0	3.7
$10,000–$11,999	232	324	−92	625	2.5	2.2
$12,000–$14,999	237	385	−148	692	1.8	1.8
$15,000–$24,999	235	500	−265	806	3.4	3.4
$25,000 and over	238	1189	−951	1498	−	−

33. The values for the top income class actually correspond to an income of $40,000.

34. There are, of course, additional health expenses that are not covered in this analysis; for example, dental care, ophthalmic services, certain drugs.

The additional marginal gross tax rate—the rate at which premiums and taxes increase as income increases—is shown in column 6. The additional marginal net tax rate, the rate at which benefits net of premiums and taxes falls as income increases, is shown in column 7.[35] These rates are generally very low, suggesting that disincentive effects of the standard plan are likely to be minimal. (These estimates must, however, be treated with caution because combining demographic groups leads to an underestimate of the marginal rates that would prevail for individual family types.)[36]

The uniformly distributed dollar (UDD) measures provide a convenient summary of the progressiveness of the plan. With $\alpha = 0$ the UDD value of benefits is simply the average benefit per family, $217. As α rises, that is, as preferences become more egalitarian, the UDD value of benefits falls: at $\alpha = 1$ it is $184 and at $\alpha = 2$ it is $165. This reflects the regressive nature of benefits shown in column 2. For net benefits the opposite is true. When $\alpha = 0$, the UDD value is of course zero (in the aggregate, families pay as much as they receive in benefits).[37] With $\alpha = 1$ the UDD value of net benefits is $93; with $\alpha = 2$ it is $120. For $\alpha = 1$ the implication is that if the weight given to a marginal dollar of benefits or taxes to a family is inversely proportional to income, the standard plan has beneficial effects equivalent in social value to a net gain by every family of $93.

Table 10.6 reexamines the benefit and financing impact for families of two adults and two children. The anomalous result of regressive benefits is now gone. Benefits fall from $477 at the lowest income level to $252 at the highest. Premium plus tax cost still increases very rapidly. The break-even point rises to somewhere between $10,000 and $12,000, reflecting the fact that these families generally have higher incomes than the population as a whole.

The average total cost, shown in column 3, is greater than in table 10.5 at every income level because the family size is greater than average. The average total cost remains a relatively small fraction of income at each income level. Column 8 shows the maximum out-of-pocket cost at each income level, a measure of how well the insurance coverage succeeds in protecting the family against excessive financial risk. For families with incomes between $2,500 and $10,000 the maxi-

35. Both tax rates are, of course, incremental to the taxes and progressive benefits that otherwise exist.

36. For individual family types the maximum additional marginal tax rate is less than 11 percent and the maximum additional marginal gross tax rate is 3.5 percent.

37. This, of course, ignores the welfare gain from the risk-spreading aspect of insurance and the welfare loss due to medical price distortions and taxes (see M. Feldstein chapter 6).

Table 10.6. Distribution of benefits and financing, standard plan, families of two adults and two children

Income bracket (1)	Benefits (2)	Cost to family (3)	Net benefits (4)	Average total payment (5)	Additional marginal gross tax rate (percent) (6)	Additional marginal net tax rate (percent) (7)	Maximum direct payment (8)
Less than							
$2,000–$2,999	$477	$ 63	$414	$ 173	1.5	1.5	$212
$3,000–$3,999	477	85	392	195	2.3	9.6	252
$4,000–$4,999	404	108	296	291	3.0	5.8	308
$5,000–$5,999	350	164	186	401	2.9	5.1	420
$6,000–$6,999	326	191	135	452	3.2	5.2	476
$7,000–$7,999	306	223	83	504	3.2	5.0	532
$8,000–$9,999	279	271	8	578	2.9	4.3	616
$10,000–$11,999	252	330	−78	665	2.3	2.3	868
$12,000–$14,999	252	387	−135	722	1.8	1.8	868
$15,000–$24,999	252	507	−255	842	3.5	3.5	868
$25,000 and over	252	1203	−951	1538	–	–	868

mum out-of-pocket expenditure is slightly less than 10 percent of income. At higher income levels the absolute maximum is higher, but the percentage of income is lower.[38]

The uniformly distributed dollar measures provide additional insight into the distributional impact of the program on these families. For gross benefits the UDD value is $288 when $\alpha = 0$. This exceeds the $216 for all families because of the greater family size. The progressivity of the benefits is reflected in the UDD for $\alpha = 1$ of $328 and for $\alpha = 2$ of $400. The UDD value for $\alpha = 0$ is negative (−$38), indicating that on average these families pay more in premiums and taxes than they expect to receive in benefits. The progressivity is substantial, however, so that with $\alpha = 1$ the UDD value is $89 and with $\alpha = 2$ it is $256.

We may consider the sensitivity of the results to the assumption that the entire payroll tax is borne by labor. If we substitute the assumption that half of the tax is shifted forward in the form of higher prices, there is a slight change in the estimated distribution of net benefits in favor of middle-income families. More specifically, very low income families (below $3,000) lose an average of about $3 per family; families between $3,000 and $15,000 gain average amounts of less than $10 per family. Families between $15,000 and $25,000 lose $12 per family, while those with income above $25,000 lose an average of $88. The concentration of gains on middle-income families implies that the overall effect on progressivity is minimal. With α values below 1 there is no change (to the nearest dollar). For $\alpha = 2$ the assumption of 50 percent shifting reduces the UDD value from $120 to $118. In short, the analysis appears quite insensitive to the degree of forward shifting that is assumed.

Effects of Incremental Program Changes

The standard plan provides a point of departure for considering modifications in the basic insurance coverage (the parameters of the deductible, coinsurance, and upper limit formulas) and the method of financing (the payroll tax rate and ceiling and the parameters of the premium formula). The effect of these changes on the distribution of net benefits is generally nonlinear. As an approximation, therefore, we consider the effects of separate and small incremental changes from the standard package.

Table 10.7 shows the effect on the distribution of net benefits for all

38. This is more than offset by the higher taxes paid by these families. The ratio of maximum total cost continues to rise as a percentage of income.

Table 10.7. Distributional effects of incremental changes in coverage and financing, all families combined

Plan changes	Change in net benefits by income class					
	<$2,000	$2,000–	$3,000–	$4,000–	$5,000–	$6,000–
Standard plan	$124	$145	$112	$99	$89	$64
Deductible: +$100 per family	−31	−12	−13	−13	−13	−11
Deductible: +$10 per $1,000 of income	7	6	0	−2	−3	−4
Coinsurance: +0.05 at all incomes	−6	−7	−5	−5	−5	−4
Coinsurance: +0.01 per $1,000 of income	2	3	1	−1	−2	−3
Coinsurance: +$100 in upper limit	−1	0	0	−1	−1	−1
Payroll tax: Increase taxable income to $12,000						
Payroll tax: +0.001 in tax rate	0	0	0	−1	−2	−2
Premium: +$25 per family	−13	−12	−13	−13	−13	−11
Premium: +0.1 percent of income	0	1	1	0	0	−1
Premium: Substitute $15 per adult and $10 per child	15	13	13	12	9	6

a. Net benefits (not change) for standard plan (first row).

families combined of ten incremental changes. The UDD values for $\alpha = 0.5$, 1.0, and 2.0 are also shown.

Consider first the changes in the insurance coverage. The introduction of an additional $100 deductible per family is quite regressive. Families with incomes below $8,000 lose, while those above $8,000 gain.[39] The UDD value at $\alpha = 1$ falls from $93 to $73. An increase in the income-related component of the deductible, from $50 per $1,000 of income to $60 per $1,000 of income, benefits both the two lowest and the two highest income classes while making those in between slightly worse off. The increased UDD values show that on balance

39. All the changes in this table also result in a corresponding change in income taxes.

$7,000–	$8,000–	$10,000–	$12,000–	$15,000–	$25,000+	UDD value of net benefits		
						$\alpha = 0.5$	$\alpha = 1.0$	$\alpha = 2.0$
$29	$18	$92	$148	$265	$951	$56	$93	$120
−9	−3	2	12	39	222	44	73	92
−5	−5	−5	−3	1	31	58	97	126
−3	−1	2	6	15	78	53	89	114
−3	−4	−4	−2	4	48	56	94	122
−1	−1	2	0	4	30	56	93	120
−2	−3	−2	−1	5	56	56	93	120
−9	−3	2	12	39	222	49	83	107
−1	−2	−3	−2	3	37	56	93	120
3	−3	−9	−14	−28	−123	63	104	134

this is a progressive change. The table also shows that a general increase in the coinsurance rate is somewhat regressive while an increase in the income-related component of the coinsurance rate is somewhat progressive.[40] A $100 increase in the limit on the coinsurance rate (to $1,500) has almost no effect.

Raising the level of individual taxable payroll income from a maximum of $9,000 to a maximum of $12,000, favors those with incomes below $10,000 and above $25,000. Between these limits, single-earner

40. It is difficult to compare the relative progressivity of two types of changes since the UDD values depend on the absolute amounts. It might, however, be reasonable to say that the deductible change was more progressive because the fall of UDD at $\alpha = 2$ compared with the fall at $\alpha = 1$ was relatively greater for the deductible change.

and two-earner families lose more in additional payroll taxes than they gain by reduced income taxes.

Among the other changes, the most significant were the increase in the basic premium (a regressive change) and the change to a premium schedule of $15 per adult and $10 per child (a progressive change).

The distributional effects of each of these changes reflects not only the change itself but the induced change in the income taxes that provide the "residual" finance for the plan. A more detailed analysis could show the separate components of this distributional change and the differences in impact by family composition.[41]

The design of national health insurance benefits and financing will have important distributional effects. This chapter has developed and applied a framework for assessing alternative plans. The analysis takes into account the probabilistic character of health expenditures and the joint importance of income and family characteristics.

A simulation method for calculating the actuarial value of the benefits of different insurance coverages and different price elasticities of demand is developed. It is implemented with information from a large sample of expenditures and is used to derive distributions for families of different composition.

Special tabulations of data collected in the Survey of Economic Opportunity provide the basis for analyzing the impact of different financing methods. The complex relationship between income distribution and family size is brought out by comparing the distributional impact for all families together and for families of two adults and two children.

Several distribution criteria for evaluating the distributional impact of a national health insurance plan are suggested. These are then applied to a "standard plan" which is shown to have generally desirable properties. A number of alternative modifications in the "standard plan" are then examined.

Appendix: Evaluating Insurance Options

Alternative insurance options were evaluated with the aid of individual data on the experience of 335,000 federal employees and their families in 1968. Separate distributions were available for employed adults under age sixty five, for their spouses, and for dependent children.

41. A supplement available from the authors contains full tables of benefit distribution and financial impact for all families combined for each of the changes considered in table 10.7.

The basic model of price sensitivity implies a constant price elasticity:

$$\tilde{E}_i = k_\beta \tilde{X}_i \tag{A1}$$

where $\tilde{E}_i$ is the actual expenditure of the ith individual, k is the share of expense paid out of pocket at the margin,[42] and $\tilde{X}_i$ is the expenditure that would have occurred in the absence of insurance.[43] The tilde over $\tilde{E}_i$ and $\tilde{X}_i$ serves as a reminder that these are random variables. Obviously, if expenditure is not sensitive to price ($\beta = 0$), the observed expenditure distributions are also equivalent to the underlying $\tilde{X}_i$ distributions. More generally, we use the observed $\tilde{E}_i$ distributions (for employees and children) and the values of k implied by the federal employee insurance to derive the $\tilde{X}_i$ distributions corresponding to two alternative price elasticities, $\beta = -0.33$ and $\beta = -0.67$.[44]

Table 10.A1. Cumulative probability distributions of total covered expenditure, 1969

	Cumulative probability			
	Two adults, two children		Two adults, four children	
Upper limit of expenditure	$\beta = 0$	$\beta = -0.67$	$\beta = 0$	$\beta = -0.67$
$ 65	0.3151	0.5967	0.1987	0.4963
130	0.4225	0.7370	0.3054	0.6652
260	0.5472	0.8716	0.4192	0.8246
390	0.6478	0.9028	0.5319	0.8807
520	0.7132	0.9411	0.6166	0.9248
650	0.7522	0.9526	0.6733	0.9437
1,300	0.8871	0.9922	0.8520	0.9894
2,600	0.9484	0.9998	0.9371	0.9997
6,500	0.9935	1.0000	0.9914	1.0000
13,000	1.0000	1.0000	1.0000	1.0000

42. k equals one in the deductible range and equals the coinsurance rate above that. Beyond the upper limit (when the actual coinsurance rate equals zero), demand was constrained by assuming an "effective" coinsurance rate of 0.10 in order to represent the nonmonetary costs that in practice serve to prevent demand from becoming infinite.

43. No attempt is made in this analysis to allow the price of care to respond to changes in insurance.

44. In each case, the $\tilde{X}_i$ distribution is also adjusted to 1969 levels by a constant proportional increase equal to the average claim increase among federal employees with this coverage.

The $\tilde{X}_i$ distributions for individuals are then convoluted numerically to obtain distributions for a wide variety of family compositions.[45] Table 10.A1 shows two such family expenditure distributions. The first is for a family of two adults and two children, the second for a family of two adults and four children. Both distributions are shown for price elasticities of zero and −0.67.

Family $\tilde{X}$ distributions are used to calculate the actuarial value and expected out-of-pocket expenditures of different insurance coverage plans. For each deductible and coinsurance rate in the plan a large number of random drawings are made from the $\tilde{X}$ distribution of each family type. The expenditure corresponding to each value $\tilde{X}$ is then calculated using equation (A1). The sample of drawings is then used to calculate the average family benefit (the actuarial value of the payments by the insurance plan) and the average direct expense (out-of-pocket payment) of the family.

45. This procedure involves the approximations of (1) assuming stochastic independence of illness within families and (2) assuming that the appropriate distribution for a particular type of individual is independent of the composition of his family. Attempts to improve on these assumptions would have to be based on very inadequate data.

11 The Effect of National Health Insurance on the Price and Quantity of Medical Care

In this chapter a microsimulation model is used to estimate the effects of alternative national health insurance policies. Unlike previous microsimulation studies, this analysis uses an explicit model of the supply and price response in the markets for hospital care and physicians' services. Indeed, two quite different models of supply and price response are examined and their implications are contrasted.

A microsimulation model of household demand is necessary if the analysis is to provide useful results in the comparison of specific health insurance proposals. The effects of alternative national health insurance policies depend crucially on the stochastic character of health-care demand. More specifically, the effects of different sets of deductibles, coinsurance rates, and other parameters of insurance policies depend on particular stochastic distributions of health expenditures. Aggregate specification of demand behavior cannot capture the subtle differences in the response of demand to different types of insurance policies. The stochastic simulation model of demand used in this chapter is based on the actual experience of more than three hundred thousand families. The basic demand model, described in detail in the first section, is an extension of the simple aggregate health-care demand model used in chapter 10.

A serious weakness of all previous microsimulation studies of national health insurance including our own (Feldstein, Friedman, and

This chapter was written with Bernard Friedman. Reprinted with permission from *The Role of Health Insurance in the Health Services Sector,* ed. Richard N. Rosett (New York: National Bureau of Economic Research, 1976). The methods and computer programs used in this paper were developed in a project supported by the Department of Health, Education, and Welfare and described in more detail in unpublished technical reports: "National Health Insurance Simulation Model" (August 1972) and "Supply and Price Response in National Health Insurance Analysis" (September 1972).

Luft 1972) has been the neglect of the supply and price response to national health insurance. The analysis in this chapter shows how an aggregate model of supply and price response can be combined with a microsimulation model of demand. Although there are no explicit aggregate demand equations, the complete model is solved for prices that equate supply and demand. The supply model and the method of finding the equilibrium are described in the second section. Some illustrative results are then presented in the third section.

The supply and price response of the second and third sections is based on the simplest model of aggregate supply and the assumption of market-clearing equilibrium. The markets for hospital care and for physicians' services may not behave in this way. Hospital prices may rise in response to increases in demand because hospitals change the nature of their product and not because it is more expensive to produce a larger quantity of the old product. Physicians may increase prices in response to greater demand or increased insurance without setting a market-clearing price. The fourth section develops a model with these characteristics, describes the simultaneous interaction of demand with this supply behavior, and presents some illustrative results.

Most of the debate about the effects of national health insurance has focused on the uncertainty about the responsiveness of household demand. This chapter shows that uncertainty about supply response may be even more important.

A Microsimulation Model of Demand

The annual health-care expenditures of a group of families with the same demographic composition, income, and insurance coverage can be described by a joint frequency distribution of expenditures on hospital services and medical services. Each such distribution is conditional on the gross prices charged for hospital and physician services. Let $F^i(E_h, E_m \mid P_h, P_m)$ be such a distribution for insurance coverage i with

E_h = family's total expenditure for hospital services,
E_m = family's total expenditure for medical services,
P_h = gross price per unit of hospital services,
P_m = gross price per unit of medical services.

An associated distribution of net out-of-pocket expense $G^i(N \mid P_h, P_m)$ is related to F^i by the insurance reimbursement formula.

The expenditure distribution associated with any particular insurance structure and prices is derived from a "baseline" quantity distribution that would prevail in the absence of any insurance and with prices equal to unity: $F^0(X_h, X_m | P_h = 1, P_m = 1)$. There is, of course a different baseline expenditure distribution for each family type. A specific national health insurance proposal can be described in terms of the deductibles, coinsurance rates, and maximum net out-of-pocket expenditure for each type of family. D_h and D_m denote the deductibles, C_h and C_m the coinsurance rates, and MAX the maximum net out-of-pocket expenditure.

The equations relating expenditure in the presence of insurance to the baseline distribution and the prevailing gross prices are extensions of a traditional constant-elasticity demand model. The most appropriate way to extend a constant-elasticity specification to deal with deductibles and a maximum net spending limit is uncertain. One approach, offered as a tentative specification until better empirical evidence is available, assumes a constant elasticity of the quantity demanded with respect to the net price paid for expenditures over the deductible. The net price of an additional unit of hospital care depends on the family's current level of expenditure. More generally, the net price paid by the family depends on (1) the gross price charged by the hospital (P_h), (2) the effective coinsurance rate (1 for expenditures below the deductible, C_h between the deductible and the maximum net expenditure limit, and 0 above that limit) and (3) a parameter λ representing the nonmonetary costs (Acton 1972; Phelps and Newhouse 1972b) to the consumer of health services.

If there were no deductibles $(D_h = D_m = 0)$ and no maximum net expenditure (MAX $= \infty$), the two expenditure equations would be

$$E_h = P_h \cdot X_h \left[\frac{P_h(C_h + \lambda)}{1 + \lambda}\right]^{\alpha h} \left[\frac{P_m(C_m + \lambda)}{1 + \lambda}\right]^{\alpha m}, \tag{1}$$

$$E_m = P_m \cdot X_m \left[\frac{P_h(C_h + \lambda)}{1 + \lambda}\right]^{\beta h} \left[\frac{P_m(C_m + \lambda)}{1 + \lambda}\right]^{\beta m}. \tag{2}$$

If there is no insurance, then $C_h = C_m = 1$ and the equation is the usual constant-elasticity demand equation. With complete insurance $C_h = C_m = 0$, but demand remains finite because $\lambda > 0$ implies a positive nonmonetary cost.

To allow for deductibles and for the maximum net expenditure limit, it is necessary to distinguish four cases. Let $\hat{E}_h = X_h P_h^{1-\alpha h} P_m^{\alpha m}$ and $\hat{E}_m = X_m P_h^{\beta h} P_m^{1+\beta m}$, the expenditures that would occur at prices P_h, P_m if there were no insurance.

Case i. If $\hat{E}_h < D_h$ and $\hat{E}_m < D_m$, then $E_h = \hat{E}_h$ and $E_m = \hat{E}_m$. Here the insurance is irrelevant because the deductibles exceed the expenditure that would be made in the absence of insurance. The total net out-of-pocket expenditure is $N = E_h + E_m$.

Case ii. If $\hat{E}_h > D_h$ and $\hat{E}_m > D_m$, then

(a) $E_h = D_h + P_h(X_h - D_h P_h^{-1}) \left[\dfrac{P_h(C_h + \lambda)}{1 + \lambda} \right]^{\alpha_h} \left[\dfrac{P_m(C_m + \lambda)}{1 + \lambda} \right]^{\alpha_m}$,

$\qquad E_m = D_m + P_m(X_m - D_m P_m^{-1}) \left[\dfrac{P_h(C_h + \lambda)}{1 + \lambda} \right]^{\beta_h} \left[\dfrac{P_m(C_m + \lambda)}{1 + \lambda} \right]^{\beta_m}$,

$\qquad N = D_h + D_m + C_h(E_h - D_h) + C_m(E_m - D_m) < \text{MAX}$,

or

(b) $E_h = D_h + P_h(X_h - D_h P_h^{-1}) \left[\dfrac{P_h \lambda}{1 + \lambda} \right]^{\alpha_h} \left[\dfrac{P_m \lambda}{1 + \lambda} \right]^{\alpha_m}$,

$\qquad E_m = D_m + P_m(X_m - D_m P_m^{-1}) \left[\dfrac{P_h \lambda}{1 + \lambda} \right]^{\beta_h} \left[\dfrac{P_m \lambda}{1 + \lambda} \right]^{\beta_m}$,

$\qquad N = \text{MAX}$.

Case iii. If $E_h > D_h$ and $\hat{E}_m < D_m$ then either[1]

(a)
$\qquad E_h = D_h + P_h(X_h - D_h P_h^{-1}) \left[\dfrac{P_h(C_h + \lambda)}{1 + \lambda} \right]^{\alpha_h} \left[\dfrac{P_m(C_m + \lambda)}{1 + \lambda} \right]^{\alpha_m}$,

$\qquad E_m = \hat{E}_m$,
$\qquad N = D_h + C_h(E_h - D_h) + \hat{E}_m < \text{MAX}$,

or

(b) $E_h = D_h + P_h(X_h - D_h P_h^{-1}) \left[\dfrac{P_h \lambda}{1 + \lambda} \right]^{\alpha_h} \left[\dfrac{P_m \lambda}{1 + \lambda} \right]^{\alpha_m}$,

$\qquad E_m = P_m X_m \left[\dfrac{P_h \lambda}{1 + \lambda} \right]^{\beta_h} \left[\dfrac{P_m \lambda}{1 + \lambda} \right]^{\beta_m}$,

$\qquad N = \text{MAX}$.

Case iv. If $\hat{E}_h < D_h$ and $\hat{E}_m > D_m$, the results bear an obvious analogy to case iii.

These four sets of demand equations can be used to generate the distribution F^i corresponding to any gross prices, insurance characteristics, and demand parameters. More specifically, given a baseline distribution $F^0(X_h, X_m)$, we can draw values (X_h, X_m) with the appropriate probability and calculate the corresponding E_h, E_m. Average gross and net expenditures $(\overline{E}_h, \overline{E}_m,$ and $\overline{N})$ are then readily computed. This procedure is done separately for each family type. These cal-

---

1. For simplicity, the actual calculations assume $E_m = \hat{E}_m$ in both subcases.

culations and the aggregates produced by combining the averages for different family types could be used to assess the effects of alternative national health insurance proposals if supplies were infinitely elastic at fixed values of P_h and P_m. This was essentially the procedure used in chapter 10 with a simpler model that did not distinguish hospital and medical services.

The primary data for this model are the individual insurance claims for more than three hundred thousand federal government employees and their dependents in 1970. All these persons had the very comprehensive Aetna High-Option coverage. A tabulation of the joint frequency distribution of hospital and medical services (a 24-by-24 matrix of relative frequencies with an associated matrix of cell means) was derived for all male employees. Similar tabulations were derived separately for female employees, dependent spouses, and children. The Aetna coverage uses a $50 deductible per individual (except that the first $1,000 of hospital room and board is fully reimbursed) and a coinsurance rate of 20 percent for both hospital and medical services. For each category of individual the observed bivariate frequency distribution was used to infer the baseline distribution corresponding to each of several alternative sets of demand parameters (α's, β's and λ). This procedure uses the inverse of the demand function with $D_h = 0$, $D_m = 50$, $C_h = C_m = 0.20$, and MAX $= \infty$. The prices were both normalized to be one.

Family baseline distributions for sixteen family compositions (for example, husband and wife; husband, wife, and three children) were produced by convoluting the baseline distributions for individuals.[2] Persons over sixty-five were assumed to be excluded from the basic national health insurance plan and were therefore ignored in calculating family distributions. For each of the sixteen family compositions twelve income categories were defined in order to implement national health insurance specifications that are income related and to assess the tax burdens that balance the new government expenditures.

The demand simulation model provides average gross and net expenditures for each of the 192 family types. These are also aggregated to national averages and subaverages by using population counts computed from the Current Population Survey of 1971.

Although the experience of the federal employees with Aetna

2. Although the independence assumption seems strong, several countervailing forces may produce such independence. Some preliminary comparisons of convoluted "synthetic" family distributions and actual family distributions supported the assumption of independence.

High-Option coverage is an extremely rich and valuable source of data, these employees are not a representative sample of all U.S. families, particularly in regard to geographic distribution, employment status, and occupation. For each set of demand parameter assumptions $(\alpha_n, \alpha_m, \beta_n, \beta_m, \lambda)$ the following additional steps are taken to calibrate the baseline distributions to known national aggregates for 1970. The typical family insurance coverage in 1970 was assumed to be $D_h = 100$, $D_m = 100$, $C_h = 0.25$, $C_m = 0.40$, and MAX $= \infty$.[3] This typical coverage is used for a preliminary simulation to estimate the national aggregate expenditures corresponding to each set of demand parameters. Suppose that the estimated expenditures for some set of demand parameters are E_h^* and E_m^* and that the actual expenditures are E_h^0 and E_m^0. The ratios E_h^*/E_h^0 and E_m^*/E_m^0 are then used to deflate the expenditure units of the corresponding baseline distributions. With this calibration completed, the implications of various national health insurance plans may be compared for the given set of demand parameters.

A Supply Response Model and the Equilibrium Solution

In the supply response model the usual interaction of supply and demand provides a market-clearing reaction of quantities and prices to a change in insurance coverage. The computational problems and novelty of the model occur because there are no aggregate demand equations but only individual demand equations and a microsimulation model.

The basic idea and computational procedure for the supply response model can be described most easily by ignoring the distinction between hospital and medical services. The solution for the more general case will be discussed later in this chapter. Let Q be the aggregate quantity of health services consumed by all households, P the price level, and E the expenditure $(E = Q \cdot P)$. Since there are no natural units in which to measure Q, we take the current price prevailing in the absence of national health insurance (P_0) to have the value one and thus define the quantity in the absence of national health insurance (Q_0) to be equal to the expenditure (E_0).

An aggregate supply function with constant price elasticity can be written

$$\ln Q = \ln Q_0 + \gamma \ln P. \tag{3}$$

---

3. This assumption for "typical" coverage is based on Reed (1969) and information supplied by the Department of Health, Education, and Welfare.

In an *aggregate* market demand function could be written in terms of the gross market price and the features of the national health insurance program, the two equations could be solved for the changes in P and Q that would accompany alternative national health insurance (NHI) plans. However, such an aggregate demand function is the outcome of a very complex and stochastic set of individual demand functions that cannot be given an aggregate parametric summary. Only by operating the demand simulation model described in the first section can points on the demand curve be calculated. The market equilibrium is found by combining the aggregate supply function of equation (3) with demand generated by the simulation model.

The process of convergence to an equilibrium solution of this iterative simulation process is best described with the aid of a diagram. Figure 11.1 shows the change in the price-quality equilibrium that results from the introduction of national health insurance. More specifically, in the absence of NHI the market is in equilibrium at point A. The demand curve ($D1$) relates the quantity demanded to the *gross* price for the structure of private health insurance prevailing before NHI. The $D1$ curve is not actually known, but points on it can be found by using the demand simulation model. The supply function S

Figure 11.1

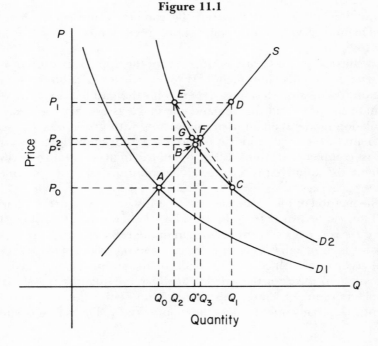

corresponds to equation (3). The introduction of NHI shifts the demand function to D2 and the equilibrium to B. The computational problem is to determine the coordinates of the point B even though the two demand curves are not directly observable.

The following feasible and efficient procedure is used. First, the demand simulation model is used to find the aggregate quantity that would be purchased under NHI if price were unchanged — that is, it locates the point C and the quantity Q_1. Second, the supply function is used to solve for the price P_1 at which the quantity Q_1 would be supplied. Third, the demand simulation model is used again to find the aggregate quantity demanded in the presence of NHI but with the gross market price P_1; this is Q_2 at point E. It is clear from figure 11.1 that (if the aggregate demand function is well behaved) the equilibrium price after NHI (P^*) lies between P_0 and P_1. Similarly, the new equilibrium quantity (Q^*) lies between Q_1 and Q_2. The fourth step in the analysis is to approximate the unknown demand curve (D2) in the relevant range by the straight line connecting points C and E. This is shown as a broken line in the figure. For computational purposes it is defined by the equation

$$Q = Q_2 - \frac{Q_1 - Q_2}{P_1 - P_0}(P_1 - P).$$ (4)

Equations (3) and (4) may now be combined and solved for the equilibrium price-quantity point. This corresponds to point F and thus to P_2 and Q_3.

The next step checks on the closeness of the approximations of F to the true new equilibrium B. Since, by construction, F is on the supply funtion, the test of closeness depends on the gap between the trial solution (point F) and the demand curve. To assess this, the demand simulation model is again used. Simulating with gross price P_2 yields the point G. If the quantities at G and F are sufficiently close, the analysis is complete. If they differ by more than some prespecified amount, the iterative procedure can be continued in order to achieve greater accuracy.

The method of increasing accuracy is illustrated in figure 11.2, with notation carried over from figure 11.1. If Q_3 is greater than Q_4, the curve D2 is convex toward the origin in the relevant range. If the inequality is reversed, the curve is concave and the calculations are modified accordingly. Since the equation for the supply curve is given, it is possible to solve for the price P_3 at which the quantity Q_4 would be supplied. Demand simulation then identifies the point H and the quantity Q_5 that would be demanded at price P_3. The points G and H

Figure 11.2

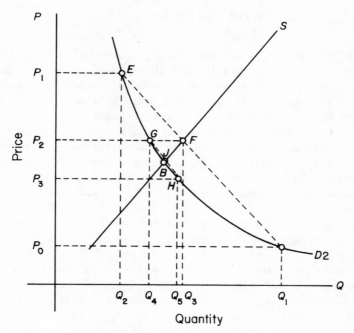

are analogous to the old points E and C. The equation of the line joining G and H is found and used as a local approximation to the demand curve. The intersection of this approximation and the supply curve identifies the point J, which is much closer to B than F was. This is verified and the accuracy evaluated by a further simulation at the price corresponding to J.

This iterative simulation method of finding the post-NHI market equilibrium is easily extended to separate markets for hospital care and medical services. The procedure begins by using the demand simulation model described in the first section to calculate the hospital and medical expenditures E_h and E_m, that would prevail with NHI if the prices remained unchanged.[4] Since the pre-NHI prices are normalized at one, these expenditures are also equivalent to quantities. This yields quantities that may be denoted QH_1 and QM_1, corresponding to point C of figure 11.1.

4. The simulation model of the first section permits specifying a separate set of deductibles, coinsurance rates, and MAX value for each of the 192 family demographic types and income classes.

The two aggregate constant elasticity supply functions are

$$\ln QH = \ln QH_0 + \gamma_H \ln PH,$$
$$\ln QM = \ln QM_0 + \gamma_M \ln PM, \tag{5}$$

where QH_0 and QM_0 are the aggregate quantities before NHI, PH and PM are prices of hospital and medical care ($PH_0 = PM_0 = 1$), and γ_H and γ_M are supply elasticities. Substituting the values QH_1 and QM_1 into QH and QM yields the prices PH_1 and PM_1 at which these quantities would be supplied; these prices correspond to point 'D of figure 11.1. The demand simulation model is then repeated using PH_1 and PM_1 and the deductibles, coinsurance rates, and values of MAX provided for by the NHI plan. The aggregate quantities demanded at these prices, QH_2 and QM_2, correspond to point E of figure 11.2.

Although the coordinates of two points such as C and E were sufficient to define a linear demand equation when hospital and medical services were not distinguished, a third point is now needed if the cross-price effects are to be taken into account. A new price corresponding to the average of PH_1 and the pre-NHI price ($PH_0 = 1$) is selected for hospital care. A similar value is selected for medical care. At these prices (PH_2 and PM_2), a new set of quantities (QH_3 and QM_3) is obtained by simulation. The coordinates of the three quantity-price points (QH_1, QM_1, 1, 1), (QH_2, QM_2, PH_1, PM_1), and (QH_3, QM_3, PH_2, PM_2) can be used to evaluate the parameters of the two linear equations that approximate the demand function in the presence of NHI. More specifically, we take the aggregate demand equations to be

$$QH = a_1 + a_2 PH + a_3 PM \quad \text{and} \quad QM = b_1 + b_2 PH + b_3 PM. \tag{6}$$

The three parameters of each equation can be obtained by substituting the values of the variables for each of the three price-quantity points. The two supply equations (5) and the two demand equations (6) are then solved simultaneously to obtain trial equilibrium values (QH_4, QM_4, PH_3, PM_3) that correspond to point F of figure 11.1. This set of values corresponds to a point on the supply functions. To check the accuracy of the approximation to the demand, the demand simulation is recomputed for prices PH_3 and PM_3. This yields a point that is analogous to G of figure 11.1. If this is not sufficiently accurate, a further iteration is computed as described for figure 11.2.

An Analysis of Two National Health Insurance Plans

The first NHI plan (NHI-1) has low annual deductibles of $50 for hospital care and $50 for medical services and very low coinsurance rates of 10 percent for both types of services. There is no limit, however, to the family's maximum net expenditure (MAX = ∞). These characteristics of the NHI plan are the same for all income levels and all family demographic compositions. The second NHI plan (NHI-2) has the same $50 deductible but a coinsurance rate of 20 percent for both types of expenditure. Each family's net expenditure is limited to 10 percent of family income. This is a substantial reduction in risk, especially for lower- and middle-income families.

The individual demand equations are simplified by assuming no cross-price elasticities ($\alpha_m = \beta_h = 0$ in the demand equations of the first section). Although hospital services and other services are substitutes for some purposes, they are also complements in other contexts. The assumption of zero cross elasticity may therefore be a reasonable starting point for a preliminary analysis.[5] Two sets of price elasticities have been used. The "moderate" price elasticities assume that the own-price of hospital care (α_h) is 0.5 and the own-price elasticity of medical care (β_m) is 0.4. The "low" elasticity pair assumes that $\alpha_h = 0.25$ and $\beta_m = 0.20$. The relative nonmonetary cost parameter λ is assumed to be 0.10 in all the calculations. The same baseline distributions are used in all income classes; this implicitly assumes that there is zero income elasticity of demand.

Table 11.1 analyzes the first NHI plan. Column 1 presents baseline figures for 1970 with no NHI program. Total expenditure on covered services for the population under age sixty-five is $23.3 billion. This corresponds to hospital services of $12.9 billion and other medical care expenditure of $10.4 billion.[6] Because the pre-NHI prices are normalized to be unity, these expenditures can also serve as measures of quantities for comparison with the post-NHI quantities.

Column 2 shows the impact that NHI-1 would have if prices remained unchanged. Total national expenditures on the covered health services would increase 38 percent to $32.2 billion. The quantity of hospital services rises 38 percent to 17.8, and the quantity of other medical services rises 38 percent to 14.4. The effective coinsurance rates are 17 percent for hospital care and 25 percent for other medical care. The cost to the government is therefore $25.6 billion.

An analysis with supply elasticities of 0.8 for both hospital-care and other services is presented in column 3. The results are substantially different from the pure demand case of column 2. Prices rise by ap-

5. Davis and Russell (1972) provided some evidence of positive cross-price elasticities, but medical services in their study were limited to hospital outpatient care.

6. Actual costs in 1970 were $13.2 billion for hospital services and $10.1 billion for medical services. The calibration method does not yield these exact figures because of the nonlinearity of the insurance schedules. These dollar amounts refer to persons under age sixty-five; see Cooper et al. (1973).

Table 11.1. Effects of NHI plan 1

	Baseline simulation (no NHI) (1)	"Moderate" demand elasticities				"Low" demand elasticities			
		Supply ∞ (2)	Elasticities 0.8 (3)	0.2 (4)	Price response model (5)	Supply ∞ (6)	Elasticities 0.8 (7)	0.2 (8)	Price response model (9)
National health expenditure[a]	23.3	32.2	37.0	42.3	38.1	27.2	30.5	35.9	35.0
Cost to government[a]	—	25.7	29.9	34.5	30.8	21.0	23.9	28.6	27.8
Quantity of hospital care[a]	12.9	17.8	15.7	14.1	14.3	15.0	14.5	13.8	13.7
Quantity of medical care[a]	10.4	14.4	12.9	11.6	10.4	12.2	11.8	11.3	10.4
Price of hospital care	1.00	1.00	1.28	1.58	1.55	1.00	1.15	1.40	1.44
Price of medical care	1.00	1.00	1.31	1.72	1.54	1.00	1.17	1.48	1.47
Effective coinsurance rate, hospital care	—	0.17	0.16	0.16	0.16	0.19	0.19	0.18	0.18
Effective coinsurance rate, medical care	—	0.25	0.23	0.21	0.23	0.27	0.25	0.23	0.24

Note: The moderate demand elasticities are $\alpha_n = 0.5$ and $\beta_m = 0.4$; the low elasticities are $\alpha_n = 0.25$ and $\beta_m = 0.20$.
a. Billions of 1970 dollars.

proximately 30 percent. Total expenditure of $37 billion is 15 percent higher than the estimate that ignored the endogenous price increase. The higher gross prices also imply a smaller increase in the quantities of care. The quantity of hospital services is 15.7, indicating that the rise from the pre-NHI value of 12.9 is only 22 percent, or about half of the estimated increase when the price response was ignored. The comparison is similar for medical services. National spending increases $13.7 billion, but the extra volume of services is worth only $5.3 billion at the pre-NHI prices. Column 4 shows comparable results for lower supply elasticities of $\gamma_H = \gamma_M = 0.2$. The total spending increases are greater, but the quantity increases are smaller.

Columns 6–8 present the same comparison of supply elasticities but with a lower pair of demand elasticities.[7] Although the effects of the NHI plan are now smaller, the implications of different supply elasticities are still very important. It is clear, moreover, that plausible differences in supply elasticities are at least as important as a source of uncertainty in total expenditure and in the cost to the government as the plausible differences in demand elasticities.

Table 11.2 presents a corresponding analysis for the second national health insurance option. The higher coinsurance rates ($C_H = C_M = 0.2$) decrease total expenditure, but the maximum out-of-pocket expenditure of 10 percent of income increases total expenditure. If prices remained constant, the net effect of these two changes in the NHI program would be a small reduction in total cost; with the moderate demand elasticities, total expenditure is $31.9 billion under plan NHI-2 in contrast to $32.2 billion under plan NHI-1. The effect of less elastic supply is to increase prices under both plans. The higher price substantially increases the probability that each family's expenditure will exceed 10 percent of income. At this point the MAX limit becomes effective and the coinsurance rate ends. Although demand is limited by the nonmonetary price $[\lambda/(1 + \lambda)]$, there is a substantial increase in demand. The result is that NHI-2 becomes more expensive than NHI-1. The government's cost is generally lower under the second plan because the higher coinsurance rate on relatively small expenditures more than outweighs the extra cost of providing complete protection for expenditures above 10 percent. Only if the supply elasticities are very low would prices rise enough to reverse this situation and make NHI-2 more expensive; this happens here with $\gamma_H = \gamma_M = 0.2$. With the lower demand elasticities the rise in expenditure is always sufficiently small that NHI-2 entails lower total expenditure and lower cost to the government.

7. Columns 5 and 9 present results that are discussed in the fourth section.

Table 11.2. Effects of NHI plan 2

	Baseline simulation (no NHI) (1)	"Moderate" demand elasticities				"Low" demand elasticities			
		Supply ∞ (2)	Elasticities 0.8 (3)	Elasticities 0.2 (4)	Price response model (5)	Supply ∞ (6)	Elasticities 0.8 (7)	Elasticities 0.2 (8)	Price response model (9)
National health expenditure[a]	23.3	31.9	37.3	43.8	36.5	26.5	29.5	34.9	31.7
Cost to government[a]	–	24.2	28.9	34.6	28.3	19.0	21.4	25.9	23.2
Quantity of hospital care[a]	12.9	18.4	16.3	14.5	15.4	14.8	14.4	13.8	14.1
Quantity of medical care[a]	10.4	13.4	12.4	11.4	10.4	11.7	11.5	11.1	10.4
Price of hospital care	1.00	1.00	1.34	1.77	1.45	1.00	1.15	1.42	1.28
Price of medical care	1.00	1.00	1.25	1.59	1.37	1.00	1.13	1.37	1.31
Effective coinsurance rate, hospital care	–	0.19	0.18	0.17	0.18	0.24	0.23	0.22	0.23
Effective coinsurance rate, medical care	–	0.31	0.29	0.27	0.30	0.34	0.33	0.31	0.32

Note: The moderate demand elasticities are $\alpha_n = 0.50$ and $\beta_m = 0.40$; the low demand elasticities are $\alpha_n = 0.25$ and $\beta_m = 0.20$.
a. Billions of 1970 dollars.

The supply elasticity can also affect the distributional impact of a national health insurance plan. Because the current simulations assume a zero income elasticity of demand for health services, the first NHI plan provides the same expected benefits at all income levels to families with any fixed demographic composition. NHI-2, on the other hand, limits each family's net expenditure to no more than 10 percent of family income. For low-income families this is a substantial reduction in the net price of health services, whereas for higher-income families the effect on price is much smaller. The result is a more substantial increase in spending at lower incomes.

These distributional effects are presented in table 11.3. The analysis refers to the second NHI plan and to the moderate price elasticities. Columns 1–3 describe the impact on families of two adults and two children in the case in which prices are unchanged—that is, infinitely elastic supplies of hospital and medical services at the original prices. Column 1 presents the average net benefit received by families at each income level—the average cost to the government as insurer. These net benefits fall rapidly for the first few income classes and then fall more slowly, reflecting the highly skewed distribution of health spending. Similarly, the average direct out-of-pocket payments by the family (column 2) increase rapidly for the first few income classes and then more slowly. The total quantity of care received is, with prices fixed at unity, the sum of the net benefits and direct payments; these quantities are shown in column 3. The quantity of care consumed also falls rather rapidly at first and then more slowly.

All three columns show that substantial progression is introduced by the single feature of a 10 percent maximum limit on direct payments, even when there is a relatively low 20 percent coinsurance rate. It is convenient to have a summary measure of the distributional impact and a method of combining the benefits (or payments or quantities) in different income classes into a single measure that reflects a constant value judgment about distributional equity. The uniformly distributed dollar (UDD) measure is useful for this purpose. For example, the UDD value of benefits is a weighted sum of the average benefits per family in each income class:

$$B_{\text{UDD}} = \sum_i B_i W_i N_i / \sum_i W_i N_i, \tag{7}$$

where B_i is the benefit per family in income class i, W_i is the weight given to a marginal dollar of a family in income class i, and N_i is the number of families in class i. If $B_i = 1$, $B_{\text{UDD}} = 1$; thus one unit in the B_{UDD} measure is the social value of one dollar given to each family — that is, the social value of a uniformly distributed dollar. It is conve-

Table 11.3. Distributional aspects of NHI plan 2: supply response model

Income class	Two adults, two children						All families		
	$\gamma_H = \gamma_M = \infty$			$\gamma_H = \gamma_M = 0.8$			$\gamma_H = \gamma_M = \infty$		
	Net benefits (1)	Direct payments (2)	Quantity (3)	Net benefits (4)	Direct payments (5)	Quantity (6)	Net benefits (7)	Direct payments (8)	Quantity (9)
Less than $2,000	$823	$ 87	910	$968	$ 90	814	$201	$ 28	229
$2,000–$2,999	700	132	832	830	140	745	202	42	245
$3,000–$3,999	647	143	790	770	154	709	261	62	323
$4,000–$4,999	620	151	771	735	163	689	297	77	374
$5,000–$5,999	589	157	746	709	170	675	346	95	441
$6,000–$6,999	564	162	726	678	176	656	365	107	473
$7,000–$7,999	536	165	701	651	180	638	387	120	507
$8,000–$9,999	513	169	682	617	185	617	409	134	543
$10,000–$11,999	487	172	659	586	189	596	424	148	572
$12,000–$14,999	465	175	640	551	192	576	429	158	586
$15,000–$24,999	434	178	612	520	197	552	424	168	592
$25,000 and over	413	179	592	484	199	527	395	167	562
UDD values									
$\alpha = 0.0$	497	169	667	596	186	602	351	112	462
$\alpha = 0.5$	522	165	687	626	180	620	307	86	393
$\alpha = 1.0$	562	156	718	672	170	647	262	62	324
$\alpha = 1.5$	623	141	765	742	153	688	231	45	276
$\alpha = 2.0$	696	122	819	825	131	735	214	36	250

Note: All calculations use moderate demand elasticities, $\alpha_n = 0.5$ and $\beta_m = 0.4$.

nient to relate the W_i's to income by a simple functional relation. The constant-elasticity function $W_i = Y_i^{-\alpha}$ is both familiar and convenient. For $\alpha = 1$ it implies that the weight given to a marginal dollar of income varies inversely with the income of the recipient family. The higher the value of α, the more egalitarian the implied preferences.

Table 11.3 shows the B_{UDD} values corresponding to values of α between 0 and 2. The value of $\alpha = 0$ corresponds to the simple average of benefits with no weighting for distribution. The average benefit (cost to the government) per family with two adults and two children is thus $497. For someone whose distributional preferences correspond to $\alpha = 1$, these benefits are equivalent to $562 distributed uniformly to all such families. With more egalitarian preferences ($\alpha = 2$), the benefits are equivalent to $696 distributed uniformly. Conversely, the average value of direct out-of-pocket payments is $169 per family of two adults and two children, but this amount is equivalent to a smaller uniformly distributed payment of $156 for $\alpha = 1$ and $122 for $\alpha = 2$. Finally, the average quantity of services is $667 per family. Applying the same UDD evaluation to these benefits implies that for $\alpha = 1$, they are equivalent to a constant $718 per family.

The effect of introducing supply elasticities of 0.8 for hospital and medical services is to increase prices and therefore expenditures at all income levels. The equilibrium quantities are now smaller than before. Benefits rise by about 18 percent in the lower-income classes and by about 14 percent in the higher-income classes. Direct costs rise by about 7 percent in the lower-income classes and about 11 percent in the higher-income classes. Thus in both ways the NHI-2 plan is slightly more redistributive when the supply response is explicitly recognized. But the relatively greater direct payments by higher-income families just about offset the relatively lower benefits from the insurer and make the proportional change in the quantity of services approximately equal at all income levels; the quantities shown in column 6 are almost exactly 90 percent of the quantities in column 3.

Although the NHI-2 plan is very progressive with respect to income when attention is focused on families with a single demographic composition, this characteristic is diguised when all family types are combined. Average family size increases with family income; there are fewer single-person families and larger average numbers of children. Columns 7–9 show that this has striking effects on the distribution of average benefits, direct payments, and quantities of care. Average benefits rise with income until $15,000 and then fall only slightly. Average direct payments rise much more sharply with income. The net effect is that quantity increases with family income up to $25,000, despite the income-related limit on direct payments. This comparison demonstrates the importance of taking demographic structure into account in evaluating the distributional impact of alternative NHI plans.

A Price Response Model

Neither hospitals nor physicians are like the typical economic agents to which the traditional theory of price and quantity determination applies. These differences—the nonprofit nature of hospitals, the special expertise of physicians, and the physicians' professional interest—may not be enough to vitiate the applicability of the traditional theory in the preceding sections. Nevertheless, it seems useful to provide an alternative response model that contains special features of the health-care sector. The price response model presented in this section incorporates ideas about the markets for physicians' services and hospital care that were previously developed by M. Feldstein (1970c; 1971b; chapters 2, 3). An important characteristic of this alternative model is that the price-quantity equilibrium need not be market clearing; excess demand and nonprice rationing may prevail in equilibrium.

Consider first the model of physicians' behavior. The price response model specifies that the effect of NHI is to raise the gross price of physicians' services by an amount that depends on the increased insurance coverage of physicians' services. More complete insurance raises the physicians' price not only because it increases demand, but also because physicians take into account the financial impact of their fees on their patients. Moreover, physicians may seek to maintain excess demand in order to have the opportunity to select the types of patients and diagnoses that they like to treat; an increase in insurance permits gross prices to be raised without reducing the desired degree of excess demand.[8]

More specifically, the change from the pre-NHI price PM_0 to the post-NHI price PM_1 is given by the function

$$\frac{PM_1}{PM_0} = \left[\frac{NPM_1}{NPM_0}\right]^{-\delta_M}, \tag{8}$$

where NPM_0 is the average *net* price of physicians' services prevailing before NHI (the product of PM_0 and the effective coinsurance rate before NHI) and NPM_1 is the average *net* price that would prevail

8. These ideas are developed more fully in M. Feldstein (1970c) and in chapter 2.

after NHI if physicians did not alter their gross price.[9] The computational procedure for deriving PM_1 is straightforward. The demand simulation model is used to calculate NPM_0 as the ratio of aggregate *direct* patient expenditure on physicians' services to aggregate *total* expenditure on those services. The insurance coverage is then changed to the NHI plan and the calculation is repeated to obtain NPM_1. Since NPM_1 depends on the gross price PM_0, no iterative procedure is necessary. Applying equation (8) then yields the new price that prevails under NHI.

The supply function of the physician now indicates the *desired* supply at each price. The same constant elasticity function is used:

$$\ln QM_1 = \ln QM_0 + \gamma_M \ln PM_1. \tag{9}$$

If the aggregate demand at price PM_1 (and corresponding hospital price PH_1) is less than or equal to the desired supply QM_1, the equilibrium quantity is demand determined; that is, each family gets the quantity of physicians' services that it wants at the new prevailing price. If, however, as seems more likely, the aggregate demand exceeds supply, the new equilibrium is supply determined. Each family obtains only some fraction of the services that it would like to purchase with the new prices and insurance coverage. In the absence of better information about nonprice rationing, this model specifies that each family receives the same fraction of the quantity that it demands regardless of income, demographic composition, or desired expenditure. More specifically, the rationing constant for physicians' services is defined as

$$RM = QM_1/QMD, \tag{10}$$

where QMD is the aggregate quantity of physicians' services demanded at prices PM_1 and PH_1 under the NHI plan, and QM_1 is the desired aggregate supply defined in equation (9). Each individual family then obtains RM times the quantity that it demands according to the basic demand equations in the first section, with $P_h = PH_1$ and $P_m = PM_1$.

The use of nonprice rationing increases the likelihood that some families would receive less care than in the absence of NHI even if NHI improves everyone's coverage. This clearly happens when the supply elasticity is zero but the demand elasticity is nonzero. NHI then increases demand and results in a rationing parameter RM less than one. Unless all families' demands are increased in exactly the

9. This model of price response is clearly a simplification that is used because no more specific hypothesis seems either theoretically or empirically superior.

same proportion, the NHI reduces the quantity of care received by some families.

Although the hospital services section of the price response model has the same formal structure as the model of physicians' services, the interpretation of this behavior is quite different. An analysis of hospitals' response to the growth of private insurance in the 1960s and to the introduction of Medicare and Medicaid suggests that hospitals respond to insurance by increasing the cost per patient-day through more sophisticated care and higher staff wages. Prices rise in response to additional insurance, not because of a greater unit cost of providing more of the same type of care (a rising supply curve in the traditional sense), but because hospitals produce a different product and choose to pay higher wages. To analyze this as a response to NHI, one would use the price response model with a demand-determined equilibrium. The price of hospital services after the introduction of NHI is given by

$$\frac{PH_1}{PH_0} = \left[\frac{NPH_1}{NPH_0}\right]^{-\delta_H}, \tag{11}$$

where NPH_0 is the average net price of hospital services prevailing before NHI and NPH_1 is the average net price that would prevail after NHI if hospitals did not alter their gross price. The analysis in chapter 3 suggests this type of behavior with $0 < \delta_H \leq 1$ and with the actual quantity determined by household demand. The model is thus completed by using PH_1 and PM_1 to calculate each family's demand and assuming that hospitals will supply this quantity.

Alternatively, the price response model may be evaluated with a supply-determined equilibrium by using the hospital supply equation

$$\ln QH_1 = \ln QH_0 + \gamma_H \ln PH_1,$$

where γ_H is the elasticity of supply. The hospital rationing parameter *(RH)* is then defined by an equation analogous to (10). The individual demand equations and *RH* are then combined to determine the allocation of the rationed hospital care.

The price response model in which the quantities are constrained by supply can also be used to examine the case in which price controls are used to limit the price rise. The prices PM_1 and PH_1 are then determined by the price control agency instead of by equations (8) and (11). The corresponding supplies are then calculated with equations (9) and (12). The individual demand simulations yield rationing parameters *RM* and *RH* and the rationed allocation services corresponding to the NHI plan, the controlled prices, and the quantities supplied.

The two alternative NHI options discussed in the third section have been reanalyzed with this price response model. More specifically, the price response parameters δ_H and δ_M are both assigned the value 0.5; a 20 percent decrease in the effective coinsurance rate (for example, from 0.40 to 0.32) thus raises the gross prices by approximately 10 percent and therefore also lowers the net price by about 10 percent. For medical services the total supply is assumed fixed: $\gamma_M = 0$. The equilibrium quantities of medical services are therefore supply determined. For hospital services a positive supply elasticity ($\gamma_H = 0.5$) is assumed. The two alternative demand specifications used in the third section are again investigated. With the moderate demand elasticities ($\alpha_n = 0.5$, $\beta_m = 0.4$), the increase in demand exceeds the increase in supply and the allocation of hospital services is also supply determined. Only with the low demand elasticities ($\alpha_n = 0.25$, $\beta_m = 0.2$) is there no excess demand and a demand-determined allocation.

The aggregate implications of these price response models are shown in columns 5 and 9 of tables 11.1 and 11.2. With the moderate demand elasticities the total cost implications are quite similar to the previous analysis with supply elasticities of 0.8 and market-clearing prices. Total national spending under NHI-1 is $38.1 billion, in comparison with the earlier value of $37 billion; for NHI-2 the figures are $36.5 billion and $37.3 billion. Estimated costs to the government are also quite similar. The underlying price and quantity changes are, however, very different; price rises are greater and quantity increases are smaller. For NHI-1 total national spending increases by $14.8 billion to buy only $1.4 billion worth of additional services valued at original prices (quantity increases from 23.3 billion to 24.7 billion). With NHI-2 the extra spending of $13.2 billion induces only an extra quantity worth $2.5 billion at original prices.

Although the prices and aggregate quantities are quite different under the two models, for the two sets of assumptions examined here the distributional implications are approximately the same. Table 11.4 shows the distributions of benefits, direct out-of-pocket payments, and quantities for families with two adults and two children under the price response model and under the supply response model with $\gamma_H = \gamma_M = 0.8$. Although benefits and direct payments are lower under the price response model, the ratios of corresponding values under the two models are approximately constant. Similarly, quantities are some 10 percent lower at each income level. Of course, this result depends on the assumptions made for this comparison.

Table 11.4. Distributional aspects of NHI plan 2: comparison of price response and supply response models

Income class	Price response model			Supply response model		
		$\gamma_H = 0.5$	$\gamma_M = 0$		$\gamma_H = \gamma_M = 0.8$	
	Net benefits (1)	Direct payments (2)	Quantity (3)	Net benefits (4)	Direct payments (5)	Quantity (6)
Less than $2,000	$945	$ 89	730	$968	$ 90	814
$2,000–$2,999	812	137	669	830	140	745
$3,000–$3,999	750	150	634	770	154	709
$4,000–$4,999	723	159	621	735	163	689
$5,000–$5,999	696	166	607	709	170	675
$6,000–$6,999	664	172	589	678	176	656
$7,000–$7,999	638	176	574	651	180	638
$8,000–$9,999	604	181	554	617	185	617
$10,000–$11,999	572	185	534	586	189	596
$12,000–$14,999	543	188	516	551	192	576
$15,000–$24,999	506	193	494	520	197	552
$25,000 and over	470	195	470	484	199	527
UDD variables						
$\alpha = 0.0$	582	182	539	596	186	602
$\alpha = 0.5$	611	176	556	626	180	620
$\alpha = 1.0$	657	166	581	672	170	647
$\alpha = 1.5$	725	149	617	742	153	688
$\alpha = 2.0$	806	128	659	825	131	735

Note: All calculations use moderate demand elasticities and refer to families of two adults and two children.

With a more complex insurance structure (for example, deductibles related to income) or different elasticities of demand and supply, the two models of provider behavior may imply quite different distributional patterns.

The primary purpose of this chapter has been to emphasize that any analysis of the effects of alternative national health insurance plans should take into account the effect of insurance on the prices and supplies of health services. An operational method was presented for combining a stochastic microsimulational model of household demand with aggregate supply and price determination equations.

The supply models used in this analysis are preliminary and can only be regarded as illustrative. Neither the traditional supply model nor the price response model can be eliminated as completely inconsistent with the data. More econometric research is therefore required to provide conditional estimates of the parameters of both models. We hope that this evidence of the importance of these parameters will encourage others to continue work on these empirical issues.

Postscript

A well-meaning and seemingly innocuous government policy to encourage private health insurance has played a central role in the cumulative erosion of the health-care market. The favorable tax treatment of health insurance purchases has grown over time to become a $10 billion inducement to overinsurance. The resulting excess insurance has raised the demand for sophisticated health services, driven up the cost of care, and thereby increased the demand for even more insurance. The rising cost of care also generated the pressures on the government that resulted in the creation of Medicare and Medicaid. Costs have continued to rise, inducing a call for more government controls and for more government finance through some form of national health insurance.

The future of health care in the United States is now uncertain. With the existing insurance coverage, a rapid rise in hospital costs is likely to continue and to bring with it growing pressure for more regulation and controls. The variety of national health insurance proposals that continue to be debated would increase the extent of insurance and enlarge the government's role in the provision of health care. These developments toward a more centralized and government-controlled provision of health care are encouraged by some health policy specialists who believe that "health care is different," that individuals (and their doctors) cannot choose health care intelligently so that it must be chosen for them by a wise and benign government, and that any inequality in health care is ethically wrong. Still others favor more government finance and control of health care, even though they do not regard health care as special, because they welcome any opportunity for more egalitarian policies and a reduced role for the private market.

At the same time pressures in the opposite direction are growing.

There is an increasing recognition of the problems caused by excess insurance, of the inappropriateness of increased regulation, and of the desirability of maintaining individual freedom of choice in medical care. The political process is now giving more attention to the idea of restructuring the system of health insurance and health-care finance in ways that would strengthen the private market and the role of competition. An essential features of such reforms is to limit the tax subsidy to private insurance and to stop the growth of government health insurance programs. Although the gains that would result from such changes could in principle make everyone better off, these policies may not be adopted. Individuals may focus on the immediate potential loss of health insurance benefits that appear to be paid for by "someone else" rather than on the indirect benefits of lower health-care costs, higher wages, and reduced tax rates. Myopia is the enemy of reform.

Whatever the outcome of these conflicting forces, the experience of the health-care sector contains a useful general lesson that goes beyond tax subsidies, health insurance, and hospital costs. In the health-care sector a relatively small but critically positioned government interference with the private market has created a cumulative process of market collapse and of increasing government control that is difficult if not impossible to reverse. What has happened in the health-care sector could happen in other ways in other parts of the economy. Although the decentralized market process can function successfully with some imperfection and some government intervention, beyond a critical level of government interference the natural market forces become adverse and destroy the viability of the market process itself. Extending this conclusion to the economy as a whole may not be inappropriate.

References

Acton, J. P. 1972. *Demand for Health Care among the Urban Poor, with Special Emphasis on the Role of Time.* Rand Publication R-1151-OEO-NYC.

——— 1970. Evaluation of a Life Saving Program. Doctoral dissertation, Harvard University.

Altman, S. H. 1971. *Present and Future Supply of Registered Nurses.* Washington, D.C.: U.S. Government Printing Office.

American Hospital Association. 1968. *Selected Characteristics of the Physician Population, 1963–1967.* Chicago.

——— 1974. *Hospital Statistics, 1973.* Chicago: American Hospital Association, Department of Human Resources Management.

——— *Hospitals.* Journal of the American Hospital Association, Guide Issue, pt. 2 (issues from 1950–1969).

Andersen, R., and O. W. Anderson. 1967. *A Decade of Health Services.* Chicago: University of Chicago Press.

Anderson, R., and L. Benham. 1970. Factors Affecting the Relationship between Family Income and Medical Care Consumption. In *Empirical Studies in Health Economics,* ed. H. Klarman. Baltimore, Md.: Johns Hopkins Press.

Annual Report of the Secretary of the Treasury for 1968. 1969. Washington, D.C.: U.S. Government Printing Office.

Arrow, K. J. 1976. Welfare Analysis of Changes in Health Insurance Rates. In *The Role of Health Insurance in the Health Services Sector,* ed. R. Rosett. New York: National Bureau of Economic Research.

———1974. Optimal Insurance and Generalized Deductibles. *Scandinavian Actuarial Journal,* pp. 1–42.

——— 1965. *Aspects of the Theory of Risk Bearing.* Yrjo Jahnsson Lectures. Helsinki: Yrjo Jahnsson Foundation.

——— 1964. The Role of Securities in the Optimal Association of Risk-Bearing. *Review of Economic Studies* 31:91–96.

——— 1963. Uncertainty and the Welfare Economics of Medical Care. *American Economic Review* 53:941–973.

Auster, R. D., I. Leveson, and D. Sarachek. 1969. The Production of Health: An Exploratory Study. *Journal of Human Resources* 4:411–436.

Bailey, N. T. J. 1957. Operational Research in Hospital Planning and Design. *Operational Research Quarterly,* p. 149.

Bailey, R. M. 1970. Economies of Scale in Medical Practice. In *Empirical Studies in Health Economics,* ed. H. Klarman. Baltimore, Md.: Johns Hopkins Press.

Balestra, P., and M. Nerlove. 1966. Pooling Cross-Section and Time-Series Data in the Estimation of a Dynamic Model: The Demand for Natural Gas. *Econometrica* 34:585–612.

Barlow, R. 1967. The Economic Effects of Malaria Eradication. *American Economic Review* 57:130–147.

Barzel, Y. 1969. Productivity and the Price of Medical Services. *Journal of Political Economy* 77:1014–28.

Benham, L. 1971. The Labor Market for Registered Nurses: A Three-Equation Model. *Review of Economics and Statistics* 50:246–252.

Benham, L., A. Maurizi, and M. Reder. 1968. Migration, Location, and Renumeration of Medical Personnel: Physicians and Dentists. *Review of Economics and Statistics* 50:332–347.

Berry, R. E., Jr. 1970. Product Heterogeneity and Hospital Cost Analysis. *Inquiry* 7:67–75.

Borch, K. H. 1968. *The Economics of Uncertainty.* Princeton, N. J.: Princeton University Press.

Bridges, B., Jr. 1971. Family Need Differences and Family Tax Burden Estimates. *National Tax Journal* 24:423–448.

Brinker, P. A., and B. Walker. 1962. The Hill-Burton Act: 1948–1954. *Review of Economics and Statistics* 44:208–212.

Brown, D. M., and H. E. Lapan. 1972. The Rising Price of Physicians' Services: A Comment. *Review of Economics and Statistics* 54:101–104.

Carr, W. J., and P. J. Feldstein. 1967. The Relationship of Cost to Hospital Size. *Inquiry* 4:45–65.

Chiswick, B. 1976. Comment on Feldstein and Friedman. In *The Role of Health Insurance in the Health Services Sector,* ed. R. Rosett. New York: National Bureau of Economic Research.

Cohen, H. A. 1970. Hospital Cost Curves with Emphasis on Measuring Patient Care Output. In *Empirical Studies in Health Economics,* ed. H. Klarman. Baltimore, Md.: Johns Hopkins Press.

Cooper, B. S., N. L. Worthington, and M. F. McGee. 1973. *Compendium of National Health Expenditures Data.* Washington, D.C.: U.S. Department of Health, Education, and Welfare.

Cooper, B., et al. 1973. *Medical Care Expenditures, Prices, and Costs: Background Book.* Washington, D.C.: U.S. Department of Health, Education, and Welfare.

Cost of Living Council. 1974. Health Care: Final Phase IV Regulations. *Federal Register* 39, part 2.

Crew, M. 1969. Coinsurance and the Welfare Economics of Medical Care. *American Economic Review* 59:906–908.

Davis, K. 1973. Theories of Hospital Inflation: Some Empirical Evidence. *Journal of Human Resources* 8:181–201.

——— 1972a. Economic Theories of Behavior in Nonprofit Private Hospitals. *Economic and Business Bulletin* 24:1–13.

——— 1972b. An Empirical Investigation of Alternative Models of the Hospital Industry. Paper presented at the American Economic Association Meetings, December, Toronto, Ontario.

——— 1971. Relationship of Hospital Prices to Costs. *Applied Economics* 3: 115–125.

Davis, K., and L. B. Russell. 1972. The Substitution of Hospital Outpatient Care for Inpatient Care. *Review of Economics and Statistics* 54: 109–120.

Drèze, J. H. 1962. L'Utilité Sociale d'une Vie Humaine. *Revue Française de Recherche Operationnelle* 23, 2e Trimestre.

Dubos, R. 1959. *Mirage of Health.* New York: Harper and Co.

Economic Report of the President. 1976. Washington, D.C.: U.S. Government Printing Office.

Edelson, N. M. 1971. The Influence of Skill Mix, Monopsony Power, and Philanthropy on Hospital Wage Rates. Discussion Paper No. 211, Wharton School of Finance and Commerce, University of Pennsylvania.

Ehrlich, I., and G. Becker. 1972. Market Insurance, Self-Insurance, and Self-Protection. *Journal of Political Economy* 80:623–648.

Eilers, R. 1969. Postpayment Medical Expense Coverage: A Proposed Salvation for Insured and Insurer. *Medical Care* 7:191–208.

Evans, R. G. 1970a. Efficiency Incentives in Hospital Reimbursement. Doctoral dissertation, Harvard University.

——— 1970b. "Behavioral" Cost Functions for Hospitals. Discussion Paper No. 35, Department of Economics, University of British Columbia, April 1970.

Fein, R. 1967. *The Doctor Shortage: An Economic Diagnosis.* Washington, D.C.: Brookings Institution.

——— 1958. *Economics of Mental Illness.* New York: Basic Books.

Fein, R., and G. Weber. 1971. *Financing Medical Education.* A general report prepared for the Carnegie Commission on Higher Education and the Commonwealth Fund. New York: McGraw-Hill Book Co.

Feldstein, M. S. 1974a. Unemployment Compensation: Adverse Incentives and Distributional Anomalies. *National Tax Journal* 27:231–244.

——— 1974b. The *Economics of Health and Medical Care.* Proceedings of a conference held by the International Economic Association at Tokyo, March 1973. London: Macmillan and Company.

——— 1973a. Technical Change and the Demand for Physicians' Services. Mimeographed.

——— 1973b. An Econometric Model of the Medicare System: Reply. *Quarterly Journal of Economics* 87:490–494.

——— 1973c. The Medical Economy. *Scientific American* 229:151–159.

——— 1972. Distributional Equity and the Optimal Structure of Public Prices. *American Economic Review* 62:32–36.

———— 1971a. An Econometric Model of the Medicare System. *Quarterly Journal of Economics* 85:1–20.

———— 1971b. *The Rising Cost of Hospital Care.* Published for the National Center for Health Services Research and Development, Department of Health, Education, and Welfare. Washington, D.C.: Information Resources Press.

———— 1970a. Health Sector Planning in Developing Countries. *Economica* 37: 139–163.

———— 1970b. Improving Medical Care Price Statistics. In 1969 Proceedings of the Business and Economics Statistics Section of the American Statistical Association, pp. 361–365.

———— 1970c. The Rising Price of Physicians' Services. *Review of Economics and Statistics* 52:121–133.

———— 1968. The Use of an Econometric Model for Health Sector Planning. In *Federal Programs for the Development of Human Resources:* A compendium of papers submitted to the Subcommittee on Economic Progress of the Joint Economic Committee, Congress of the U.S. Washington, D.C.: U.S. Government Printing Office.

———— 1967. *Economic Analysis for Health Service Efficiency: Econometric Studies of the British National Health Service,* Contributions to Economic Analysis, vol. 51. Amsterdam: North-Holland Publishing Company.

Feldstein, M. S., and E. Allison. 1972. Current Tax Subsidies of Private Health Insurance. Mimeographed.

Feldstein, M. S., and B. Friedman. 1972. The Demand for Supplementary Private Insurance, Discussion Paper No. 382, Harvard Institute of Economic Research.

Feldstein, M. S., and H. Luft. 1973. Distributional Constraints in Public Expenditure Planning. *Management Science.* 19:1414–22.

Feldstein, M. S., M. Piot, and T. K. Sundaresan. 1973. *Resource Allocation Model for Public Health Planning.* Published as a supplement to vol. 48 of the *Bulletin of the World Health Organization.*

Feldstein, M. S., and A. Taylor. 1976. *Differences among Hospitals in the Rates of Increase of Cost and Related Characteristics.* A report to the Council on Wage and Price Stability.

Feldstein, P. J.: 1966. Research on the Demand for Health Services. *Milbank Memorial Fund Quarterly* 43:128–165.

———— 1964. The Demand for Medical Care. In *Report of the Commission on the Cost of Medical Care.* Chicago: American Medical Association.

———— 1961. *An Empirical Investigation of the Marginal Cost of Hospital Services: Studies in Hospital Administration.* Chicago: Graduate Program in Hospital Administration, University of Chicago.

Feldstein, P. J., and W. J. Carr. 1964. The Effect of Income on Medical Care Spending. *Proceedings of Social Statistics Section of American Statistical Association* 7.

Feldstein, P. J., and S. Kelman. 1970. A Framework for an Econometric Model of the Medical Care Sector. In *Empirical Studies in Health Economics,* ed. H. Klarman. Baltimore, Md.: Johns Hopkins Press.

Fisher, F. M. 1965. Dynamic Structure and Estimation in Economy-Wide Econometric Models. In *Brookings Quarterly Econometric Model of the United States*, ed. J. S. Duesenberry et al. Chicago: Rand McNally and Co.

Frech, H. E., III, and P. B. Ginsburg. 1972a. Physician Pricing: Monopolistic or Competitive? *Southern Economic Journal* 35:573–577.

——— 1972b. Imposed Health Insurance in Monopolistic Markets. National Center for Health Services Research and Development, Department of Health, Education, and Welfare.

Friedman, Bernard 1974. Risk Aversion and the Consumer Choice of Health Insurance Options. *Review of Economics and Statistics* 56:209–214.

——— 1971. A Study of Uncertainty and Health Insurance. Doctoral dissertation, Massachusetts Institute of Technology.

Friedman, M., and S. Kuznets. 1945. *Income from Independent Professional Practice*. New York: National Bureau of Economic Research.

Friedman, M., and L. J. Savage. 1948. The Utility Analysis of Choices Involving Risk. *Journal of Political Economy* 56:279–304.

Fuchs, V. 1976. The Earnings of Allied Health Personnel: Are Health Workers Underpaid? *Explorations in Economic Research.* 3, no. 3:408–432.

——— 1975. Are Health Workers Underpaid? National Bureau of Economic Research, Working Paper no. 108. Stanford, California.

——— 1965. Some Economic Aspects of Mortality in the U.S. Mimeographed.

Fuchs, V., and M. Kramer. 1972. *Determinants of Expenditures for Physicians' Services in the United States, 1948–68*. Published for the National Center for Health Services Research and Development, Department of Health, Education, and Welfare. Washington, D.C.: U.S. Government Printing Office.

Gillespie, W. I. 1965. Effect of Public Expenditures on the Distribution of Income. In *Essays in Fiscal Federalism*, ed. R. A. Musgrave. Washington, D.C.: Brookings Institution.

Ginsburg, P. 1974. Price Controls and Hospital Costs. Presented at AEA-HERO session of Allied Social Science Association meetings. San Francisco, December.

——— 1972a. Resource Allocation in the Hospital Industry: The Role of Capital Financing. *Social Security Bulletin* 35:20–30.

——— 1972b. Capital Investment by Nonprofit Firms: The Voluntary Hospital. Michigan State University, Econometrics Workshop Paper No. 7205.

——— 1970. Capital in Nonprofit Hospitals. Doctoral thesis. Harvard University.

Ginsburg, P., and L. Manheim. 1972. The Effect of Coinsurance and Deductibles on Health Services Utilization and Expenditure: A Survey. Economic Analysis Branch, National Center for Health Services Research and Development, Department of Health, Education, and Welfare.

Gould, J. P. 1969. The Expected Utility Hypothesis and the Selection of Optimal Deductibles for a Given Insurance Policy. *Journal of Business* 42:143–151.

Gramlich, E. M. 1969. State and Local Governments and Their Budget Constraint. *International Economic Review* 10:163–182.

Griliches, Z., ed. 1971. *Price Indexes and Quality Change.* Cambridge, Mass.: Harvard University Press.

Grossman, M. 1972a. *The Demand for Health: A Theoretical and Empirical Investigation.* New York: National Bureau of Economic Research.

———— 1972b. On the Concept of Health Capital and the Demand for Health. *Journal of Political Economy* 80:223–256.

Hansen, W. L. 1964. Shortages and Investment in Health Manpower. In *The Economics of Health and Medical Care,* ed. S. Axelrod. Ann Arbor, Mich.: University of Michigan.

Harberger, A. C. 1971. Three Basic Postulates for Applied Welfare Economics. *Journal of Economic Literature* 9:785–797.

———— 1964. The Measuremment of Waste. *American Economic Review* 54: 58–76.

Hartley, M., H. O. Hartley, and L. Pondy. 1972. The Use of Integer Programming to Estimate Leontief and Mixed Cobb-Douglas-Leontief Production Functions. Discussion Paper No. 153, Economic Research Group, Department of Economics, State University of New York at Buffalo.

Health Insurance Institute. n.d. *Source Book of Health Insurance Data,* 1973–74. New York.

———— n.d. *Source Book of Health Insurance Data,* 1959–1968. New York.

Hefty, T. R. 1969. Returns to Scale in Hospitals: A Critical Review of Recent Research. *Health Services Research* 4:267–280.

Henderson, J. M. 1968. Local Government Expenditures: A Social Welfare Analysis. *Review of Economics and Statistics* 50:156–163.

Holtman, A. G. 1972. Prices, Time, and Technology in the Medical Care Market. *Journal of Human Resources* 7:177–190.

Hotelling, H. 1938. The General Welfare in Relation to Problems of Taxation and of Railway and Utility Rates. *Econometrica* 6:242–269.

Houthakker, H. S., and L. D. Taylor. 1966. *Consumer Demand in the United States 1929–1970.* Cambridge, Mass.: Harvard University Press.

Hughes, E. F. X., V. R. Fuchs, J. E. Jacoby, and E. M. Lewit. 1972. Surgical Workloads in Community Practice. *Surgery* 71:315–327.

Ingbar, M. L., and L. D. Taylor. 1969. *Hospital Costs in Massachusetts: An Econometric Study.* Cambridge, Mass.: Harvard University Press.

Inman, R. 1971. Three Essays on Fiscal Federalism. Doctoral dissertation, Harvard University.

Jones, K., and R. Sidebotham. 1962. *Mental Hospitals at Work.* London: Routledge and Kegan Paul.

Joseph, H. 1971. Empirical Research on the Demand for Health Care. *Inquiry* 8:61–71.

Kessel, R. A. 1970. The American Medical Association and the Supply of Physicians. *Law Contemporary Problems* 35:267–283.

———— 1958. Price Discrimination in Medicine. *Journal of Law and Economics* 1: 20–53.

Klarman, H. W., ed. 1970. *Empirical Studies in Health Economics.* Baltimore, Md.: Johns Hopkins Press.

———— 1969a. Approaches to Moderating the Increases in Medical Care Costs. *Medical Care* 7:175–190.

———— 1969b. Reimbursing the Hospital: The Differences the Third Party Makes. *Journal of Risk and Insurance* 36:553–566.

———— 1967. Present Status of Cost-Benefit Analysis in the Health Field. *Americal Journal of Public Health* 57:1948–53.

———— 1965a. *The Economics of Health.* New York: Columbia University Press.

———— 1965b. Syphilis Control Programs. In *Measuring Benefits of Government Investments,* ed. R. Dorfman. Washington, D.C.: Brookings Institution.

———— 1964. The Increased Cost of Hospital Care. In *The Economics of Health and Medical Care,* ed. S. J. Axelrod. Ann Arbor, Mich.: Bureau of Public Health Economics and Department of Economics, University of Michigan.

Kolodrubetz, W. W. 1971a. Trends in Employee Benefit Plans in the Sixties. *Social Security Bulletin* 34, no. 4:21–34.

———— 1971b. Employee Benefit Plans in 1969. *Research and Statistics Note.* Social Security Administration.

Lave, J., and L. Lave. 1970. Hospital Cost Functions: Estimating Cost Functions for Multi-Product Firms. *American Economic Review* 60:379–395.

Lee, M. L. 1971. A Conspicuous Production Theory of Hospital Behavior. *Southern Economic Journal* 38:48–58.

Livernash, R. E. 1970. Wages and Benefits. In *A Review of Industrial Relations Research,* vol. 1, ed. W. L. Ginsburg, A. Weber, and F. Cassell. Madison, Wisc.: Industrial Relations Research Association.

Long, M. F. 1964. Efficient Use of Hospitals. In *The Economics of Health and Medical Care,* ed. A. Axelrod. Ann Arbor, Mich.: University of Michigan Press.

Luft, H. 1972. *Poverty and Health: An Empirical Investigation of the Economic Interactions.* Doctoral dissertation, Harvard University.

———— 1970. Determinants of the Flow of Physicians to the United States. Rand Corporation Paper P-4538.

McNerney, W. J., and study staff. 1962. *Hospital and Medical Economics* (Study of Populations, Services, Costs. Methods of Payments, and Controls), vol. 2. Chicago: Hospital Research and Educational Trust.

Mann, J. K., and D. E. Yett. 1968. The Analysis of Hospital Costs: A Review Article. *Journal of Business of the University of Chicago* 41:191–202.

Mitchell, B., and C. Phelps. 1975. *Employer-Paid Group Health Insurance and Costs of Mandated National Coverage* (n.p.).

Mitchell, B., and R. J. Vogel. 1974. *Health and Taxes: An Assessment of the Medical Deduction.* New York: Rand Publications.

Mossin, J. 1968. Aspects of Rational Insurance Purchasing. *Journal of Political Economy* 76, part 1:553–568.

Mueller, M. S. 1972. Private Health Insurance in 1971: Population Coverage, Enrollment, and Financial Experience. *Social Security Bulletin* 35:3–19.

Muller, C., and P. Worthington. 1970. Factors Entering into Capital Decisions of Hospitals. In *Empirical Studies in Health Economics,* ed. H. Klarman. Baltimore, Md.: Johns Hopkins Press.

Musgrave, R., J. Carroll, L. Cook, and L. Frane. 1951. Distribution of Tax Payments by Income Groups: A Case Study for 1948. *National Tax Journal* 4:1–53.

National Advisory Commission on Health Manpower. 1967. *Report,* 2 vols. Washington, D.C.: U.S. Government Printing Office.

National Center for Health Statistics. 1971. *Current Estimates from the Health Interview Survey, United States, 1969.* Series 10, no. 63. Washington, D.C.: U.S. Government Printing Office.

———— 1970. *Inpatient Utilization of Short-Stay Hospitals by Diagnosis in the U.S., 1965.* Series 13, no. 6. Washington, D.C.: U.S. Government Printing Office.

———— 1967. *Family Hospital and Surgical Insurance Coverage, United States, July 1962–June 1963.* Series 10, no. 42. Washington, D.C.: U.S. Government Printing Office.

———— 1966a. *Personal Health Expenses: Per Capita Annual Expenses, United States: July-December 1962.* Series 10, no. 27. Washington, D.C.: U.S. Government Printing Office.

———— 1966b. *Hospital Discharges and Length of Stay: Short-Stay Hospitals, United States, July 1963-June 1964.* Series 10, no. 30. Washington, D.C.: U.S. Government Printing Office.

U.S. Bureau of the Census. 1971a. *Current Population Survey 1970.* Series P-60, no. 75. Washington, D.C. U.S. Government Printing Office.

———— 1971b. *Census of Government,* vol. 3, no. 2.

———— 1970. *Current Population Reports.* Series P-60, no. 75. Income in 1969 of Families and Persons in the U.S. Washington, D.C.: U.S. Government Printing Office.

———— 1969. *Current Population Reports.* Series P-60, no. 66. Income in 1968 of Families and Persons in the U.S. Washington, D.C.: U.S. Government Printing Office.

———— 1967. *Census of Government,* vol. 3, no. 2.

———— 1967. *Current Population Reports.* Series P-60, no. 53. Income in 1966 of Families and Persons in the U.S. Washington, D.C.: U.S. Government Printing Office.

———— 1964. *U.S. Census of Population: 1960.* Vol. 1: *Characteristics of the Population,* part 1. Washington, D.C.

Nerlove, M. 1967. Experimental Evidence on the Estimation of Dynamic Economic Relations from a Time Series of Cross Sections. *Economic Studies Quarterly* 18:42–74.

Newhouse, J. P. 1970a. Toward a Theory of Nonprofit Institutions: An Economic Model of a Hospital. *American Economic Review* 60:64–74.

———— 1970b. A Model of Physician Pricing. *Southern Economic Journal* 37: 174–183.

Newhouse, J. P., and F. Sloan. 1972. A Model of Physician Pricing: Comment and Reply. *Southern Economic Journal* 38:577–580.

Newman, P. 1965. *Malaria Eradication and Population Growth.* Bureau of Public

Health Economics Research Series, no. 10. Ann Arbor, Mich.: University of Michigan.

Okner, B. A. 1972. Constructing a New Data Base from Existing Microdata Sets: The 1966 Merge File. *Annals of Economic and Social Measurement* 1: 325–342.

Pashigian, B. P., L. L. Schkade, and G. H. Menefee. 1966. The Selection of an Optimal Deductible for a Given Insurance Policy. *Journal of Business* 39: 35–44.

Pauly, M. 1974. Overinsurance and the Public Provision of Insurance: The Roles of Moral Hazard and Adverse Selection. *Quarterly Journal of Economics* 88:44–62.

——— 1971. *Medical Care at Public Expense.* New York: Praeger Publishers.

——— 1969a. A Measure of the Welfare Cost of Health Insurance. *Health Services Research* 4:281–292.

——— 1969b. Notes on a New Model of Non-Profit Hospital Behavior and Investment. Mimeographed. Department of Economics, Northwestern University.

——— 1968. The Economics of Moral Hazard. *American Economic Review* 58: 531–537.

Pauly, M., and D. F. Drake. 1970. Effect of Third-Party Methods of Reimbursement on Hospital Performance. *Empirical Studies in Health Economics,* ed. H. Klarman. Baltimore, Md.: Johns Hopkins Press.

Pauly, M., and M. Redisch. 1973. The Not-for-Profit Hospital as a Physicians' Cooperative. *American Economic Review* 61, part 3:87–100.

Pechman, J. A. 1966. *Federal Tax Policy.* Washington, D.C.: Brookings Institution.

Phelps, C. 1975. Effects of Insurance on Demand for Medical Care. In R. Andersen et al., *Equity in Health Services.*

——— 1973. *The Demand for Health Insurance: A Theoretical and Empirical Investigation* New York: Rand Publications.

Phelps, C., and J. P. Newhouse. 1972a. *Coinsurance and the Demand for Medical Services.* Rand Publication R-964-OEO.

——— 1972b. Effect of Coinsurance: A Multivariate Analysis. *Social Security Bulletin* 35:20–44.

Pratt, J. W. 1964. Risk Aversion in the Small and in the Large. *Econometrica* 32:122–136.

Projector, D. S., and G. Weiss. 1966. *Survey of Financial Characteristics of Consumers.* Washington, D.C.: Board of Governors of the Federal Reserve System.

Rafferty, J. A. 1972. Output Determination and Product-Mix in the Hospital. Discussion Paper, Economic Analysis Branch, National Center for Health Services Research and Development, Department of Health, Education, and Welfare.

——— 1971. Patterns of Hospital Use: An Analysis of Short-Run Variations, *Journal of Political Economy* 79:154–63.

Reder, M. W. 1969. Some Problems in the Measurement of Productivity in the Medical Care Industry. In *Production and Productivity in the Service*

Industries, Studies in Income and Wealth, vol. 34, ed. V. Fuchs. New York: Columbia University Press (NBER).

—— 1965. Some Problems in the Economics of Hospitals. *American Economic Review* 55:472–481.

Reed, L. S. 1969. Private Health Insurance in the United States, 1968: Enrollment, Coverage, and Financial Experience. *Social Security Bulletin* 32:19–35.

Reed, L. S., and W. Carr. 1968. *The Benefit Structure of Private Health Insurance,* Social Security Research Report no. 32. Washington, D.C.: U.S. Government Printing Office.

Reed, M., and G. Sadowsky. 1969. *The 1966 and 1967 Survey of Economic Opportunity,* Files and Related Software. Brookings Computer Center Memorandum no. 48.

Reinhardt, U. 1972. A Production Function for Physician Services. *Review of Economics and Statistics* 54:55–66.

Revelle, C., F. Feldmann, and W. Lynn. 1969. An Optimization Model of Tuberculosis Epidemiology. *Management Science* 16:B190–B211.

Rice, D. P. 1968. The Direct and Indirect Cost of Illness. In *Federal Programs for the Development of Human Resources:* A Compendium of Papers Submitted to the Subcommittee on Economic Progress of the Joint Economic Committee, U.S. Congress. Washington, D.C.: U.S. Government Printing Office.

Rice, D. P., and B. S. Cooper. 1970. National Health Expenditures, 1929–1968. *Social Security Bulletin* 33:3–20.

——, 1968. National Health Expenditures, 1950–1966. *Social Security Bulletin* 31:3–22.

Rice, R. G. 1966. Skill Earnings and the Growth of Wage Supplements. *American Economic Review* 61:583–593.

Rimlinger, G. V., and H. B. Steele. 1963. An Economic Interpretation of the Spatial Distribution of Physicians in the U.S. *Southern Economic Journal* 30:1–12.

Roemer, M. I. 1961. Bed Supply and Hospital Utilization: A Natural Experiment. *Hospitals* 35:36–42.

Roemer, M. I., and M. Shain. 1959. *Hospital Utilization and Insurance.* Chicago: American Hospital Association.

Rosenthal, G. 1970. Price Elasticity of Demand for Short-Term General Hospital Services. In *Empirical Studies in Health Economics,* ed. H. Klarman. Baltimore, Md.: Johns Hopkins Press.

—— 1964. *The Demand for General Hospital Facilities.* Chicago: American Hospital Association.

Rosett, R. N., and L. F. Huang. 1973. The Effect of Health Insurance on the Demand for Medical Care. *Journal of Political Economy* 81, part 1: 281–305.

Rothschild, M., and J. E. Stiglitz. 1976. Equilibrium in Competitive Insurance Markets: An Essay on the Economics of Imperfect Information. *Quarterly Journal of Economics* 90, no. 4:629–649.

Russell, L. 1973. An Econometric Model of the Medicare System: Comment. *Quarterly Journal of Economics* 87:482–489.

Salkever, D. 1972. A Microeconometric Study of Hospital Cost Inflation. *Journal of Political Economy* 80:1144–66.

———1970. Studies in the Economics of Hospital Costs. Doctoral dissertation, Harvard University.

Schelling, T. C. 1968. The Life You Save May Be Your Own. In *Problems in Public Expenditure Analysis,* ed. S. B. Chase. Washington, D.C.: Brookings Institution.

Scitovsky, A. 1967. Changes in the Costs of Treatment of Selected Illnesses, 1951–65. *American Economic Review* 57:1182–95.

Scitovsky, A., and N. Snyder. 1972. Effect of Coinsurance on the Use of Physician Services. *Social Security Bulletin* 35:3–19.

Shannon, G., R. Bashur, and C. Metzner. 1969. The Concept of Distance as a Factor in Accessibility and Utilization of Health Care. *Medical Care Review* 26:143–161.

Sloan, F. A. 1973. A Microanalysis of Physicians' Hours of Work Decisions. Presented at IEA Conference on Economics of Health and Medical Care, Tokyo, April 2–7.

——— 1971. The Demand for Medical Education: A Study of Medical School Applicant Behavior. *Journal of Human Resources* 6:466–489.

——— 1970. Lifetime Earnings and Physicians' Choice of Specialty. *Industrial Labor Relations Review* 24:47–56.

——— 1968. Economic Models of Physician Supply. Doctoral dissertation, Harvard University.

Smith, K., M. Miller, and F. Golladay, 1972. An Analysis of the Optimal Use of Inputs in the Production of Medical Services. *Journal of Human Resources* 7:208–225.

Smith, V. L. 1968. Optimal Insurance Coverage. *Journal of Political Economy* 76:68–77.

Spence, M., and R. Zeckhauser. 1971. Insurance, Information, and Individual Action. *American Economic Review* 61:360–387.

Steele, H. B., and G. V. Rimlinger. 1965. Income Opportunities and Physician Location Trends in the United States. *Western Economic Journal* 3, no. 2: 182–194.

Taylor, A. K. 1975a. Hospital Wage Inflation: An Empirical Model of the Hospital Sector with Endogenous Wages. Mimeographed.

——— 1975b. The Demand for Labor in Non-Profit Institutions: Studies of the Hospital Industry. Doctoral dissertation, Harvard University.

Taylor, V. D. 1969. *The Price of Hospital Care.* Santa Monica, Calif.: Rand Corporation.

U.S. Department of Commerce. 1970. *Survey of Current Business,* July.

——— 1969. *Input-Output Structure of the U.S. Economy, 1963,* vol. 1. Washington, D.C.: U.S. Department of Commerce, Office of Business Economics.

U.S. Bureau of Labor Statistics. 1975. *Industry Wage Survey: Earnings and Supplementary Benefits in Hospitals,* Boston.

———— 1971. *Employee Compensation and Payroll Hours in the Private Non-Agricultural Economy (Production and Non-Production Worker)*. Bulletin 1728.

———— 1970a. *Handbook of Labor Statistics 1970*. Washington, D.C.: U.S. Government Printing Office.

———— 1970b. *Annual Earnings and Employment Patterns of Private Non-Agricultural Employees, 1965*. Bulletin 1675.

———— 1970c. *Employment and Earnings* 16, no. 9.

———— 1968. *Employee Compensation and Payroll Hours, 1968*. Bulletin 1728.

———— 1966. *Employee Compensation in the Private Non-Farm Economy, 1966*. Bulletin 1627.

———— 1965a. *Railroads*. Bulletin 335-3.

———— 1965b. *Building Construction*. Report 335-9.

———— 1965c. *Supplementary Compensation for Non-Production Workers: Employee Expenditures and Practices*. Bulletin 1470.

———— 1964a. *Air Transportation*. Bulletin 1571.

———— 1964b. *Motor Passenger Transport*. Bulletin 1561.

———— 1964c. *Water Transportation*. Bulletin 1577.

———— 1964d. *Trucking*. Bulletin 1577.

———— 1960. *Mining*. Bulletin 1332.

U.S. Civil Service Commission, Bureau of Retirement and Insurance. 1970. *Fiscal Year 1968 Report*. Washington, D.C.: U.S. Government Printing Office.

U.S. Department of Health, Education, and Welfare. 1967. *A Report to the President on Medical Care Prices*. Washington, D.C.: U.S. Government Printing Office.

U.S. Internal Revenue Service. 1972. *Statistics of Income 1970, Individual Income Tax Returns*. Washington, D.C.: U.S. Government Printing Office.

———— 1970. *Statistics of Income for 1968*. Washington, D.C.: U.S. Government Printing Office.

Waldman, S. 1969. *Tax Credits for Private Health Insurance*. Washington, D.C.: Social Security Administration, U.S. Department of Health, Education, and Welfare.

Weisbrod, B. A. 1971. Costs and Benefits of Medical Research: A Case Study of Poliomyelitis. *Journal of Political Economy* 79:527–544.

———— 1965. Some Problems of Pricing and Resource Allocation in a Non-Profit Industry: The Hospitals. *Journal of Business* 38:18–28.

———— 1961. *Economics of Public Health*. Philadelphia, Pa.: University of Pennsylvania Press.

Weisbrod, B. A., and R. J. Fiesler. 1961. Hospitalization Insurance and Hospital Utilization. *American Economic Review* 51:126–132.

Weiss, J., J. Greenlick, and J. Jones. 1971. Determinants of Medical Care Utilization: Impact of Spatial Factors. *Inquiry* 8:50–57.

Wilensky, G., and J. Holahan. 1972. National Health Insurance: Costs and Distributional Effects. Urban Institute Paper 957–1.

Woman's Bureau. 1970. *Handbook on Women Workers*. Bulletin 294. Washington, D.C.: U.S. Government Printing Office.

Worthington, Nancy L. 1975. National Health Expenditures, 1929–74. *Social Security Bulletin* 38, no. 2:3–20.

Yett, D. E. 1971. The Chronic "Shortage" of Nurses. A Public Policy Dilemma. *Empirical Studies in Health Economics,* ed. H. Klarman. Baltimore, Md.: Johns Hopkins Press.

Yett, D. E., and F. Sloan. 1971. Analysis of Migration Patterns of Recent Medical School Graduates. Presented at the Health Services Research Conference on Factors in Health Manpower Performance and the Delivery of Health Care, Chicago, December 9.

Yett, D., L. Drabek, M. Intriligator, and L. Kimball. 1971. The Use of an Econometric Model to Analyze Selected Features of National Health Insurance Plans. University of Southern California Research Institute for Business and Economics, Los Angeles.

Zeckhauser, R. 1970. Medical Insurance: A Case Study of the Trade-off between Risk Spreading and Appropriate Incentives. *Journal of Economic Theory* 2:10–26.

Zeckhauser, R., and M. Spence. 1971. Insurance, Information, and Individual Action. *American Economic Review* 61:380–387.

Index